国家教育部新世纪网络课程建设工程项目　　总主编　肖云南
商务英语系列课程教材

国际支付与结算
International Payments and Settlements

（第3次修订本）

主　编　王益平
副主编　莫再树

清华大学出版社
北京交通大学出版社
·北京·

内 容 简 介

本书共14章，涵盖了国际贸易支付与结算的主要方式、结算工具、单据和结算规则等，全面介绍了国际支付与结算领域最新的知识与规则。本书以英语介绍专业知识，相对原版教材而言，语言简练，通俗易懂，而且内容丰富、新颖，实务性和可操作性强。

本书可供商务英语、国际金融、国际贸易、经济管理、法律、财税等专业三、四年级的学生作为复合型专业英语教材使用，亦可供具有一定英语基础知识且正在从事或准备从事国际商务活动的读者及专业人士学习参考。

本书封面贴有清华大学出版社防伪标签，无标签者不得销售。
版权所有，侵权必究。侵权举报电话：010－62782989　13501256678　13801310933

图书在版编目（CIP）数据

国际支付与结算／王益平主编．—修订本．—北京：清华大学出版社；北京交通大学出版社，2008.12（2020.11修订）
（商务英语系列课程教材／肖云南总主编）
国家教育部新世纪网络课程建设工程项目
ISBN 978－7－81082－065－3

Ⅰ．国…　Ⅱ．王…　Ⅲ．①国际贸易－支付方式－英语－高等学校－教材　②国际结算－英语－高等学校－教材　Ⅳ．H31

中国版本图书馆CIP数据核字（2008）第190143号

国际支付与结算
GUOJI ZHIFU YU JIESUAN

责任编辑：	张利军
出版发行：	清 华 大 学 出 版 社　邮编：100084　电话：010－62776969　http：//www．tup．com．cn
	北京交通大学出版社　邮编：100044　电话：010－51686414　http：//www．bjtup．com．cn
印 刷 者：	北京鑫海金澳胶印有限公司
经　　销：	全国新华书店
开　　本：	185 mm×260 mm　印张：20　字数：500千字
版 印 次：	2020年11月第1版第3次修订　2020年11月第20次印刷
印　　数：	57 501～59 000册　定价：49.00元

本书如有质量问题，请向北京交通大学出版社质监组反映。对您的意见和批评，我们表示欢迎和感谢。
投诉电话：010－51686043，51686008；传真：010－62225406；E-mail：press@bjtu.edu.cn。

前 言

(第3次修订本)

迈入新世纪和加入WTO,我国正逐步地参与国际竞争,同世界接轨。随着全球经济的发展和市场化的运作,英语作为国际贸易用语变得越来越重要,社会上也越来越迫切地需要既有专业知识又能熟练运用英语的人才。在这一新形势下,一些有条件的院校纷纷开设商务英语专业,商务英语已经进入了很多高校的课程之中。21世纪是一个充满机遇和挑战的时代,它为当前的商务英语教学提出了更新、更高的要求。怎样才能有效地提高学生的实际语言运用能力,培养既有专业知识又能熟练运用英语的人才,使学生所学的知识跟上时代的节奏,符合社会经济生活的实际需求,已成为英语教育工作者的历史责任,也是日益发达的经济和社会发展的需要。

为了适应新的形势,满足高等院校商务英语等专业学生和社会上各阶层商务工作者的需求,我们组织编写了这套《商务英语系列课程教材》。目的是帮助商务英语、国际贸易等专业的学生有效地解决学习中出现的问题,让更多的人通过商务英语系列课程的学习,快速提高商务英语听、说、读、写、译等各方面的能力,掌握国际商务领域最新的知识和动态,不断提高自身素质和专业水平,迎接国际竞争的挑战,为祖国的现代化建设服务。

《商务英语系列课程教材》是国家教育部新世纪网络课程建设工程项目之一,本系列教材包括《商务英语听说》(修订本)、《商务英语阅读(精读本)》、《商务英语选读(泛读本)》(第2版)、《商务英语写作》(修订本)、《商务英语笔译》、《商务英语口译》、《国际商务英语综合教程》、《国际商务谈判》(修订本)、《国际贸易实务》、《国际市场营销》(修订本)、《国际支付与结算》(第3次修订本)、《国际商法》、《国际商务导论》、《国际金融》、《世界贸易组织导论》等。随着国际商务的发展和读者的需要,我们还将不断对这一系列教材进行补充和修订,以期形成受读者欢迎的动态系列教材。本系列教材可作为高等院校商务英语等相关专业的普及教材,也可供社会上从事外贸和商务工作的读者使用。

本系列教材具有以下特色。

(1) 本系列教材内容新、全面,专业性、可操作性强。

(2) 本系列教材强调专业基础,重视语言运用,各书均配有大量练习,注重全面提高学生运用商务知识和英语的能力。

(3) 本系列教材中的部分教材设计有配套的课程软件,便于学生自主学习。操作上可灵活掌握,不仅可供在校生课堂学习,还可以面向全国网络课程的学生和在职人员自学,覆盖面广。

(4) 本系列教材的编写者均为从事商务英语教学的一线教师,具有多年丰富的教学经验和极强的事业心和敬业精神。大部分教材由作者根据自身教学经验编写了配套的课后练习参考答案,可与同行交流,便于教师授课和辅导学生进行课后实践。

随着中国对外贸易的发展,国际结算业务面临着前所未有的发展局面。结算业务是否能够顺利进行将直接影响到贸易货款的收付和银行的声誉，而且国际支付与结算中又涉及大量的国际惯例，对这些惯例理解和掌握的程度如何将直接影响到结算的质量。因此，不管是从事国际贸易的业务人员，还是办理国际业务的银行工作人员，都需要对国际支付与结算的理论和实践知识有较全面的了解。

为了适应对外贸易及银行外汇业务的发展，培养和造就大批既懂国际贸易和国际金融业务，又能运用英语从事商务和国际银行业务的复合型人才，使之系统地掌握与国际结算有关的理论知识和实务性操作，我们于2004年编写了出版了本书的第一版，受到了各兄弟院校师生和广大的国际结算从业人员的厚爱，已经多次重印。如今，由于国际银行业务的发展，特别是从2007年7月1日起，作为规范国际信用证结算业务重要规则的《跟单信用证统一惯例（2007年修订本）》（UCP 600）和《审核跟单信用证项下单据的国际标准银行实务》（ISBP 681）开始实行，使得本书的内容有了修订的需求，因此我们对本书的内容进行了全面细致的修订，以期符合目前形势的发展。修订后，本书共14章，涵盖了国际贸易支付与结算的主要方式、结算工具、单据和结算规则等，全面介绍了国际支付与结算领域最新的知识与规则。本书以英语介绍专业知识，相对原版教材而言，语言简练，通俗易懂，并且具有内容丰富、新颖、实务性和可操作性强等特点，适合作为商务英语、国际金融、国际贸易等专业"国际支付与结算"课程的双语教材使用。本书每章都配有针对性很强的练习，以便于学习者复习和巩固所学的知识。

本书由王益平担任主编，负责编写第1、2、3、6、7、8章；莫再树担任副主编，负责编写第4、5、9、10、11、12、13、14章。全书由王益平负责大纲的编写和统稿，加拿大的Ian Winchester博士负责审稿。在本书的编写过程中，我们得到了招商银行总行国际业务部同仁们的大力支持，他们为本书的编写提供了大量的最新材料；同时，使用本书第一版的读者也给了我们许多宝贵的建议和鼓励，在此一并表示衷心的感谢！

由于编著者水平有限，书中不妥之处在所难免，敬请广大读者批评指正。

编 者

于长沙市岳麓山

2020年11月

注：本书课后练习答案及相关资料可发邮件至 cbszlj@jg.bjtu.edu.cn 索取。

学习指导

本书系统地介绍了与国际贸易支付与结算有关的各种工具、方法、单据、规则等，内容广泛，简明易懂。

本书可供商务英语、国际金融、国际贸易、经济管理、法律、财税等专业三、四年级的学生作为复合型专业英语教材使用，亦可供具有一定英语基础知识、正在从事或准备从事国际商务活动的读者及专业人士学习参考。本书每章都配有词汇表、注释、练习及免费的电子版参考答案，以便学习者在提高业务知识的同时熟悉相关的语言知识。本书课时可安排为54学时。关于本书的学习建议如下。

(1) 了解各个章节的内容（详见中英文目录），每章包括学习目标、基本理论、词汇、注释和针对性练习。相关理论、国际惯例、基本操作是本书每章的重点。对于一些有关结算实务的实际操作章节，要特别注意操作的流程。

(2) 国际支付与结算中要用到各种单据，对于每种单据，要了解它的基本内容，并且能够制作各种单据。

(3) 每章都提供了一些相关的学习网站，读者在学习时可以查阅相关网站的内容以巩固和加深对本章内容的理解。

(4) 建议在学习本书的同时，阅读一些有关支付与结算的中英文书籍，这将有助于更好地理解各个章节的主要内容。

编 者
2020年11月

Contents

Chapter 1 Brief Introduction to International Trade ······ (1)
国际贸易简介

  1.1 Introduction to International Trade ······ (1)
      国际贸易概述

  1.2 Trade Terms ······ (3)
      贸易术语

  1.3 Basic Methods of International Payments and Settlements ······ (11)
      国际支付与结算的主要方式

  1.4 Summary ······ (14)
      小结

Chapter 2 Introduction to International Payments and Settlements ······ (20)
国际支付与结算概述

  2.1 Definition of International Payments and Settlements ······ (20)
      国际支付与结算的定义

  2.2 Evolution of International Payments and Settlements ······ (21)
      国际支付与结算的演变

  2.3 Characteristics of Modern International Payments and Settlements ······ (22)
      现代国际支付与结算的特点

  2.4 Major Points Concerning International Payments and Settlements ······ (23)
      国际支付与结算应注意的主要问题

  2.5 Correspondent Banking Relationship ······ (24)
      代理行关系

Chapter 3 Credit Instruments ······ (33)
信用工具

  3.1 Negotiable Instruments ······ (33)
      流通票据

  3.2 Bill of Exchange (Draft) ······ (35)
      汇票

  3.3 Promissory Note ······ (42)
      本票

3.4 Check ⋯⋯⋯⋯⋯⋯⋯⋯⋯⋯⋯⋯⋯⋯⋯⋯⋯⋯⋯⋯⋯⋯⋯⋯⋯⋯⋯⋯⋯⋯ (43)
　　 支票

Chapter 4　International Bank Remittance ⋯⋯⋯⋯⋯⋯⋯⋯⋯⋯⋯ (56)
　　　　　　国际银行汇兑

4.1 Introduction to International Bank Remittance ⋯⋯⋯⋯⋯⋯⋯⋯ (56)
　　 国际银行汇兑概述

4.2 Practice of International Bank Remittance ⋯⋯⋯⋯⋯⋯⋯⋯⋯⋯ (61)
　　 国际银行汇兑实务

4.3 Functions of Remittance in International Trade ⋯⋯⋯⋯⋯⋯⋯⋯ (69)
　　 汇兑在国际贸易中的功能

Chapter 5　Collection ⋯⋯⋯⋯⋯⋯⋯⋯⋯⋯⋯⋯⋯⋯⋯⋯⋯⋯⋯⋯⋯ (75)
　　　　　　托收

5.1 Introduction to Collection ⋯⋯⋯⋯⋯⋯⋯⋯⋯⋯⋯⋯⋯⋯⋯⋯⋯ (75)
　　 托收方式概述

5.2 Practice of Documentary Collection ⋯⋯⋯⋯⋯⋯⋯⋯⋯⋯⋯⋯⋯ (80)
　　 跟单托收实务

5.3 Risk Protection and Financing under Collection ⋯⋯⋯⋯⋯⋯⋯⋯ (87)
　　 托收业务的风险防范与资金融通

Chapter 6　Letter of Credit ⋯⋯⋯⋯⋯⋯⋯⋯⋯⋯⋯⋯⋯⋯⋯⋯⋯⋯ (96)
　　　　　　信用证

6.1 Introduction to Letter of Credit ⋯⋯⋯⋯⋯⋯⋯⋯⋯⋯⋯⋯⋯⋯⋯ (96)
　　 信用证概述

6.2 Types of Letter of Credit ⋯⋯⋯⋯⋯⋯⋯⋯⋯⋯⋯⋯⋯⋯⋯⋯⋯ (104)
　　 信用证的种类

Chapter 7　L/C Practice ⋯⋯⋯⋯⋯⋯⋯⋯⋯⋯⋯⋯⋯⋯⋯⋯⋯⋯⋯ (149)
　　　　　　信用证实务

7.1 The Operation of Import Credit ⋯⋯⋯⋯⋯⋯⋯⋯⋯⋯⋯⋯⋯⋯ (149)
　　 进口信用证实务

7.2 The Operation of Export Credit ⋯⋯⋯⋯⋯⋯⋯⋯⋯⋯⋯⋯⋯⋯ (163)
　　 出口信用证实务

7.3 Credit as a Means of Finance ⋯⋯⋯⋯⋯⋯⋯⋯⋯⋯⋯⋯⋯⋯⋯ (172)
　　 信用证融资

7.4 Risk Protection of L/C ⋯⋯⋯⋯⋯⋯⋯⋯⋯⋯⋯⋯⋯⋯⋯⋯⋯⋯ (174)
　　 信用证的风险防范

Chapter 8　Documents under the Credit ……………………… (182)
　　　　　　信用证项下的单据

8.1　Introduction to Documents ………………………………… (182)
　　　单据概述

8.2　Types of Documents ……………………………………… (183)
　　　单据的种类

8.3　Invoice ……………………………………………………… (184)
　　　发票

8.4　Transport Documents ……………………………………… (191)
　　　运输单据

8.5　Insurance Documents or Certificates …………………… (203)
　　　保险单据或保险证明

8.6　Miscellaneous Documents ………………………………… (205)
　　　其他单据

Chapter 9　International Factoring and Forfeiting …………… (217)
　　　　　　国际保理与福费廷

9.1　Factoring …………………………………………………… (217)
　　　账款保理

9.2　Forfeiting ………………………………………………… (224)
　　　福费廷

9.3　Differences between Factoring and Forfeiting ………… (227)
　　　保理与福费廷的不同之处

Chapter 10　Letter of Guarantee ………………………………… (232)
　　　　　　　银行保函

10.1　Introduction to Letter of Guarantee …………………… (232)
　　　　保函概述

10.2　Bid Bond ………………………………………………… (237)
　　　　投标保函

10.3　Performance Bond ……………………………………… (239)
　　　　履约保函

10.4　Advance Payment Bond ………………………………… (240)
　　　　预付款保函

10.5　Standby Letter of Credit ………………………………… (241)
　　　　备用信用证

10.6　Repayment Guarantee …………………………………… (241)
　　　　还款保函

10.7 Overdraft Guarantee ……………………………………………… (242)
　　　 透支保函
10.8 Others ……………………………………………………………… (243)
　　　 其他保函

Chapter 11　Rules of International Payments and Settlements …………… (249)
　　　　　　国际支付与结算的规则
11.1 URC ………………………………………………………………… (249)
　　　 《托收统一规则》
11.2 UCP ………………………………………………………………… (252)
　　　 《跟单信用证统一惯例》
11.3 ICC 525 ……………………………………………………………… (257)
　　　 《跟单信用证项下银行偿付统一规则》
11.4 URDG ……………………………………………………………… (259)
　　　 《见索即付担保统一规则》
11.5 Basic Features of International Settlement Rules ………………… (260)
　　　 国际结算规则的基本特征

Chapter 12　International Payment Systems ………………………………… (267)
　　　　　　国际支付体系
12.1 Introduction to International Payment Systems ………………… (267)
　　　 国际支付体系概述
12.2 Some Major Payment Systems …………………………………… (268)
　　　 几种主要的支付体系

Chapter 13　International Non-trade Payments and Settlements ………… (280)
　　　　　　国际非贸易支付与结算
13.1 Traveler's Check …………………………………………………… (280)
　　　 旅行支票
13.2 Credit Card ………………………………………………………… (283)
　　　 信用卡
13.3 Traveler's Letter of Credit ………………………………………… (285)
　　　 旅行信用证

Chapter 14　Cyber-payments ………………………………………………… (291)
　　　　　　电子支付
14.1 Introduction to Cyber-payments ………………………………… (291)
　　　 电子支付概述
14.2 Cyber-payments Today …………………………………………… (293)
　　　 电子支付的现状

14.3　Transfer of Money on Internet ……………………………………………（294）
　　　网上支付
14.4　Control of the Electronic Money ………………………………………（299）
　　　电子货币的管理
14.5　Cyber-payments in the Future …………………………………………（300）
　　　电子支付的未来
References ……………………………………………………………………（308）
参考文献

Brief Introduction to International Trade
国际贸易简介

> 📢 **In this chapter, you will learn:**
> ☑ Some concepts about international trade
> ☑ Trade terms
> ☑ Basic international payment and settlement methods

International payments and settlements refer to the money transfer via banks to settle accounts, debts and claims among different countries. They are originated from both international trade transactions such as the sales of tangible goods and intangible service transactions and international non-trade transactions such as international lendings and investments. While international non-commercial settlement is of equal importance in international banking business, international commercial settlement will constitute the core part of international payment and settlement. So in this chapter we are going to give a brief introduction to international trade.

1.1 Introduction to International Trade
国际贸易概述

1.1.1 Definition of International Trade 国际贸易的定义

International trade is the exchange of goods and services produced in one country for those produced in another country. In most cases countries do not trade the actual goods and services. Rather they use the income or money from the sale of their products to buy the products of another country.[1]

1.1.2 Major Participants in International Trade 国际贸易的主要参与者

(1) The buyer who purchases the goods.
(2) The seller who provides the goods.
(3) Banks that facilitate the payment of the transaction.

1.1.3 Points to Be Considered for Both the Buyer and the Seller in International Trade　国际贸易中买卖双方应注意的事项

(1) The creditworthiness of the opposing party.
(2) Payment methods.
(3) Trade terms.
(4) The exchange risks.

1.1.4 Major Processes of International Trade　国际贸易的主要程序

1. Business Negotiation

(1) Enquiry (the act of requesting information on the availability of specific products).
(2) Offer/quotation (a promise to supply goods on the terms stated).
(3) Counter offer (offer made in reply to an offer made by somebody else).
(4) Acceptance/order (an offer to buy).

2. Sales Contract

The sales contract is a written agreement that clearly states the rights and responsibilities of both parties to a transaction.[2]

No matter where you are doing business you must keep in mind that international contracts must be prepared and negotiated in a completely different context than domestic ones. An international sales contract is not merely a document setting forth quantity, price, delivery arrangement of the product; it must also take into account the local legal system and political and exchange risks in the country involved. An international sales contract usually contains the following parts.

(1) Quality clause (including the goods description, quality, specifications, etc.).
(2) Quantity clause (including weight, numbers, length, dimension, volume, capacity, etc.).
(3) Package clause (including the mode of packing, and its material).
(4) Price clause (including the unit price, pricing currency and the price terms used).
(5) Delivery terms (including time of delivery, port of loading & port of destination, transshipment, partial shipment and the mode of transportation, such as charter, liner, railway, airline, post, multi-mode transportation).
(6) Insurance clause (the risks to be covered, the percentage of insurance and the party effecting the insurance).
(7) Payment clause (the payment method and its content).
(8) Commodity inspection clause (including how the right of inspection is determined, the time, place and organization of inspection).
(9) Claim clause, arbitration clause & force majeure clauses.

3. Settlement of the Proceeds

There are many ways to settle the proceeds of international trade, we'll discuss them in detail in the next chapters.

1.2　Trade Terms　贸易术语

1.2.1　Introduction to Trade Terms　贸易术语介绍

When quoting prices to his overseas buyer, an exporter will naturally take into account payment of the various expenses involved in getting the goods from the factory or warehouse in his own country to the buyer's premises. If the seller and the buyer in international contracts want their deals to be successfully completed, they have, at the very beginning of the deal, to make clear to each other their respective obligations and find the full expression of those in the trade terms.

Trade terms are also called "price terms" or "delivery terms". They are sets of uniform rules codifying the interpretation of trade terms defining the rights and obligations of the buyer and the seller in international transactions.[3]

The most important trade terms in history are as follows:

(1) Warsaw-Oxford Rules, made by International Law Association in 1932. It only defines CIF contracts.

(2) Revised American Foreign Trade Definition, made by nine American business groups in 1941. It is the revised form for six price terms defined in 1919. These price terms are Ex Point of Origin, Free on Board, Free Alongside, Cost & Freight, Cost, Insurance and Freight and Ex Docks.

(3) Incoterms, developed and issued by the International Chamber of Commerce (ICC) in Paris. The International Chamber of Commerce first published in 1936 a set of international rules for the interpretation of the most commonly used trade terms in foreign trade. These rules were known as "Incoterms 1936". Since then, expert lawyers and trade practitioners have updated them six times to keep pace with the development of international trade.[4] The current version is "Incoterms 2000" (also called ICC560), which began from Jan. 1, 2000. They aim to provide a set of standardized terms which mean exactly the same to both parties to a contract and which will be interpreted in exactly the same way by courts in every country. Incoterms are not part of national or international law, but they can be binding on buyers or sellers provided the sales contract specifies that a particular Incoterms will apply. "Incoterms 2000" includes 13 terms.

1.2.2　Detailed Interpretation of "Incoterms 2000"
《国际贸易术语2000》详细释义

Group E expresses departure from the seller's premises.

1. Ex Works (…Named Place) (EXW)

Ex Works (EXW) means that the seller fulfills his obligation to deliver when he has made the goods available to the buyer at his premises or another named place (i.e., works, factory, warehouse, etc.) not cleared for export and not loaded on any collecting vehicle. Title and risk pass to the buyer including payment of all transportation and insurance costs from the seller's door.

This term thus represents the minimum obligation for the seller. It shouldn't be used when the buyer cannot carry out the export formalities directly or indirectly. It can be used for any mode of transportation.

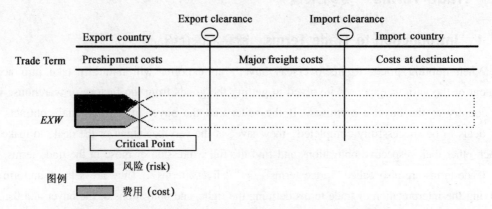

Case: 每套 10 美元天津卖方工厂交货（USD10.00 per set Ex seller's works Tianjin）

Group F expresses main carriage paid by the seller.

2. Free Carrier (...Named Place) (FCA)

Title and risk pass to the buyer including transportation and insurance costs when the seller delivers goods cleared for export to the carrier nominated by the buyer at the named place. It should be noted that the chosen place of delivery has an impact on the obligations of loading and unloading the goods at that place. If delivery occurs at the seller's premises, the seller is responsible for loading. If delivery is at any other place, the seller is not responsible for unloading. This term may be used for any mode of transport.

"Carrier" means any person who, in a contract of carriage, undertakes to perform or to procure the performance of transport by rail, road, air, sea, inland water or by a combination of such modes.

If the buyer nominates any other person to receive the goods, the seller is deemed to have fulfilled his obligation to deliver the goods when they are delivered to that person.

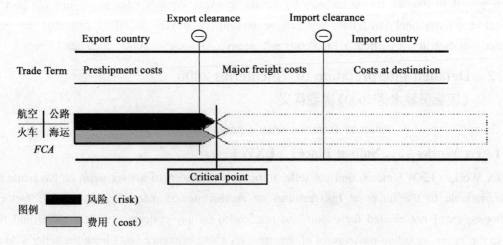

Case: 每件 15 美元上海虹桥机场交货（USD15.00 per piece FCA Hengchiao Airport, Shanghai）

3. Free Alongside Ship (...Named Port of Shipment) (FAS)

Title and risk pass to the buyer including payment of all transportation and insurance cost when the goods are placed alongside the vessel at the named port of shipment by the seller. The export clearance obligation rests with the seller. This is a reversal from previous Incoterms versions, which required the buyer to arrange for export clearance. However, if the parties wish the buyer to clear the goods for export, this should be made clear by adding explicit wording to this effect in the contract of sale.[5]

It is used for sea or inland waterway transportation.

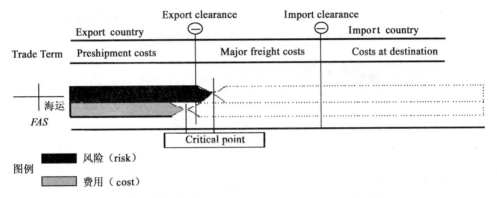

Case: 每吨 120 美元青岛港船边交货 (USD120.00 per metric ton FAS Chingdao)

4. Free on Board (...Named Port of Shipment) (FOB)

Title and risk pass to buyer including payment of all transportation and insurance cost when the goods pass the ship's rail at the named port of shipment. This means that the buyer has to bear all costs and risks of loss or damage to the goods from that point.

The FOB term requires the seller to clear the goods for export.

It is used only for sea or inland waterway transportation.

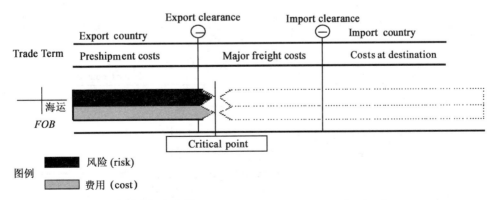

Case: 每件 28 美元广州港船上交货 (USD28.00 per set FOB Guangzhou)

Group C expresses main carriage paid by the seller.

5. Cost and Freight (...Named Port of Destination) (CFR)

The seller delivers when the goods pass the ship's rail in the port of shipment. The seller must pay the costs and freight necessary to bring the goods to the named port of destination but the risk of loss of or damage to the goods, as well as any additional costs due to events occurring after the time of delivery, are transferred from the seller to the buyer.

This term requires the seller to clear the goods for export.

It is used for sea or inland waterway transportation.

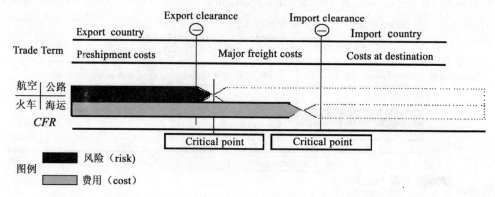

Case: 每公斤 12 美元成本加运费至纽约交货 (USD12.00 per kilo CFR New York)

6. Cost, Insurance and Freight (...Named Port of Destination) (CIF)

The seller delivers when the goods pass the ship's rail in the port of shipment. The seller must pay the costs and freight necessary to bring the goods to the named port of destination but the risk of loss or damage to the goods, as well as any additional costs due to events occurring after the time of delivery, are transferred from the seller to the buyer. However, in CIF the seller has also to procure marine insurance against the buyer's risk of loss or damage to the goods during the carriage. Consequently, the seller should contract for insurance and pay the insurance premium.

This term requires the seller to clear the goods for export.

It is used for sea or inland waterway transportation.

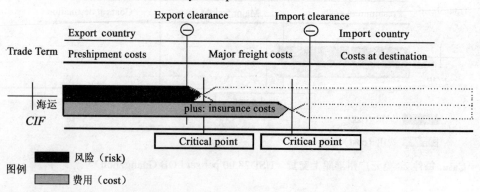

Case: 每箱 30 美元成本加运保费至神户 (USD30.00 per case CIF Kobe)

Chapter 1 Brief Introduction to International Trade

7. Carriage Paid to (...Named Port of Destination) (CPT)

Title, risk and insurance cost pass to buyer when the seller delivers the goods to the carrier nominated by him and pays transportation cost to the named destination.

This term requires the seller to clear the goods for export.

It is used for any mode of transportation.

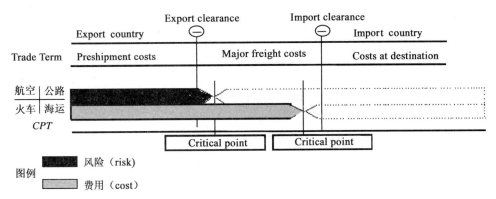

Case: 每个纸板箱68美元运费付至芝加哥交货 (USD68.00 per carton CPT Chicago)

8. Carriage and Insurance Paid to (...Named Port of Destination) (CIP)

Title and risk pass to buyer when the seller delivers the goods to the carrier nominated by him but the seller must in addition pay the cost of carriage necessary to bring the goods to the named destination. This means that the buyer bears all risks and any additional costs occurring after the goods have been so delivered. The seller also has to procure insurance against the buyer's risk of loss or damage to the goods during the carriage.

It is used for any mode of transportation.

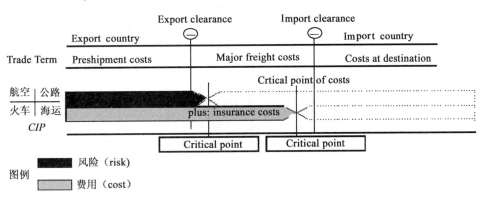

Case: 每个纸板68美元运保费付至芝加哥交货 (USD68.00 per carton CIP Chicago)

Group D expresses arrival of the goods.

9. Delivered at Frontier (...Named Place) (DAF)

Title, risk and responsibility for import clearance pass to buyer when goods are placed at the disposal of the buyer on the arriving means of transport not unloaded, cleared for export, but not cleared for import at the named point and place at the frontier, but before the customs border of the adjoining country. The term "frontier" may be used for any frontier including that of the country of export. Therefore, it is of vital importance that the frontier in question be defined precisely by always naming the point and place in the term.

It is used for any mode of transportation.

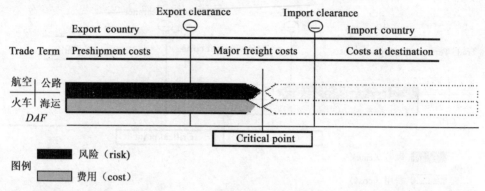

Case: 每套 120 法国法郎 Lanslebourg（法意边境）交货 (FFR120.00 per set DAF Lanslebourg France)

10. Delivered EX Ship (...Named Port of Destination)(DES)

Title, risk, responsibility for vessel discharge and import clearance pass to buyer when the goods are placed at the disposal of the buyer on board the ship not cleared for import at the named port of destination. The seller has to bear all the costs and risks involved in bringing the goods to the named port of destination before discharging.

This term can only be used when the goods are to be delivered by sea or inland waterway or multimodal transport on a vessel in the port of destination.

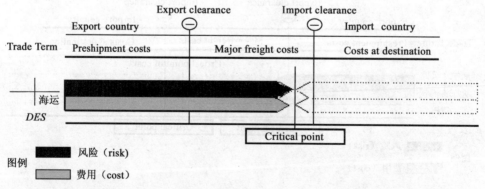

Case: 每吨 150 美元在悉尼港船上交货 (USD150.00 per metric ton DES Sydney)

11. Delivered EX Quay (...Named Port of Destination)(DEQ)

Title and risk pass to buyer when goods are placed at the disposal of the buyer not cleared for import on the quay (wharf) at the named port of destination. The seller has to bear costs and risks

Chapter 1 Brief Introduction to International Trade

involved in bringing the goods to the named port of destination and discharging the goods on the quay (wharf). This term requires the buyer to clear the goods for import and to pay for all formalities, duties, taxes and other charges upon import.

This is a reversal from previous Incoterms versions, which required the seller to arrange for import clearance.

It is used for sea or inland waterway or multimodal transport on discharging from a vessel onto the quay (wharf) in the port of destination.

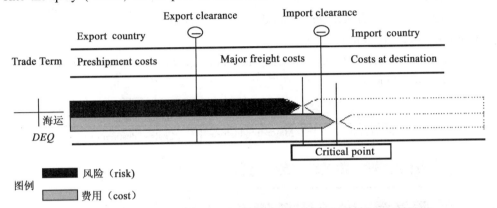

Case: 每吨58英磅伦敦目的港码头交货（关税已付）(GBP58.00 per metric ton DEQ (Duty Paid) London)

12. Delivered Duty Unpaid (...Named Place of Destination) (DDU)

The term means that the seller delivers the goods to the buyer, not cleared for import, and not unloaded from any arriving means of transport at the named place of destination. The seller has to bear the costs and risks involved in bringing the goods thereto, other than, where applicable, any "duty" (which term includes the responsibility for the risks of the carrying out of customs formalities, and payment of formalities, customs duties, taxes and other charges) for import in the country of destination. Such "duty" has to be borne by the buyer as well as any costs and risks caused by failure to clear the goods for import in time.

It is used for any mode of transportation. Buyer is obligated for import clearance.

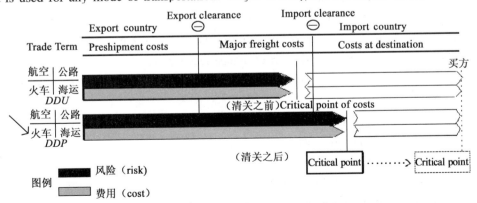

Case: 每纸板箱20美元未付关税，交货在华盛顿14号街321号（USD20.00 per carton DDU at 321, 14th Street N.W. Washington D.C.）

13. Delivered Duty Paid (...Named Place of Destination)(DDP)

It means that the seller delivers goods to the buyer, cleared for import, and not unloaded from any arriving means of transport at the named place of destination. The seller has to bear all the costs and risks involved in bringing the goods thereto including, where applicable, any "duty" (which term includes the responsibility for the risks of the carrying out of customs formalities and the payment of formalities, customs duties, taxes and other charges) for import in the country of destination. This term represents the maximum obligation for the seller. It should not be used if the seller is unable directly or indirectly to obtain the import license.

It is used for any mode of transportation.

While the EXW (Ex Works) term represents the minimum obligation for the seller, DDP represents the maximum obligation.

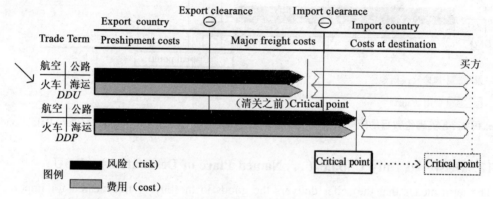

Case: 每套 15.40 美元运载工具到达纽约付关税交货 (USD15.40 per set DDP upon arrival of the vehicle at New York)

1.2.3 Objectives of "Incoterms" 国际贸易术语的目的

(1) Trade terms are key elements of international contracts of sale, since they tell the parties what to do with respect to:

① delivery terms (carriage of the goods from the seller to the buyer and division of costs and risks between the parties);

② price terms (stipulating what are included in the price the buyer paid to the seller, e.g. cost, freight, insurance, export and import clearance fees etc.);

③ delivery obligation (the documents the seller should provide, e.g. bill of lading, insurance policy, etc.).

(2) To establish clear and binding rules for:

① The division of transport cost;

② The division of transport risks;

③ The handling liabilities, for example:

— Furnishing of documents;

— Export and import clearance;

— Notifications to the parties concerned.

1.2.4 What "Incoterms" Do Not Deal With 国际贸易术语不涉及的问题

"Incoterms" do not deal with the following aspects:
(1) Transfer of property/legal title;
(2) Breach of contract/deficiency in the merchandise;
(3) Terms of payment;
(4) Place of jurisdiction.

1.3 Basic Methods of International Payments and Settlements 国际支付与结算的主要方式

1.3.1 Key Factors Determining the Payment Method 决定结算方式的主要因素

(1) The business relationship between the seller and the buyer.
(2) The nature of the merchandise.
(3) Industry norms.
(4) The distance between the buyer and the seller.
(5) The potential for currency fluctuation.
(6) Political and economic stability in both the buyer and the seller's country.

1.3.2 Relative Security of Payment Methods 结算方式的相对安全性

In international business, the seller and the buyer are far from each other. It is, of course, the desire of all parties for a transaction to have absolute security. The seller wants to be absolutely sure that he gets paid, while the buyer wants to make absolutely certain he gets what he has ordered. In fact, there can't be absolutes of certainty for both parties to a transaction. If one has absolute security, the other party correspondingly loses a degree of security. Also, a buyer or seller who insists on having the transaction work only for himself will find that he is losing a great deal of business. International business, therefore, often requires a compromise on the part of the seller and the buyer that leads to relative security for both parties.

1.3.3 Settlement on Commercial Credit 基于商业信用的结算

The following categories are the usual methods of payment to settle international transactions on commercial credit. All have variations and permutations that are the subject of this course. Here it is described briefly; a detailed discussion is developed in the next chapters.

1. Payment in Advance

It is also called advance payment. The buyer places the funds at the disposal of the seller prior to shipment of the goods or provision of services. While this method of payment is expensive and contains a degree of risk, it is quite common when the manufacturing process or services delivered are specialized and capital intensive. In such circumstances the parties may agree to fund the operation by partial payment in advance or by progress payment. It provides greatest security for the seller and involves greatest risk for the buyer.

Characteristics:

(1) Provides greatest security for the seller and greatest risk for the buyer;

(2) Requires that the buyer have a high level of confidence in the ability and willingness of the seller to deliver the goods as ordered.

Basic points to be considered in using advance payment:

(1) The credit standing of the exporter must be exceedingly good;

(2) The economic and political conditions in the exporter's country should be very stable;

(3) The importer should have sufficient balance sheet liquidity or be confident of obtaining working capital by way of import financing;

(4) The importer should have the knowledge that the exchange control authorities in his country will permit advance payment to be made.

2. Open Account

An arrangement between the buyer and seller whereby the goods are manufactured and delivered before payment is required. Open account provides for payment at some stated specific future date and without the buyer issuing any negotiable instrument evidencing his legal commitment. The seller must have absolute trust that he will be paid at the agreed date. It provides the least risk for the buyer, and the greatest risk for the seller.

Essential features of open account business are as follows:

(1) The credit standing of the importer must be very good;

(2) The exporter is confident that the government of the importer's country will not impose regulations deferring or blocking the transfer of funds;

(3) The exporter has sufficient liquidity to extend any necessary credit to the importer or has access to export financing.

3. Remittance

Remittance refers to the transfer of funds from one party to another among different countries. That is, a bank (the remitting bank), at the request of its customer (the remitter), transfers a certain sum of money to its overseas branch or correspondent bank (the paying bank) instructing them to pay to a named person or corporation (the payee or beneficiary) domiciled in the country.

4. Collection

An arrangement whereby the goods are shipped and the relevant bill of exchange is drawn by the seller on the buyer, and documents are sent to the seller's bank with clear instructions for collection through one of its correspondent banks located in the domicile of the buyer.

(1) Documentary collection. Documentary collection may be described as collection on financial instruments being accompanied by commercial documents or collection on commercial documents without being accompanied by financial instruments, that is, commercial documents without a bill of exchange.

① The seller ships the goods and obtains the shipping documents, and usually draws a draft, either at sight or with a tenor of ×× days on the buyer for the value of the goods.

② The seller submits the draft(s) and/or document(s) to his bank, which acts as his agent.

③ The bank acknowledges that all documents as noted by the seller are presented.

④ The seller's bank sends the draft and other documents along with a collection letter to a correspondent bank usually located in the same city as the buyer.

⑤ Acting as an agent for the Remitting Bank, the Collecting Bank notifies the buyer upon receipt of the draft and documents.

⑥ All the documents, and usually title to the goods, are released to the buyer upon his payment of the amount specified or his acceptance of the draft for payment at a specified later date.

(2) Clean collection. Clean collection is collection on financial instruments without being accompanied by commercial documents, such as invoice, bill of lading, insurance policy, etc.

① It is an arrangement whereby the seller draws only a draft on the buyer for the value of the goods/services and presents the draft to his bank.

② The seller's bank sends the draft along with a collection instruction letter to a correspondent bank usually in the same city as the buyer.

An essential feature of collection is that although it is safer than on open account for the seller, there is the possibility of the buyer or his banker refusing to honor the draft and take up the shipping documents, especially at a time when the market is falling. In such a case, the seller may not receive his payment although he is still the owner of the goods.

1.3.4　Settlement on Bank Credit　基于银行信用的结算

1. Letter of Credit

A letter of credit is an undertaking issued by a bank for the account of the buyer (the Applicant) or for its own account, to pay the Beneficiary the value of the draft and/or documents, provided that the terms and conditions of the documentary credit are complied with.

A letter of credit provides the most satisfactory method of settling international transactions. Its primary function is relying on the bank's undertaking to pay, thereby enabling the seller or the exporter to receive payment as soon as possible after the shipment of his goods and also enabling the buyer or the importer to arrange with his bank for the financing of the payment. It is, therefore, of great importance in the sense that it contributes to the smooth conducting of international trade.

2. Bank Guarantee

In international trade, the buyer wants to be certain that the seller is in a position to honor his commitment as offered or contracted. The former therefore makes it a condition that appropriate security is provided. On the other hand, the seller must find a way to be assured of receiving payment if no special security is provided for the payment such as in open account business and documentary collections. Such security may be obtained through banks in the form of a guarantee. A bank guarantee is used as an instrument for securing performance or payment especially in international business.

A bank guarantee is a written promise issued by a bank at the request of its customer, undertaking to make payment to the beneficiary within the limits of a stated sum of money in the event of default by the principal. It may also be defined as the irrevocable obligation of a bank to pay a sum of money in the event of non-performance of a contract by the principal.

1.4 Summary 小结

In international trade, a buyer normally wants to defer payment to favor his cash flow, whereas a seller wants to receive payment as soon as possible. The terms offered by the exporter will depend very much on his knowledge of the overseas customer — the latter's financial standing and competitiveness of other suppliers in the same line of business. As to the importer, he should consider the credit standing of the exporter. Can he receive the goods after making its payment? Is the quality of the goods up to standard? Therefore, the terms and methods of payment in international trade should be agreed on by the exporter and importer in their sales contract.

New Words and Expressions

Word	Pronunciation	Part	Meaning
transshipment	[træn'ʃipmənt]	n.	转运
capacity	[kə'pæsiti]	n.	容量，生产量
inspection	[in'spekʃən]	n.	检查，视察，检验，商检
arbitration	[ˌɑːbi'treiʃən]	n.	仲裁，公断
inquiry	[in'kwaiəri]	n.	质询，调查，询盘，问价
quotation	[kwəu'teiʃən]	n.	价格，报价单，行情表，报价
facilitate	[fə'siliteit]	v.	便利，使容易
		n.	便利，方便
domestic	[də'mestik]	a.	家庭的，国内的
consideration	[kənsidə'reiʃən]	n.	体谅，考虑，需要考虑的事项，报酬，因素
dimension	[di'menʃən]	n.	尺寸，尺度，维（数），体积
warehouse	['wɛəhaus]	n.	仓库
		v.	存仓
premises	['prəmisiz]	n.	房屋及周围的土地（这里表示"公司或企业的所在地"）
amendment	[ə'mendmənt]	n.	改善，改正，修改
update	[ʌp'deit]	v.	使现代化，使跟上最新的发展
reversal	[ri'vəːsəl]	n.	颠倒，逆转，反转，倒转
fulfill	[ful'fil]	v.	履行，实现，完成（计划等）
formality	[fɔː'mæliti]	n.	拘谨，礼节，正式手续
quay	[kiː]	n.	码头

lighter	[ˈlaitə]	n.	驳船
procure	[prəˈkjuə]	v.	获得，取得
breach	[briːtʃ]	n.	违背，破坏，破裂
frontier	[ˈfrʌntjə]	n.	国境，边疆，边境
adjoin	[əˈdʒɔin]	v.	邻接，临近，毗邻
adjoining	[əˈdʒɔiniŋ]	a.	邻接的，隔壁的，临近的
furnish	[ˈfəːniʃ]	v.	供应，提供（相当于"supply"）
deficiency	[diˈfiʃənsi]	n.	缺乏，不足
jurisdiction	[ˌdʒuərisˈdikʃən]	n.	权限，司法权，裁判权
norm	[nɔːm]	n.	标准，规范，准则，规则
fluctuation	[ˌflʌktjuˈeiʃən]	n.	波动，起伏
variation	[ˌvɛəriˈeiʃən]	n.	变更，变化，变异，变种
permutation	[ˌpəːmjuː(ː)ˈteiʃən]	n.	置换，彻底改变，兑变
commitment	[kəˈmitmənt]	n.	委托事项，许诺，承担义务，承诺
domicile	[ˈdɔmisail]	n.	住处，法定居住地

currency/foreign exchange fluctuation　汇率波动
multi-modal transportation　多式联运
percentage of insurance　投保比例
force majeure　不可抗力
opposing party　对方
delivery arrangement　交货安排
sales contract　销售合同
respective obligation　各自的责任
International Chamber of Commerce　国际商会
Incoterms　国际贸易术语
uniform rules　统一规则
trade practitioner　从事贸易工作的人员
current version　最近或最新的版本
ship's rail　船舷
clear the goods for export　出口清关
insurance premium　保费

import license　进口许可证
Warsaw-Oxford Rules　《华沙－牛津规则》
Revised American Foreign Trade Definition
《美国对外贸易定义修订本》
absolute security　绝对安全
advance payment　预付款
place . . . at the disposal of　将……交由……处置
progress payment　（按施工）进度（分批）付款
working capital　流动资本，周转资金
blocking the transfer of funds　冻结资金的流动
for the account of　以……的名义
primary function　主要功能
open account　赊账方式，记账交易
financial standing　财务状况
the same line of business　同一行业
credit standing　信用状况

Notes

1. International trade is the exchange of goods and services produced in one country for those produced in another country. In most cases countries do not trade the actual goods and services. Rather they use the income or money from the sale of their products to buy the

products of another country. 国际贸易是以一国的产品和劳务交换另一国的产品和劳务。通常情况下，国与国之间并不直接用产品和劳务相交换，而是以销售产品所得的收入来购买另一国的产品。

2. The sales contract is a written agreement that clearly states the rights and responsibilities of both parties to a transaction. 销售合同是一个明确规定交易各方权利和义务的书面协议。

3. Trade terms are also called "price terms" or "delivery terms". They are a set of uniform rules codifying the interpretation of trade terms defining the rights and obligations of the buyer and the seller in international transactions. 贸易术语又叫"价格术语"或"交货条件"，它们是确定国际贸易中买卖双方责任和义务的一套统一的规则和有关规则的释义。
此句有两个分词短语，要注意它们各自所修饰的成分。

4. Since then, expert lawyers and trade practitioners have updated them six times to keep pace with the development of international trade. 从此以后，专业律师、贸易从业人员等多次对它进行修改，以使它适应贸易新形势的发展。
"update"意为"to make more modern or up to date"（使现代化，使跟上最新的发展）。

5. However, if the parties wish the buyer to clear the goods for export, this should be made clear by adding explicit wording to this effect in the contract of sale. 然而，如果双方希望由买方办理出口清关的手续，则应在销售合同中对此予以明确规定。
"to ... effect"意为"with ... general meaning"，例如：
He called me a fool, or words to that effect.
他称我为呆子诸如此类的话。
He has made a declaration to the effect that all fighting must cease at once.
他做了宣布，大意是说战斗必须立刻停止。

1. Fill in the blanks to complete each sentence.

（1）An international sales contract is not merely a document setting forth quantity, price, delivery arrangement of the product; it must also take into account the _____ and _____ and _____ in the country involved.

（2）Settlement on commercial credit usually includes _____, _____, _____ and _____.

（3）Settlements on bank credit include _____ and _____.

（4）Trade terms are also called _____ or _____.

Chapter 1　Brief Introduction to International Trade

（5）While the EXW（Ex Works）term represents the _____ obligation for the seller, DDP represents the _____ obligation.

（6）_____ is most advantageous to the seller.

（7）_____ is least advantageous to the seller.

（8）Collection can be divided into _____ and _____.

2. Define the following terms.

（1）international trade

（2）trade terms

（3）open account

（4）advance payment

（5）sales contract

3. Translate the following terms or sentences into English.

（1）以银行信用为基础的结算　　（2）货币波动的可能性

（3）出口清关　　　　　　　　　（4）支付保费

（5）办理出口手续　　　　　　　（6）国际贸易的主要参与者

（7）商品检验条款　　　　　　　（8）履行交货责任

（9）货物已越过船舷

（10）国际贸易合同是在与国内贸易合同完全不同的环境下进行的。

4. Decide whether the following statements are true or false.

（1）Incoterms set out the obligation of the buyer. （　）

（2）Under the term CFR, it is the seller's responsibility to procure the insurance for the goods transported. （　）

（3）Documentary credit offers a high degree of safety for both the buyer and seller. （　）

（4）Advance payment, open account, documentary collection and letter of credit are the usual means of payment to settle international trade transactions. （　）

（5）To the seller of the goods, the most satisfactory arrangement as far as payment is concerned is to receive it in advance. （　）

（6）The term FAS can only be used for sea or inland waterway transport. （　）

（7）The term EXW represents the minimum obligation for the importer. （　）

（8）The trade term DES should be followed by named port of destination. （　）

（9）Clean collection is collection for financial documents without commercial documents being attached. （　）

（10）Trade on open account terms usually satisfies the seller's desire for cash and the importer's desire for credit. （　）

5. Choose the best answer to each of the following statements.

（1）To the exporter, the fastest and safest method of settlement is _____.

A. letter of credit B. cash in advance C. open account D. banker's draft

(2) To the importer, the fastest and safest method of settlement is _____.
   A. letter of credit B. cash in advance C. open account D. collection

(3) Under a letter of credit, the exporter can receive the payment only when _____.
   A. he has shipped the goods
   B. he has presented the documents
   C. the documents presented comply with the credit terms
   D. the importer has taken delivery of the goods

(4) Settlement by documentary credit is fair to _____.
   A. the banks involved   B. the trading companies concerned
   C. the shipping company   D. all of the above

(5) An additional risk borne by the seller when granting a credit to the buyer is that the latter will not _____.
   A. accept the bill   B. take up the documents
   C. take delivery of the goods   D. make payment at maturity

(6) _____ is a compromised method between open account and cash in advance.
   A. letter of guarantee   B. remittance
   C. treasury bill   D. documentary collection

(7) The trade term FOB means Free on Board (named _____).
   A. port of shipment   B. port of destination
   C. premises   D. place of destination

(8) Under the trade term _____, the seller might undertake to clear the goods for import into the buyer's country.
   A. EXW   B. FOB   C. DDP   D. FAS

(9) The trade term CIF should be followed by _____.
   A. named port of destination   B. named port of shipment
   C. named place of destination   D. named place

(10) Under the trade term FOB Tokyo, the freight should be _____.
   A. pre-paid by the exporter   B. paid
   C. payable at destination   D. payable at the port of loading

(11) Under the trade term _____, the importer undertakes the least obligation.
   A. CIP   B. DDP   C. DDU   D. EXW

(12) Under the trade term _____, the exporter undertakes the least obligation.
   A. CIP   B. DDP   C. DDU   D. EXW

(13) According to Incoterms 2000, there are _____ different trade terms.
   A. 6   B. 11   C. 14   D. 13

(14) The trade term CPT should be followed by _____.
   A. named port of destination   B. named port of shipment
   C. named place of destination   D. named place

(15) The trade term DAF should be followed by _____.
    A. named port of destination   B. named port of shipment
    C. named place of destination   D. named place
(16) In the Incoterms, any obligation which does not appear in a particular Incoterms must be the responsibility of the _____.
    A. bank   B. seller   C. exporter   D. buyer
(17) Which of the following is based on commercial credit? _____.
    A. Letter of credit   B. Bank letter of guarantee
    C. Collection   D. Insurance policy
(18) In credit transactions, the goods and the documents are sent to the importer _____.
    A. in different ways   B. in different directions
    C. in the same way   D. at one time
(19) In documentary collection, after the goods have been shipped, the exporter presents the documents to _____.
    A. the collecting bank   B. the reimbursing bank
    C. the remitting bank   D. the opening bank
(20) The instructions for collection are mainly _____.
    A. those given in the contract   B. written on the bill of exchange
    C. given by the importer   D. given by the exporter

Introduction to International Payments and Settlements
国际支付与结算概述

> 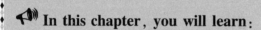 **In this chapter, you will learn:**
> - ☑ The concept and evolution of international payments and settlements
> - ☑ Correspondent banking relationship
> - ☑ Inter-bank accounts

2.1 Definition of International Payments and Settlements
国际支付与结算的定义

International payments and settlements are financial activities conducted among different countries in which payments are effected or funds are transferred from one country to another in order to settle accounts, debts, claims, etc. emerged in the course of political, economic or cultural contacts among them.[1]

As everybody knows, most international payments originate from transactions in the world trade. They are money transfers as a result of international clearing, such as:

(1) Visible trade. The main weight of international money transfer is importing/exporting of commodities and goods between the buyers and the sellers. Importers in one country must make payment to exporters in another country for their imported goods. On the other hand, exporters must receive payment from the overseas buyers.

(2) Invisible trade. It covers not only service trade, but also technology transfer, patent, copyright contracts, etc. Services include all receipts and payments between the residents and foreigners on transportation, insurance, travel, communications, postage and bank service, etc.

(3) Financial transaction. International financial transaction covers foreign exchange market transactions, government supported export credits, syndicated loans, international bond issues, etc.

(4) Payments between governments. The government of one country may make payment to

Chapter 2　Introduction to International Payments and Settlements

that of another country for political, military, or economic reasons, such as giving aids and grants, providing disaster relief, etc.

(5) Others. Other international payments such as overseas remittances, educational expenses, inheritances, etc., should also be settled among countries.

1. International Trade Settlement

With the expansion of global trade amongst countries, the role of banks in international trade finance is becoming more and more important. Most transactions must be settled through banks. Without the bank's participation, international trade would not have been developed to the stage we have reached today.

2. International Non-trade Settlement

There are many ways by which funds can be transferred from one country to another under trade service. When the tourists, merchants, delegations or other people go abroad, they need money to spend, to buy something, or to pay for various expenses and charges there. The most common means for them to carry funds are cash, traveler's check, traveler's letter of credit and credit card. These are within the scope of non-trade settlement.

2.2　Evolution of International Payments and Settlements
国际支付与结算的演变

2.2.1　From Cash Settlement to Non-cash Settlement　从现金结算到非现金结算

1. Cash Settlement

Before the sixth century B.C., goods were exchanged between traders in different countries on a barter basis. A barter system put the trading parties at great inconvenience. Then, a medium of exchange was created in the form of coins at the beginning of the fifth century B.C., thereby ending the barter transactions. These coins were measured and exchanged by weight and fineness among trading countries for settling international payments. Since then, international payments have been effected by shipping precious metals taking the form of coins, bars or bullions to or from the trading countries. This direct transfer of precious metals is called cash settlement.

2. Non-cash Settlement

The shipment of gold or silver across national boundaries was both expensive and risky. Freight costs were high, the risk of being lost, stolen or robbed was omnipresent, and what is more, the speed of transferring funds depended on the speed of transportation facilities, which often slowed the turnover of funds. From the thirteenth century A.D., bills of exchange were created, gradually taking the place of coins in international payments, and the bill of exchange market began to develop. With the establishment of foreign exchange banks at the end of the eighteenth century, international payments could be settled by way of transferring funds through the accounts opened in these banks. From then on, the non-cash settlement era began. Nowadays non-cash settlements are universally adopted all over the world. There is no denying the fact that the establishment of foreign exchange markets does play a very important role in creating and developing non-cash settlements, for foreign exchange banks are allowed to buy and sell foreign exchange freely in these markets so as to meet the needs of international banking business.

2.2.2 From Direct Payment Made between International Traders to Payment Effected through a Financial Intermediary
从贸易商之间直接支付到通过金融中介进行支付

As mentioned above, initially, international trade payments were made by the buyers directly to the sellers by means of precious metal shipments. As foreign exchange banks were set up over time in different regions the world over, the payment channel has changed, especially after a new means of payment, namely the bill of exchange, had been widely used in international payments and settlements. These banks acted as intermediaries effecting international payments by the buyers to the sellers. With the worldwide banking network and modern banking technicality, banks can not only provide easy and quick transfer of funds needed for conducting international trade but also furnish their customers with valuable economic and credit information. Nowadays they have become the center of international settlement.[2]

2.2.3 From Payments under Simple Price Terms to Payments under More Complex Price Terms   从使用简单贸易术语支付到使用复杂贸易术语支付

In the past, international trade payments were settled on very simple price terms, such as cash on delivery, cash on shipment, cash with order, cash before shipment, etc. In modern international trade, a more comprehensive and exact set of terms has been developed.

As indicated in INCOTERMS 2000 (International Rules for the Interpretation of Trade Terms) ICC Publication, the price terms available for use are multifarious and more complicated than before.

2.2.4 International Payments and Settlements in the Internet Era
互联网时代的国际支付与结算

With the development of computer technology, business is done and payments and settlements are effected by means of all kinds of payment systems, which makes it quicker and safer and more convenient for both the buyer and seller. Nowadays, Internet is developing very fast and people are trying to make payment on line. This new type of business transaction is called net banking. Although there are a lot of problems to be solved, net banking is very promising.

2.3 Characteristics of Modern International Payments and Settlements
现代国际支付与结算的特点

(1) Various instruments are widely used in international payments and settlements. In the early days when international trade is less developed, cash is the major medium of exchange used

Chapter 2 Introduction to International Payments and Settlements

in international payment and the international settlement of this period is called cash-settlement. With the passage of time, financial instruments gradually took the place of cash to settle accounts for the traders. Financial instruments are made against the creditworthiness of the relevant parties. With the major forms such as bill of exchange, promissory note and check, funds can be transferred, debts can be offset and accounts will be cleared. The international shipment of cash is replaced by the international movement of financial instruments, not only the security of payment is greatly enhanced, but also the time is largely saved and the costs are significantly reduced.

(2) Banks become the center of international settlement. As modern society requires large volumes of daily transactions of goods and services to satisfy its economic wants, these large volumes of daily transactions may involve a great number of traders in many different countries as well as large but varied sums of money. It may be very inconvenient and frustrating for the traders themselves to match the amounts and settle the accounts. Such problems in settlement greatly affected the development of international trade. With the development of the worldwide banking network as well as modern banking technicality, banks have moved in as a reliable intermediary between the traders with the result that both the buyer and the seller can maintain accounts with banks. As a result, the arrangements of funds transfer via banks "smooth-out" the inconvenience of direct payment, especially when long distance and a large sum of money is involved.

(3) Vehicle currencies are more diversified than before. More key currencies are now used in international payment and settlement instead of being concentrated on one or two major international currencies such as Pound sterling and US dollar.[3]

(4) Electronic devices are widely used in international payment. The development of the international banking network with electronic communications creates the integration of international settlement operations with electronic messages such as SWIFT, CHIPS and CHAPS, etc. to facilitate the international funds transfer.

Taking further steps to develop, the international payment operations will incorporate with electronic data interchange services (EDI). EDI enables all paper-based trade documentation to be sent, received and acknowledged by all parties electronically so that no documents or data need to be made on paper and send manually. It eliminates the repetitive and tedious paper work and thus reduces the opportunities for errors and helps to save time and resources.

(5) International lending is often combined with international payment. In so doing, large transactions, such as the export business of capital goods and engineering projects can be promoted.

2.4 Major Points Concerning International Payments and Settlements
国际支付与结算应注意的主要问题

(1) International payment and settlement methods.

(2) The financial instruments that facilitate international payments and settlements.
(3) Documents used in international payments and settlements.
(4) The currencies used in international payments and settlements.
(5) Rules and regulations on international payments and settlements.

2.5 Correspondent Banking Relationship 代理行关系

2.5.1 Definition of Correspondent Bank 代理行的定义

International banking is effected through the cooperation of commercial banks all over the world. This cooperation comes from the establishment of correspondent relationships between banks. The so-called correspondent bank may be defined as "a bank having direct connection or friendly service relations with another bank".[4]

Correspondent banking is an arrangement under which one bank (correspondent) holds deposits owned by other banks (respondents) and provides payment and other services to those respondent banks. Such arrangements may also be known as agency relationships in some domestic contexts. In international banking, balances held for a foreign respondent bank may be used to settle foreign exchange transactions. Reciprocal correspondent banking relationships may involve the use of so-called nostro and vostro accounts to settle foreign exchange transactions. Even for large international banks such as the Bank of China, the establishment of correspondent relationship is still very important because they cannot do any international business without the cooperation of local banks.

Under an agency arrangement, a Chinese bank, for example, may have a prior agreement with a foreign bank to the effect that each will function as the agent of the other in its own country. The banks may open deposit accounts with, and entrust business to each other on a reciprocal basis.

1. Samples of Agency Arrangements

<u>Sample of Proposal for an Agency Arrangement</u>

In order to cope with the increasing trading opportunities between customers of our two banks, it is our pleasure to propose the conclusion of an Agency Arrangement with your esteemed bank.

Anticipating your agreement to our proposal, we have taken the liberty of drafting a schedule of Agency Arrangements, which is enclosed herewith for your study. We would appreciate your returning to us a signed copy filling in the blank spaces with your comments, if any.

As regards our control documents, we are sending you under separate cover. We trust our proposal will be found mutually beneficial and wish to assure you that our services will be entirely at your disposal.

Chapter 2　Introduction to International Payments and Settlements

Sample of Agency Arrangement

Date: Dec. 18th, 2019

Bank A and Bank B through friendly negotiation and on the basis of equality and mutual benefits agree to establish correspondent relationship for the cooperation of banking business as follows:

Offices concerned:

Bank A including its ×× branches;

Bank B including its ×× branches;

Additional branches will be included through negotiation whenever business requires.

Control documents:

(1) Each party will send its Booklet of Authorized Signatures and Schedule of Terms and Conditions to the other party;

(2) Bank A's telegraphic test key is supplied to Bank B's office for mutual use.

Currencies for transactions:

US dollars, Hong Kong dollars, Pound sterling, Deutsche mark, Swiss franc;

Other currencies will be included through negotiation whenever it is necessary;

Account will be opened through negotiation according to the development of business.

Business transactions:

(1) Remittance. Each party may ask the other party to pay by draft, mail transfer, telegraphic transfer. At time of drawing, cover is to be remitted to the designated account of the paying party.

(2) Letter of credit. Each party may issue by mail or by cable the letter of credit to the other party nominated as advising bank. Appropriate instruction is to be embodied in each credit advice with regard to reimbursement.

(3) Collection. Each party may send collections directly to the other party with specific instruction in each individual case regarding the disposal of proceeds.

(4) Each party may request the other party to provide the credit standing of the clients.

(5) Credit facilities. Credit facilities furnished by each bank shall be subject to separate agreement.

This arrangement becomes effective immediately on the date of signing of both parties and will terminate after receipt of each party's advise three months prior to the date of termination.

Bank A　　　　　　　　　　　　Bank B
Authorized Signature　　　　　　Authorized Signature

<u>Sample of Cooperation Agreement</u>

Date: Dec. 18th, 2019

This Agreement is concluded to strengthen the cooperation of banking business and promote the development of business transactions between Bank A and Bank B; both parties agree on the basis of equality and mutual benefit as follows:

(1) Establish the correspondent relationship between two Banks;

(2) Exchange information in the financial field and provide advisory service to each other;

(3) Bank A will provide Bank B with loans and/or credit facilities at favorable conditions;

(4) Bank A undertakes to prepare and carry out at its own expense, trainee programs for senior officers from Bank B.

This cooperation agreement shall take effect on the day of signing.

Bank A	Bank B
Authorized Signature	Authorized Signature

2. Selecting a Best Bank

The exercise of intelligent selection in making banking connections is very important. Factors are taken into account about:

(1) the reputation of the bank;

(2) size of the bank;

(3) location of the bank;

(4) services offered by the bank;

(5) fundamental policies and strength of the bank;

(6) physical features and personnel;

(7) momentum of early start, etc.

2.5.2　Control Documents　控制文件

When establishing a correspondent banking relationship, two banks concerned will exchange information on the services they can perform or cooperate with each other. Usually "A" Bank and "B" Bank shall be supplied with the control documents when they are establishing an agency banking relationship. The control documents include:

1. Lists of Specimen of Authorized Signatures

The authorized signatures are used for authentication of the messages, letters, remittances, letters of credit, etc. addressed by the bank to its correspondent bank.[5] A bank's signature book contains facsimiles of signatures of authorized officers. A bank draft will not be paid if it bears no authorized signatures. When signatures thereon, such as letters of credit are found out of their previous shapes compared with the specimen in authorized signature book, they have to be confirmed by tested telex.

2. Telegraphic Test Keys

The telegraphic test keys are code arrangements that enable the banks to receive cables from other banks to verify that the cables/telexes are authentic in the absence of written signatures. These codes are strictly confidential. In compliance with the request in "A" Bank, "B" Bank is enclosing under sealed cover a table of his serial and rotation numbers to be used in conjunction of Telex/Cable messages from "B" to "A". It is important to destroy the testing documents and confirm that fact by returning letter duly signed as soon as "A" receives the canceling letter.

3. Terms and Conditions

By negotiation, both correspondent banks may reach some agreements on the terms and conditions of their business. For example, "If instructions to cancel a collection are received prior to the presentation of bills to drawees, commission will be charged at minimum rate for collections. Postage, cable charges and any other expenses arising from transactions entrusted to our care are to be collected from you at their actual costs."

4. SWIFT Authentic Key

This is an electronic "key" that is used between SWIFT member banks for authenticating all messages to be transmitted through SWIFT.

2.5.3 Inter-bank Accounts 银行往来账户

A current account or a checking account may be opened between banks with the establishment of a correspondent banking relationship. Any bank before opening an account in its correspondent bank, must be aware of the detailed conditions of this connection, such as amount of initial deposit, minimum credit balance for covering the cost of services provided, interest rate of the account, overdraft permission, and how often the statement of account is sent.

1. Nostro Account

The Italian word "Nostro" means our. Nostro account is the foreign currency account (due from account) of a major bank with the foreign banks abroad to facilitate international payments and settlements.

Case: From the point of view of a UK bank, a nostro account is our bank's account in the books of an overseas bank, denominated in foreign currency. An example would be an account in the name of Midland Bank, in the books of Bank of New York, denominated in USD. Midland Bank is a customer of Bank of New York.

2. Vostro Account

The word "vostro" means your. As the counterpart of nostro account, vostro account is an account (due to account) held by a bank on behalf of a correspondent bank.

Case: From the point of view of a UK bank, a vostro account is an overseas bank's account with us, denominated in GBP.

When funds are remitted from the United Kingdom, nostro account is used if the payment is denominated in foreign currency, and vostro account is used if payment is denominated in GBP.

Banks treat their nostro accounts in the same way as any other customer would treat his bank account. The bank will maintain its own record of the nostro account, known as a mirror account, and it will reconcile the bank statements against these mirror accounts.

In order to maintain accurate records, the bank tries to value-date all transactions. The bank estimates the date on which authorized transactions will actually be debited or credited to the nostro account, and it uses these dates in its mirror account.

3. Samples of Reimbursement Methods

When requesting the other party to effect payment, the instructing party must give clear instructions as to the reimbursement methods. Here are some examples of reimbursement instructions:

"*In cover, we have credited the sum to your account with us.*"

"*Please debit the sum to our account with you.*"

"*In cover, we have authorized The Bank of Tokyo, New York to debit our account and credit your account with them.*"

"*In cover, please reimburse yourselves to the debiting of our account with The Bank of Tokyo New York.*"

2.5.4　Services Provided by Correspondents　往来行所提供的服务

(1) Collecting checks, drafts, and other credit instruments.

(2) Making loan or investments as agents for their customer banks.

(3) Making credit investigations of firms that borrow in the open market.

(4) Providing banks with foreign exchange facilities, including commercial and traveler's checks.

(5) Providing banks with funds/loans in case of need.

New Words and Expressions

transfer　[trænsˈfə:]		n.	转账，过户，转让
		v.	转移，转让
claim　[kleim]		n.	（根据权利提出）要求，要求权
		v.	索赔
resident　[ˈrezidənt]		n.	居民
		a.	居住的，常驻的
intercourse　[ˈintə(:)kɔ:s]		n.	交往，交流，交际，沟通
omission　[əuˈmiʃən]		n.	冗长，错误，遗漏
bullion　[ˈbuliən]		n.	金银，金条，金块
fineness　[ˈfainnis]		n.	出色，优良，纯度，含金量
omnipresent　[ɔmniˈprezənt]		a.	无所不在的

Chapter 2 Introduction to International Payments and Settlements

turnover	['tə:n,əuvə]	n.	流通量,营业额,周转
cover	['kʌvə]	n.	抵补,抵偿,冲销,保证金,准备金,资金头寸
entrust	[in'trʌst]	v.	委托
reciprocal	[ri'siprəkəl]	a.	互惠的
		n.	互相起作用的事物
schedule	['skedʒjul]	n.	时间表,进度表,费率表
authentication	[ɔ:,θenti'keiʃən]	n.	证实,验证
facsimile	[fæk'simili]	n.	传真,复制本,摹本
confidential	[kɔnfi'denʃəl]	a.	秘密的,机要的,机密的
overdraft	['əuvədrɑ:ft]	n.	透支,透支额
counterpart	['kauntəpɑ:t]	n.	极相似的人或物,对手,对应物
momentum	[məu'mentəm]	n.	动力,要素,推动力
multifarious	[,mʌlti'fɛəriəs]	a.	种种的,各式各样的
reconcile	['rekənsail]	v.	使和解,调解,一致
technicality	[tekni'kæliti]	n.	专门性,技术性
intermediary	[,intə'mi:diəri]	n.	中介,媒介,中间物
		a.	中间的,媒介的

visible trade　有形贸易
invisible trade　无形贸易
financial transaction　金融交易
syndicated loan　银团贷款
international payment system　国际支付体系
international settlement rules　国际结算规则
customs and practices　惯例
current account　经常账户
capital account　资本账户
balance account　平衡账户
unilateral transfer　单边(资金)转移
medium of exchange　交换媒介
precious metal　贵金属
transportation facility　交通设施
financial intermediary　金融中介
modern banking technicality　现代银行技术
on line　在线(服务)
net banking　网上银行业务
electronic business　电子商务
SWIFT　全球银行金融电讯协会
electronic telecommunications　电子通信系统

correspondent relationship　代理行关系
current account　经常账户,活期账户
agency arrangement　代理安排
take the liberty of　冒昧地做某事
control documents　控制文件
under separate cover　另外(寄送),单独(寄送)
fundamental policy　基本政策,基本制度
strength of a bank　银行的实力
booklet of authorized signature　授权签字样本
authorized signature　授权签字
tested telex　加押电传
test key　加押密码
serial number　卷宗号
rotation number　流转号,业务流程号
on conjunction of　与……有联系
checking account　支票账户,活期账户
initial deposit　初始存款
credit balance　贷方余额,信贷余额
mirror account　镜子账户
reimbursement method　偿付方式
commercial credit　商业信用

engineering project 工程项目	bank credit 银行信用
equality and mutual benefit 平等互利	nostro account 往账
appropriate instruction 有关指示	vostro account 来账
credit advice 贷记通知	credit standing 资信
commercial bank 商业银行	

Notes

1. International payments and settlements are financial activities conducted among different countries in which payments are effected or funds are transferred from one country to another in order to settle accounts, debts, claims, etc. emerged in the course of political, economic or cultural contacts among them. 国际支付与结算是各国之间进行的金融活动,它涉及一个国家向另一个国家支付款项或转移资金以清算各国在政治、经济、文化往来过程中所产生的账户和债权、债务。
本句的中心词"financial activities"后面的定语很长,定语里包含了定语和目的状语。

2. With the worldwide banking network and modern banking technicality, banks can not only provide easy and quick transfer of funds needed for conducting international trade but also furnish their customers with valuable economic and credit information. Nowadays they have become the center of international settlements. 由于这些银行具有全球性的银行网络和现代化的银行技术,它们不仅能使进行国际贸易所需要的资金转移得更快、更方便,而且还能给客户提供宝贵的经济信息和资信调查。现今,这些银行已经变成了国际清算中心。

3. Vehicle currencies are more diversified than before. More key currencies are now used in international payments and settlements instead of being concentrated on one or two major international currencies such as Pound sterling and US dollar. 交易货币比以前更加多样化。在国际支付与结算中,人们不只是使用诸如英镑或者美元等一两种货币进行交易,而是使用越来越多的主要货币。
"vehicle currencies"在这里指"交易货币"。以前国际结算中使用的结算货币主要是英镑或者美元等硬通货。现在,随着贸易的发展,交易货币越来越多样化了。

4. The so-called correspondent bank may be defined as "a bank having direct connection or friendly service relations with another bank". 所谓往来行,可以定义为"与另一家银行有着直接的或友好的服务关系的一家银行"。

5. The authorized signatures are used for authentication of the messages, letters, remittances, letters of credit, etc. addressed by the bank to its correspondent bank. 授权签字是用于验证由一家银行向其往来银行发出的信息、信函、汇款和开出的信用证的真实性。

Chapter 2 Introduction to International Payments and Settlements

Exercises

1. **Fill in the blanks to complete each sentence.**

   (1) Before the sixth century B.C., goods were exchanged between traders in different countries on a _____ basis.

   (2) A _____ ended the barter transactions.

   (3) The shipment of gold or silver across national boundaries was both _____ and _____.

   (4) Nostro account means _____ account.

   (5) _____ account means your account.

   (6) To Bank of China, a RMB account held by Bank of England is called _____ account.

   (7) If a British bank has an account in Paris with a French bank, it will refer to that account as _____ account.

   (8) Control documents are lists of _____, _____, _____ and _____.

2. **Define the following terms.**

   (1) correspondent relationship
   (2) international settlements
   (3) visible trade
   (4) financial transaction
   (5) vostro account

3. **Translate the following terms into English.**

   (1) 商业信用   (2) 控制文件
   (3) 账户关系   (4) 现金结算
   (5) 金融中介   (6) 贷记通知
   (7) 代理安排   (8) 贷方余额
   (9) 偿付方式   (10) 加押密码

4. **Decide whether the following statements are true or false.**

   (1) Under non-trade settlement, the most common means to carry funds are cash, traveler's check, traveler's letter of credit and credit card. (   )

   (2) Nostro account is an account (due to account) held by a bank on behalf of a correspondent bank. (   )

(3) Bills of exchange were created in the sixteenth century. ( )

(4) The authorized signatures are used for authentication of the messages, letters, remittances, letters of credit, etc. addressed by the bank to its correspondent bank. ( )

(5) From an American bank's view, a nostro account is a dollar account held for its overseas correspondents. ( )

5. **Choose the best answer to each of the following statements or questions.**

   (1) From the point of view of a Chinese bank, _____ is our bank's account in the books of an overseas bank, denominated in foreign currency.
   - A. a vostro account
   - B. a nostro account
   - C. a mirror account
   - D. a record account

   (2) There are four main methods of securing payment in international trade: ① payment under documentary credit, ② open account, ③ collection, ④ payment in advance. From an exporter's point of view, the order of preference is _____.
   - A. ①, ②, ③, ④
   - B. ④, ③, ①, ②
   - C. ④, ①, ③, ②
   - D. ②, ④, ①, ③

   (3) The documentary collection provides the seller with a greater degree of protection than shipping on _____.
   - A. documentary credit
   - B. banker's letter of guarantee
   - C. banker's draft
   - D. open account

   (4) An exporter sells goods to a customer abroad on FOB terms and on CIF terms. Who is responsible for the freight charges in each?
   - A. Importer, exporter.
   - B. Exporter, importer.
   - C. Importer, importer.
   - D. Exporter, exporter.

   (5) Foreign trade can be conducted on the following terms except for _____.
   - A. open account
   - B. documentary collection
   - C. documentary credit
   - D. public bonds

   (6) A bank gets to know its exact position of funds by _____.
   - A. reflecting the credit balance
   - B. examining the mirror account
   - C. consulting a foreign bank
   - D. checking the nostro account

   (7) If Bank of China instructs Bank of America to pay a sum of US$1,000,000.00 to Midland, its nostro account will be _____.
   - A. credited
   - B. debited
   - C. increased
   - D. decreased

   (8) Statements of balance of international payment don't include _____.
   - A. current account
   - B. capital account
   - C. balancing account
   - D. visible account

   (9) Cash settlement is effected by shipping _____ taking the form of coins, bars or bullions.
   - A. precious metals
   - B. gold
   - C. silver
   - D. notes

   (10) International cash settlement has the following disadvantages except _____.
   - A. expensive
   - B. safe
   - C. risky
   - D. time-consuming

Credit Instruments
信用工具

> 📢 **In this chapter, you will learn:**
> ☑ The three important negotiable instruments—bill of exchange, promissory note and check
> ☑ The functions of a negotiable instrument
> ☑ The characteristics of each instrument
> ☑ The essentials of each instrument

A credit instrument is a written or printed paper by means of which funds are transferred from one person to another.[1] Credit instruments most commonly used in international payments and settlements are bills of exchange, promissory notes and checks. They are also known as negotiable instruments. Credit instruments may also take such forms as traveler's checks, certificates of deposit, treasury bills, treasury bonds, etc.

3.1 Negotiable Instruments 流通票据

3.1.1 Definition of Negotiable Instrument 流通票据的定义

Bills of exchange, checks, promissory notes, dividend warrants, bearer bonds, bearer scrips, debentures payable to bearer, share warrants payable to bearer, Treasury Bills, certificates of deposit are all negotiable instruments, providing they are in a deliverable state, i.e. in favor of "the bearer". D. Richardson defines a negotiable instrument as: "A negotiable instrument is a chose in action, the full and legal title to which is transferable by delivery of the instrument (possibly with the transferor's endorsement) with the result that complete ownership of the instrument and all the property it represents passes freely from equities to the transferee, providing the latter takes the instrument in good faith and for value."[2]

3.1.2 Functions of Negotiable Instrument 流通票据的功能

(1) As a means of payment.

(2) As a credit instrument.

(3) As a transferable instrument.

3.1.3　Parties to Negotiable Instrument　流通票据的当事人

(1) Drawer. A drawer is the person who draws a bill of exchange or a check upon the drawee for the payment of a certain amount of money.

(2) Drawee. A drawee is the person upon whom a bill of exchange or a check is drawn. He is also known as the addressee of a draft.

(3) Payee. A payee is the person to whose order the drawee is to make payment or to whom the money is to be paid.

(4) Acceptor. If and when the drawee agrees and assents to the order in writing addressed to him on a bill of exchange by signing his name on its face, indicating that he will pay on due date, the drawee will become an acceptor.

(5) Endorser. When a payee or a holder signs his name on the back of an instrument for the purpose of transferring it to another person, he is called an endorser. He is liable to his subsequent endorser, his endorsee or any subsequent holder of the instrument.

(6) Endorsee. An endorsee is the person to whom an instrument is endorsed. He is the holder of an instrument, which has been transferred by the endorser.

(7) Acceptor for honor. The person who himself is not a party liable on a bill of exchange but with the consent of the holder may intervene and accept the bill supra protest.

(8) Guarantor. A guarantor is the person who guarantees the acceptance and payment of a bill of exchange, though he is not a party liable thereto. The obligations of the guarantor are the same as those of the guarantee.

(9) Holder. A holder is the possessor of an instrument, namely the payee, the endorsee or bearer. He may sue, if needed, on the instrument in his own name.

(10) Holder for value. A holder for value is the person who possesses an instrument for which value has been given by himself or by some other person.

(11) Holder in due course. The person who is in possession of an instrument that is ① complete and regular on its face, ② taken before maturity without notice of its previous dishonor, ③ taken in good faith and for value, and ④ taken without notice of any infirmity in the instrument or defect in the title of the person negotiating it. He is also called a bona fide holder, who may claim payment from all parties liable on the instrument.

3.1.4　Essentials of Negotiable Instrument　流通票据的要素

(1) An unconditional order or promise in writing to pay a sum certain in money.

(2) Addressed by one person to another.

(3) Payable to bearer or to order.

(4) Payable on demand or at a definite future time.

3.2 Bill of Exchange (Draft) 汇票

3.2.1 Definition of Bill of Exchange 汇票的定义

A bill of exchange is an unconditional order ① in writing ⑥, addressed by one person (the Drawer) ② to another (the Drawee) ③, signed by the person giving it ④, requiring the person to whom it is addressed (the Drawee, who when he signs becomes the Acceptor) ⑤ to pay on demand, or at a fixed or determinable future time ⑦, a sum certain in money ⑧ to or to the order of a specified person, or to bearer (the payee) ⑨.³ (Bills of Exchange Act, 1882 of the United Kingdom)

👉 **SAMPLE 3-1**

---

⑥ Exchange for ⑧US$25,000.　　　　　　　Shanghai, March 19ᵗʰ, 2019

⑦ At sight ①pay to the order of ⑨ the Bank of China

The sum of ⑧twenty-five thousand US dollars only.

Value received.

To: ③⑤The Citi Bank　　　　　　　For ②China National Chemicals Import & Export

New York, N.Y., U.S.A.　　　　　　　　　　Corporation, S.B.

　　　　　　　　　　　　　　　　　　　　　　　(Signed)④

3.2.2 Essentials of Bill of Exchange 汇票的要素

In conformity with the Bills of Exchange Act 1882 of the United Kingdom and the Uniform Law on Bills of Exchange and Promissory Notes 1930 of Geneva, a bill of exchange must fulfill the following requirements.

(1) The word "Exchange".
(2) An unconditional order in writing.
(3) Name and address of the drawee.
(4) Drawer's signature(s).
(5) Date and place of issue.
(6) Name or business entity of the payee.
(7) Tenor.
(8) Place of payment.
(9) Amount.

3.2.3 Acts of Bill of Exchange 汇票的票据行为

(1) Issuance. To issue a draft comprises two acts to be performed by the drawer. One is to

draw and sign a draft; the other is to deliver it to the payee.

(2) Endorsement. It is an act of negotiation.

Prerequisites for a valid endorsement:

① It should be normally effected on the back of a draft and signed by the endorser;

② It must be made for the whole amount of the draft.

Four kinds of endorsements:

① Blank endorsement. An endorsement in blank is one that shows an endorser's signature only and specifies no endorsee. It is also called a general endorsement. A draft so endorsed becomes payable to bearer.

SAMPLE 3-2 Blank Endorsement

② Special endorsement. A special endorsement is one that specifies an endorsee to whom or to whose order the draft is to be paid, in addition to the signature of an endorser. For example, "Pay John Smiths".

SAMPLE 3-3 Special Endorsement

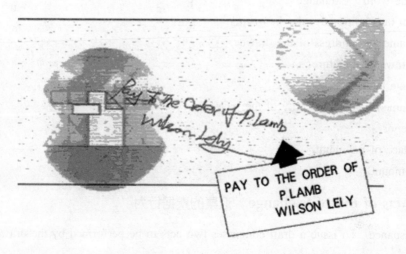

③ Restrictive endorsement. An endorsement is restrictive when it prohibits further transfer of the draft. For example, "Pay John Smiths only".

👉 SAMPLE 3-4 Restrictive Endorsement

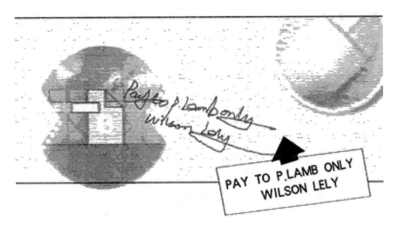

PAY TO P.LAMB ONLY
WILSON LELY

④ Conditional endorsement. A conditional endorsement is a special endorsement adding some words thereto that create a condition bound to be met before the special endorsee is entitled to receive payment. The endorser is liable only if the condition is fulfilled. For example, "Pay to John Smith upon his delivery of warehouse receipt of 100 cases of corn". [4]

(3) Presentment. A draft must be duly presented for payment if it is a sight bill or duly presented for acceptance first and then presented for payment at maturity if it is a time bill.

(4) Acceptance. Acceptance of a draft is a signification by the drawee of his assent to the order given by the drawer. He engages, by signing his name across the face of the bill that he will pay when it falls due. So presentment for acceptance is legally necessary to fix the maturity date of a draft payable after sight. Valid acceptance requires:

① The word "accepted" must be written on the bill to be followed by the signature of the acceptor and the date of acceptance. A mere signature of the acceptor without additional words is also justified.

② It ought not be expressed that the drawee will carry out his promise by any other means than the payment of money.

(5) Payment. Act of payment is performed when a bill of exchange is paid. A bill is discharged by payment in due course only when such payment is made by or on behalf of the drawee or the acceptor.

(6) Dishonor. Act of dishonor is a failure or refusal to make acceptance on or payment of a draft when presented.

(7) Notice of dishonor. A notice on which default of acceptance or of payment by the drawee or the acceptor is advised, to be given by holder of a draft to the drawer and all the endorsers whom he seeks to hold liable for payment. A notice of dishonor must be given by

or on behalf of the holder or an endorsee on the next business day after the dishonor of the draft.

(8) Protest. A written statement under seal drawn up and signed by a notary public or other authorized person for the purpose of giving evidence that a bill of exchange has been presented by him for acceptance or for payment but dishonored.[5]

(9) Right of recourse. In the event of a draft being dishonored, the holder has a right of recourse against the other parties thereto, that is, a right to claim compensation from the drawer or any endorser.

(10) Guarantee. Act of guarantee is performed by a third party called guarantor, who engages that the bill will be paid on presentation if it is a sight bill or accepted on presentation and paid at maturity if it is a time bill.

(11) Discounting. Discounting a bill of exchange is to sell a time bill already accepted by the drawee but not yet fallen due to a financial institution at a price less than its face value.

Figure 3-1 is an illustration of procedures of bill of exchange.

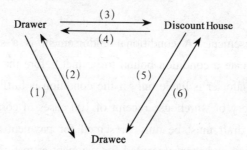

Figure 3-1 The procedures of bill of exchange

(1) To issue a bill, present it for acceptance.
(2) To accept it.
(3) To sell it to the discounting house.
(4) To pay the amount (i.e. less than the face value).
(5) To present it for payment at maturity.
(6) To pay the face value.

For example, suppose an accepted bill for USD50,000 falls due on June 30 and the exporter takes it to a discount bank on April 6. If the discount rate is 10%, the discount interest is calculated as follows:

$$D = V \times T \times R/360$$

D = discount interest
V = face value of the bill
T = tenor (days)
R = discount rate (n% p.a.)

Hence:

$$D = 50,000 \times 85 \times 10\%/360 = 1,180$$

The amount the exporter can get is:
$$USD\ 50,000 - USD\ 1,180 = USD\ 48,820$$

3.2.4 Classification of Bill of Exchange 汇票的分类

1. According to the Drawer

(1) Banker's draft or bank draft. It is a draft drawn by a bank on another bank.

SAMPLE 3-5

```
No. _____
Date _____
EXCHANGE FOR _____

    At _____ sight of this First of Exchange, second of the
same tenor and date unpaid, pay to the order of _____
the sum of _____
Drawn under _____
_____

To: China Construction Bank        For and on behalf of
    Hongkong Branch                China Construction Bank

                                       (Signature)
```

(2) Trade bill. It is a bill issued by a trader on another trader or on a bank.

SAMPLE 3-6

BILL OF EXCHANGE

```
DRAFT NO. _____                    (PLACE AND DATE)
DRAWN UNDER _____ L/C NO. _____ DATED _____
EXCHANGE FOR _____
                                        (PLACE)      (DATE)
AT _____ SIGHT OF THIS SECOND OF EXCHANGE
(FIRST OF EXCHANGE BEING UNPAID) PAY TO THE ORDER OF

_____
            (PAYEE'S NAME)
THE SUM OF _____  VALUE RECEIVED
            (AMOUNT IN WORDS)
TO _____
       (DRAWEE)
                                AUTHORIZED SIGNATURE _____
   SPECIMEN                                          (DRAWER)
```

2. According to the Acceptor

(1) Trader's acceptance bill. It is a time bill drawn on a trader and has been accepted and signed by him for payment at maturity.

👉 **SAMPLE 3-7   Trader's Acceptance Bill**

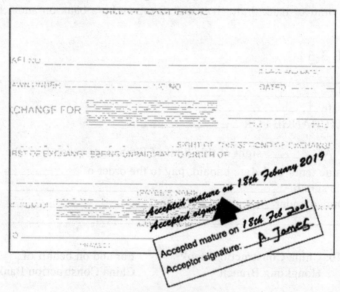

(2) Banker's acceptance bill. It is a time bill drawn on a bank and accepted and signed by this bank for payment at maturity. This kind of bill is more preferable and negotiable than the trader's acceptance bill and more acceptable in the discount market because of the creditworthiness of banks.

👉 **SAMPLE 3-8   Banker's Acceptance Bill**

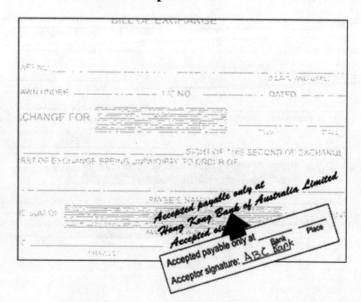

3. According to the Tenor

(1) Sight bill. It is a bill payable on demand or at sight or on presentation.

☞ **SAMPLE 3-9**

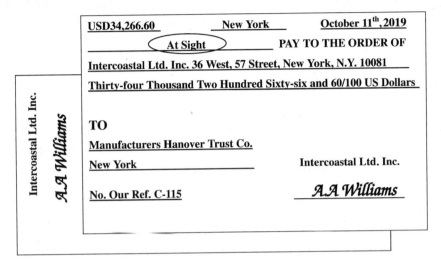

(2) Time bill or usance bill. It is a bill payable at a fixed or determinable future time.

☞ **SAMPLE 3-10**

```
USD182,400.00        New York         October 11th, 2019
         At 180 days sight        PAY TO THE ORDER OF
Derkshire Industries Inc, 102 Madison Ave, New York, N.Y. 10088
One Hundred Eighty-two Thousand and Four Hundred US Dollars

TO
Manufacturers Hanover Trust Co.
New York                           Derkshire Industries Inc.

No. Our Ref. C-113                     A. Friser
```
(Derkshire Industries Inc. / A. Friser)

4. According to Whether Commercial Documents Are Attached Thereto

(1) Clean bill. It is a bill without shipping documents attached thereto.
(2) Documentary bill. It is a bill with shipping documents attached thereto.

5. According to the Currency Denominated

(1) Local currency bill. It is a bill on which the amount is denominated in local currency.

(2) Foreign currency bill. It is a bill on which the amount is denominated in foreign currency.

3.2.5　Functions of Bill of Exchange　汇票的功能

The Bill of Exchange performs many functions in international trade including the following.

(1) Facilitates the granting of trade credit in a legal format by permitting payments on agreed future dates.

(2) Provides formal evidence of the demand for payment from a seller to a buyer.

(3) Provides the seller with access to finance by permitting them to transfer their debts to a bank or other financier by merely endorsing the Bill of Exchange to that bank or financier.

(4) Permits the banker or financier to retain a valid legal claim on both the buyer and the seller. In certain circumstances a bank or financier may have a stronger legal claim under a Bill than the party that sold them the debt.

(5) Permits a seller to obtain greater security over the payment by enabling a bank to guarantee a drawee's acceptance (guarantee to pay on the due date) by signing or endorsing the Bill.

(6) Allows a seller protect their access to the legal system in the event of problems, while providing easier access to that legal system.

3.3　Promissory Note　本票

3.3.1　Definition of Promissory Note　本票的定义

A promissory note is an unconditional promise ① in writing ⑦ made by one person (the maker) ② to another (the payee or the holder) ③ signed by the maker ④ engaging to pay ⑤, on demand or at a fixed or determinable future time ⑧, a sum certain in money ⑥, to or to the order of a specified person, or to bearer.[6]

☞ **SAMPLE 3-11**

---

⑦Promissory Note　　　　　　　　　　　　　New York, April 1, 2019

For⑥ USD99,999.00

On⑧ the 20th June, 2019 fixed by the promissory note ①we promise⑤to pay③BA the sum of⑥ninety-nine thousand nine hundred and ninety-nine US Dollars only.

　　　　　　　　　　　　　　　　　　　　　　　For and on behalf of
　　　　　　　　　　　　　　　　　　　　　　　　　　②CD
　　　　　　　　　　　　　　　　　　　　　　　　(signed)④

3.3.2 Characteristics of Promissory Note 本票的特征

(1) It is an unconditional promise in writing.

(2) The basic parties to a promissory note are the maker and the payee. The maker corresponds to the drawer as well as the drawee of a bill of exchange.

(3) There is no need to accept the instrument if it is payable at a fixed or determinable future time. In all cases the maker is the primarily liable party.

(4) Promissory notes other than those issued by banks are not very widely used in modern commercial transactions. Bearer promissory notes payable on demand and issued by banks are equivalent to bank notes of large denomination, which may cause inflation and are prohibited by the government in many countries.

3.3.3 Essentials of Promissory Note 本票的要素

(1) The words "promissory note" clearly indicated.

(2) An unconditional promise to pay.

(3) Name of the payee or his order.

(4) Maker's signature.

(5) Place and date of issue.

(6) Period of payment.

(7) A certain amount of money.

(8) Place of payment.

3.3.4 Differences between Promissory Note and Bill of Exchange 汇票与本票的不同之处

(1) A promissory note is a promise to pay, whereas a bill of exchange is an order to pay.

(2) There are only two essential parties to a promissory note, namely the maker and the payee (or the holder in the case of a bearer note), whereas there are three parties to a bill of exchange, namely the drawer, the drawee and the payee.

(3) The maker is primarily liable on a promissory note, whereas the drawer is primarily liable, if it is a sight bill, and the acceptor becomes primarily liable, if it is a time bill.

(4) When issued, a promissory note has an original note only, whereas a bill of exchange may be either a sole bill or a bill in a set, i.e. a bill drawn with second of exchange and third of exchange in addition to the original one.

3.4 Check 支票

3.4.1 Definition of Check 支票的定义

A check is an unconditional order ① in writing ② addressed by the customer (the drawer) ③ to a bank (the drawee) ⑤ signed by that customer ④ authorizing the bank to pay on demand ⑥ a specified sum of money ⑦ to or to the order of a named person or to bearer (the payee) ⑧.⁷

SAMPLE 3-12

②Check for ⑦USD10,000.00   Shanghai, May 4, 2019

①⑥Pay to the order of ⑧ John Smith the sum of ⑦ ten thousand US Dollars only

To:⑤ Bank of China,   ③For China National Arts & Crafts
Shanghai, China   Import & Export Corp.
                                 ④(Signed)

3.4.2 Essentials of Check 支票的要素

(1) The word "check" clearly indicated.
(2) An unconditional order in writing.
(3) Name of the paying bank.
(4) Drawer's signature.
(5) Place and date of issue.
(6) Address of the paying bank.
(7) A sum certain in money.
(8) Name of the payee.

3.4.3 Features of Check 支票的特征

(1) A check must be unconditional.
(2) A check must be drawn on a bank.
(3) A sum certain in money must be written on a check, which should be signed by or per procurement for the drawer.
(4) The date of a check is not essential in that it can be antedated, post-dated or dated on a non-business day.
(5) The payee may be bearer, a specified person or his order.

3.4.4 Parties to Check 支票的当事人

(1) Drawer: the customer who writes the check.
(2) Drawee: the banker on whom the check is drawn and to whom the order to pay is given.
(3) Payee: the person to whom a check is stated to be payable.

3.4.5 The Banker's Duty to Honor Checks 银行兑付客户支票的责任

The banker is obliged to honor a customer's checks up to the amount of his credit balance or available overdraft limit.[8] The banker's duty to honor the check ends:

(1) on countermanding of payment by the customer — commonly known as "stop";

(2) on receiving notice that the customer has died or dissolved;

(3) on receiving notice of bankruptcy or liquidation of the customer;

(4) on receiving order that is made against the customer;

(5) on receiving notice of mental disorder of the customer;

(6) on receiving a garnishee order against the customer's account;

(7) on receiving a court order freezing the customer's account.

1. Countermand of Payment

Countermand of payment denotes the cancellation by the customer (the drawer) of his mandate to the drawee bank or paying bank of the check, but in order to be effective the countermand must actually come to that bank's notice. Mere constructive countermand, such as the bank is supposed to be in a position to learn of the stop payment, is not enough. The drawer is the only person who can instruct the drawee bank to stop payment on a particular check.

2. Position When a Banker Wrongfully Pays a Check

If a banker pays a check without authority, if the customer's signature is forged, or the check is void because of material alteration, prima facie the banker cannot debit its customer's account. But:

(1) The customer must bear any loss caused by breaching his duty to carefully draw a check in such a way that no alteration could have been made;

(2) Sometimes the customer is estopped, for example, if the banker suffers detriment from the customer's failure to notify him promptly after discovering that his signature has been forged.

3.4.6 Check Clearing 支票的清算

The process of obtaining payment for his customers for checks that are paid into the branch from customers of other branches. This process identifies two key roles that banks have to play in the check clearing system. These are the roles of collecting bank and paying bank.

1. Collecting Bank: the Bank Who Accepts a Check for Credit into an Account of His Customer

To carry out the role of collecting bank, it is important that all the checks accepted for deposit should be carefully scrutinized. The points to be checked are as follows:

(1) Date.

① Out of date. A check is valid for six months from the date of issue, unless a shorter period is written on the face of the check. For example, if a check dated 8th March, 2008 is presented on

10th September the same year, it would be out of date.

② Post dated. In some cases it is also called ante-dated. This means that the check is dated later than the day on which it is presented. In the above example, if the check was presented on any day before 8th March, 2008, it would be "post-dated".

③ Undated. If a check is presented undated, the payee can insert a date and should be asked to do so by the bank cashier. If any undated checks are mistakenly accepted, the date stamp can be used to insert it. However, once a date is entered on a check, it cannot be altered by the payee.

(2) Payee. The payee's name should be the same as the one shown on the account that the check is being paid into. If the name is different, an endorsement is required.

(3) Words and figures. Both words and figures should be written and should agree. If they disagree, the check should be returned to the drawer for amendment or for a new check to be issued.

(4) Signature. The check must be examined to see if it is signed. A check without a signature written in is not an effective check.

(5) Endorsement. If a check is transferred to a third party, it should be endorsed by the payee, and if it is transferred for more than once, the endorsement should agree and be consistent.

(6) Crossing. When a check is crossed, it must be paid into a bank account and cannot be cashed over the counter.

2. Paying Bank: the Bank Who Effects Payment of the Check Drawn by His Customer

The points to pay attention:

(1) The check is drawn on the paying bank and its branch;
(2) The check has the correct date;
(3) The words and figures agree;
(4) The signature complies with the authority;
(5) The check must be complete and regular;
(6) There is no material alteration;
(7) The check is payable to a specified person or bearer;
(8) There is no countermand of payment;
(9) There is sufficient funds;
(10) There is no legal bar.

3. Process of Check Clearing

(1) The payee presents the check to his own bank and requests the bank to collect it.
(2) The collecting bank examines the check to insure that it is in order.
(3) The collecting bank presents the check to the paying bank.
(4) The paying bank pays the collecting bank when it is satisfied that the check is properly drawn and there are sufficient funds or overdraft balance in the drawer's account.
(5) The collecting bank credits the payee's account when he receives the funds from the

paying bank.

Figure 3-2 shows the process of check clearing.

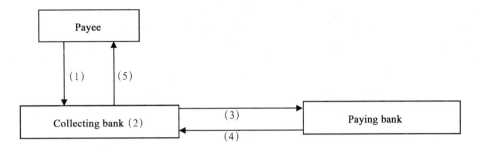

Figure 3-2　The process of check clearing

3.4.7　Types of Check　支票的分类

Broadly speaking, checks are of four types.

1. Open Check

A check is called "open" when it is possible to get cash over the counter at the bank. The holder of an open check can do the following.

(1) Receive its payment over the counter at the bank.

(2) Deposit the check in his own account.

(3) Pass it to some one else by signing on the back of a check.

2. Crossed Check

Since open check is subject to risk of theft, it is dangerous to issue such checks. This risk can be avoided by issuing another types of check called "crossed check". The payment of such check is not made over the counter at the bank. It is only credited to the bank account of the payee. A check can be crossed by drawing two transverse parallel lines across the check, with or without the writing "Account payee" or "Not Negotiable".

1) Meaning

A crossing is in effect an instruction to the paying bank from the drawer or holder to pay the fund to a bank only. Hence, such checks will not be paid over the counter of the paying bank and must be presented for payment by a collecting bank.[9]

2) General crossing

Where a check bears across its face an addition of:

(1) the words "and company", or any abbreviation thereof, between two parallel transverse lines, either with or without the words "not negotiable";

(2) two parallel transverse lines simply, either with or without the words "not negotiable", that addition constitutes a crossing, and the check is crossed generally.

The effect of a general crossing is to make the check payable only through another banker (it must be deposited into a bank account for clearing).

SAMPLE 3-13

_____	Not negotiable	Account payee	Not negotiable a/c payee
(A)	(B)	(C)	(D)

3) Special crossing

Where a check bears across its face an addition of the name of a bank, either with or without the two parallel transverse lines, that addition constitutes a special crossing. If a check is crossed specially, only the bank mentioned in the check can receive payment from the drawee bank.

SAMPLE 3-14

ABC Bank	ABC Bank	A/C Payee
	ICBC Bank for collection	BOC Bank
(A)	(B)	(C)

3. Bearer Check

A check which is payable to any person who presents it for payment at the bank counter is called "bearer check". A bearer check can be transferred by mere delivery and requires no endorsement.

4. Order Check

An order check is one which is payable to a particular person. In such a check the word "bearer" may be cut out or cancelled and the word "order" may be written. The payee can transfer an order check to someone else by signing his or her name on the back of it.

3.4.8　Differences between Check and Bill of Exchange　支票与汇票的区别

(1) A bill of exchange may be drawn upon any person, whereas a check must be drawn upon a banker.

(2) Unless a bill is payable on demand, it is usually accepted, whereupon the acceptor is the primarily liable party. A check need not be accepted for it is payable only on demand and the drawer is the party primarily liable.

(3) A bill must be presented for payment when due, or else the drawer will be discharged. A check must be presented for payment within a reasonable time or within a certain time, such as 30 days according to the regulations of the country concerned. The drawer of a check is not discharged even though it has not been presented for payment within the stipulated time unless the delay in presentation incurs losses to the drawer.

New Words and Expressions

acceptance	[əkˈseptəns]	n.	接受，承兑
dishonor	[disˈɔnə]	n.	不兑现，拒付（票据），不履行付款义务
debenture	[diˈbentʃə]	n.	债券
title	[taitl]	n.	权利，物权
intervene	[ˌintəˈviːn]	v.	干涉，干预，插入，介入
maturity	[məˈtʃuəriti]	n.	成熟，完备，（票据）到期
discount	[diskaut]	n.	折扣，贴现
endorsee	[indɔːˈsiː]	n.	被背书人
endorsement	[inˈdɔːsmənt]	n.	背书，签注（文件），认可
equity	[ˈekwiti]	n.	公平，产权，（复数）普通股，股本
essential	[iˈsenʃəl]	n.	本质，实质，要素，要点
garnishee	[ˌgɑːniˈʃiː]	n.	第三债务人
mandate	[ˈmændeit]	n.	（书面）命令，支付命令
infirmity	[inˈfəːmiti]	n.	缺点，缺陷，虚弱
prerequisite	[ˈpriːˈrekwizit]	n.	先决条件，必备条件
insolvent	[inˈsɔlvənt]	a.	破产的，无偿还能力的
protest	[prəˈtest]	n.	主张，抗议，拒绝证书
tenor	[ˈtenə]	n.	（汇票）的期限
verify	[ˈverifai]	v.	检验，校验，核对
validity	[vəˈliditi]	n.	有效性，合法性，有效期
vindicate	[ˈvindikeit]	v.	证明……真实或正确，还……清白
estop	[isˈtɔp]	v.	禁止，禁止翻供
detriment	[ˈdetrimənt]	n.	损害，损害物
scrutinize	[ˈskrutinaiz]	v.	细察
crossing	[ˈkrɔsiŋ]	v.	横越
		n.	横越，交叉口，（支票的）划线
inventory	[ˈinvəntri]	n.	详细目录，存货，财产清册，总量
submission	[səbˈmiʃən]	n.	屈服，降服，服从，谦恭，投降
affix	[əˈfiks]	v.	使附于，粘贴
bulky	[ˈbʌlki]	a.	大的，容量大的，体积大的

acceptance bill　承兑汇票　　　　　　　　discounting bank　贴现银行
acceptance for honor　参加承兑　　　　　dishonored bill　被拒付的票据
accepted bill　已承兑汇票　　　　　　　　dividend warrant　股息（利）单，领取股息通知书
accepting bank　承兑银行　　　　　　　　expiry date　到期日
acceptor for honor　参加承兑人　　　　　financial instrument　金融工具
after date　出票后　　　　　　　　　　　freeze the customer's account　冻结客户的账户
after sight　见票后　　　　　　　　　　　garnishee order　向第三债务人下达的扣押（债务人财产）令

ante-dated 出票日期比实际日期早	general crossed check 一般划线支票
at a fixed period after date 出票后固定日期	general endorsement 空白背书
at a fixed period after sight 见票后固定日期	holder for value 付对价持票人
banker's draft 银行汇票	holder in due course 正当持票人
bearer bill 不记名汇票	in good faith 善意
bill of exchange 汇票	local clearing house 同城票据交换所
blank endorsement 空白背书	negotiable instrument 流通票据
bona-fide holder 善意持票人	notary public 法定公证人
check's serial number 支票序号	notice of dishonor 拒付通知
chose in action 法律（权利）上的动产，无形资产	payable to bearer 付持票人
	payable to order 付指定人
claim compensation 要求赔偿	payment in due course 正当付款
clearing bank 清算银行	payment instrument 支付工具
commercial paper 商业票据	post-dated 填写日期迟于实际日期
conditional acceptance 有条件承兑	printed facsimile 刊印的签字样本
conditional endorsement 有条件背书	promissory note 本票
countermand of payment （票据）止付	right of recourse 追索权
crossed check 划线支票	sole bill 单张汇票，无副本的汇票
date of presentation 提示日期	special crossed check 特殊划线支票
discharged bill 已清偿汇票，付讫票据	special endorsement 特别背书
discharged by payment 解除付款义务，履行了付款义务	subsequent endorser 后手背书人
	subsequent holder 后手持票人
discount charges 贴现费用	usance bill/draft 远期汇票
discount house 贴现行	

Notes

1. A credit instrument is a written or printed paper by means of which funds are transferred from one person to another. 信用工具是可凭以将资金从某人转移给他人的一张书写的或印制好的凭证。

2. "A negotiable instrument is a chose in action, the full and legal title to which is transferable by delivery of the instrument (possibly with the transferor's endorsement) with the result that complete ownership of the instrument and all the property it represents passes freely from equities to the transferee, providing the latter takes the instrument in good faith and for value." "流通票据是一种法定的财产，这种财产的全部或法定的权益可以通过交付进行转让（可以凭转让方的背书），其转让的结果是只要受让人是正当取得或者支付对价而取得该财产，该票据的全部所有权及其所代表的财产权益将转移给受让人。"

3. A bill of exchange is an unconditional order in writing, addressed by one person (the drawer) to another (the drawee), signed by the person giving it, requiring the person to whom it is addressed (the drawee, who when he signs becomes the acceptor) to pay on demand, or at a fixed or determinable future time, a sum certain in money to or to the order of a specified person, or to bearer (the payee). 汇票是一人开给另一人的无条件书面命令,由发出命令的人签名,要求接受命令的人立即或在可以确定的将来时间把一定金额的货币支付给一个特定的人,或他的指定人,或持票人。

4. A conditional endorsement is a special endorsement adding some words thereto that create a condition bound to be met before the special endorsee is entitled to receive payment. The endorser is liable only if the condition is fulfilled. For example, "Pay to John Smith upon his delivery of warehouse receipt of 100 cases of corn". 有条件背书是在特别背书的基础上加上背书取得付款的一些特殊条件的词语。只有符合了这些条件,背书人才有义务付款。例如:"如果约翰·史密斯将100箱玉米运至仓库了即付款给他"。
背书有空白背书(Blank Endorsement)、特别背书(Special Endorsement)、限制性背书(Restrictive Endorsement)和有条件背书(Conditional Endorsement)等几种形式。

5. A written statement under seal drawn up and signed by a notary public or other authorized person for the purpose of giving evidence that a bill of exchange has been presented by him for acceptance or for payment but dishonored. (拒绝证书是)法定公证人或其他有权出具证书者出具并签署的加封书面声明,以证明汇票经其提示承兑或提示付款但被退票。

6. A promissory note is an unconditional promise in writing made by one person (the maker) to another (the payee or the holder) signed by the maker engaging to pay, on demand or at a fixed or determinable future time a sum certain in money, to or to the order of a specified person, or to bearer. 本票是一人向另一人开立,由出票人签字,保证对某一特定的人或其指定人或持票人即期或在固定的或可以确定的某一日期支付一定货币金额的书面的无条件的付款承诺。

7. A check is an unconditional order in writing addressed by the customer (the drawer) to a bank (the drawee) signed by that customer authorizing the bank to pay on demand a specified sum of money to or to the order of a named person or to bearer (the payee). 支票是由银行的客户向银行开出,由出票人签字,授权银行对某人或其指定人或持票人即期支付一定货币金额的书面的无条件支付命令。

8. The banker is obliged to honor a customer's checks up to the amount of his credit balance or available overdraft limit. 只要客户在银行有足够的存款余额或透支额度,银行就有责任兑现客户的支票。
此处的"overdraft limit"意为"透支额度"。

9. A crossing is in effect an instruction to the paying bank from the drawer or holder to pay the fund to a bank only. Hence, such checks will not be paid over the counter of the paying bank and must be presented for payment by a collecting bank. 支票的划线实际上是出票人或持

票人指示付款银行只能将资金入银行账户的指示。因此,划线支票不能在付款银行取现,必须由代收行向付款行提示付款。

1. **Define the following terms.**

    (1) negotiable instrument

    (2) bill of exchange

    (3) check

    (4) documentary bill

    (5) crossing

2. **Translate the following terms into English.**

    (1) 一般划线支票　　　　　　　(2) 特殊划线支票

    (3) 过期支票　　　　　　　　　(4) 未到期支票

    (5) 大小写金额　　　　　　　　(6) 空白背书

    (7) 特别背书　　　　　　　　　(8) 限制性背书

    (9) 跟单汇票　　　　　　　　　(10) 即期汇票

    (11) 远期汇票　　　　　　　　　(12) 承兑汇票

    (13) 可确定的未来某一天　　　　(14) 光票

    (15) 流通票据　　　　　　　　　(16) 贴现行

    (17) 商人银行　　　　　　　　　(18) 无条件的付款承诺

    (19) 负连带责任　　　　　　　　(20) 出票后 90 天付款

3. **Decide whether the following statements are true or false.**

    (1) In a promissory note, the drawer and the payer are the same person. (　)

    (2) A promissory note is an unconditional order in writing. (　)

    (3) There is no acceptor in a promissory note. (　)

    (4) A bank draft is a check drawn by one bank on another. (　)

    (5) A trade bill is usually a documentary bill. (　)

    (6) The interest in the bill of exchange can only be transferred by endorsement. (　)

    (7) An endorser of a bill is liable on it to subsequent endorsers and holders of the bill. (　)

    (8) The person who draws the bill is called the drawer. (　)

    (9) Bills of exchange drawn by and accepted by commercial firms are known as trade bills. (　)

    (10) Trade bills are usually documentary bills. (　)

    (11) Endorsements are needed when checks in favor of a sole payee are credited to a joint

account. (　)

(12) An open check can be paid into a bank account. (　)
(13) An open check can be cashed over the counter. (　)
(14) A crossed check can be cashed over the counter. (　)
(15) The payment of a check cannot depend upon certain conditions being met. (　)
(16) In a check, the drawer and the payer are the same person. (　)
(17) If a check is presented undated, the payee can insert a date. (　)
(18) A draft is a conditional order in writing. (　)
(19) If a bill is payable "at 30 days after date", the date of payment is decided according to the date of acceptance. (　)
(20) A bill payable "at 90 days sight" is a sight bill. (　)

4. Choose the best answer to each of the following statements.

(1) The person paying the money is a ____ of a check.
　　A. payee　　　　B. endorser　　　　C. drawer　　　　D. endorsee

(2) A check is valid for ____ months from the date of issue, unless a shorter period is written on the face of it.
　　A. six　　　　B. nine　　　　C. three　　　　D. one

(3) If a check dated 1st Feb., 2020 was presented on the 5th Nov., 2019, it would be ____.
　　A. pre-dated　　B. out of date　　C. post dated　　D. undated

(4) If a check dated 1st Feb., 2020 was presented on the 5th Oct., 2020, it would be ____.
　　A. pre-dated　　B. out of date　　C. post dated　　D. undated

(5) The effect of a blank endorsement is to make the check payable to the ____.
　　A. order of a specified person　　　B. specified person
　　C. bearer　　　　　　　　　　　　　D. named person

(6) Banks usually ask for endorsements when checks in favor of ____ payees are credited to a ____ account.
　　A. joint … joint　　　　　　　B. joint … sole
　　C. sole … joint　　　　　　　D. sole … sole

(7) Payee J. Smith endorsed "James Smith pay to L. Green", this is a ____ endorsement.
　　A. specific　　B. blank　　C. general　　D. restrictive

(8) If a bill is payable "60 days after date", the date of payment is decided according to ____.
　　A. the date of acceptance　　　　B. the date of presentation
　　C. the date of the bill　　　　　　D. the date of maturity

(9) A ____ carries comparatively little risks and can be discounted at the finest rate of interest.
　　A. sight bill　　　　　　　　　B. bank draft

C. commercial bill   D. trade bill

(10) A term bill may be accepted by the ____.
   A. drawer   B. drawee   C. holder   D. payee

(11) The party to whom the bill is addressed is called the ____.
   A. drawer   B. drawee   C. holder   D. payee

(12) When financing is without recourse, this means that the bank has no recourse to the ____ if such drafts are dishonored.
   A. payer   B. drawee   C. payee   D. drawer

(13) Only by endorsement can the interest in the bill be transferred by ____.
   A. the drawer   B. the drawee
   C. the holder   D. any person to the bill

(14) A promissory note is "inchoate" until it has been delivered to the ____.
   A. payer or bearer   B. payee or drawee
   C. payee or bearer   D. holder or drawer

(15) The ____ of a promissory note has prime liability while the other parties have secondary liability.
   A. holder   B. drawee   C. maker   D. acceptor

(16) An acceptance with the wording "payable on delivery of bill of lading" is ____.
   A. a general acceptance   B. qualified acceptance
   C. non acceptance   D. partial acceptance

(17) ____ must be accepted by the drawee before payment.
   A. A sight bill   B. A bill payable ×× days after sight
   C. A promissory note   D. A bill payable ×× days after date

(18) A(n) ____ is a financial document.
   A. bill of exchange   B. bill of lading
   C. insurance policy   D. commercial invoice

(19) In order to retain the liabilities of the other parties, a bill that has been dishonored must be ____.
   A. protested   B. given to the acceptor
   C. retained in the files   D. presented to the advising bank

(20) "A check payable to ABC Company is credited to the personal account of Mr. Li", the bank ____.
   A. is correct in crediting the account
   B. is merely doing what is requested by its customer
   C. has committed an act of negligence
   D. will make a claim on its principal

5. Read the following draft and give your answer to each of the following questions.

```
Exchange for GBP5,000.00                    Shanghai, Jan 15, 2019
   At 90 days sight pay this first bill (Second unpaid) to the order of the Bank of China
   The sum of Five Thousand Pounds only.
   Value received.


   To: ABC Company              For China National Crafts Import & Export
       London                       Corporation, S.B.
                                              (Signed)
```

(1) Who is the drawer?
(2) Who is the drawee?
(3) Who is the payee?
(4) Is this a demand draft or a tenor draft?
(5) Is this a sola bill or a bill of exchange in two sets?
(6) Where is the bill drawn?

6. Please draw a draft according to the following conditions.

Drawer: ABC Company, Shanghai   Amount: USD 100,000.00
Drawee: DEF Bank, New York   Payee: G&H Company
Date of Issue: August 25, 2020

7. Complete the following check according to the following information.

Mrs. Warren asks Joe Williams to draw out to her a crossed check for USD2,300.00. She is to pay the amount to her account with Pacific Bank, City Office. Joe Williams signed the check (No. 12345) on March 21, 2020 as requested.

```
             HONGKONG AND SHANGHAI BANKING CORP., LTD.
                            (3) _____
                                    Date (1) ____ , _____
   Pay (2) _____    USD(4) _____
                                       (5) _____
       (6) _____
```

International Bank Remittance
国际银行汇兑

> **In this chapter, you will learn:**
> ☑ Methods, parties and procedures of remittance
> ☑ Advantages and disadvantages of remittance
> ☑ Practice of remittance
> ☑ The function of remittance in international trade

4.1 Introduction to International Bank Remittance
国际银行汇兑概述

In international business, the settlement of claims and debts and the transfer of money are carried out by several methods of transmission.

International remittance happens when a client (remitter) asks his bank to send a sum of money to a beneficiary abroad by one of the transfer methods at his option. The beneficiary can be paid at the designated bank, which is either the remitting bank's overseas branch or its correspondent.

Remittance refers to a bank (the remitting bank), at the request of its customer (the remitter), transfers a certain sum of money to its overseas branch or correspondent bank (the paying bank) instructing it to pay a named person (the payee/beneficiary) domiciled in that country. Remittance is used for the settlement of both commercial and non-commercial settlements. Therefore, it is an important payment method in international banking business.

4.1.1 Parties Concerned and Methods 汇兑的当事人及方式

1. Parties Concerned

Parties involved in international bank remittance include the following.

(1) The remitter. The remitter is the person who requests his bank to remit funds to a beneficiary in a foreign country. The remitter is also the payer.

(2) Remitting bank. Remitting bank is the bank transferring funds at the request of a remitter to its correspondent or its branch in another country and instructing the latter to pay a certain amount of money to a beneficiary.[1]

(3) The payee. The payee (beneficiary) is a person who is addressed to receive the remittance.

(4) Paying bank. Paying bank is the bank entrusted by the remitting bank to pay a certain amount of money to a beneficiary named in the remittance advice.[2]

2. Methods

There are three basic ways for a bank to transfer funds for its client from the home country to abroad. They are mail remittance, telegraphic remittance and remittance by demand draft.

1) Remittance by Airmail

Remittance by airmail transfers funds by means of a payment order, a mail advice, or sometimes an advice issued by a remitting bank, at the request of the remitter. It is more generally known as mail transfer or M/T.

A payment order, mail advice or credit advice/please debit advice is an authenticated order in writing addressed by one bank to another instructing the latter to pay a sum certain in money to a specified person or a beneficiary named thereon.[3]

2) Remittance by Cable/Telex/SWIFT

Remittance by cable/telex/SWIFT is often referred to as cable transfer or telegraphic transfer, namely T/T. It is exactly the same as a mail transfer, except that instructions from the remitting bank to the paying bank are transmitted by cable instead of by airmail.

It is therefore quicker, but more expensive than mail transfer is. It is often used when the remittance amount is large and the transfer of funds is subject to a time limit.

The only means of authenticating a cable transfer is the test key. However, remittance by SWIFT should be authenticated by SWIFT authentic key.

3) Remittance by Banker's Demand Draft

Remittance by banker's demand draft is often referred to as demand draft (D/D). A banker's draft is a negotiable instrument drawn by a bank on its overseas branch or its correspondent abroad ordering the latter to pay on demand the stated amount to the holder of the draft. It is often used when the client wants to transfer the funds to his beneficiary himself. The process of a demand draft is as follows:

(1) First of all the draft is drawn;

(2) After the draft is drawn, it is handed to the remitter, who may send or carry it abroad to the person in whose favor it is drawn;

(3) Upon receipt of the draft, the payee namely the beneficiary can either present it for payment at the counter of the drawee bank or collect the proceeds through his own bank for his account.

4.1.2 Procedures 汇兑的业务流程

1. Procedures for M/T and T/T

The operations conducted by the remitting bank are called the outward remittance and those carried out by the paying bank are called the inward remittance. The procedures for bank remittance by mail or by cable usually comprise the following steps.

(1) The remitter (a bank's customer) makes out the necessary application form and gives his signed written application to his bank instructing it to make an M/T or T/T, indicating the beneficiary's full name, address and the name of beneficiary's banker (if any).

This actually means that the remitter sends a written order to the remitting bank to pay to the debit of the remitter's account or against cash deposit.

(2) The remitting bank debits his customer's account with the amount to be remitted together with its commission and expense (if any).

(3) The remitting bank issues a payment order to its branch or correspondent in the place where the beneficiary is domiciled.

The payment order specifies the details of the payment: amount, name and address of the beneficiary, and name of the remitter. The payment order must be authenticated with the authorized signatures of the remitting bank.

(4) Upon receipt of the payment order, the paying bank verifies the authorized signatures, notifies the beneficiary, and pays to him the stated amount minus expenses charged by itself.

(5) The paying bank claims reimbursement from the remitting bank in accordance with the latter's instructions.

The whole procedure virtually is done by entries over banking accounts, where remitting bank debits his account and credits the account of the correspondent bank. On receipt of the payment instructions, the latter (the paying bank) passes a reciprocal entry over its account with the remitting bank and pays the money over to the exporter. Figure 4-1 illustrates the procedures.

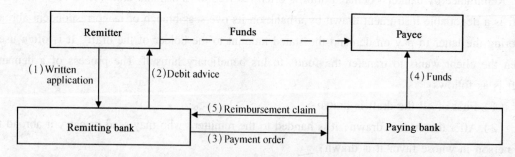

Figure 4-1 A simplified remittance diagram

2. Procedures for D/D

The usually adopted procedure for D/D is as follows:

(1) A written request to issue a draft is made by the remitter (a bank's customer).

(2) The remitting bank (the draft-issuing bank) debits the customer's account with the amount of the draft plus bank commission (if any), issues a bank draft and hands it to the remitter.[4]

(3) The issuing bank sends an advice (a special letter of advice or a non-negotiable copy of the draft) by airmail to the drawee bank, namely its overseas branch or its correspondent abroad, instructing the latter to pay it on presentation of the original draft as well as how to reimburse it.[5] Nowadays most banks usually omit airmailing the advice to the drawee bank.

(4) The remitter forwards the draft to the payee.

(5) The payee presents the draft to the drawee bank for payment.

(6) The drawee bank verifies the signatures, pays the draft, and claims back the amount that is paid according to its agency arrangement with the remitting bank. If the signatures can not be identified, the paying bank will only pay the draft on collection basis.

Figure 4-2 illustrates the procedures.

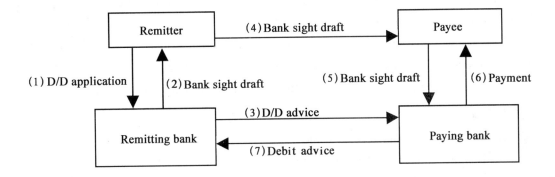

Figure 4-2　A demand draft diagram

4.1.3　Advantages and Disadvantages　汇兑的利与弊

1. Advantages

1) Advantages of remittance by demand draft

(1) Demand draft can be used for paying small amounts.

(2) Demand draft is a negotiable instrument, which can be transferred from one person to another by endorsement, so that it is more convenient in use for payment.

(3) In time of war, one can transfer funds out of the enemy country by means of the demand draft in virtue of its negotiability.

2) Advantages of remittance by airmail

It involves bank-to-bank instructions with banks responsible for making payments, so it is rather reliable.

3) Advantages of remittance by cable

(1) It is the fastest way to transfer funds.

(2) It involves bank-to-bank instructions with banks responsible for making payments, so it is quite safe, especially when large amount is transferred.

2. Disadvantages

1) Disadvantages of remittance by demand draft

(1) As a remitter himself is responsible for mailing the demand draft, its transmission is slower than that of T/T and cannot serve the purpose of quick payment.

(2) It is possible for a demand draft to be lost, stolen or destroyed. The remitting bank is generally reluctant to stop payment on a draft issued by itself for this would mean an act of dishonor on its part which will have an unfavorable effect on its credit-worthiness. To stop payment on lost draft is time consuming.

2) Disadvantages of remittance by airmail

(1) It is possible for the mail transfer order to be delayed or lost in the post, thus causing difficulty for its payment.

(2) As the mail transfer exclusively depends on international airmail service, its transmission is slower than that of T/T and cannot serve the purpose of quick payment.

(3) Unlike the remittance by demand draft, the beneficiary must await notification from the bank concerned.

3) Disadvantages of remittance by cable

(1) It is more expensive as compared with M/T or D/D, but if the amount transferred is large, the interest cost which should be otherwise incurred due to time delay can be saved.

(2) The beneficiary must await notification from the bank concerned.

4.1.4 Summary 小结

The advantages and disadvantages of the three methods of fund transfer have to be balanced when transferring funds.

Generally speaking, airmail remittance is less used than T/T or D/D nowadays, except for small amount remittances made by individuals for family maintenance, cash gift, etc.

T/T is favorable to the seller. He can get money at an early date, speed up the turnover of funds, increase the income of interests and avoid the risk of fluctuation in the exchange rate.

However, the buyer has to pay more cable expenses and bank charges. Therefore, if T/T is not definitely stipulated in the transaction, the buyer makes payment only by M/T.

Chapter 4 International Bank Remittance

Sometimes the amount of payment is comparatively large, the money market fluctuates greatly and the currency of settlement being used is likely to devaluate. In these cases, T/T is preferable, and T/T should be definitely stipulated in the contract. However, the seller should prevent the buyer from forcing the contractual price down under the pretext of bearing more expenses.

A large number of international remittances are carried out by telecommunications. SWIFT, an automated payment system, is commonly used among member banks, which provides the member banks with faster, safer, cheaper, and more reliable handling of their customers' transactions.

Swiftness, reliability, safety, and inexpensiveness are major advantages of transmission by means of SWIFT messages.

4.2 Practice of International Bank Remittance 国际银行汇兑实务

4.2.1 Outward Remittance 汇出汇款

Outward remittance refers to the settlement or transferring of foreign exchange funds according to the requirement of the remitter to the designated account overseas. When the home bank is acting as the remitting bank, the remittance handled by him is called an outward remittance. The remitting bank, at the remitter's request, sends M/T advice or payment order (in M/T), or a telegram or a telex with test key enclosed (in T/T) to the paying bank as a payment authorization, directing it to offer the fund to the payee on behalf of the remitter.

1. Procedures for Handling Outward Remittance

(1) The customer presents the application form of remittance with a seal on to the remitting bank.

(2) For outward remittance in the case of Cash on Delivery, the customer shall present the original customs declaration, verified statement of payment for imports, standby import remittance payment form (if required), and the declaration form of statement of balance of payment.

(3) First-time companies that require the remittance service shall present the documents below: a duplicate copy of the business license; a duplicate copy of the authorized permit for exporting and importing; memorandum account for payment of imports (if required); and specimen signature to be saved with the remitting bank.

(4) The remitting bank sends the currency and the instructions or the trust deed of mail transfer by SWIFT or telex, or opens a draft.

(5) The remitting bank checks the remitted currency regularly, and urges the overseas bank to credit the currency in time.

The operation flow of outward remittance is shown as Figure 4-3 (telegraphic transfer and mail transfer are expressed in bold line, and draft transfer in dotted line).

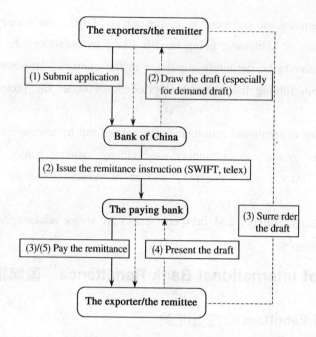

Figure 4-3 The operation flow of outward remittance

Attentions:

In China, when handling outward remittances, it should be presented to the bank the following materials: ① application for outward remittance, ② drawing note of foreign exchange account/RMB check for purchasing foreign exchange; when handling the outward remittance, it must comply with the state regulations on foreign exchange management. Following valid documents required by foreign exchange regulations should be submitted: the relevant approval files for purchasing foreign exchange, the report form of BOP (if needed), and Verification Certificate of Import Payment (if needed).

2. Return of Outward Remittance

In cases of telegraphic transfer and/or mail transfer, the remitting bank will propose return of remittance to the debiting bank on the basis of both the application in written form and the receipt provided by the remitter. Return of remittance shall not be handled unless the remitting bank receives the reply of agreeing remittance return and the currency of remittance from the debiting bank. In the case of a draft, the remitting bank will handle return of remittance on the basis of verification after the remitter proposes it in written form and sends the original draft with endorsement.

4.2.2 Inward Remittance 汇入汇款

Inward remittance refers to the settlement of funds that the overseas remitter transfers to a paying bank via an overseas bank (remitting bank). When the home bank is acting as the paying bank, the remittance handled by him is called an inward remittance. The paying bank shall credit the designated payee's account according to the instructions of the remitting bank.

1. Procedures for Handling Inward Remittance

(1) On receipt of the advice, the paying bank shall, following relevant stipulations, credit the stated amount to the client account on the same day. The payee will receive the advice of receipt the following working day.

(2) If the payee is not locally residing, the paying bank shall transfer the said remittance within two banking days after receipt of the money supply by way of an optimal channel route.

(3) On receipt of the remittance, the paying bank will credit the vostro account in the original currency or settle the remittance, and prepare the statement of balance of payment.

(4) Mail transfer is credited based on the verified trust deed, and a demand draft is credited based on the verified original draft.

The operation flow of inward remittance is shown as Figure 4-4 (telegraphic transfer is expressed in bold line and draft transfer in dotted line).

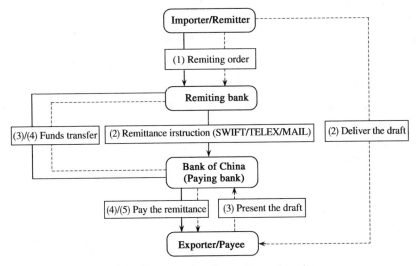

Figure 4-4 The operation flow of inward remittance

2. Principles for Handling Inward Remittance

(1) Telegraphic Transfer is fulfilled not later than the second banking day after receipt, and Mail Transfer is fulfilled not later than the fifth banking day after receipt.

(2) When handling remittance, the observed principle is "crediting to the account of the designated payee".

(3) When responding to inquiries, the paying bank observes the principles of "checking for every inquiry, replying to every customer, and inside checking first before making external inquiries on behalf of the client". Checking by phone shall receive a reply within two banking days, and checking by mail within five.

(4) The paying bank respects the privacy rights of its customers, and shall not entertain any inquiries by any persons other than the remitter and/or the payee.

3. Return of Inward Remittance

(1) The paying bank shall return the remittance on its own initiative if the said amount remains uncredited for three months due to incomplete information on the payee, account number

or mailing address.

(2) If return of remittance is proposed by the remitting bank, the paying bank will handle it after confirming that the currency has been received and has not been credited yet. If, on the other hand, the currency has been credited, the remitter shall contact directly the payee for its return.

(3) If return of remittance is proposed by the payee who refuses to accept the remittance, the paying bank shall debit the currency from the vostro account after verification based on the reasons stated by the payee.

4.2.3 Specimen Forms of Remittance 汇兑业务的表格样本

1. Application for Mail/Telegraphic Transfer

☞ **SAMPLE 4-1**

To
The Manager,
Bank Of India,
Singapore Branch

Pls use **BLOCK CAPITAL LETTERS** & **STRIKE OUT** which is not applicable

Sir,

APPLICATION FOR MAIL TRANSFER /TELEGRAPHIC TRANSFER TO BANK OF INDIA

I/We request you to effect to the debit of my /our account/accepting cash/cheque for the following remittance by cable/telex/swift/mail through your correspondent as per details furnished by me/us. It is distinctly understood that this fund transfer is sent entirely at my/our risk and cost, and that the bank is not to be held responsible for any mistake, omission or delay for misinterpretation of the message when received or transmitted on the part of its official failure/mistakes on the part of intermediary/ agent banks in carrying our instructions or technical snags or postal delays for what so ever reason may be or for any incorrect/incomplete information furnished by me/us.

BANK OF INDIA _____ BRANCH
(Please refer to the bank's BRANCH DIRECTORY FOR CORRECT NAME OF BRANCH)

DETAILS OF BENEFICIARY

NAME: _____

ACCOUNT: NRE/NRNR/FCNR/NRO   SB/DBD/FD/QIC/MIC

ACCOUNT NO. _____

PERIOD OF TERM DEPOSIT: _____ MONTHS.

MT	
TT	

DETAILS OF REMITTANCE

AMOUNT IN INR _____ RATE _____ SGD _____

COMMISSION _____
POSTAGE _____
CABLE _____
CASH IN LIEU _____
TOTAL AMOUNT _____

PAYMENT INSTRUCTIONS

DEBIT MY A/C NO. _____

BY CASH

BY CHEQUE NO. _____ DATED _____ BANK _____

SPECIAL INSTRUCTION _____

APPPLICANT'S DETAILS

NAME: _____ NRIC/PPNO. _____

ADDRESS: _____
_____ SINGAPORE

TELE NO. HP _____ OFF. _____ RESI. _____

EMAIL _____

SIGNATURE _____ DATE: _____

Chapter 4 International Bank Remittance

Application for Real Time Gross Settlements ("RTGS") / and Telegraphic Transfer ("TT")

BankWest
Bank of Western Australia Ltd.
ABN 22 050 494 454

Service Centre Name

I/We request the Bank of Western Australia ABN 22 050 494 454 ("**BankWest**") to make the payment mentioned in this request by: ☐ Real Time Gross Settlements ☐ Telegraphic Transfer

Method of payment to beneficiary: ☐ Advise and Credit ☐ Advise and Pay ☐ Pay on application and identification

Correspondent Bank(s) Charge(s): ☐ Charges to Remitter ☐ Charges to Beneficiary

Financial Markets Ref. No. (where applicable)	Currency and Amount		
☐ Booking Number	Exchange Rate		
☐ Debit Foreign Currency Account		RTGS / TT Fee	
☐ Forward Exchange Contract (FEC) No.	**TOTAL**		

Remitter (full name and address "PO Box" **NOT ALLOWED**)

Beneficiary (full name and address)

Beneficiary's Bank (full name, address and BSB number)

Beneficiary Account Number   Payment Message

I/We agree to the following terms and conditions:

(a) BankWest may not be able to make the payment on the day of this request due to cut off times imposed by payment delivery systems. If this occurs then BankWest will try to make the payment no later than the close of business on the next banking day following the request.

(b) The time taken for a payment to reach the Beneficiary depends on the banking systems of the countries or institutions through which the payment is made and the provision of correct and complete Beneficiary information. A payment sent overseas will normally arrive within one week.

(c) Once a payment is made it is irrevocable.

(d) The receiving institutions may charge a fee and deduct it from the payment.

(e) BankWest will not be liable for any loss resulting from delays in making the payment by it or anyone else or failure of the Beneficiary to receive payment.

(f) I/We acknowledge that my details above are required by the Financial Transactions Reports, act 1988 (Cth), will be used and disclosed (including transferred overseas) by BankWest to give effect to this requisition and that I/We may at any time gain access to those details.

(g) If the Beneficiary is an individual, I/We will advise the Beneficiary that the Beneficiary's information set out above has been provided to BankWest to give effect to this requisition and in accordance with the requirements of the Financial Transaction Reports, Act 1988 (Cth) and that it can be accessed by the Beneficiary.

Authorised Signature(s) of Remitter

BSB, Account Number and/or Foreign Currency Acct. to debit (including fee)   Date

Signature of Authorised Officer of BankWest   BankWest Staff Name and Number   Bank Stamp

S20-9/02

2. Demand Draft Application

 SAMPLE 4-2

Chapter 4 International Bank Remittance

3. Telegraphic Transfer Tracer/Cancellation/Amendment Request

☞ **SAMPLE 4-3**

TELEGRAPHIC TRANSFER TRACER / CANCELLATION / AMENDMENT REQUEST

Your Particulars

Name ....

NRIC/PP No. ....

Contact No. – Tel .... Pager .... Handphone ....

TT Details

Please send a tracer for the following transaction, details are as follows :

TT Reference No. ....

Date of Transaction ....

Currency & Amount ....

Reason for Request :

☐ Beneficiary claims non-receipt of funds.

☐ Amendment of TT details : ....
....

☐ Cancellation of payment.

☐ Others (please specify) : ....
....

Charges Details

Payment of handling charge and any agent charges that may arise from the above request is as follows :

☐ Debit my/our account No. ....

☐ Cash : NRIC/PP No. ....

Terms and Conditions of Request

I/We acknowledge that my request for cancellation of payment will be made only when you are in possession of the funds in respect of the above telegraphic transfer payment. This is subject to the beneficiary and/or his bank agreeing to my/our request for cancellation and returning the funds to you. I/We agree that you will have no responsibility or liability towards me/us if the beneficiary fails to return the funds to you.

I/We agree that any refund is to be made at the prevailing buying rate and less your charges if any.

_____   _____
Authorised Signature(s) with Company Stamp (if applicable)   Date

For Bank Use

Special Instruction from Branch ....
....

☐ Faxed original TT application form to Payment Operations (REM).

Name & Signature .... Branch ....

Specimen No. .... Contact No ....

Fax to : Payment Operations (Rem) – Investigation Team, Fax No. 6878-1053

DBS BANK LTD
Co. Reg. No. 196800306E

REM-03(11/2003)

4.2.4 Methods of Reimbursement 偿付的方法

There are varieties of methods of reimbursement.[6]

(1) Crediting vostro account of the paying bank. If the paying bank opens a current account with the remitting bank, the reimbursement instructions should be written as:

"*In cover, we have credited the sum to your account with us.*"

(2) Debiting remitting bank's nostro account. If the paying bank maintains the remitting bank's account, the reimbursement may be instructed as:

"*Please debit the sum to our account with you.*"

"*You are authorized to debit the sum to our account with you.*"

After effecting payment, the paying bank debits the sum to the account of the remitting bank with them.

(3) Instructing a reimbursing bank to effect payment by debiting the remitting bank's nostro account. If the remitting bank does not open an account with the paying bank, the former may instruct its correspondent with which it maintains an account, to debit this account and credit the paying bank's account if the paying bank has an account with that correspondent, too, or to pay the amount to another bank with which the paying bank maintains an account. The reimbursement clause is thus written as:

"*In cover, we have authorized The Bank of Tokyo, New York to debit our account and credit your account with the above sum.*"

"*In cover, we have instructed The Bank of Tokyo, New York to pay the proceeds to your account with The Standard Chartered Bank, New York.*"

(4) Instructing the paying bank to claim reimbursement from another branch of the same bank or another bank with which the remitting bank opens an account. The instructions are written as:

"*In cover, please reimburse yourselves to the debiting of our account with The Bank of Tokyo, New York.*"

"*In cover, please claim on The Bank of Tokyo, New York.*"

(5) According to the payments agreement between two countries. In case there is a payment agreement signed by two countries concerned, the reimbursement instructions must abide by the terms in that agreement. The instructions are thus written as:

"*In cover, you are authorized to debit our Central Bank's clearing account with your Central Bank.*"

"*In cover, we have requested our Central Bank to credit the sum to the clearing account of your Central Bank with them.*"

4.2.5 Cancellation of the Remittance 汇兑的取消

1. Cancellation of Mail Transfer or Telegraphic Transfer

Mail transfer or telegraphic transfer can be cancelled before its payment is made. It is usually done at the request of the remitter or the payee who refuses to receive the payment.

Whenever the paying bank receives an advice from the remitting bank to cancel the latter's payment order, it will do so accordingly.

Once the payment has been made, the remittance cannot be cancelled. The remitter himself may contact the payee to claim back the remittance payment.

2. Cancellation of a Bank Draft Already Issued

If the remitter requests the remitting bank to cancel a bank draft already issued by reason of its being lost or stolen, the latter is generally reluctant to do so because the remitting bank assumes the responsibility of guaranteeing the draft's payment once it is issued.

However, the remitting bank may issue a duplicate of draft against a letter of indemnity from the remitter, if the paying bank confirms that the original one has not yet been paid.

4.3 Functions of Remittance in International Trade 汇兑在国际贸易中的功能

In international trade, remittance as a settlement of claims and debts, according to the time of shipment and of payment, falls into two categories: the so called "cash before shipment" method and "shipment at first settlement later" method. The former is known as payment in advance, and the latter open account.

Whichever of these two methods of settlement is decided upon, the same methods of payment are available to the importer: SWIFT or telegraphic transfer, mail transfer or demand draft.

However, these two methods of settlement are not popularly used in international trade, because of the risk involved for the importers or exporters.

4.3.1 Payment in Advance Made by Remittance 用汇兑支付预付货款

Payment in advance signifies that the importer pays the exporter before delivery of the goods. In fact, importers are seldom prepared to make full payment in advance of the shipment of goods. It is more common to find that they are prepared to pay in advance only a certain percentage of the value of the goods, that is, the so called down payment.

Payment in advance usually appears in transactions in small amount or in particular business lines. The buyer has to advance the capital too early and undertake the risk of late delivery or non-delivery.

Any of the following methods of transfer may be used to transfer the payment before delivery of the goods from the importer to the exporter through banks: remitting the payment by a banker's draft, by mail transfer, by telegraphic transfer, by SWIFT message, and by an international money order.

4.3.2 Open Account Business 赊账业务

Open account business is also called payment after arrival of goods. The seller may be prepared to ship his goods on open account when the exporter is well acquainted with the financial status of the buyer and entertains no doubt about his solvency, or when the exporter sells goods to his overseas branch or subsidiary.

Under open account business, the exporter sends his shipping documents to the buyer who remits in due course or at agreed intervals the agreed price either by T/T, M/T, or D/D through a bank.

The exporter makes no precise date for payment of the goods shipped. Instead, he is prepared to rely on his past experience of the buyer's integrity to effect settlement at the proper time.

New Words and Expressions

remittance	[ri'mitəns]	n.	汇款,汇款额
transmission	[trænz'miʃən]	n.	播送,发射,传动,传送,传输,转播
designate	['dezigneit]	v.	指明,指出,任命,指派,指定
correspondent	[ˌkɔris'pɔndənt]	n.	代理行
claim	[kleim]	v.	(根据权利提出)要求
		n.	要求权
remitter	[ri'mitə]	n.	汇款人
payee	[pei'i:]	n.	收款人,领款人
domicile	['dɔmisail]	n.	住所,住宅
		v.	(使)定居,居住
authenticate	[ɔ:'θentikeit]	v.	鉴别
negotiate	[ni'gəuʃieit]	v.	谈判,磋商,让渡(支票、债券等)
negotiability	[niˌgəuʃiə'biliti]	n.	可磋商性,可转让性,流通性
entertain	[ˌentə'tein]	v.	娱乐,招待,款待,抱有,持有
subsidiary	[səb'sidjəri]	a.	辅助的,补充的
		n.	子公司
solvency	['sɔlvənsi]	n.	(债务等的)偿付能力
duplicate	['dju:plikeit]	n.	复制品,副本
surrender	[sə'rendə]	v.	交出,放弃
		n.	交出,放弃,投降,取消
beneficiary	[ˌbeni'fiʃəri]	n.	受惠者,受益人

remitting bank　汇出行　　　　　　　　　home country　母国
paying bank　汇入行,解付行　　　　　　outward remittance　汇出
telegraphic transfer　电汇　　　　　　　　inward remittance　汇入
demand draft transfer　票汇　　　　　　cash deposit　预存现款,现金存款
mail transfer　信汇　　　　　　　　　　in line with　根据,按照
mail remittance　信汇　　　　　　　　　letter of indemnity　赔偿保证书
money order　邮政汇票,汇款单　　　　cash before shipment　付款后装运
payment in advance　预付　　　　　　shipment at first settlement later　先装运后结算

Chapter 4   International Bank Remittance

debit advice 借记通知单	down payment 首批付款，定金
payment order 支付委托书	in due course 在适当的时候
on one's own initiative 主动地	financial status 财务状况
designated bank 指定银行	clearing account 清算账户

Notes

1. Remitting bank is the bank transferring funds at the request of a remitter to its correspondent or its branch in another country and instructing the latter to pay a certain amount of money to a beneficiary.   汇出行是应汇款人的请求将资金转移给它在国外的代理行或分行，并指示后者解付一定货币金额给受益人。

2. Paying bank is the bank entrusted by the remitting bank to pay a certain amount of money to a beneficiary named in the remittance advice.   解付行是受汇出行委托将一定货币金额解付给汇款通知书上指定的受益人。

3. A payment order, mail advice or credit advice/please debit advice is an authenticated order in writing addressed by one bank to another instructing the latter to pay a sum certain in money to a specified person or a beneficiary named thereon.   支付委托书、信汇通知书或借记报单是一家银行向另一家银行开出的书面的真实支付命令，指示后者支付一定货币金额给委托书上指定的某一特定的人或受益人。

4. The remitting bank (the draft-issuing bank) debits the customer's account with the amount of the draft plus bank commission (if any), issues a bank draft and hands it to the remitter.
汇出银行（开汇票银行）将汇票金额加上银行手续费（如有的话）借记客户账户，开出银行汇票并将它交给汇款人。

5. The issuing bank sends an advice (a special letter of advice or a non-negotiable copy of the draft) by airmail to the drawee bank, namely its overseas branch or its correspondent abroad, instructing the latter to pay it on presentation of the original draft as well as how to reimburse it.   开票行航寄通知书（特殊的通知函或汇票的不可流通副本）给付款银行，即其海外分行或国外代理行，指示后者在汇票提示时付款及如何偿付票款。

6. 常见的偿付方式(Reimbursement Methods)有以下几种：
   (1) 贷记解付行的来账(crediting vostro account of the paying bank);
   (2) 借记汇出行的往账(debiting remitting bank's nostro account);
   (3) 指示偿付行借记汇出行的往账来偿付解付行(instructing a reimbursing bank to pay the paying bank by debiting the remitting bank's nostro account);

(4) 指示解付行向同一家银行的另一家分行或汇出行开有账户的另一家银行索偿 (instructing the paying bank to claim reimbursement from another branch of the same bank or another bank with which the remitting bank opens an account);

(5) 按照两国的支付协定 (according to the payments agreement between two countries)。

7. In cover, we have credited the sum to your account with us. 作为偿付，我行已将汇款金额贷记你行在我行的账户。

 Exercises

1. Fill in the blanks to complete each sentence.

(1) International remittance happens when a client (payer) asks his bank to send a sum of money to a _____ abroad by one of the transfer methods at his option.

(2) A _____, _____ or _____ is an authenticated order in writing addressed by one bank to another instructing the latter to pay a sum certain in money to a specified person or a beneficiary named thereon.

(3) Telegraphic transfer is often used when _____ and _____. The only means of authenticating a cable transfer is the _____.

(4) Under D/D, upon receipt of the draft, the beneficiary can either present it for payment at the counter of the drawee bank or _____.

(5) The whole procedure virtually is done by entries over banking accounts, where the buyer's bank (remitting bank) _____ his account and _____ the account of the correspondent bank.

(6) In time of war, one can transfer funds out of the enemy country by means of the _____ in virtue of its negotiability.

(7) The remitting bank under D/D is generally reluctant to stop payment on a draft issued by itself for this would mean an _____ on its part which will have an unfavorable effect on its credit-worthiness.

(8) A large number of international remittances are carried out by telecommunications. _____, _____, _____, and _____ are major advantages of transactions among member banks by means of SWIFT messages.

(9) If the paying bank maintains the remitting bank's account, the reimbursement may be effected by _____.

(10) Any methods of transfer may be used to transfer the payment before _____ from the importer to the exporter through banks.

Chapter 4 International Bank Remittance

2. Define the following terms.

(1) international remittance

(2) remitting bank

(3) mail transfer

(4) demand draft transfer

(5) cancellation of the remittance

3. Translate the following terms into English.

(1) 汇款通知单   (2) 汇出汇款
(3) 国际汇款单   (4) 往来账户
(5) 自动支付系统   (6) 作为偿付
(7) 赔偿保证书   (8) 信汇通知书
(9) 汇票的不可流通副本   (10) 首期付款

4. Choose the best answer to each of the following statements.

(1) A payment order, mail advice or credit advice/please debit advice is an authenticated order in writing addressed by one bank to another instructing the latter to pay a sum certain in money to a specified person or a ____ named thereon.
  A. bank   B. beneficiary   C. remitter   D. acceptor

(2) The only means of authenticating a cable transfer is the ____.
  A. SWIFT authentic key   B. payment order
  C. test key   D. authorized signatures

(3) ____ is often used when the client wants to transfer the funds to his beneficiary himself.
  A. Demand draft   B. Mail transfer
  C. Telegraphic transfer   D. Remittance by SWIFT

(4) The same methods of transfer may be used both in advance payment and open account business: remitting the payment by a banker's draft, by mail transfer, by telegraphic transfer, by SWIFT message, and by a(n) ____.
  A. postal money order   B. international money order
  C. payment order   D. reimbursement

(5) If the paying bank opens a current account with the remitting bank, the reimbursement may be effected by ____.
  A. instructing the paying bank to claim reimbursement from another branch of the same bank or another bank with which the remitting bank opens an account
  B. debiting remitting bank's nostro account
  C. instructing a reimbursing bank to pay the paying bank by debiting the remitting bank's nostro account
  D. crediting vostro account of the paying bank

(6) If a London bank makes a payment to a correspondent abroad, ____.

A. it will remit the sum abroad
B. the foreign bank's vostro account will be credited
C. the London bank's nostro account will be credited
D. either A or B

(7) If Barclay Bank instructs Citibank to pay a sum of USD2,000,000 to Midland, its nostro account should be ____.
A. credited   B. debited   C. increased   D. decreased

(8) Mail transfers are sent to the correspondent bank ____, unless otherwise instructed by clients.
A. by courier service   B. by ordinary mail   C. by airmail   C. by seamail

(9) The various methods of settlement all involve the same book keeping. The only difference is ____.
A. the method by which the overseas bank is advised about the transfer
B. the method by which the beneficiary is advised about the transfer
C. the speed
D. the beneficiary

(10) Suppose that a UK firm which is to pay a debt to a West German supplier in Deutschmarks. The firm will give a written instruction to its bank in the UK to issue a mail transfer. Then the UK bank ____.
A. debit the UK firm's account as authorized
B. credit the UK firm's account as authorized
C. debit the account of the West German bank
D. credit the West German supplier's account

Collection
托 收

> 📣 **In this chapter, you will learn:**
> ☑ Definition, parties and types of collection
> ☑ Procedure, outward and inward collection
> ☑ Risk protection and financing under collection methods

5.1 Introduction to Collection 托收方式概述

5.1.1 Definition of Collection 托收的定义

Collection is an arrangement whereby the goods are shipped and a relevant bill of exchange is drawn by the seller on the buyer, and/or shipping documents are forwarded to the seller's bank with clear instructions for collection through one of its correspondent bank located in the domicile of the buyer.[1]

According to the definition given in the Uniform Rules for Collections (ICC Publication No. 522), collection means the handling by banks, on instructions received, of documents, in order to:

(1) obtain acceptance and/or, as the case may be, payment;

(2) deliver commercial documents against acceptance or, as the case may be, against payment;

(3) deliver documents on other terms and conditions.

A documentary collection is distinguished from a typical cash on delivery transaction in two ways:

(1) Instead of an individual, shipping company, or postal service collecting the payment, a bank handles the transaction;

(2) Instead of cash on delivery for goods it is cash on delivery for a title document (bill of lading) that is then used to claim the goods from the shipping company.

Banks, therefore, act as intermediaries to collect payment from the buyer in exchange for the transfer of documents that enable the holder to take possession of the goods. The procedure is easier than a documentary credit, and the bank charges are lower. The bank, however, does not act as surety of payment but rather only as collector of funds for documents.

For the seller and buyer, a documentary collection falls between a documentary credit and open account in its desirability. A documentary collection offers more protection to an exporter than he would have when selling on open account, for if title documents are part of the collection packet, access to the merchandise can be controlled. Moreover, payment is always effected in readily available funds so the exporter is not faced with accepting a check, which would ultimately have to be collected.

The importer is also protected by the documentary collection process for he knows that his merchandise has been shipped, as evidenced by the shipping documents. It is a far better arrangement than payment by cash in advance. For both exporter and importer the documentary collection is cost-effective as collection fees are typically modest.

The disadvantage of selling on a documentary collection basis is that while the merchandise may be protected, it is still in a foreign port. If the drawee fails to pay, an alternate buyer must be found or the goods must be returned at the expense of the seller.

5.1.2 Parties to the Operation of Collections 托收业务的当事人

There are four main parties to a collection transaction. Note that each party has several names. This is because business people and banks each have their own way of thinking about and naming each party to the transaction.

For instance, as far as business people are concerned there are just buyers and sellers and the buyer's bank and the seller's bank. Banks, however, are not concerned with buying and selling. They are concerned with remitting (sending) documents from the principal (seller) and presenting drafts to the drawee (buyer) for payment.

The main parties are as follows:

1. The Principal (Seller/Exporter/Drawer)

The principal is generally the customer of a bank who prepares documentation (collection documents) and submits (remits) them to his bank (remitting bank) with a collection order for payment from the buyer (drawee). The principal is also sometimes called the remitter.

2. The Remitting (Principal's/Seller's/Exporter's) Bank

The remitting bank is the bank receiving documentation from the seller for forwarding to the buyer's bank along with instructions for payment.

3. The Collecting or Presenting Bank

This can be any bank other than the remitting bank involved in processing the collection. Specifically, this is the bank that presents the documents to the buyer and collects cash payment or a promise to pay in the future from the buyer in exchange for the documents.

Normally the collecting bank is a correspondent or branch of the remitting bank in the importer's country. If the collecting bank is not located near the importer, it will send the documents to a presenting bank in the importer's city.

4. The Drawee (Buyer/Importer)

The drawee is the party that makes cash payment or accepts a draft according to the terms of the collection order in exchange for the documents from the presenting/collecting bank and takes possession of the goods. The drawee is the one on whom a draft is drawn and who owes the indicated amount.

Sometimes, in case of non-acceptance and/or non-payment, there may be another party, and that is case of need.

5. Case of Need

The case of need is the representative appointed by the principal to act as case of need in the event of non-acceptance and/or non-payment, whose power should be clearly and fully stated in the collection. [2]

5.1.3 Types of Collection 托收的种类

1. Documentary Collection vs Clean Collection

1) Documentary collections

- Definition

Documentary collections may be described as collections on financial instruments being accompanied by commercial documents or collections on commercial documents without being accompanied by financial instruments, that is, commercial documents without a bill of exchange. [3]

- Alternative Definition

Documentary collection is a payment mechanism that allows the exporters to retain ownership of the goods until they receive payment or are reasonably certain that they will receive it.

- Bank's role in documentary collection

In a documentary collection the bank, acting as the exporter's agent, regulates the timing and sequence of the exchange of goods for value by holding the title documents until the importer either pays the draft or accepts the obligation to do so.

- Basic forms of documentary collections

(1) Documents against payment (D/P)

- Definition

The collecting bank may release the documents only against full and immediate payment, insofar as national, federal or local laws or regulations do not prevent it.

- Precautions

In practice buyers prefer to postpone the takeover of the documents and the payment until after the arrival of the goods. In order to take precautions against such a practice on the part of the importer, a clear term "payment on first presentation of the documents" should be included in the collection order.

- Advantage

This type of collection offers the greatest security to the exporter.

According to the time of making payment, D/P can be divided into two kinds: documents against payment at sight (D/P at sight) and acceptance documents against payment (acceptance D/P).

— Documents against payment at sight (D/P at sight)

Under this method, the seller issues a sight draft. The collecting bank presents the sight draft to the buyer. When the buyer sees it he must pay the money at once, then he can get the shipping documents. This method is also called "payment against documents".

— Acceptance against payment (Acceptance D/P)

Bills of exchange against payment are usually sight bills. But sometimes, the drafts under D/P may be payable on a certain date in the future.

It works like this:

① The collecting bank presents a bill of exchange to the buyer for acceptance;

② The accepted bill is kept at the collecting bank together with the documents up to maturity;

③ The buyer pays the bill of exchange at maturity;

④ At maturity of the accepted bill, the collecting bank releases the documents to the buyer who takes possession of the shipment;

⑤ The collecting bank sends the funds to the remitting bank, which then in turn sends them to the seller.

- Comment

① This gives the buyer time to pay for the shipment but gives the seller security that title to the shipment will not be handed over until payment has been made.

② If the buyer refuses to accept the bill or does not honor payment at maturity, the exporter will have time to take appropriate measures or possibly to look for another customer for the goods.

③ This type of collection is seldom used in actual practice. Acceptance D/P can still be subdivided into two types: D/P after sight and D/P after date.

(2) Documents against acceptance (D/A)

- Definition

The presenting bank may release the documents to the buyer against the buyer's acceptance of a draft, drawn payable 30~180 days after sight or due on a definite date.

- Advantage to the buyer

After acceptance, the buyer gains possession of the goods before the payment is made and is able to dispose of the goods as he wishes.

- Disadvantage to the seller

The seller, however, bears the risk of the buyer's non-payment. If the seller intends to have the shipping documents released against acceptance, he must be sure that the buyer will be in a position to pay the time bill at maturity because he will lose control of the goods and rely on the creditworthiness and integrity of his overseas customer to pay on due date.

- What the seller should know

The draft is held by the collecting bank and presented to the buyer for payment at maturity, after which the collecting bank sends the funds to the remitting bank, which in turn sends them to the principal/seller. The seller should be aware that he gives up title to the shipment in exchange for the acceptance of the bill of exchange that now represents his only security in the transaction.

2) Clean collections

- Definition

Clean collections are collections on financial instruments without being accompanied by commercial documents, such as invoice, bill of lading, insurance policy, etc.

- Features

(1) Under clean collection, only the draft and, if necessary, an instruction letter are sent out for collection. The documents are sent directly by the exporter to the importer or the exporter's foreign agent.

(2) The exporter is, in fact, shipping on open-account terms. Clean collection may also be used when the goods are shipped to agents overseas on consignment.

(3) A clean collection may represent an underlying trade transaction or a purely financial transaction involving no movement of merchandise and, therefore, no documents.

(4) This method lacks the protection of the documentary collection. It is generally used in countries where a draft is needed for legal purposes or because it is required by the exchange control authorities.

- Typical clean items

Typical clean items that may be handled on a collection basis are any of the following items.

(1) Checks.

(2) Dividend warrants drawn on foreign banks.

(3) Promissory notes.

(4) Clean drafts.

(5) Acceptances.

(6) Certificates of deposit issued by foreign banks.

(7) Savings passbooks issued by foreign banks, governments, and post offices.

(8) Drafts drawn under a traveler's letter of credit from a foreign bank.

2. Direct Collection vs Indirect Collection

Usually collection is sent by the remitting bank to the collecting bank, but sometimes it can be sent directly to the correspondent bank by the seller itself.

- Definition

Direct collection is an arrangement whereby the seller obtains his bank's pre-numbered direct collection letter, thus enabling him to send his documents directly to his bank's correspondent bank for collection. This kind of collection accelerates the paperwork process.

- Features

(1) The seller sends to his bank — remitting bank — a copy of the respective instruction/collection letter that has been forwarded directly by him to the correspondent bank — collecting bank.

(2) The remitting bank treats this transaction in the same fashion as a normal documentary collection item, as if it were completely processed by the remitting bank.

(3) By using this service, the exporter foregoes the chance of having the bank examine his documents before they are mailed out. The exporter benefits, however, from the bank's follow-up services.

(4) The collection bank will usually charge the same collection fee that it would apply when a bank sends the item directly.

5.2 Practice of Documentary Collection 跟单托收实务

5.2.1 Procedures of Documentary Collection 跟单托收业务的程序

1. Features of Documentary Collection Procedure

(1) The documentary collection procedure involves the step-by-step exchange of documents giving title to goods for either cash or contracted promise to pay at a later time.

(2) The collection procedure is chronological. The banks in a documentary collection transaction do not act until the preceding steps have been completed. This means that the exporter does not receive payment until his or her bank has received the funds from its correspondent, the overseas collecting bank.

2. Procedure for D/P

The transaction flow of the documents-against-payment goes in the following.

(1) The exporter ships the goods to the importer's location as agreed in the sales contract.

(2) The exporter submits to his bank, the remitting bank, documents, a sight draft drawn on the importer, and written instructions governing the collection.

The documents include a title document, usually the bill of lading, plus any other documents required by the importer or by the Customs in the importer's country. The remitting bank is under no obligation to examine the documents except to verify that they appear to be those stipulated by the exporter.

(3) The remitting bank sends documents, draft, and collection order to the collecting/presenting bank in the importer's country that notifies the importer.

(4a) The importer pays the face amount of the draft plus any charges the importer is responsible for, as stated in the collection order.

(4b) The collecting/presenting bank releases the documents to the importer, who can then claim the goods.

(5) The collecting bank deducts its fee and sends the importer's payment to the bank from which the collecting order was received.

(6) The remitting bank credits the exporter's account for the face value of the draft minus any fees and charges for which the exporter is responsible.

Figure 5-1 illustrates the documents-against-payment transaction flow.

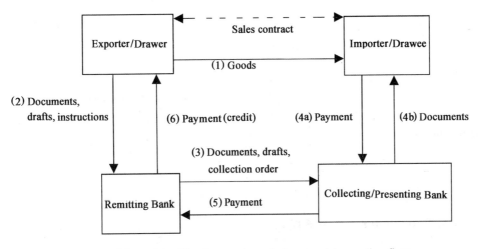

Figure 5-1　The documents-against-payment transaction flow

3. Procedure for D/A

The transaction flow of the documents-against-acceptance goes like the following.

(1) The exporter ships the goods to the importer's location as agreed in the sales contract.

(2) The exporter submits to the remitting bank documents, including a time draft drawn on the importer and a written order giving complete, precise instructions governing the collection.

(3) The remitting bank sends documents, time draft, and collection order to the collecting/presenting bank in the importer's country, which notifies the importer.

(4a) The importer writes "Accepted" and the date and signs across the face of the draft, thereby creating a trade acceptance.

(4b) The collecting/presenting bank releases the documents to the importer, who can then claim the goods.

(5a) At maturity the collecting/presenting bank presents the acceptance to the importer.

(5b) The importer pays the face amount of the acceptance plus any fees or other transaction costs that are the buyer's responsibility.

(6) The collecting bank deducts its fee and either sends the payment to the remitting bank or credits the remitting bank's account if they have a correspondent relationship.

(7) The remitting bank credits the exporter's account for the face value of the draft less whatever fees and charges the exporter is responsible for.

Figure 5-2 illustrates the documents-against-acceptance transaction flow.

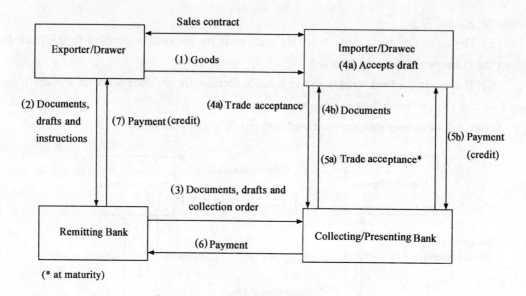

Figure 5-2　The documents-against-acceptance transaction flow

5.2.2　Collection Order　托收委托书

1. Importance of Collection Order

All documents sent for collection must be accompanied by a collection order giving complete and precise instructions. Banks are only permitted to act upon these instructions and in accordance with the Uniform Rules for Collections. If the collecting bank cannot, for any reason, comply with the instructions given in the collection order, it must immediately advise the party from whom it received the collection order.

2. Specific Instructions

The collection order is a standard form of authority that enables the exporter to include specific instructions to his bank regarding the documentary collection. Specific instructions are required on the following points.

1) D/P or D/A

Release documents to the importer against payment (D/P) or against acceptance (D/A). Normally D/P will apply with sight drafts and D/A will apply with term drafts. It is, however, possible to arrange for D/P instructions to be given with term drafts and this can often arise in trade with the Far East.

2) Store and insure clause

(1) If documents are not taken up on arrival of goods, instructions are required on whether to warehouse and insure the goods. This clause is known as a store and insure clause.

(2) If the importer does not pay or accept the Bill of Exchange, he cannot obtain the goods. However, the goods will be at the docks or airport, or container depot, in the

overseas country.

(3) If the store and insure clause is adopted, the overseas bank will be instructed to warehouse and insure the goods if documents are not taken up. The cost of this operation will be claimed from the exporter's bank, which will debit their customer, the principal.

(4) If the goods are warehoused and insured, then they are protected, giving the exporter time to find an alternative buyer or to ship the goods back.

3) Bank and other charges

The collection order will state whether bank and other charges have to be collected in addition to the face value of the Bill of Exchange. The exporter should complete the clause in accordance with the details agreed in the sales contract.

4) About protest

Specific instructions are required on whether or not to protest in the event of dishonor by either non-payment or non-acceptance.

If a Bill of Exchange is protested, a lawyer in the overseas country will undertake formal procedures whereby he asks the drawee the reason for dishonor and makes appropriate notes.

It will be the overseas bank that instructs the lawyer to protest. The overseas bank will have to be reimbursed by the exporter's bank that will then debit their customers.

In some countries, the law requires a dishonored Bill of Exchange to be protested within one working day, otherwise the drawer cannot sue on the bill.

5) Advice of dishonor

Advice of dishonor, with reasons, should be given by airmail or cable. Cable is most desirable, but again the cost will ultimately be borne by the exporter.

6) Prior presentation

When goods are transported by sea and documents go by air, it is quite common for the collection to be presented to the drawee before the arrival of the goods. If this clause is adopted, the overseas bank will be authorized to await the arrival of the goods before pressing the drawee for payment or acceptance.

7) Case of need

The case of need referred to on the collection order is an agent of the exporter who is resident in the importer's country. The case of need can act in an advisory capacity or have full powers. The latter will allow the case of need to overrule the instructions contained in the collection schedule. If a case of need is named, the overseas bank will refer to him in the event of dishonor for guidance or instruction.

8) Method of settlement

Instructions as to the method of settlement are required. Obviously urgent SWIFT would be best from the exporter's point of view, but this is a more costly method than mail transfer is.

SAMPLE 5-1

Specimen of Collection Order (1)
Please Collect the Under-mentioned Foreign Bill and/or Documents

Full Name and Address of Drawer / Exporter				For Bank Use Only	Date		I.S.B. Collection No.
				Drawers reference (to be quoted in all correspondence)			
				For Bank Use Only	Due Date		Correspondents Reference
Consignee — Full Name and Address				Drawee (if not Consignee) — Full Name and Address			
				For Bank Use Only			Fate Dates
To Barclays Bank PLC SWIFT ADDRESS BARC GB22				Drawers Bankers Barclays Bank Account No.	Sorting Code No. 20		Ref. No.

PLEASE FORWARD DOCUMENTS ENUMERATED BELOW BY AIRMAIL. FOLLOW SPECIAL INSTRUCTIONS AND THOSE MARKED X

Bill of Exchange	Commercial Invoice	Cert'd / Cons. Invoice	Certificate of Origin	Insurance policy / cert.	Bill of Lading	Parcel post Receipt	Air Waybill
Combined Transport Document			Other Documents and whereabouts of any missing Original Bill of Lading				

Release Documents On	ACCEPTANCE		PAYMENT		If unaccepted And advise reason by	Protest	Do Not protest
						Cable	Airmail
If documents are not taken up on arrival of goods	Warehouse Goods		Do Not Warehouse		If unpaid And advise reason by	Protest	Do Not protest
						Cable	Airmail
	Insure Against Fire		Do Not insure		Acceptance / Payment may be deferred until arrival of goods.	Yes	No
Collect ALL Charges		Yes		No	After final–payment remit proceeds by	Cable	Airmail
Collect Correspondent's Charges ONLY		Yes		No			
Goods and carrying vessel							
For Bank Use Only							
In case of need refer to					For Guidance	Accept their Instructions	

SPECIAL INSTRUCTIONS 1. Represent on arrival of goods if not honored on first presentation.

Date of Bill of Exchange	Tenor		Amount of Collection	
Bill of Exchange claused	Please apply proceeds of this collection as indicated with an "x".		Credit us in Sterling	
			Credit our Foreign Currency Account	
			Apply to Forward Contract No.	
For Bank use Only	We agree that you shall not be liable for any loss, damage or delay however caused which is not directly due to the negligence of your own officers and servants. Any charges and expenses not recovered from the drawees, including any costs of protecting the merchandise may be charged to us.			
	Date & Signature			

SAMPLE 5-2

Specimen of Collection Order (2)

BANK OF CHINA
COLLECTION ORDER

ADDRESS:
CABLE:
TELEX: DAY-MONTH-YEAR
SWIFT:
FAX:

WHEN CORRESPONDING
PLEASE QUOTE OUR REF. NO

MAIL TO: (COLLECTING BANK)

Dear Sirs,
We enclose the following draft(s) / documents as specified hereunder which please collect in accordance with the instructions indicated herein.
DRAWER:

DRAWEE:

Deliver documents against	Due date / Tenor
Drawer's Ref. No.	AMOUNT

DOCUMENTS

Draft	Comm. invoice	CUST CONSUL. INV	PACK WT LIST	ORIGN CERT	QUAL QUAN WT CERT	INSP ANALY CERT	E L SHIP CERT VISA INV	INS POLICY DECLAR	B/L P.P.R. A.W.B. C.R.				

Special instructions: (See box marked "x")
☐ Please acknowledge receipt of this Collection Order.
☐ All your charges are to be borne by the drawees.
☐ In case of a time bill, please advise us of acceptance giving maturity date.
☐ In case of dishonor, please do not protest but advise us of non-payment/non-acceptance by telex, giving reasons.

Disposal of proceeds upon collection:

REMARKS

Yours faithfully,
For BANK OF CHINA

Authorized signature(s)

Unless otherwise specified this Collection is subject to Uniform Rules for Collections (ICC Brochure No. 522)

5.2.3 Outward Collection 出口托收

1. Classification

Operationally banks classify collection items as either outward collections or inward collections. For the remitting bank in the exporter's country, the item is called an outward collection or payable overseas. For the collecting bank in the importer's country, the item is called an inward collection or payable domestic.

2. Outward Collection

In outward collection, a bank acting as the remitting bank sends the draft drawn against an exporter with or without shipping documents attached, to an appropriate overseas bank, namely, the collecting bank, to get the payment or acceptance from the importer.

5.2.4 Inward Collection 进口托收

1. Inward Collection

In inward collection, a bank acting as the collecting bank receives the draft with or without shipping documents attached as well as the instructions from a bank abroad, namely, the remitting bank. On behalf of the remitting bank, the collecting bank endeavors to collect the payment or obtain the acceptance from the importers.

2. Importance of Collections

Collections serve as a compromise between open account and advance payment in settlement of international transactions concluded by the importer and the exporter. This service offered by banks facilitates a creditor in one country to obtain settlement from a debtor in another at a minimum cost. The handling of inward collections received by banks from their overseas correspondents is considered to be a very important service which, if not taken seriously, can result in monetary loss and also damage a banking relationship.

3. Bank's Responsibility

(1) Banks are only permitted to act upon the instructions given in the collection orders giving complete and precise instructions. Any deviation from these instructions at the request of the drawee will be at the responsibility of the collecting bank.

(2) Banks will act in good faith and exercise reasonable care and must verify that the documents received appear to be as listed in the collection order and must immediately advise the party from whom the collection order was received of any documents missing.[4]

(3) Banks have no further obligation to examine the documents.

4. Presentation

(1) In the case of documents payable at sight, the presenting bank must make presentation for payment without delay.

(2) In the case of documents payable at a tenor other than sight the presenting bank must,

where acceptance is called for, make presentation for acceptance without delay and where payment is called for, make presentation for payment on maturity date.

5.3 Risk Protection and Financing under Collection
托收业务的风险防范与资金融通

5.3.1 Risks Involved under Collection 托收业务的风险防范

At first glance, the use of foreign collection terms seems to be the most satisfactory procedure from the point of view of both the exporter and the importer. Closer examination of collection practices shows, however, that there are a number of risks, especially for the seller but also for the buyer.

1. Risks for Exporter

1) Brief introduction

Seldom does a seller accept payment by D/P or D/A unless the buyer is of unquestionable integrity or if there is a special relation between the seller and the buyer. Generally speaking, most of the risks the exporter assumes include: acceptance risk, credit risk of the importer, political risk of the importer's country, foreign exchange transfer risk and documentary risk that the shipment may fail to clear customs.

2) Risks for exporter

- Non-acceptance of merchandise

One common danger is that the importer may refuse to accept the merchandise. The importer may base the refusal on some small, inadvertent infraction of the sales contract.

The real reason for the non-acceptance of merchandise is that between the time the order was placed and the draft received, there has been a significant drop in the market price. When this happens, the exporter is stuck with his merchandise in a foreign port, probably incurring a heavy storage charge and a market at a greatly reduced price.

Taking court action against the importer is, in most cases, not a satisfactory solution due to the expense and time delay involved.

Usually the foreign collecting bank will offer its assistance in arranging for storage and insurance at the port of destination. Often the bank can help in finding an alternate buyer for the merchandise, although a substantial discount is still required in most cases.

- Non-payment of trade acceptance

Generally, shipping on a time-draft basis is more risky for the seller than a sight draft. In the latter case, at least the seller maintains control over the merchandise until he is paid. Otherwise, the exporter takes not only the risk that the time draft will not be accepted, but also the risk that the trade acceptance will not be paid at maturity. If the acceptance is not paid, the importer has control over the merchandise, thus preventing the exporter from selling it elsewhere.

- Possession of goods

Another danger an exporter might face is that the importer, due to local regulations, can get possession of the goods without paying or accepting the draft. Certain governments, for instance, may demand that the buyer show them the shipping documents before they allocate the needed foreign exchange. In this and similar cases, the document may have to be released to the importer on trust receipt. Thus, the exporter and his agent bank lose control over the merchandise before payment.

- Exchange restrictions

It may occur that the importer is perfectly willing to pay, but that local exchange regulations do not permit him to obtain the necessary foreign exchange. The merchandise in question may not be approved for importation and, in this case, exchange will never be made available. Alternatively, those requiring foreign exchange may have to go on a waiting list that may extend several months or even years.

3) Exporter's measures against risks

In order to avoid or minimize these risks, the seller, besides having a clear picture of these common risks, should take some measures.

First, the exporter should always make sure that the overseas importer is of good reputation and of good financial standing. Otherwise, an importer without satisfactory creditworthiness may reject the goods on some pretext after its arrival, in the hope of driving the seller into a price reduction. Failing to take delivery of the goods promptly upon its arrival at the final destination will result in substantial demurrage and insurance costs, as well as damages to the goods especially to those perishable goods.

Secondly, the exporter should take into account the economic and political conditions in the importing country. For instance, if the market price of the imported goods falls, the importer may also find a pretext to refuse payment.

Thirdly, the exporter should also pay attention to the foreign exchange regulations in the importing country so that the outward payment made by the importer will present no problem.

Furthermore, the exporter should take precautions, such as by hedging operations or by immediate settlement of the accounts denominated in a foreign currency, to avoid losses on foreign exchange transactions.

2. Risks for Importer

1) Brief introduction

A transaction based on collection terms is not entirely without risk for the importer. The importer has the risk that the goods shipped may not be as ordered. He must rely primarily on the exporter's good reputation, honesty, and ability to deliver merchandise of the grade, quality, and quantity ordered.

On sight or arrival draft terms, the importer can not inspect the merchandise before making payment. On time draft terms, the importer can inspect, but only after having obligated himself — at least against holders in due course — by accepting the draft.

The importer may be able to protect himself against faulty merchandise by requiring an inspection certificate as part of the documentation.

2) Risks for importer

(1) Payment may have to be made prior to the arrival of the goods. No opportunity is then available to inspect the goods before making payment. Whether the goods are of the contract description entirely depends on the exporter's credit standing.

(2) By accepting a bill of exchange under the documents against acceptance collection, the importer incurs two separate legal liabilities, that is, he will have another legal liability on the bill of exchange besides his liability on the sales contract.

(3) In some countries, if a bill of exchange is protested, this can ruin the reputation of a trader and may be considered an act of bankruptcy. Therefore the consequences of non-acceptance or non-payment on the part of the importer will be worse than anything else.

5.3.2 Financing under Collection 托收业务的资金融通

1. Collection Bill Purchased

1) Definition

Financing by banks for exporters under documentary collection methods takes the form of collection bill purchased. Collection bill purchased means that the remitting bank purchases the documentary bill drawn by the exporter on the importer.[5]

2) Process

(1) When the exporter hands the bill and the full set of shipping documents over to the remitting bank for collection of payment, the bank may purchase the documentary bill if the export goods enjoy great popularity in the market abroad and both the exporter and the importer are thought reliable.

(2) The bank then sends the exporter the net amount after deducting from the face value the bank fees and the interest incurred.

(3) Thus, the remitting bank becomes the holder of the documentary bill and sends the bill and documents to the collecting bank for presentation to the importer.

(4) When the collection is paid, the collecting bank remits it to the remitting bank that has given the advance.

3) Comment

Collection bill purchased, however, involves great risk for the remitting bank due to lack of a guarantee and, so, many remitting banks are unwilling to do so.

2. Trust Receipt

1) Definition

Financing by banks for importers under collection methods takes the form of trust receipt. On collection terms basis, if the collecting bank has a great degree of trust in the importer, the bank may be willing to release the negotiable bill of lading, and thereby also the goods, to the importer against the signing of a trust receipt. After the importer has made his final sale and received the proceeds, he can pay the collecting bank that granted the advance.⁶

2) Application

Trust receipt is given by the importer to the collecting bank when he asks the bank to release documents of title to the goods which have pledged to the bank as security for credit facilities, without repaying the credit or giving other security.

This happens when the importer has to get hold of the goods (by means of the documents of title) in order to warehouse them or sell them at good prices, but is not yet in a position to repay the credit which is financing the purchase of the goods.

Parties: At this point, the importer acts as a trustee with the bank as the entruster. Since this is an operation of "trust", the legal title to the goods remains with the entruster.

3) The obligations of the trustee

(1) To arrange for the goods to be warehoused and insured in the bank's name.

(2) To pay all the proceeds of sale to the bank or to hold them on behalf of the bank.

(3) Not to put the goods in pledge to other persons.

(4) To return the goods or the proceeds to the bank at any time when requested.

(5) To settle claims of the bank before liquidation in case of the trustee's bankruptcy.

4) Risks for the collecting bank

(1) The collecting bank authorizing the release of title documents on trust receipt must realize that certain risks are being taken that have to be evaluated. After all, physical possession of the goods is being turned over to the trustee in the hope that he will turn over the proceeds of any sale to the entruster.

(2) It should be noted that in this case the bank might bear some risk, as the protection afforded by the trust receipt against a dishonest customer is slight. This is because the letter of trust does not prevent the passing of title to a purchaser who buys the goods from the importer for value and without notice of trust.

(3) Consequently, trust receipt financing, as the term implies, requires a great degree of trust in the reputation, honesty, and integrity of the customer acting as trustee.

New Words and Expressions

forward	[fɔːwəd]	v.	转寄,提交,运送
instruction	[inˈstrʌkʃən]	n.	指示,指导,指令
domicile	[dɔmisail]	n.	住所,住宅
		v.	(使)定居
principal	[ˈprinsəp(ə)l]	n.	委托人,负责人,本金
		a.	主要的,首要的
passbook	[ˈpæsˌbuk]	n.	存款簿,银行存折
paperwork	[ˈpeipəwəːk]	n.	文书工作

Chapter 5 Collection

forego	[fɔː'gəu]	v.	（在位置时间或程度方面）走在……之前，居先
dispose	[di'pəuz]	v.	处理，处置，部署，布置，安排，除去，使愿意
chronological	[ˌkrɔnə'lɔdʒikl]	a.	按年代顺序排列的
verify	['vərifai]	v.	检验，校验，查证，核实
stipulate	['stipjuleit]	v.	规定，保证
warehouse	['weəhaus]	n.	仓库，货栈，大商店
		v.	贮入仓库
demurrage	[di'mʌridʒ]	n.	逾期费，滞纳金
proceeds	['prəusiːdz]	n.	款项
advance	[əd'vɑːns]	n.	预付（款）
representative	[ˌrepri'zentətiv]	n.	代表
		a.	典型的，有代表性的
consignment	[kən'sainmənt]	n.	发货，寄货
accelerate	[æk'seləreit]	v.	加速，促进
integrity	[in'tegriti]	n.	诚实，信誉，正直
overrule	[ˌəuvə'ruːl]	v.	驳回，否决，支配，制服
pledge	[pledʒ]	n.	保证，抵押，抵押品
		v.	保证，使发誓，抵押，典当

inadvertent infraction 无意中造成的伤害，不小心造成的疏忽
faulty merchandise 质量有问题的商品
documentary collection 跟单托收
clean collection 光票托收
collection order 托收委托书
financial instrument 金融单据
remitting bank 托收行
collecting bank 代收行
presenting bank 提示行
outward collection 出口托收
documents against payment 付款交单

documents against acceptance 承兑交单
collection bill purchased 托收出口押汇
trust receipt 信托收据
Uniform Rules for Collections 《托收统一规则》
title documents 物权单据
presentation of the document 提示单据
be in a position to 能够
exchange restrictions 外汇管制
perishable goods 易变质货物
hedging operations 套期保值操作
negotiable bill of lading 可转让提单

Notes

1. Collection is an arrangement whereby the goods are shipped and a relevant bill of exchange is drawn by the seller on the buyer, and/or shipping documents are forwarded to the seller's bank with clear instructions for collection through one of its correspondent bank located in the domicile of the buyer.　托收是这样一种安排，即出口商在货物装运后，开出以进口商

为付款人的相关汇票,将汇票和(或)货运单据连同其明确的托收指示交给出口地银行,委托出口地银行通过其在进口商所在地的往来银行向进口商收取货款。

2. The case of need is the representative appointed by the principal to act as case of need in the event of non-acceptance and/or non-payment, whose power should be clearly and fully stated in the collection. 需要时的代理人(委托人的代表)就是委托人指定的代表。他在汇票遭到拒绝承兑和(或)遭到拒绝付款时充当需要时的代理人。其权利应在托收委托书上有明确而充分的规定。

3. Documentary collections may be described as collections on financial instruments being accompanied by commercial documents or collections on commercial documents without being accompanied by financial instruments, that is, commercial documents without a bill of exchange. 跟单托收可以是附带商业单据的金融票据托收或不附带金融票据的商业单据托收,即并无汇票,单是商业单据的托收。

4. Banks will act in good faith and exercise reasonable care and must verify that the documents received appear to be as listed in the collection order and must immediately advise the party from whom the collection order was received of any documents missing. 银行办理托收业务应遵守信用,谨慎从事,检查所收到的单据为托收委托书中所规定的单据,并应将任何遗失的单据立即通知寄送托收委托书的一方。

5. Financing by banks for exporters under documentary collection methods takes the form of collection bill purchased. Collection bill purchased means that the remitting bank purchases the documentary bill drawn by the exporter on the importer. 跟单托收项下银行向出口商融资常采用托收出口押汇的形式。托收出口押汇是指托收银行买入出口商向进口商开立的汇票。

6. Financing by banks for importers under collection methods takes the form of trust receipt. On collection terms basis, if the collecting bank has a great degree of trust in the importer, the bank may be willing to release the negotiable bill of lading, and thereby also the goods, to the importer against the signing of a trust receipt. After the importer has made his final sale and received the proceeds, he can pay the collecting bank that granted the advance. 跟单托收项下银行向进口商融资常采用信托收据的形式。以托收为支付条件时,如果代收银行对进口商有较高的信任度,代收银行愿意凭进口商签署信托收据而将可流通的提单进而将货物交给进口商。进口商销货并收回货款后再行偿付代收银行。

Exercises

1. Fill in the blanks to complete each sentence.

(1) If the collecting bank is not located near the importer, it would send the documents to a

_____ in the importer's city.

(2) In a documentary collection the bank, acting as the exporter's agent, regulates the timing and sequence of the exchange of goods for value by holding the _____ until the importer either _____ or _____.

(3) The clean collection method lacks the protection of the documentary collection. It is generally used in countries where a draft is needed for _____ purposes or because it is required by _____.

(4) Under documents against acceptance, after acceptance, the buyer gains possession of the goods before _____ and is able to dispose of the goods as he wishes.

(5) Collections serve as a compromise between _____ and _____ in settlement of international transactions concluded by the importer and the exporter.

(6) _____ is a banking business in which a bank acting as the collecting bank receives the draft with or without shipping documents attached as well as the instructions from a bank abroad and endeavors to collect the payment or obtain the acceptance from the importers.

(7) Collection bill purchased involves great risk for _____ for lack of bank's guarantee, so they are seldom willing to do so.

(8) The collecting bank authorizing the release of title documents on _____ must realize that this financing requires a great degree of confidence in the reputation, honesty, and integrity of the customer acting as trustee.

(9) Under _____, the seller issues a draft. The collecting bank presents the draft to the buyer. When the buyer sees it he must pay the money at once, then he can get the shipping documents.

(10) The remitting bank sends _____ to the collecting/presenting bank in the importer's country that notifies the importer.

2. Define the following terms.

(1) collection
(2) case of need
(3) documentary collection
(4) outward collection
(5) collection bill purchased

3. Translate the following terms into English.

(1) 承兑交单
(2) 商业承兑汇票
(3) 需要时的代理人
(4) 出口押汇
(5) 物权单据
(6) 以寄售方式
(7) 直接托收
(8) 货运单据
(9) 付款交单
(10) 远期汇票

4. Choose the best answer to each of the following statements or questions.

(1) The principal is generally the customer of a bank who prepares documentation and submits them to the ____ bank with a collection order for payment from the buyer (drawee).
   A. remitting
   B. collecting
   C. presenting
   D. correspondent

(2) Which type of collection offers the greatest security to the exporter?
   A. Documents against acceptance.
   B. Documents against payment.
   C. Clean collection.
   D. Acceptance D/P.

(3) ____ is an arrangement whereby the seller obtains his bank's pre-numbered direct collection letter, thus enabling him to send his documents directly to his bank's correspondent bank for collection.
   A. Clean collection
   B. Documents against payment
   C. Direct collection
   D. Documents against acceptance

(4) Which of the following is not the obligation of the trustee?
   A. To arrange for the goods to be warehoused and insured in the trustee's name.
   B. To pay all the proceeds of sale to the bank or to hold them on behalf of the bank.
   C. Not to put the goods in pledge to other persons.
   D. To settle claims of the bank prior to liquidation in case of the trustee's bankruptcy.

(5) Which of the following is not a risk that the exporter assumes on documentary collection basis?
   A. Non-acceptance of merchandise.
   B. Harm to the reputation due to dishonor.
   C. Exchange restrictions.
   D. Non-payment of trade acceptance.

(6) _____ is the bank to which the principle has entrusted the collection.
   A. The remitting bank
   B. The collecting bank
   C. The presenting bank
   D. Both A and B

(7) _____ has the right of first choice in selecting a collecting bank.
   A. The presenting
   B. The drawee
   C. The remitting bank
   D. The principle

(8) Any expenses incurred by a bank in connection with protesting a bill will be charged to _____.
   A. the principal
   B. the remitting bank
   C. the collecting bank
   D. the drawee

(9) The commission charged by a third bank involved in the collection should be paid by _____.
   A. the exporter
   B. the importer

C. the correspondent bank   D. the remitting bank
(10) The importance of distinction between financial documents and commercial documents lies in that it helps decide whether it is _____.
A. inward collection or outward collection
B. bill collection or goods collection
C. cash collection or check collection
D. clean collection or documentary collection

Letter of Credit
信用证

> 📢 **In this chapter, you will learn:**
> ☑ Characteristics of a letter of credit
> ☑ Benefits of the documentary credit
> ☑ Basic documentary credit procedure
> ☑ Different types of credits

6.1 Introduction to Letter of Credit 信用证概述

6.1.1 Definition of Letter of Credit 信用证的定义

The letter of credit is the most widely used instrument of international banking. It has had a long and successful history as a means of facilitating international trade, particularly during times of economic and political uncertainty.

In international trade it is almost impossible to match payment with physical delivery of the goods, which constitutes conflicting problems for trade. Since the exporter prefers to get paid before releasing the goods and the importer prefers to obtain control over the goods before paying the money. And collection also involves great risks for both the buyer and seller as is mentioned in Chapter 5. The letter of credit is an effective means to solve the problems. Its objective is to facilitate international payment by means of the creditworthiness of the bank. This method of payment offers security to both the seller and the buyer. The former has security to get paid provided he presents impeccable documents while the latter has the security to get the goods required through the documents he stipulated in the credit.[1]

The documentary credit or letter of credit is an undertaking issued by a bank for the account of the buyer (the applicant) or for its own account, to pay the beneficiary the value of the draft and/or documents provided that the terms and conditions of the documentary credit are complied with.[2]

The documentary credit achieves a commercially acceptable compromise between the conflicting interests of buyer and seller by matching time of payment for the goods with the time of their delivery.³ It does this, however, by making payment against documents representing the goods rather than against the goods themselves.

6.1.2 Characteristics of Letter of Credit 信用证的特点

A letter of credit places a bank's credit instead of a commercial credit. It is guaranteed by the issuing bank's creditworthiness. Its main characteristics are as follows:

(1) The issuing bank undertakes to effect payment, quite independent of whether the applicant is bankrupt or is in default or not, provided the documents presented are in compliance with the terms and conditions of the credit.

(2) A letter of credit stands independent of the sales contract. Although the credit is issued on the basis of the contract, banks are in no way concerned with or bound by it, even if any reference whatsoever to such contract is included in the credit. The bank, when issuing the credit has no regard for the sales contract but follows an application handed in by the buyer.

(3) In letter of credit business, banks deal with documents and not with goods, services or other performances to which the documents may relate. They check exclusively on the basis of the documents presented to them to see whether the terms of the credit are fulfilled. They are not in a position to verify whether the goods supplied actually conform to those specified in the credit.

(4) Banks engaged in letter of credit business assumes no responsibility for the form, sufficiency, accuracy, genuineness, falsification or legal effect of any documents presented. Their main responsibility in this respect is to examine each document presented to see whether it appears on the face to be in compliance with the credit terms.

(5) Banks dealing letter of credit business assume no responsibility for the acts of third parties taking part in one way or another in the credit transaction.

6.1.3 Benefits of Documentary Credit 信用证的优点

The documentary credit provides a high level of protection and security to both buyers and sellers engaged in international trade. The seller is assured that payment will be made by a party independent of the buyer so long as the terms and conditions of the credit are complied with. The buyer is assured that payment will be made to the seller only after the bank has received the title documents called for in the credit.

1. Facilitates Financing the Documentary Credit

(1) Provides a specific transaction with an independent credit backing and clear-cut promise of payment.

(2) Satisfies the financing needs of the seller and buyer by placing the bank's credit standing, distinguished from the bank's funds, at the disposal of both parties.

(3) Reduces or eliminates the commercial credit risk since payment is assured by the bank

which issues an irrevocable documentary credit. The seller no longer needs to rely on the willingness and capability of the buyer to make payment.

(4) Reduces certain exchange and political risks while not necessarily eliminating them.

(5) May not require actual segregation of cash, since the buyer is not always required to collateralize his documentary credit obligation to the issuing bank.[4]

(6) Expands sources of supply for the buyer since certain sellers are willing to sell only against cash in advance or a documentary credit.

2. Provides Legal Protection

Although not forced, documentary credits are supported by a wide variety of laws and customs.

(1) Legislative and semi-legislative law.

(2) Codified law — in most countries, the law for documentary credit has been codified.

(3) Decision law — statutory laws governing documentary credits are found in various jurisdictions. There are also extensive legal cases that have interpreted these statutory provisions and are well known in judicial circles.

(4) Contractual law/customary law — in addition to codified law and case law. Documentary credits are usually governed by the ICC Uniform Customs and Practices for Documentary Credits[5]. These rules, which are periodically revised, have been in effect since 1933 and are the set of universally recognized rules governing documentary credit operation. The current version is UCP600 that was put into effect on July 2007. The UCP rules are adopted by banks through collective notification to the ICC, by the respective National Committees of the ICC, by the national bank association of the country, by a bank's individual adherence and notification to the ICC, or by incorporation of the UCP in the documentary credit itself.

3. Assures Expert Examination of Documents

(1) The buyer is assured that the documents required by the documentary credit (if issued subject to UCP rules) must be presented in compliance with the terms and conditions of the documentary credit and the UCP rules.

(2) The buyer is assured that the documents presented will be examined by banking personnel knowledgeable in the documentary operations.

(3) The buyer is confident that payment will only be made to the seller after the terms and conditions of the documentary credit and the UCP rules are complied with.[6]

6.1.4 Parties to Documentary Credit 信用证的当事人

There are four main parties to a documentary credit transaction and some other parties, which facilitate the transaction. Each party has multiple names. The name used for each party to the transaction depends upon who is speaking. Business people like to use the names buyer, seller, buyer's bank and seller's bank. The banks prefer to use the names applicant, beneficiary, issuing bank, advising bank, confirming bank, nominated paying/negotiating/accepting bank and transferring bank, if any.

(1) Applicant/importer/the buyer. The applicant is always an importer or a buyer, who fills out and signs an application form, requesting the bank to issue a credit in favor of an exporter or a seller abroad.

(2) Issuing/opening bank/the buyer's bank: the bank which issues a letter of credit at the request of an applicant. By issuing a credit the issuing bank undertakes full responsibility for payment against proper documents presented by the beneficiary.

(3) Advising bank: correspondent bank or branch of the issuing bank to whom the letter of credit is routed for transmission to the beneficiary. It has the task of informing the beneficiary that the credit has been issued in his favor so that the beneficiary may make necessary preparation for shipping the goods and drafting the documents stipulated in the credit.

(4) Beneficiary/exporter/the seller: the exporter or the seller in whose favor the credit is issued, because such a credit is considered to benefit the exporter by its assurance of payment to him.

(5) Confirming bank: a bank, usually the advising bank, which adds its undertaking to those of the issuing bank and assumes liability under the credit.

(6) Negotiating bank: a bank that purchases the documents under the credit. If all the credit terms are met, the negotiating bank will buy the exporter's drafts with or without recourse and then it will send the drafts and documents to the issuing bank for reimbursement.

(7) Paying bank/drawee bank: a bank who is authorized by the issuing bank to pay the beneficiary according to the terms and conditions of the credit.

(8) Accepting bank: the bank accepting the drafts under the credit.

(9) Reimbursing bank: the bank from which the nominated paying bank or any negotiating bank that has made a payment under the credit may obtain reimbursement. It can be the issuing bank itself, or an authorized bank of the issuing bank.

6.1.5 Basic Procedures of Documentary Credit 信用证的基本程序

The documentary credit procedure involves the step-by-step exchange of documents giving title to the goods for either cash or a contracted promise to pay at a later time. There are four major groupings of steps in the procedure.

1. Issuance

Issuance describes the process of the buyer's applying for and opening a documentary credit at the issuing bank and the issuing bank's formal notification of the seller through the advising bank.

Figure 6-1 shows the process of issuance.

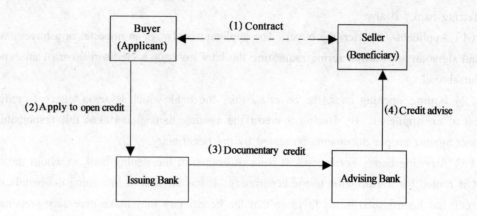

Figure 6-1　The process of issuance

The following numbered steps correspond to the above diagram.

(1) The buyer and seller agree on the terms of the sale.

① Specifying a documentary credit as the means of payment.

② Naming an advising bank.

③ Listing the required documents.

(2) The buyer applies to his bank for the opening of the credit and the conclusion of the security agreement between the applicant and the issuing bank.

(3) The issuing bank sends the documentary credit to the advising bank named in the credit.

(4) The advising bank informs the seller of the documentary credit.

2. Amendment

Amendment is the process whereby the terms and conditions of a documentary credit may be modified after the credit has been issued.

Upon receipt of the documentary credit, the beneficiary should review it closely to see that the terms and conditions:

(1) reflect the agreement of the buyer and the seller;

(2) can be met within the time stipulated;

(3) does not contain any conditions which are unacceptable or impossible to comply with.

Upon examination, the seller may find problems, and if he wants to proceed with the transaction, but with modification to the terms of the contract, he or she should contact the buyer immediately and request an amendment. Amendments must be authorized by the buyer and issued by the issuing bank to the seller through the same channel as the original documentary letter of credit.

Figure 6-2 shows the process of amendment.

Chapter 6　Letter of Credit

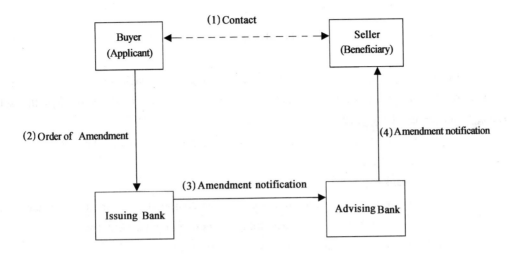

Figure 6-2　The process of amendment

The following numbered steps correspond to the above diagram.

(1) The seller requests that the buyer make an amendment to the credit. This can be done by a telephone call, a fax, or by face-to-face negotiation.

(2) If the buyer agrees, he instructs the issuing bank to issue the amendment.

(3) The issuing bank makes the amendment and notifies the advising bank of the amendment.

(4) The advising bank notifies the seller of the amendment.

3. Utilization

Utilization refers to the procedure for the seller's shipping of the goods, the transmission of documents from the seller to the buyer through the banks, and the transfer of the payment from the buyer to the beneficiary through the banks (settlement).

Figure 6-3 shows the process of utilization.

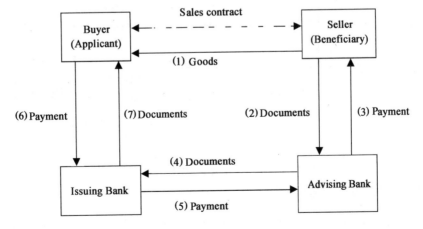

Figure 6-3　The process of utilization

The following numbered steps correspond to the above diagram.

(1) The seller ships the goods to the buyer and obtains the title documents from the shipping

line.

(2) The seller prepares and presents all the documents as required by the credit to the nominated bank.

(3) The advising/confirming bank reviews the document package making certain the documents are in conformity with the terms and conditions of the credit and pays the seller according to the terms of the credit.

(4) The advising/confirming bank sends the documents to the issuing bank by mail or by courier or other telegraphic means.

(5) The issuing bank:

① reviews the documents making certain that they are in conformity with the terms of the credit;

② pays the advising/confirming bank according to their reimbursement agreement;

③ advises the buyer that the documents have been received.

(6) The buyer:

① reviews the documents making certain that they are in conformity with the terms of the credit;

② makes payment to the issuing bank.

(7) The issuing bank sends the documents to the buyer who then takes possession of the shipment.

4. Settlement

Settlement (a subpart of utilization) concerns with the different ways in which payment may be effected to the beneficiary from the buyer through the banks.

Figure 6-4 shows the process of settlement.

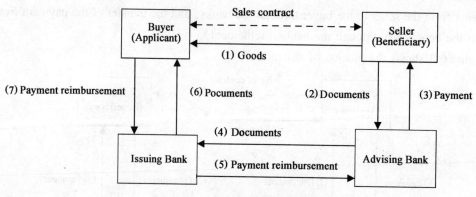

Figure 6-4　The process of settlement

6.1.6　Some Commonsense Rules about Letter of Credit
有关信用证的一些基本规则

An irrevocable documentary credit (especially a confirmed one) is, therefore, an excellent instrument of payment. Also, if appropriate documents are called for, and provided reliance can be placed on the integrity of the seller, it is an effective means of obtaining delivery of the goods. It is, nevertheless, a precision instrument, and must be properly handled by all concerned.[7]

Thus, both the buyer and seller should observe certain rules of commonsense.

1. First Rule

1) Buyer

His instructions to the issuing bank must be clear, correct and precise, and free from excessive details.[8] The bank cannot be expected to guess what he wants, nor can it check complicated, and often technical specifications, etc.

2) Seller

Although considerable time may elapse between the receipt of a credit and its utilization, he should not delay studying it and requesting any necessary changes.

2. Second Rule

1) Buyer

The purpose of the credit is to pay for his purchase, not to "police" the commercial transaction. Its terms and conditions, and the documents called for, should, therefore, be in agreement with the sales contract on which it may be based.

2) Seller

He should satisfy himself that the terms, conditions and documents called for are in agreement with the sales contract. (Banks are not concerned with such contracts.) Their examination of the documents will take into consideration only the terms of the credit and any amendments to it.

3. Third Rule

1) Buyer

Any inspection of the goods prior to, or at the time of shipment must be evidenced by a document. The precise nature and issuer of such documents must be stated in the credit.

2) Seller

When it is time to present the documents, he should:

(1) present the required documents exactly as called for by the credit; (They must be in accordance with the terms and conditions of the credit and not, on their face, inconsistent with one another.)

(2) present the documents to the bank as quickly as possible, and in any case within the validity of the credit and within the period of time after issuance of the transport document specified in the credit or applicable under UCP 600 Article 14.

4. Fourth Rule

1) Buyer

The credit should not call for documents that the seller cannot provide, nor set out conditions that he cannot meet. (This is particularly important with changes in traditional documentation resulting from trade facilitation developments and changes in transport technology.)

2) Seller

He must remember that non-compliance with the terms stipulated in the credit, or irregularities in the documents, oblige the bank to refuse settlement.

6.2 Types of Letter of Credit 信用证的种类

Letter of credit may be classified from different angles such as time of payment, commitment of banks, special purpose of credit, etc.

6.2.1 According to Whether It Can Be Revoked or Not 按是否可撤销分类

1. Revocable Credit

It is a credit that may be amended or cancelled or revoked by the Issuing Bank without the Beneficiary's consent and even without prior notice to the Beneficiary up to the moment of payment by the bank at which the Issuing Bank has made the documentary credit available.

The revocable credit therefore does not constitute an undertaking by the issuing bank to make payment. It involves risks to the beneficiary since the documentary credit may be amended or cancelled while the goods are in transit and before the documents are presented, or although documents may have been presented, before payment has been made, or, in the case of a deferred payment documentary credit, before documents have been taken up. So it is normally accepted as a usage between affiliated parties or subsidiary companies, or as a usage of a particular trade, or as a substitute for a promise to pay or a payment order. At present days, revocable credits are seldom used.

Function clause:

"This credit is subject to cancellation or amendment at any time without prior notice to the beneficiary."

"We undertake to honor your drafts drawn and negotiated in conformity with the terms of this credit provided such negotiation has been made prior to receipt by your notice of cancellation."

"This advice, revocable at any time without notice, is for your guidance only in preparing drafts and documents and conveys no engagement or obligation on our part or on the part of our above mentioned correspondent."

"This revocable credit may be cancelled by the issuing bank at any moment without prior notice."

2. Irrevocable Credit

It is a credit that constitutes a definite undertaking of the issuing bank, provided that the stipulated documents are presented to the nominated bank or to the issuing bank and that the terms and conditions of the documentary credit are complied with, to pay, accept drafts and/or document(s) presented under the documentary credit. It can't be cancelled/modified without the express consent of the issuing bank, the confirming bank (if any) and the beneficiary. Therefore, it constitutes an undertaking by the issuing bank to make payment.

Function clause:

"We (The Issuing Bank) hereby issue in your favor this irrevocable documentary credit that is available by payment/negotiation of your draft."

"We hereby engage with you that all drafts drawn in conformity with the terms of this credit will be duly honored on presentation."

SAMPLE 6-1

Revocable Credit

Commercial Development Bank

Commercial Centre Building   Date: 10th August, 2019
Kuala Lumpur, Malaysia

To: Samata International Trading Co., Ltd. **Transmitted through:** Commercial Trust
International Commercial Building   Bank, Jakarta, Indonesia
Jakarta, Indonesia

Revocable Letter of Credit
NO. MISC 957-321

We are hereby authorized to draw on Cavo International Trading Co., Ltd., Kuala Lumpur, Malaysia for the amounts not exceeding USD500,000 (say five hundred thousand US Dollars only) available by your draft(s) at sight, drawn in duplicate accompanied by the following documents:

1. Commercial invoice in duplicate;
2. Full set of clean "On Board" ocean Bills of Lading made out to order and indorsed blank marked "Freight Prepaid" and notify accountee;
3. Insurance policy in duplicate covering all risks plus 10% of the invoice value.

Shipment: from Indonesia to Malaysia not later than 10th October, 2019.
Partial shipments are allowed. Tran-shipments are allowed.
Covering shipment of: Materials semiconductors type-IIX10 in wooden cases.
Special instructions:

1. This advice, revocable at any time without notice, is for your guidance only in paying drafts and documents.
2. We undertake to honor your draft(s) drawn and negotiated in conformity with the terms of this credit provided such negotiation has been made prior to receipt by your notice of cancellation.
3. Documents have to be presented within 15 days after the date of issuance of the bill of lading or other shipping documents.
4. Draft(s) drawn must be inscribed with the number and date of this credit.
5. Draft(s) drawn under this credit must be presented for negotiation in Indonesia on or before 25th October, 2019.

This credit is subject to Uniform Customs and Practice for Documentary Credits (2007 Revision) fixed by International Chamber of Commerce Publication No. 600.

Commercial Development Bank
Authorized Signature

SAMPLE 6-2

Irrevocable Credit

Commercial Development Bank
Commercial Centre Building
Kuala Lumpur, Malaysia

Date: 10th August, 2019

To: Samata International Trading Co., Ltd. **Transmitted through:** Commercial Trust
International Commercial Building Bank, Jakarta, Indonesia
Jakarta, Indonesia

Irrevocable Letter of Credit
NO. MISC 957-321

We hereby issue in your favor this Irrevocable Documentary Letter of Credit for the amounts not exceeding USD500,000 (say five hundred thousand US Dollars only) available by your draft(s) at sight, drawn in duplicate accompanied by the following documents:

1. Commercial invoice in duplicate;
2. Full set of clean "On Board" ocean Bills of Lading made out to order and indorsed blank marked "Freight Prepaid" and notify accountee;
3. Insurance policy in duplicate covering all risks plus 10% of the invoice value.

Shipment: from Indonesia to Malaysia not later than 10th October, 2019.
Partial shipments are allowed. Tran-shipments are allowed.
Covering shipment of: Materials semiconductors type-IIX10 in wooden cases.

Special instructions:

1. Documents have to be presented within 15 days after the date of issuance of the bill of lading or other shipping documents.
2. Draft(s) drawn must be inscribed with the number and date of this credit.
3. Draft(s) drawn under this credit must be presented for negotiation in Indonesia on or before 25th October, 2019.

Undertaking clause:

We hereby engage with the drawers, endorsers and bona-fide holders of the draft(s) drawn under and in compliance with the terms of the credit that such draft(s) shall be duly honored on due presentation and delivery of documents as specified if drawn and negotiated within the validity date of this credit.

This credit is subject to Uniform Customs and Practice for Documentary Credits (2007 Revision) fixed by International Chamber of Commerce Publication No. 600.

Commercial Development Bank
Authorized Signature

6.2.2 According to the Adding of Confirmation 按是否加保兑分类

1. Confirmed Credit

It is a credit that carries the commitment to pay by both the issuing bank and the advising bank. It is advised to the beneficiary with another bank's confirmation added thereto. It constitutes a definite undertaking of the confirming bank, in addition to that of the issuing bank, provided that the stipulated documents are presented to the confirming bank or to any other nominated bank on or before the expiry date and the terms and conditions of the documentary credit are complied with, to pay, to accept draft(s) or to negotiate.

Confirmation is only added to an irrevocable credit at the request of the issuing bank. It is used when the seller does not have confidence that the issuing bank can effectively guarantee payment. Therefore, if the issuing bank is considered to be a first class bank, there may not be any need to have its documentary credit confirmed by another bank.

If the advising bank confirms the credit, it must pay without recourse to the seller when the documents are presented, provided they are in order and the credit requirements are met.[9]

Advantages:

(1) A double assurance of payment;

(2) Assurance of payment by the issuing bank;

(3) Assurance of payment from the confirming bank.

The issuing bank's authorization clause:

"*The advising bank is authorized to add your confirmation.*"

"*Please notify the beneficiary and add your confirmation.*"

"*Please add your confirmation if the beneficiary required.*"

The confirming bank's engagement clause:

"*At the request of the correspond (Issuing Bank) we (Advising Bank) have been requested to add our confirmation to this credit and we hereby undertake that all drafts drawn by you (Beneficiary) in accordance with the terms of the credit will be duly honored by us.*"

"*At the request of the correspondent bank we confirm the credit and also engage with you that drafts drawn in conformity with the terms of this credit will be paid by us.*"

"*This credit bears our confirmation and we hereby engage to negotiate, or accept on presentation to us, drafts drawn and documents presented in conformity with the terms of this credit.*"

"*We have been requested to add our confirmation to this credit and we hereby undertake to honor all drafts drawn in accordance with the terms of the credit.*"

Silent confirmation:

Silent confirmation represents an agreement between a bank and the beneficiary for that bank to "add its confirmation" to the documentary credit despite not being so authorized by the issuing bank. In this case the beneficiary and the advising bank make an independent agreement that adds the bank's confirmation to the credit for a fee.

SAMPLE 6-3

Confirmed Letter of Credit

Name of Issuing Bank: The French Issuing Bank 5th rue Francois ler 85008 Paris, France	**Irrevocable** **Documentary Credit**	Number 12345
Place and Date of Issue: Paris, 1 January, 2019	Expiry Date and Place for Presentation of Documents Expiry Date: May 29, 2019 Place for Presentation: The American Advising Bank, Tampa	
Applicant: The French Import Co. 89 rue du Commerce		
Advising Bank: Reference No. The American Advising Bank 456 Commerce Avenue Tampa, Florida	Beneficiary: The American Exporter Co. Inc. 17 Main Street, Tampa, Florida	
Partial shipments ☐ Allowed ☒ Not Allowed Transhipments ☐ Allowed ☒ Not Allowed	Amount: USD 100,000 — One Hundred Thousand US Dollars	
Confirmation: ☒ Requested ☐ Not Requested ☐ Insurance covered by buyers	Credit Available with Nominated Bank: The American Advising Bank ☒ by payment at sight ☐ by deferred payment at ☐ by acceptance of drafts at ☐ by negotiation	
Shipment From: Tampa, Florida For Transportation to: Paris, France Not Later than: May 15, 2019	Against the documents detailed herein ☐ and Beneficiary's draft(s) drawn on The French Issuing Bank, Paris, France	

Documents to be presented:

Commercial Invoice, One original and 3 copies

Multimodal Transport Document issued to the order of the French Importer Co. marked Freight Prepaid and <u>notify</u> XYZ Custom House Broker Inc.

Insurance certificate covering the Institute Cargo Clauses and the Institute War and Strike Clauses for 110% of the invoice value endorsed to the French Import Co.

Certificate of Origin evidencing goods to be of USA Origin

Packing List

Covering: Machinery and spare parts as per pro-forma invoice number 657
Dated December 17, 2018-CIP INCOTERMS 2000

Documents to be presented within ☐ days after the date of shipment but within the validity of the credit

We hereby issue the Irrevocable Documentary Credit in your favor. It is subject to Uniform Customs and Practice for Documentary Credits (2007 Revision fixed by International Chamber of Commerce No. 600) and engages us in accordance with the terms thereof. The number and the date of the credit and the name of our bank must be quoted on all drafts required. If the credit is available by negotiation, each presentation must be noted on the reverse side of this <u>advice</u> by the bank where the credit is available.

This document consists of ☐ signed page(s).

                                      The French Issuing Bank
                                      Authorized Signature

Irrevocable Documentary Credit(Confirmed)Advice

Name of Advising Bank The American Advising Bank, 456 Commerce Avenue Tampa, Florida Reference Number of Advising Bank: 2417 Place and date of Notification: Jan. 14, 2019. Tampa	Notification of Irrevocable Documentary Credit
Issuing Bank: The French Issuing Bank 5th rue Francois ler 85008 Paris, France	Beneficiary: The American Exporter Co. Inc.17 Main Street, Tampa, Florida
Reference Number of Issuing Bank: 12345	Amount: USD100, 000 — One Hundred Thousand US Dollars

We have been informed by the above-mentioned issuing bank that the above-mentioned Documentary Credit have been issued in your favor.

Please find enclosed the advice intended for you.

Check the Credit terms and conditions carefully. In the event that you do not agree with the terms and conditions, or if you feel unable to comply with any of those terms and conditions, kindly arrange an amendment of the Credit through your contracting party (the Applicant).

☐ This notification and the enclosed advice are sent to you without any engagement on our part.

☒ As requested by the Issuing Bank, we hereby add our confirmation to this Credit in accordance with the stipulations under UCP 600 Article 8.

The American Advising Bank
Authorized Signature
_____

2. Unconfirmed Credit

It is a credit that bears no confirmation of the correspondent bank. It only has the commitment of the issuing bank.

Function clause—when this kind of credit is advised to the beneficiary, the advising bank should clearly state in its credit advice:

"*We advise this credit to you without engagement on our part.*"

The beneficiary therefore has to rely solely on the foreign bank that issues the credit. This means that an unconfirmed irrevocable credit is appropriate only if the political and transfer risks are small.

SAMPLE 6-4

Unconfirmed Letter of Credit

Name of Issuing Bank: The French Issuing Bank 5th rue Francois ler 85008 Paris, France	Irrevocable Documentary Credit	Number 12345
Place and Date of Issue: Paris, 1 January, 2019	Expiry Date and Place for Presentation of Documents Expiry Date: May 29, 2019 Place for Presentation: The Americ an Advising Bank, Tampa	
Applicant: The French Import Co. 89 rue du Commerce		
Advising Bank: Reference No. The American Advising Bank 456 Commerce Avenue Tampa, Florida	Beneficiary: The American Exporter Co. Inc. 17 Main Street, Tampa, Florida	
Partial shipments ☐ Allowed ☒ Not Allowed Transhipments ☐ Allowed ☒ Not Allowed	Amount: USD 100,000 — One Hundred Thousand US Dollars	
Confirmation: ☐ Requested ☒ Not Requested ☐ Insurance covered by buyers	Credit Available with Nominated Bank: The American Advising Bank ☐ by payment at sight ☐ by deferred payment at ☐ by acceptance of drafts at ☐ by negotiation	
Shipment From: Tampa, Florida For Transportation to: Paris, France Not Later than: May 15, 2019	Against the documents detailed herein ☐ and Beneficiary's draft(s)drawn on The French Issuing Bank, Paris, France	

Documents to be presented:
Commercial Invoice, One original and 3 copies

Multimodal Transport Document issued to the order of the French Importer Co. marked Freight Prepaid and <u>notify</u> XYZ Custom House Broker Inc.

Insurance certificate covering the Institute Cargo Clauses and the Institute War and Strike Clauses for 110% of the invoice value endorsed to the French Import Co.

Certificate of Origin evidencing goods to be of USA Origin

Packing List

Covering: Machinery and spare parts as per pro-forma invoice number 657
Dated December 17, 2018-CIP INCOTERMS 2000

Documents to be presented within 7 days after the date of shipment but within the validity of the credit

We hereby issue the Irrevocable Documentary Credit in your favor. It is subject to Uniform Customs and Practice for Documentary Credits (2007 Revision fixed by International Chamber of Commerce No. 600) and engages us in accordance with the terms thereof. The number and the date of the credit and the name of our bank must be quoted on all drafts required. If the credit is available by negotiation, each presentation must be noted on the reverse side of this <u>advice</u> by the bank where the credit is available.

This document consists of ☐ signed page(s).

The French Issuing Bank
Authorized Signature

Irrevocable Documentary Credit(Unconfirmed)Advice

Name of Advising Bank The American Advising Bank, 456 Commerce Avenue Tampa, Florida Reference Number of Advising Bank: 2417 Place and date of Notification: Jan. 14, 2019. Tampa	Notification of Irrevocable Documentary Credit
Issuing Bank: The French Issuing Bank 5th rue Francois ler 85008 Paris, France	Beneficiary: The American Exporter Co. Inc. 17 Main Street, Tampa, Florida
Reference Number of Issuing Bank: 12345	Amount: USD100, 000 — One Hundred Thousand US Dollars

We have been informed by the above-mentioned issuing bank that the above-mentioned Documentary Credit have been issued in your favor.
  Please find enclosed the advice intended for you.
  Check the Credit terms and conditions carefully. In the event that you do not agree with the terms and conditions, or if you feel unable to comply with any of those terms and conditions, kindly arrange an amendment of the Credit through your contracting party (the Applicant).

☒ This notification and the enclosed advice are sent to you without any engagement on our part.
☐ As requested by the Issuing Bank, we hereby add our confirmation to this Credit in accordance with the stipulations under UCP 600 Article 8.

The American Advising Bank
Authorized Signature
_____

6.2.3 According to the Tenor 按期限分类

1. Sight Credit

It is a letter of credit calling for payment upon the presentation of the documents either with or without a sight draft. Under such a credit, the beneficiary (the drawer) is entitled to receive payment at once on presentation of his draft to the drawee bank or to the issuing bank if drawn on the issuing bank, once the relevant documents have been checked and found to be in order. Payment is sometimes effected only against a receipt issued by the beneficiary but usually against correct documents without any receipt.

Function clause:
  "Available by sight draft drawn on issuing bank against complying documents."
  "Payment is to be made upon presentation of the complying documents at the counters of ... bank."

SAMPLE 6-5

Irrevocable Sight Documentary Letter of Credit

Exim-bank Ltd. Malaysia International Commercial Building 10th/F. BOX 100815	Tel: 762-2215 Telex: 762517N
Issuing Bank: Exim-bank Ltd. Malaysia **Irrevocable Documentary Credit**	**Date and Place of Issue:** June 25, 2019, Malaysia **Credit Number:** Of Issuing Bank: S-01-Y-825 Of Advising Bank: MS810
Advising Bank: Development Bank, (Ltd.) International Trading Building, Singapore P.O. Box 401016	**Applicant:** Dearmei Trading Co., Ltd, Malaysia 10th/F. Lisi Building P.O. Box 288125
Beneficiary: Kam Dor Bo Trading Co., Ltd 8th/F. Forrum Building Singapore	**Expiry Date:** 25th August, 2019 In the country of the beneficiary

At the request of Dearmei Trading Co., Ltd, Malaysia, we open this Irrevocable Documentary Letter of Credit No. S-01-Y-825 in your favor for an amount not exceeding total of USD1,000,000 (One million US Dollar only) available by your drafts drawn at sight on us covering 100% invoice value accompanied by the following documents:
1. Commercial invoice in triplicate
2. Insurance policy in duplicate covering all risks plus 10% of invoice value
3. Full set of clean "On board" ocean Bills of Lading made out to our order notify buyers and marked "Freight Prepaid".
4. Certificate of origin in duplicate
5. Packing list in duplicate
6. Certificate of inspection in duplicate

Covering shipment of: ESP 20 kit, ESPS 10 kit, ESPSS 10 kit all in crates
Shipment from Singapore to Malaysia CIF Contract No. ESP 1245
Shipment must be effected not later than 30th July, 2019.

Special Clause:
1. This credit is available by draft drawn on issuing bank at sight.
2. Partial shipments are prohibited. Tran-shipments are prohibited.
3. Draft against this credit must be drawn and negotiated on or before August 25, 2019.
4. The number and date of this credit must appear on the draft drawn.
5. The amount of the draft must be endorsed on the back hereof and this credit is to be returned to us when exhausted or expired.

We hereby guarantee that drafts drawn under and in compliance with the terms and conditions of this credit shall be duly accepted and paid at sight.

For the **Exim-bank Ltd. Malaysia**
Authorized Signature

2. Time Credit/Usance Credit

If a letter of credit specifies that drafts are to be drawn at any length of time, such as 60 days, 90 days or 180 days, after sight, it is called a time or usance credit. Under such a credit, the issuing bank engages that the drafts drawn in conformity with the terms of the credit will be duly accepted on presentation and duly honored at maturity.

Function clause:

"Available by your draft drawn on the issuing bank at ... days after sight honored at maturity."

"Payment of the draft drawn under this credit will be effected at ... days after sight."

3. Usance Letter of Credit Payable at Sight

Under this credit, the beneficiary will receive payment at sight and the discount charges and acceptance commission are for the account of the applicant.[10] In this case, clauses in the credit are as follows:

"Available for acceptance of your drafts at 90 days sight drawn on us, drawee bank's discount or interest charges and acceptance commission are for applicant's account, and therefore the beneficiary is to receive value for term drafts as if drawn at sight."

"Usance drafts drawn under this credit are to be negotiated at sight basis. Interest is for buyer's account."

"Payments are to be made at sight basis. Discount charges, acceptance commission and stamp duty, if any, are for account of the applicant."

"The negotiating bank is authorized to negotiate the usance draft at sight for the face amount."

☞ SAMPLE 6-6

Seller's Usance Letter of Credit

Commercial Development Bank Commercial Centre Building New Delhi, India	
Irrevocable Documentary Credit Credit No. IS1125, Date of Issue: 5th Feb., 2019	
Advising Bank: United Chinese Commercial Bank, # 0509 Singapore	**Beneficiary:** Sea-Ocean Building Material Co., (Pte) Ltd. # 0721 Singapore

At the request of Tabowell International Building Materials Industry Co., Ltd., New Delhi, India, We establish an Irrevocable Credit (Seller's Usance Credit) in favor of Sea-Ocean Building Material Co., (Pte) Ltd. For the amount of USD500,000 (say five hundred thousand US Dollars only). Expiry date & place on 15th August, 2019 at the counter of the advising bank. Available by your draft(s) drawn on applicant at 120 days after sight, discount charges, stamp duty and acceptance commission are for the beneficiary's account.

Accompanied by the following documents in duplicate unless otherwise specified:
— Commercial invoice signed by general manager of Sea-Ocean Building Material Co., (Pte) Ltd.
— Insurance policy for 110% of invoice covering all risk.
— Full set of clean "On board" ocean Bills of Lading made out to order of Tabowell International Building Materials Industry Co., Ltd., New Delhi, India, marked "Freight Prepaid".

Shipping date:
Shipment to be effected not later than 15th March, 2019.

Evidencing shipment of:
Finishing materials & sanitary plumbing equipment
FM-60 boxes,   SPE-60 boxes
Shipment from Singapore to Calcutta, CIF Contract NO. IS98911

Other terms:
All negotiation and bank charges including advising charges under this credit are for account of the beneficiary.

Undertaking clause:
We hereby engage with the drawers, endorsers and bona-fide holders of the draft(s) drawn under and in compliance with the terms of the credit that such draft(s) shall be duly honored on due presentation and delivery of documents as specified if drawn and negotiated within the validity date of this credit.

This credit is subject to Uniform Customs and Practice for Documentary Credits (2007 Revision) Fixed by International Chamber of Commerce Publication No. 600.

Tel: 234666 Telex: CDB 366 Fax: DCDB 366	For Commercial Development Bank Authorized Signature

SAMPLE 6-7

Usance Letter of Credit Payable at Sight

Commercial Development Bank Commercial Centre Building New Delhi, India	
Irrevocable Documentary Credit	Credit No. IS1125 Date of Issue: 5th May, 2019
Advising Bank: United Chinese Commercial Bank, # 0509 Singapore	Beneficiary: Sea-Ocean Building Material Co., (Pte) Ltd, # 0721 Singapore

At the request of Tabowell International Building Materials Industry Co., Ltd., New Delhi, India, We issue an Irrevocable Documentary Credit in favor of Sea-Ocean Building Material Co., (Pte) Ltd. For the amount of USD500,000 (say five hundred thousand US Dollars only). Expiry date & place on 15th December, 2019 in country of the beneficiary. Usance draft(s) at 180 days to be negotiated at sight basis and discounted by us. Discount charges, stamp duty and acceptance commission are for the applicant's account.

Accompanied by the following documents in duplicate unless otherwise specified:
— Commercial invoice signed by general manager of Sea-Ocean Building Material Co, (Pte) Ltd.
— Insurance policy for 110% of invoice covering all risks.
— Full set of clean "On board" ocean Bills of Lading made out to order of Tabowell International Building Materials Industry Co., Ltd., New Delhi, India, marked "Freight Prepaid".

Shipping date:
Shipment to be effected not later than 5th June, 2019.

Evidencing shipment of:
Finishing materials & sanitary plumbing equipment
FM-60 boxes, SPE-60 boxes
Shipment from Singapore to Calcutta, CIF Contract NO. IS98911

Other terms:
All negotiation charges including advising charges under this credit are for account of the beneficiary.
Usance draft (s) 180 days drawn under this credit are to be negotiated at sight basis.

Undertaking clause:
We hereby engage with the drawers, endorsers and bona-fide holders of the draft(s) drawn under and in compliance with the terms of the credit that such draft(s) shall be duly honored on due presentation and delivery of documents as specified if drawn and negotiated within the validity date of this credit.

This credit is subject to Uniform Customs and Practice for Documentary Credits (2007 Revision) Fixed by International Chamber of Commerce Publication No. 600.

	For
Tel: 234666 Telex: CDB 366 Fax: DCDB 366	**Commercial Development Bank** Authorized Signature

6.2.4 According to Whether the Credit Can Be Transferred or Not
按信用证是否可以转让分类

1. Transferable Credit

It is a credit under which the beneficiary (the first beneficiary) may request the bank authorized to pay, incur a deferred payment undertaking, accept or negotiate (the transferring bank), or in the event of a freely negotiable credit, the bank specially authorized in the credit as the transferring bank to make the documentary credit available in whole or in part to one or more other beneficiary(ies) (second beneficiary).[11]

A credit can be transferred only if it is expressly designated as "transferable" by the issuing bank. Terms such as "divisible", "fractionable", "assignable", and "transmissible" do not render the credit transferable. If such terms are used they shall be disregarded.

A transferable credit can be transferred once. The second beneficiary cannot further transfer it.

SAMPLE 6-8

Transferable Credit

Commercial Development Bank
Commercial Centre Building
Kuala Lumpur, Malaysia

L/C NO. MS1024
Telex: 25455CDB

Transferable Letter of Credit   Date: 20th May, 2019

Applicant:	Tamali Trading Co., Ltd. Ampang Commercial Plaza Kuala Lumpur
Issuing Bank:	Commercial Development Bank
Amount:	USD100,000 (One Hundred Thousand US Dollars Only)
Expiry:	15th October, 2019 negotiation under this credit is restricted to the advising bank.
Advising Bank:	Commercial Trust Bank, Jaran Jurang Singapore
Beneficiary:	Universal Metals Trading (Pte) Co., Ltd. Jaran Jurang Singapore 584A

At the request of Tamali Trading Co., Ltd, We issue an Irrevocable Documentary Transferable Letter of Credit NO. MS1024. This credit is available by beneficiary's draft(s), drawn at sight on us in duplicate, covering 100% of the invoice value, and accompanied by the following documents marked "X".

☒ 1. Full set of clean "On Board" ocean Bills of Lading made out to order and indorsed blank marked "Freight Prepaid" and notify applicant.
☒ 2. Commercial invoice in duplicate, indicating contract No. _____.
☒ 3. Certificate of Quality in duplicate issued by the manufacturer.
☒ 4. Insurance policy in duplicate covering marine risk for 110% CIF invoice value.

Covering: Spare parts of communication equipment
　　　　　　　　　　　　　　　　　　　　　　　　　CEP — 10 cases
　　　　　　　　　　　　　　　　　　　　　　　　　CEHP — 10 cases
　　　　　　　　　　　　　　　　　　　　　　　　　CEHTP — 10 cases
Packing: Packed in wooden cases. Shipment from Singapore to Malaysia
Shipment: Partial shipment is not allowed. Tran-shipment is allowed. Shipment is to be made on or before 20th June, 2019
Special instruction:
　1. This credit is total transferable and it is transferable in Singapore only.
　2. Any negotiation and transfers under this credit is restricted to advising bank.
Undertaking clause:
　We hereby guarantee that all draft(s) drawn and negotiated in compliance with the terms and conditions of this credit shall be duly paid at maturity.
　This credit is subject to Uniform Customs and Practice for Documentary Credits (2007 Revision)fixed by International Chamber of Commerce Publication No. 600.

Commercial Development Bank
Authorized Signature

```
                          Advice of Total Transfer
                                        Tel: _____
                                        Telex: _____
                                        Date: _____
To _____
    Our Ref. No. _____
    Irrevocable Documentary Transferable credit No. _____
    In Favor of _____
    For the amount of USD _____
Dears Sirs:
    This credit has been totally transferred to _____ Co.
    Attention: Mr. _____
    We hereby authorize your draft(s) at sight on _____ Bank.
    Total transferable and transfer without substitution of invoice, this credit is transferable in
    beneficiary's country only.
    We have been authorized by issuing Bank to negotiate your draft(s) drawn in duplicate on us at sight.
    Shipping Date: _____
    Shipping from _____ to _____ 2019.

    Encl.
                                                    Yours faithfully,
    c.c.   The Original Beneficiary
           Issuing Bank                             For _____ Bank
                                                    Signature_____
```

1) Characteristics of transferable credit

(1) A transferable credit is designed to meet the requirements of international trade. It enables a middleman who is receiving payment from a buyer under a documentary to transfer his claim under the credit to his own supplier. In this way, he can carry out transactions with only a limited outlay of his own funds.

(2) The middleman gets his buyer to apply for an irrevocable credit in the middleman's favor. The issuing bank must expressly designate it as "transferable".

(3) There are two methods allowing for transferring the beneficiary's rights to a third party: assignment and transfer.

① Assignment. The beneficiary assigns or transfers to a third party his rights to the proceeds to which he may be, or may become, entitled under a documentary credit, in accordance with the provisions of the applicable law.

② Transfer. The beneficiary assigns or transfers his right to perform under the documentary credit to a third party.

2) Working flow of transferable credit

Figure 6-5 shows the working flow of transferable credit.

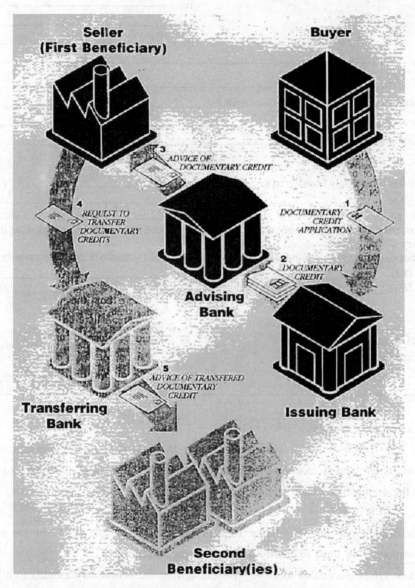

Figure 6-5 The working flow of transferable credit

3) Types of transfer
- Total transfer

Function clause:

"*The undersigned beneficiary hereby irrevocably transfers all his rights under the credit to ...*"

- Partial transfer

Function clause:

"*The undersigned beneficiary hereby irrevocably transfers partial of his rights under the*

credit to ... "
- Transfer without substitution of invoice

Function clause:

"*The undersigned beneficiary hereby irrevocably transfers all his rights under the credit to ... the undersigned beneficiary waives his right to substitute his own invoice and drafts for those of the transferee.*"

- Transfer with substitution of invoice

Function clause:

"*The undersigned beneficiary hereby irrevocably transfers all/partial of his rights under the credit to... the undersigned beneficiary retains the right to substitute his own invoice and drafts for those of the transferee.*"

- Transfer according to the original clause

It refers to a credit transferred under the terms stated in the original credit.

- Transfer with some clauses being changed

A transferable credit can be transferred only under the terms stated in the original credit. However, the intermediary may transfer the credit with the following changes.

(1) The name and address of the first beneficiary may be substituted for that of the original buyer.

(2) Unit prices and total amount of the credit may be reduced to enable the original beneficiary an allowance for profit.

(3) The expiration date, the final shipment date, and the final date for presentation of documents may all be shortened to allow the intermediary time to meet obligations under the original credit.

(4) Insurance coverage may be increased in order to provide the percentage amount of cover stipulated in the original credit.

4) Amendments to the transferable credit

Since the ultimate buyer and the actual supplier of the credit may be separated by the intermediary, there is the question of how to deal with amendments. According to UCP 600 sub-article 38(e), the beneficiary must, at the time of making a request for transfer, and prior to the transfer of the credit, irrevocably instruct whether the transferring bank may advise amendments to the secondary beneficiary.

Options for transfer rights on amendments include full or partial transfer of the credit with:

(1) retainment of rights on amendments;

(2) partial waiver of rights on amendments;

(3) waiver of rights on amendments.

2. Non-transferable Credit

It is a credit under which the beneficiary may not request the credit be transferred.

6.2.5　According to the Mode of Availability　根据付款方式分类

Depending on the way in which the credit is to be made available to the beneficiary, one or the other of the following credit types or special arrangement is employed.

1. Payment Credit/Sight Credit

It provides for payment to be made to the beneficiary immediately after presentation of the stipulated documents and on condition that the terms of the credit have been complied with.

A payment credit is a credit available by payment, under which a bank (the issuing bank/a third bank/the advising bank) specifically nominated therein is authorized to pay against the shipping documents with or without a draft presented in conformity with the terms of the credit. The paying bank indicated in the letter of credit may be the issuing bank, the advising bank or any other third bank.

(1) Available by payment with the issuing bank. It means that upon receipt of the documents by the issuing bank, it will effect the payment. The letter of credit will be expired at the place of issuing bank, that is, documents should be presented to the issuing bank within the validity of the credit. No other bank can negotiate the documents.

(2) Available by payment with a third bank. The third bank is always a clearing bank in major currency clearing centers in the world.

(3) Available by payment with the advising bank. It means that the paying bank is the advising bank and the credit will be expired at the place of advising bank. This is a typical payment credit. Whenever payment is made, it becomes a final payment without any right of recourse. The paying bank is authorized to debit the issuing bank's account if an account is opened with the bank, or the advising bank may claim reimbursement from the issuing bank by cable.[12]

2. Acceptance Credit

It is a credit available by acceptance, under which a bank specifically nominated therein is authorized to accept the draft drawn under the credit. The draft thereunder must be a time bill drawn on the issuing bank, advising bank, or any other drawee bank. The clause used in the credit is as follows: "This credit is available by acceptance of your draft drawn on XXX bank."

After presentation of the compliance documents, the nominated bank accepts the bill. The bill can be discounted in order to obtain the credit amount immediately.

The purpose of an acceptance credit is to give the importer time to make payment. If he can resell the goods before payment falls due, he can use the proceeds to meet the bill of exchange. In this way, he avoids the necessity of borrowing money to finance the transaction.

Chapter 6 Letter of Credit 121

SAMPLE 6-9

Irrevocable Payment Credit

Name of Issuing Bank: The French Issuing Bank 38 rue francois ler 75008 Paris, France	Irrevocable Documentary Credit	Number 12345
Place and Date of Issue: Paris, 1 January, 2019	**Expiry Date and Place for Presentation of Documents** Expiry Date: May 29, 2019 Place for Presentation: The American Advising Bank, Tampa	
Applicant: The French Importer Co. 89 rue du Commerce Paris, France	**Beneficiary:** The American Exporter Co. Inc. 17 Main Street Tampa, Florida	
Advising Bank: Reference No. The American Advising Bank 456 Commerce Avenue Tampa, Florida	**Amount:** USD100,000 — one hundred thousand US Dollars	
Partial shipments [x] allowed [ ] not allowed Transhipment [x] allowed [ ] not allowed [ ] insurance covered by buyers	**Credit Available with Nominated Bank:** The American Advising Bank [x] by payment at sight [ ] by deferred payment at: [ ] by acceptance of drafts at. [ ] by negotiation	
Shipment From: Tampa, Florida For transportation to: Paris, France Not later than: May 15, 2019	Against the documents detailed herein: [ ] and Beneficiary's draft (s) drawn on: The French Issuing Bank, Paris, France	

Commercial Invoice, one original and 3 copies

Multimodal Transport Document issued to the order of the French Importer Co. marked freight prepaid and notify xyz Custom House Broker Inc.

Insurance Certificate covering the Institute Cargo Clauses and the Institute War and strike Clauses for 110% of the invoice value endorsed to The French Importer Co.

Certificate of Origin evidencing goods to be of U.S.A. Origin

Packing List

Covering: Machinery and spare parts as per pro-forma invoice number 657
dated December 17, 2018-CIP INCOTERMS 2000

Documents to be presented [14] days after the date of shipment but within the validity of the Credit

We hereby issue the Irrevocable Documentary Credit in your favour. It is subject to the Uniform Customs and Practice for Documentary Credits (2007 Revision, International Chamber of Commerce, Paris, France, Publication No. 600) and engages us in accordance with the terms thereof. The number and the date of the Credit and the name of our bank must be quoted on all drafts required. If the Credit is available by negotiation, each presentation must be noted on the reverse side of this advice by the bank where the Credit is available.
This document consists of [1] signed page(s).   The French Issuing Bank

SAMPLE 6-10

Irrevocable Acceptance Credit

Name of Issuing Bank: The French Issuing Bank 38 rue francois ler 75008 Paris, France	Irrevocable Documentary Credit	Number 12345
Place and Date of Issue: Paris, 1 January, 2019	**Expiry Date and Place for Presentation of Documents** Expiry Date: May 29, 2019 Place for Presentation: The American Advising Bank, Tampa	
Applicant: The French Importer Co. 89 rue du Commerce Paris, France	**Beneficiary:** The American Exporter Co. Inc. 17 Main Street Tampa, Florida	
Advising Bank: Reference No. The American Advising Bank 456 Commerce Avenue Tampa, Florida	**Amount:** USD100,000 — one hundred thousand US Dollars	
Partial shipments [x] allowed [ ] not allowed **Transhipment** [x] allowed [ ] not allowed [ ] insurance covered by buyers **Shipment** From: Tampa, Florida For transportation to: Paris, France Not later than: May 15, 2019	**Credit Available with Nominated Bank:** The American Advising Bank [ ] by payment at sight [ ] by deferred payment at: [x] by acceptance of drafts at: [ ] by negotiation **Against the documents detailed herein:** [ ] and Beneficiary's draft (s) drawn on: The French Issuing Bank, Paris, France	

Commercial Invoice, one original and 3 copies

Multimodal Transport Document issued to the order of the French Importer Co. marked freight prepaid and notify xyz Custom House Broker Inc.

Insurance Certificate covering the Institute Cargo Clauses and the Institute War and strike Clauses for 110% of the invoice value endorsed to The French Importer Co.

Certificate of Origin evidencing goods to be of U.S.A. Origin

Packing List

Covering: Machinery and spare parts as per pro-forma invoice number 657 dated December 17, 2018-CIP INCOTERMS 2000

Documents to be presented [14] days after the date of shipment but within the validity of the Credit

We hereby issue the Irrevocable Documentary Credit in your favour. It is subject to the Uniform Customs and Practice for Documentary Credits (2007 Revision, International Chamber of Commerce, Paris, France, Publication No. 600) and engages us in accordance with the terms thereof. The number and the date of the Credit and the name of our bank must be quoted on all drafts required. If the Credit is available by negotiation, each presentation must be noted on the reverse side of this advice by the bank where the Credit is available.
This document consists of [1] signed page(s).

The French Issuing Bank

3. Deferred Payment Credit

Under a deferred payment credit, the beneficiary does not receive payment when he presents the documents, but at a later date specified in the credit. In this way, the importer gains possession of the documents (and thereby of the goods or service) before becoming liable for payment. No draft is required for this credit.

Function clause:

"*Available against presentation of the following documents . . . but payment only at . . . days after presentation of documents.*"

"*. . . payable at . . . days after bill of lading date.*"

In economic terms, a deferred payment credit is equivalent to acceptance credit, except that in the absence of a bill of exchange there is no possibility for discounting. However, the undertaking to pay established by a deferred payment credit can on certain conditions be accepted as security for an advance.

4. Negotiation Credit

A negotiation credit is one under which a bank specifically nominated therein is authorized to negotiate or one, which is freely negotiable by any bank. A freely negotiation credit assures that any bank negotiating the drafts thereunder will be duly honored by the issuing bank provided all the terms stipulated therein are complied with.

Function clause:

"*We hereby engage with the drawers, endorsers and/or bona fide holders that drafts drawn and negotiated in conformity with the terms of this credit will be duly honored on presentation.*"

A credit treated as negotiable is either a sight credit or a time credit, calling for drafts to be drawn on the issuing bank or on any other drawee bank. The so-called negotiation is to buy the draft from the beneficiary or to give value for draft and/or documents by the bank authorized to negotiate. In this case the negotiating bank becomes a holder in due course. Negotiation of drafts and/or documents is with recourse to the beneficiary unless the credit has been confirmed by the negotiating bank.

Types of negotiation credit are as follows:

(1) Free negotiation credit. If the credit is available by negotiation with any bank, it is a freely negotiable credit, and the beneficiary may present documents to and receive money from any bank of his choice.

Function clause:

"*We (Issuing Bank) hereby engage with the drawers, endorsers and bona-fide holders of the draft(s) drawn under and in compliance with the terms of the credit that such draft(s) shall be duly honored on due presentation and delivery of documents as specified.*"

"*Provided such drafts are drawn and presented in accordance with the terms of this credit, we hereby engage with drawers, endorsers and bona-fide holders that the said drafts shall be duly honored on presentation.*"

"*We hereby engage with the drawers, endorsers and bona-fide holders of the draft(s) drawn under and in compliance with the terms of the credit that the same shall be duly honored on due presentation, and negotiated at the Negotiating Bank on or before ____ 2007.*"

"*We hereby engage with the drawers, endorsers and bona-fide holders of the draft(s) drawn* under and in compliance with the terms of the credit that such drafts shall be duly honored on due presentation and paid at maturity."

(2) Restricted negotiation credit. If the credit stipulates "This credit is available by negotiation with XXX bank", it signifies that the negotiation is restricted to a bank nominated therein and the beneficiary must present his documents to the bank so nominated.

(3) Non-negotiation credit (Irrevocable straight credit). Under the irrevocable straight credit, the obligation of the issuing bank is extended only to the beneficiary in honor draft(s)/document(s) and usually expires at the counters of the issuing bank.

SAMPLE 6-11

Irrevocable Deferred Payment Credit

Name of Issuing Bank: The French Issuing Bank 38 rue francois Ier 75008 Paris, France	Irrevocable Documentary Credit	Number 12345
Place and Date of Issue: Paris, 1 January, 2019	Expiry Date and Place for Presentation of Documents Expiry Date: May 29, 2019 Place for Presentation: The American Advising Bank, Tampa	
Applicant: The French Importer Co. 89 rue du Commerce Paris, France		
	Beneficiary: The American Exporter Co. Inc. 17 Main Street Tampa, Florida	
Advising Bank: Reference No. The American Advising Bank 456 Commerce Avenue Tampa, Florida	Amount: USD100,000— one hundred thousand US Dollars	
Partial shipments [x] allowed [ ] not allowed	Credit Available with Nominated Bank: The American Advising Bank [ ] by payment at sight [x] by deferred payment at: [ ] by acceptance of drafts at: [ ] by negotiation	
Transhipment [x] allowed [ ] not allowed		
[ ] insurance covered by buyers		
Shipment From: Tampa, Florida For transportation to: Paris, France Not later than: May 15, 2019	Against the documents detailed herein: [ ] and Beneficiary's draft(s) drawn on: The French Issuing Bank, Paris, France	
Commercial Invoice, one original and 3 copies		
Multimodal Transport Document issued to the order of the French Importer Co. marked freight prepaid and notify xyz Custom House Broker Inc.		
Insurance Certificate covering the Institute Cargo Clauses and the Institute War and strike Clauses for 110% of the invoice value endorsed to The French Importer Co.		
Certificate of Origin evidencing goods to be of U.S.A. Origin		
Packing List		
Covering: Machinery and spare parts as per pro-forma invoice number 657 dated December 17, 2018-CIP INCOTERMS 2000		
Documents to be presented [14] days after the date of shipment but within the validity of the Credit		
We hereby issue the Irrevocable Documentary Credit in your favour. It is subject to the Uniform Customs and Practice for Documentary Credits (2007 Revision, International Chamber of Commerce, Paris, France, Publication No. 600) and engages us in accordance with the terms thereof. The number and the date of the Credit and the name of our bank must be quoted on all drafts required. If the Credit is available by negotiation, each presentation must be noted on the reverse side of this advice by the bank where the Credit is available. This document consists of [1] signed page(s). The French Issuing Bank		

SAMPLE 6-12
Irrevocable Negotiation Documentary Credit

Name of Issuing Bank: The French Issuing Bank 38 rue francois Ier 75008 Paris, France	Irrevocable Documentary Credit	Number 12345

Place and Date of Issue: Paris, 1 January, 2019	Expiry Date and Place for Presentation of Documents Expiry Date: May 29, 2019 Place for Presentation: The American Advising Bank, Tampa
Applicant: The French Importer Co. 89 rue du Commerce Paris, France	**Beneficiary:** The American Exporter Co. Inc. 17 Main Street Tampa, Florida
Advising Bank: Reference No. The American Advising Bank 456 Commerce Avenue Tampa, Florida	**Amount:** USD100,000 — one hundred thousand US Dollars

Partial shipments [x] allowed [ ] not allowed Transhipment [x] allowed [ ] not allowed [ ] insurance covered by buyers **Shipment** From: Tampa, Florida For transportation to: Paris, France Not later than: May 15, 2019	**Credit Available with Nominated Bank:** The American Advising Bank [ ] by payment at sight [ ] by deferred payment at: [ ] by acceptance of drafts at: [x] by negotiation Against the documents detailed herein: [ ] and Beneficiary's draft (s) drawn on: The French Issuing Bank, Paris, France

Commercial Invoice, one original and 3 copies

Multimodal Transport Document issued to the order of the French Importer Co. marked freight prepaid and notify xyz Custom House Broker Inc.

Insurance Certificate covering the Institute Cargo Clauses and the Institute War and strike Clauses for 110% of the invoice value endorsed to The French Importer Co.

Certificate of Origin evidencing goods to be of U.S.A. Origin

Packing List

Covering: Machinery and spare parts as per pro-forma invoice number 657
dated December 17, 2018-CIP INCOTERMS 2000

Documents to be presented [14] days after the date of shipment but within the validity of the Credit

We hereby issue the Irrevocable Documentary Credit in your favour. It is subject to the Uniform Customs and Practice for Documentary Credits (2007 Revision, International Chamber of Commerce, Paris, France, Publication No. 600) and engages us in accordance with the terms thereof. The number and the date of the Credit and the name of our bank must be quoted on all drafts required. If the Credit is available by negotiation, each presentation must be noted on the reverse side of this advice by the bank where the Credit is available.
This document consists of [1] signed page(s).   The French Issuing Bank

6.2.6 According to Special Function Clause 按特殊条款分类

1. Revolving Credit

It is one by which, under the terms and conditions thereof, the amount is renewed or reinstated without specific amendments to the documentary credit being required.

The so-called revolving clause can be formulated in different ways with different words stipulated in the credit.

Types of revolving credit are as follows:

1) Automatic revolving

Function clause:

"*The total amount of this credit shall be restored automatically after date of negotiation.*"

"*The amounts paid under this credit are again available to you automatically until the total of the payments reaches USD ____.*"

2) Notice revolving

Function clause:

"*The amount shall be reinstated after each negotiation only upon receipt of issuing bank's notice stating that the credit might be renewed.*"

"*The amount of each shipment shall be reinstated after each negotiation only upon receipt of credit — writing importer's issuing bank's notice stating that the credit might be renewed.*"

3) Periodic revolving

Function clause:

"*Should the negotiating bank not be advised of stopping renewal within ... days after each negotiation, this credit shall be renewed to the original amount the next month until the total payment reaches _____ USD.*"[13]

4) Cumulative revolving

Function clause:

"*Per three calendar months cumulative commencing with 15th March, 2008, revolving on the first business day of each successive month and ending with 15th December, 2008.*"

5) Non-cumulative revolving

Function clause:

"*The unused balance of each shipment is not cumulative to the following shipment.*"

SAMPLE 6-13

Revolving Letter of Credit

Commercial Development Bank
Commercial Centre Building
Kuala Lumpur, Malaysia   L/C NO. MS1024

Revolving Letter of Credit   Date: 20th May, 2019

Applicant: Tamali Trading Co., Ltd. Ampang Commercial Plaza Kuala Lumpur
Issuing Bank: Commercial Development Bank
Amount: USD100,000 (One Hundred Thousand US Dollars Only)
Expiry: 15th October, 2019 negotiation under this credit is restricted to the advising bank.
Advising Bank: Commercial Trust Bank, Jaran Jurang Singapore
Beneficiary: Universal Metals Trading (Pte) Co., Ltd. Jaran Jurang Singapore 584A

At the request of Tamali Trading Co., Ltd, We issue an Irrevocable Documentary Revolving Letter of Credit NO. MS1024. This credit is available by beneficiary's draft(s), drawn at sight on us in duplicate, covering 100% of the invoice value, and accompanied by the following documents marked "X".

☒ 1. Full set of clean "On Board" ocean Bills of Lading made out to order and indorsed blank marked "Freight Prepaid" and notify applicant.
☒ 2. Commercial invoice in duplicate, indicating contract No. _____.
☒ 3. Certificate of Quality in duplicate issued by the manufacturer.
☒ 4. Insurance policy in duplicate covering marine risk for 110% CIF invoice value.

Covering: Spare parts of communication equipment   CEP — 10 cases
                                                         CEHP — 10 cases
                                                         CEHTP — 10 cases
Packing: Packed in wooden cases. Shipment from Singapore to Malaysia
Shipment: Partial shipment is allowed. Tran-shipment is allowed.
Special instructions: This credit can be revolved three times. The amount of each shipment shall be reinstated after each negotiation only upon receipt of credit—writing importer's issuing bank's notice stating that the credit might be renewed. The total amount is USD300,000 (Three Hundred Thousand US Dollars Only)
Undertaking clause:
We hereby undertake to honor all drafts drawn in accordance with the terms of this credit.
This credit is subject to Uniform Customs and Practice for Documentary Credits (2007 Revision) fixed by International Chamber of Commerce Publication No. 600.

Commercial Development Bank
Authorized Signature
_____

2. Back-to-back Documentary Credit

A back-to-back credit may be used when the credit issued in favor of the exporter (the middleman) is not transferable or though transferable it does not meet his requirements. The exporter, namely, the beneficiary of the first credit (the master credit or prime credit), offers it as a security to the advising bank or his banker for the issuance of a second credit (back-to-back credit or subsidiary credit). In other words, the two credits are put "back to back", the one being issued on the security of the other.[14] A back-to-back documentary credit involves the following two separate documentary credits.

(1) One opened for the account of the buyer in favor of the seller.
(2) One opened for the account of the seller naming the actual supplier of the goods as the

beneficiary. The first beneficiary of the first documentary credit becomes the applicant for the second documentary credit.

SAMPLE 6-14

The Master Credit

Commercial Trust Bank	
Cable: TDB12345 Telex: CTDB11225	Manila the Philippines Date: 20th Aug., 2019
Irrevocable Credit	Credit No. M.A.2253
This letter of credit is subject to UCP600 (2007 Revision) Fixed by International Chamber of Commerce.	**Applicant:** Stanley International Trading Co. Ltd Commercial Building Manila, The Philippines
Beneficiary: Dopus Machinery Industry Co., Ltd. International Commercial Plaza, Los Angles U.S.A.	**Amount:** USD 600,000 Six Hundred Thousand U.S. Dollars Only
	Expiry Date: 20th November, 2019, in the country of Beneficiary for Negotiation
Dear Sirs, We hereby issue an irrevocable Documentary Credit which is available against beneficiary's draft(s) at sight drawn on us for full commercial invoice accompanied by the following documents: —Commercial invoice signed by Dopus Machinery Industry Co., Ltd. in duplicate. —Insurance policy or certificate issued by an insurance Co. with WPA clause covering the merchandise for 100% of the full invoice value. —Covering: Textile printing and dyeing equipments. 1. Loom HTP—Type III, 100 sets. 2. Roving Frame THE— Type II, 30 sets. 3. Winding Frame HTQ—Type III, 20 sets. 4. Drawing and Slubbing Frame HTR—Type I, 10 sets. CIF Manila including packing charge	
Documents must be presented for payment within 21 days after B/L date but within the validity of the credit	
Loading on Board from Los Angeles to Manila	Partial shipment Allowed Transhipment Prohibited
Special Conditions: 1. Full set of clean "On Board" "Freight Prepaid" ocean Bills of Lading, made out to our order marked: Notify Stanley International Trading Co., Ltd. Manila The Philippines. 2. Certificate of inspection certifying quality and quantity in Duplicate issued by Inspection Bureau of ABC. 3. Shipping Mark: TLRWPHS×120 Los Angeles—Manila.	
We hereby engage that drafts drawn in conformity with the terms of this credit will be duly honored on presentation. Authorized Signature	

Back-to-Back Credit

Commercial Associated Bank

Cable: TDB66520
Telex: CTDB22115

Commercial Centre Los Angeles U.S.A.

Date: 25th Aug., 2019

Back-To-Back Credit	Credit No. M.A 6653
This letter of credit is subject to UCP600 (2007 Revision) Fixed by International Chamber of Commerce.	**Applicant:** Dopus Machinery Industry Co., Ltd. International Commercial Plaza, Los Angles U.S.A.
Beneficiary: Akia Machinery Industry Co., Ltd. Commercial Plaza, N.Y U.S.A.	**Amount:** USD500,000 Five Hundred Thousand U.S. Dollars Only
Advising Bank: Commercial Investment Bank, New York, World Centre	**Expiry Date:** 2nd November, 2019, in the country of Beneficiary for Negotiation

Dear Sirs,

 We hereby issue an irrevocable Documentary Back to-Back Credit which is available against beneficiary's draft(s) at sight drawn on us for full commercial invoice accompanied by the following documents:

 —Commercial invoice signed by Akia Machinery Industry Co., Ltd. in duplicate.

 —Insurance policy or certificate issued by an insurance Co. with W.P.A clause covering the merchandise for 120% of the full invoice value.

 —Covering: Textile printing and dyeing equipments.

 1. Loom HTP—Type III, 100 sets.

 2. Roving Frame THE—Type II, 30 sets.

 3. Winding Frame HTQ—Type III, 20 sets.

 4. Drawing and Slubbing Frame HTR—Type I, 10 sets.

Documents must be presented for payment within 14 days after B/L date but within the validity of the credit

Loading on Board from Los Angeles to Manila	Partial shipment Forbidden Transhipment Prohibited

Special Conditions:

 1. Full set of clean "On Board" "Freight Prepaid" ocean Bills of Lading, made out to our order marked: Notify Stanley International Trading Co., Ltd. Manila The Philippines.

 2. Certificate of inspection certifying quality and quantity in Duplicate issued by Inspection Bureau of ABC

 3. Shipping Mark: TLRWPHS×120 Los Angeles–Manila.

 4. This Credit shall become operative only upon our receipt from applicant of the documents conforming to terms and conditions of the master Credit No. M.A 2253.

 We hereby engage that drafts drawn in conformity with the terms of this credit will be duly honored on presentation.

Authorized Signature

With back-to-back documentary credit, the second credit should be worded so as to produce the documents (apart from the commercial invoice) required by the primary credit, and to produce them within the time limits set by the primary credit, in order that the primary beneficiary under the first credit may be able to present his documents within the time limits of the first credit.

Function clause:

"*Payment under this Credit is to be made upon receipt of the cover of notice of acceptance from the Issuing Bank of the master credit.*"

"*This Credit shall become operative only upon receipt from of the relative documents as requested by the master Credit No. dated and made out in compliance with the terms thereof.*"

"*Payment under this Credit is to be made upon receipt of the master Credit required documents by Bank from the above-mentioned applicant which comply with the terms and conditions of the master Credit.*"

3. Reciprocal Credit

A reciprocal credit is usually concerned with a barter transaction. It is in all respects similar to an ordinary commercial credit except that the applicant of the original credit may assume the position of the beneficiary in the reciprocal credit, while the beneficiary of the original credit may become the applicant in the reciprocal credit. In other words, they are both importers and exporters in this transaction. The amounts under the two credits will be roughly the same. The relationship between the two credits can be illustrated as Figure 6-6.

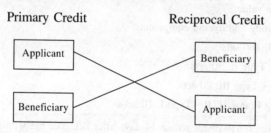

Figure 6-6 The relationship between primary credit and reciprocal credit

In order to protect the interest of all parties involved, the primary credit will incorporate a special clause as follows:

"*This credit shall not be available/operative/effective unless and until the reciprocal credit in favor of (the original applicant) for account of (the original beneficiary) is established by (the original beneficiary's bank).*"

When the reciprocal credit is established in response to the primary credit, it will normally incorporate a special clause as follows:

"*This is a reciprocal credit against (the primary issuing bank) credit No. in favor of (the original applicant) covering the shipment of.*"

☞ **SAMPLE 6-15**

Reciprocal Letter of Credit

Commercial Development Bank
Commercial Centre Building　　　L/C NO. MS1024
Kuala Lumpur, Malaysia　　　　　Telex: 25455CDB
Reciprocal Letter of Credit　Date: 20th May, 2019

Applicant: Tamali Trading Co., Ltd. Ampang Commercial Plaza Kuala Lumpur
Issuing Bank: Commercial Development Bank
We issue an Irrevocable Reciprocal Documentary Letter of Credit NO. MS1024
Amount: USD100,000 (One Hundred Thousand US Dollars Only)
Expiry: 15th October, 2019 negotiation under this credit is restricted to the advising bank.
Advising Bank: Commercial Trust Bank, Jaran Jurang Singapore
Beneficiary: Universal Metals Trading (Pte) Co., Ltd. Jaran Jurang Singapore 584A

This credit is available by beneficiary's draft(s), drawn on us in duplicate, without recourse, at 90 days, for 100% of the invoice value, and accompanied by the following documents marked "X"

☒ 1. Full set of clean "On Board" ocean Bills of Lading made out to order and indorsed Blank marked "Freight Prepaid" and notify applicant.
☒ 2. Commercial invoice in duplicate, indicating contract No. _____
☒ 3. Certificate of Quality in duplicate issued by the manufacturer.
☒ 4. Insurance policy in duplicate covering marine risk for 110% CIF invoice value.

Covering: Spare parts of communication equipment　　CEP — 10 cases
　　　　　　　　　　　　　　　　　　　　　　　　　　　　CEHP —10 cases
　　　　　　　　　　　　　　　　　　　　　　　　　　　　CEHTP —10 cases
Packing: Packed in wooden cases. Shipment from Singapore to Malaysia
Shipment: Partial shipment is not allowed. Tran-shipment is allowed.
Shipment is to be made on or before 20th July, 2019.

Special instructions: 1. This credit shall not be available unless and until the reciprocal credit is established by Trust Union Bank, Singapore in favor of Tamali Trading Co. Ltd. Ampang for amount of USD100, 000 (One Hundred Thousand US Dollars Only) covering shipment from Malaysia to Singapore.
2. The availability shall be telex advised to the beneficiary through the Trust Union Bank Singapore.
3. Universal Metals Trading (Pte) Co, Ltd, shall issue the Reciprocal Credit irrevocable before the date 20th May, 2018, specified in contract No. MS822, notice failing which the Tamali Trading Co., Ltd. has the right to resign without notice.
4. This credit is effective subject to the advising's sighting the relative export license submitted by the beneficiary.

This credit is subject to Uniform Customs and Practice for Documentary Credits (2007 Revision) fixed by International Chamber of Commerce Publication No. 600.

Undertaking clause: We here undertake to honor all drafts drawn in accordance with the terms of this credit.

　　　　　　　　　　　　Commercial Development Bank
　　　　　　　　　　　　Authorized Signature

4. Red Clause/Anticipatory Credit

It is a kind of pre-shipment financing intended to assist the exporter in the production or procurement of the goods sold. It is a credit with a special clause added thereto that authorizes the advising bank or any other nominated banks to make advances to the beneficiary before his submission of documents.[15] The red clause is so called because the clause was originally written in red ink to draw attention to the unique nature of this documentary credit. Nowadays it is seldom used.

A red clause letter of credit will be established only at the request of the applicant, it places the onus of final repayment on the applicant, who would be liable for repayment of the advances if the beneficiary fails to present the documents called for under the credit, and who would be liable for all costs — such as interest of foreign exchange hedging — incurred by the issuing bank confirming bank, if any, or any other nominated bank.

Function clause:

"*The negotiating bank is hereby authorized to make advance to the beneficiary up to an aggregate amount of USD200,000 (20% of the amount of L/C). The advances, with the interest at the ruling rate of exchange at the time of payment of such advance, are to be deducted from the proceeds of the drafts drawn under this credit.*"[16]

"*We hereby authorize you to make such advances, which are to be repaid, with interest, from the payment to be made under the credit.*"

"*It is understood that the making of the temporary advances or the payments to the above mentioned beneficiary should be optional on the part of you.*"

5. Standby Credit

The standby credit is a documentary credit or similar arrangement, however named or described, which represents an obligation to the beneficiary on the part of the issuing bank to: ① repay money borrowed by the applicant, or advanced to or for the account of the applicant, ② make payment on account of any indebtedness undertaken by the applicant, or ③ make payment on account of any default by the applicant in the performance of an obligation.[17]

SAMPLE 6-16

Anticipatory (Red Clause) Letter of Credit

Commercial Development Bank
Commercial Centre Building
Kuala Lumpur, Malaysia
Anticipatory Letter of Credit

L/C NO. MS1024
Telex: 25455CDB
Date: 20th May, 2019

Applicant:	Tamali Trading Co., Ltd. Ampang Commercial Plaza Kuala Lumpur
Issuing Bank:	Commercial Development Bank
Amount:	USD100,000 (One Hundred Thousand US Dollars Only)
Expiry:	15th October, 2019 negotiation under this credit is restricted to the advising bank.
Advising Bank:	Commercial Trust Bank, Jaran Jurang Singapore
Beneficiary:	Universal Metals Trading (Pte) Co., Ltd. Jaran Jurang Singapore 584A

At the request of Tamali Trading Co., Ltd, We issue an Irrevocable Documentary Anticipatory Letter of Credit NO. MS1024. This credit is available by beneficiary's draft(s), drawn at sight on us in duplicate, covering 100% of the invoice value, and accompanied by the following documents marked "X".

☒ 1. Full set of clean "On Board" ocean Bills of Lading made out to order and indorsed blank marked "Freight Prepaid" and notify applicant.
☒ 2. Commercial invoice in duplicate, indicating contract No._____ .
☒ 3. Certificate of Quality in duplicate issued by the manufactures.
☒ 4. Insurance policy in duplicate covering marine risk for 110% CIF invoice value.

Covering:	Spare parts of communication equipment CEP — 10 cases
	CEHP —10 cases
	CEHTP —10 cases
Packing:	Packed in wooden cases. Shipment from Singapore to Malaysia
Shipment:	Partial shipment is not allowed. Tran-shipment is allowed.
	Shipment is to be made on or before 20th Sept, 2019.

Red Clause: *We hereby authorize the Commercial Trust Bank, Jaran Jurang Singapore at your discretion to grant to the beneficiary up to 60% of the USD100,000 (One Hundred Thousand US Dollars Only). Any interest accrued thereon should be charged to you from the date of this advance to the date of repayment.*

Undertaking clause:

In consideration of your bank making such advance to the beneficiary who may eventually fail to effect shipment covered by the credit, we guarantee repayment and undertake to pay you on demand any sum owing by the beneficiary in respect of such advance together with interest thereon.

This credit is subject to Uniform Customs and Practice for Documentary Credits (2007 Revision) fixed by International Chamber of Commerce Publication No. 600.

Commercial Development Bank
Authorized Signature

☞ SAMPLE 6-17

Stand-by Letter of Credit

Commercial Development Bank
Commercial Centre Building
Kuala Lumpur, Malaysia

Date: 10th August, 2019
L/C NO. MS1024
Telex: 25455CDB

To: Otto Marine Equipment Co., Ltd. No. 2548 High Street Colombo
This credit is forwarded to the Advising Bank by airmail.
Applicant: Powell Marine Equipment Co., Ltd. P.O. Box 34258 Singapore
Issuing Bank: Commercial Development Bank, Golden Building Singapore
Advising Bank: Union Trust Bank, Commercial Building, Colombo Sri Lanka
Beneficiary: Otto Marine Equipment Co., Ltd. No. 2548 High Street Colombo

Gentlemen:

At the request of the Powell Marine Equipment Co., Ltd. as the applicant, we issue our irrevocable Stand-by Letter of Credit in favor of Otto Marine Equipment Co., Ltd. The terms and conditions as follows:

We guarantee for you that if the obligations incumbent upon in accordance with the credit are not duly fulfilled by the Buyer, we will refund the sum of USD400,000 (Four Hundred Thousand U.S. Dollars Only) with interest at the rate of 10% per annum to you against written notification and certificate issued by yours Otto Marine Equipment Co., Ltd.

Our Stand-by Letter of Credit is valid until 20th December, 2019.

This letter is to be returned to us when exhausted or expired, kindly be advised. This Stand-by Letter of Credit is subject to Uniform Customs and Practice for Documentary Credits (2007 Revision) fixed by International Chamber of Commerce Publication No. 600.

Yours Faithfully,
Commercial Development Bank
Authorized Signature

6.2.7 Credits of Combined Functions 兼具多种功能的信用证

1. Irrevocable Straight Documentary Credit

1) Definition

An irrevocable straight documentary credit conveys a commitment by the issuing bank to only honor drafts or documents as presented by the beneficiary of the credit.

2) Characteristics

Under this type of credit, the obligation of the issuing bank is only extended to the beneficiary in honoring draft(s)/document(s) and usually expires at the counters of the issuing bank. This type of credit conveys no commitment or obligation on the part of the issuing bank to persons other than the beneficiary.

3) Advantage and disadvantage

It is of greatest advantage to the applicant, because he does not incur a liability to pay the beneficiary until his own bank views the documents of the credit.[18]

4) Function clause

"We hereby engage with you that draft drawn and presented to us under and in compliance with the terms of this credit will be duly honored by us."

"We hereby agree with you that all drafts drawn under and/or documents presented to us hereunder will be duly honored by us provided the terms and conditions of the credit are complied with and the presentation is made at this office on or before the expiry date."

 SAMPLE 6-18

Irrevocable Straight Documentary Credit

Issuing bank:
The Merchant Bank 521 Market Street, 28th floor San Francisco, CA 93205
Place and date of issue: San Francisco, Sept. 20, 2019
We hereby issue our irrevocable documentary credit, No. 12345
Date of expiry: December 20, 2019   **Place of expiry:** At our counter
Applicant: US Import Company, 123 Main Street, San Francisco, California
Beneficiary: The French Export Co. 89 rue du Commerce, Paris, France
Amount: USD100,000. **Say:** One Hundred Thousand US Dollars only
Credit available with the Merchant Bank, San Francisco by payment of Beneficiary's draft at sight drawn on the Merchant Bank for 100% of invoice value accompanied by the documents detailed herein.
Partial shipments: Allowed   **Transshipments:** Not allowed
Taking in charge at: Paris, France
Not later than October 20, 2019
For transportation to San Francisco, California USA
Documents to be presented:
Commercial Invoice: one original and three copies
Clean ocean port-to-port bill of lading consigned to the applicant marked freight collect, notify applicant.
Covering: Machinery and spare parts as per Proforma Invoice No.1234, dated August 14, 2019—FOB San Francisco, Insurance effected by the applicant.
Documents must be presented at the place of expiration not later than 10 days after the date of shipment and within the validity of this credit.
Documents must be forwarded to us in one parcel and be mailed to the Merchant Bank, 28th floor, 521 Market Street, San Francisco, California CA 93205, USA.
Draft(s) must indicate the number and date of this credit.
Each draft presented hereunder must be accompanied by this original credit for our endorsement thereon of the amount of such drafts.
This credit is subject to UCP 600, by International Chamber of Commerce.
We hereby engage with you that each draft drawn and presented to us under and in compliance with the terms and conditions of this documentary credit will be duly honored by us.

The Merchant Bank
Signature

2. Irrevocable Negotiation Documentary Credit

1) Definition

An irrevocable negotiation documentary credit conveys an engagement by the issuing bank to honor drafts or documents as presented by the beneficiary or any third parties who might negotiate or purchase the beneficiary's drafts or documents as presented under the documentary credit.

2) Characteristics

Under this kind of credit, the beneficiary may ask a third bank or financial institution to negotiate or purchase and resell drafts and documents as presented under the documentary credit. This assures anyone who authorized to negotiate draft(s)/document(s) that this draft(s)/document(s) will be duly honored by the issuing bank so long as the terms and conditions of the credit are complied with.

3) Advantage and disadvantage

It is of advantage to the seller in that he does not have to wait until the issuing bank reviews the documents to get paid the proceeds under the credit.

4) Function clause

"*Credit available with any bank, by negotiation for payment of the beneficiary's draft at sight . . .*"

"*This credit is available with ABC bank, by negotiation of beneficiary's draft at 60 days after sight . . .*"

SAMPLE 6-19

Irrevocable Negotiation Documentary Credit

Issuing bank:
The Merchant Bank 521 Market Street, 28th floor San Francisco, CA93205
To: French Advising Bank, 456 Commerce Avenue, Paris, France
Place and date of issue: San Francisco, Sept. 20, 2019
We hereby issue our irrevocable documentary credit No. 12345
Date of expiry: December 20, 2019
Place of expiry: The French Advising Bank, Paris
Applicant: US Import Company, 123 Main Street, San Francisco, California
Beneficiary: The French Export Co., 89 rue du Commerce, Paris, France
Amount: USD100, 000. **Say:** One Hundred Thousand US Dollars only
Credit available with the French Advising Bank, by negotiation for payment of Beneficiary's draft at sight drawn on the Merchant Bank for 100% of invoice value accompanied by the documents detailed herein.
Partial shipments: Allowed   **Transshipments:** Not allowed
Taking in charge at: Paris, France
Not later than October 20, 2019
For transportation to San Francisco, California USA
Goods description: Machinery and spare parts as per Proforma Invoice No. 1234, dated August 14, 2019 CIF San Francisco
Documents to be presented:
Commercial Invoice: one original and three copies
Full set of clean "on board" ocean bill of lading to the order of shipper blank endorsed marked "freight prepaid" showing notify applicant
Negotiable insurance policy or certificate in 2 copies for at least 110 percent of invoice value, covering marine risks and all risks, indicating loss, if any, payable in the United States in US dollars.
Documents must be presented at the place of expiration not later than 10 days after the date of shipment and within the validity of this credit.
Documents must be forwarded to us in one parcel and be mailed to the Merchant Bank, 28th floor, 521 Market Street, San Francisco, California CA 93205, USA.
Draft(s) must indicate the number and date of this credit.
The amount of each draft negotiated under this credit must be endorsed on the reverse of this credit and presentation of any such draft to us shall be a warranty by the presenting bank that such endorsement has been made.
This credit is subject to UCP 600, by International Chamber of Commerce.
We hereby engage with you that each draft drawn and presented to us under and in compliance with the terms and conditions of this documentary credit will be duly honored by us.

The Merchant Bank
Signature

3. Irrevocable Unconfirmed Documentary Credit

1) Definition

An irrevocable unconfirmed documentary credit conveys a commitment by the issuing bank to honor drafts or documents as presented by the beneficiary of the credit.

2) Characteristics

This advising bank only undertakes to advise the credit, so the beneficiary of the credit will be paid by and has recourse to the issuing bank only.

3) Advantage and disadvantage

There is slight advantage to the applicant since he need not pay the confirmation fee.

4) Function clause

"*Confirmation instructions*: *Without.*"

☞ SAMPLE 6-20

Irrevocable Unconfirmed Documentary Credit

Korean Export & Importer Bank, Seoul, Korea
To: The Trade Bank, San Francisco, California USA
We hereby issue our irrevocable documentary credit No. 12345
Date of issue: June 15, 2019   **Date of expiry:** August 10, 2019
Place of expiry: USA
Applicant: Korean Electronic Importer Seoul, Korea
Beneficiary: American Electronics Exporter, San Jose, California USA
Amount: USD15,000.00 **Say:** Fifteen Thousand US Dollars Only
Credit available with any bank, by negotiation. Drafts payable at sight
Drawee: Korean Export & Importer Bank, Seoul, Korea
Transshipment: Prohibited   **Partial shipment:** Allowed
Loading on board San Francisco International Airport, for transportation to Kimpo Airport Seoul Korea
Latest date of shipment: July 20, 2019
Description of goods: DRAM chips Model Number MP164Ft12 per proforma invoice dated May 28, 2019
Quantity: 3,000
Unit price: USD5.00 per unit   **Total amount:** USD15,000.00 **Price terms:** EXW
Country of origin: U.S.A./Singapore/Philippines
Documents required:
1. Signed commercial invoice in triplicate
2. Airway bill consigned to Korea Export & Import Bank marked "freight collect" and notify the applicant
3. Packing list in triplicate
Additional conditions: Notify party on commercial invoice and air waybill must show Korean Electronic Importer, Seoul, Korea. Air freight should be effected by Emery Airfreight.
Charges: All banking commissions and charges, including reimbursement charges and postage outside Korea are for account of beneficiary.
Period for presentation: Documents must be presented within 14 days after the date of shipment.
Confirmation instructions: Without
Reimbursement bank: Korean Export & Importer Bank, Los Angeles, CA USA
Instructions to the paying / accepting / negotiating bank: The amount of each negotiation (draft) must be endorsed on the reverse side of this credit by the negotiating bank.
All documents must be forwarded directly by courier service in one lot to Korean Export & Importer Bank, Seoul, Korea.
If documents are presented with discrepancies, a discrepancy fee of USD40.00 or equivalent should be deducted from the reimbursement claim.
This credit is subject to UCP 600, by International Chamber of Commerce, and engages us in accordance with the terms thereof.

Korean Export & Importer Bank, Seoul, Korea
Signature

4. Irrevocable Confirmed Documentary Credit

1) Definition

An irrevocable confirmed documentary credit is an irrevocable credit that contains a commitment on the part of both the issuing bank and advising bank of payment to the beneficiary so long as the terms and conditions of the credit are met.

2) Characteristics

Assurance of payment by two banks.

3) Advantage and disadvantage

This is most secure for the beneficiary, but it is more costly.

4) Function clause

"*Confirmation instructions*: With confirmation, or confirmed."

☞ SAMPLE 6-21

Irrevocable Confirmed Documentary Credit

Korean Export & Importer Bank, Seoul, Korea
To: The Trade Bank, San Francisco, California USA
We hereby issue our irrevocable documentary credit No. 12345
Date of issue: June 15, 2019   **Date of expiry:** August 10, 2019
Place   USA
Applicant: Korean Electronic Importer Seoul, Korea
Beneficiary: American Electronics Exporter San Jose, California USA
Amount: USD15,000.00 **Say:** Fifteen Thousand US Dollars only
Credit available with: The Trade Bank   Drafts payable at sight
Drawee: Korean Export & Importer, Bank, Seoul, Korea
Transshipment: Prohibited   **Partial shipment:** Allowed
Loading on board San Francisco International Airport, for transportation to Kimpo Airport, Seoul, Korea
Latest date of shipment: July 20, 2019
Description of goods: DRAM chips Model Number MP164Ft12 per proforma invoice dated May 28, 2019
Quantity: 3,000
Unit price: USD5.00 per unit   **Total amount:** USD15,000.00 **Price terms:** EXW
Country of origin: U.S.A./Singapore/Philippines
Documents required:
1. Signed commercial invoice in triplicate
2. Airway bill consigned to Korea Export & Import Bank marked "freight collect" and notify the applicant
3. Packing list in triplicate
Additional conditions: Notify party on commercial invoice and air waybill must show Korean Electronic Importer, Seoul, Korea.
Air freight should be effected by Emery Airfreight.
Charges: All banking commissions and charges, including reimbursement charges and postage outside Korea are for account of the beneficiary.
Period for presentation: Documents must be presented within 14 days after the date of shipment.
Confirmation instructions: Confirmed
Reimbursement bank: Korean Export & Importer Bank, Los Angeles, CA USA
Instructions to the paying / accepting / negotiating bank: The amount of each negotiation (draft) must be endorsed on the reverse side of this credit by the negotiating bank.
All documents must be forwarded directly by courier service in one lot to Korean Export & Importer Bank, Seoul, Korea.
If documents are presented with discrepancies, a discrepancy fee of USD40.00 or equivalent should be deducted from the reimbursement claim.
This credit is subject to UCP 600, by International Chamber of Commerce, and engages us in accordance with the terms thereof.

Korean Export & Importer Bank, Seoul, Korea
Signature

New Words and Expressions

undertake	[ˌʌndəˈteik]	v.	承担，担任，许诺，保证
undertaking	[ˌʌndəˈteikiŋ]	n.	承诺，保证，承担
creditworthiness	[ˈkreditˈwəːðinis]	n.	信誉
bankrupt	[ˈbæŋkrʌpt]	n.	破产者
		a.	破产了的，完全丧失的
		v.	使破产
default	[diˈfɔːlt]	v./n.	违约，不履行合同
reference	[ˈrefrəns]	n.	提及，涉及，参考
exclusively	[ikˈskluːsivli]	ad.	专有地，完全地，绝对地
engage	[inˈgeidʒ]	v.	约定，承诺
accuracy	[ˈækjurəsi]	n.	精确性，正确度，准确
genuineness	[ˈdʒenjuənis]	n.	真实性
falsification	[ˌfɔːlsifiˈkeiʃən]	n.	弄虚作假，伪造，歪曲，篡改
security	[siˈkjuəriti]	n.	安全，保障
clear-cut		a.	明确的
eliminate	[iˈlimineit]	v.	排除，消除，除去，消灭
capability	[keipəˈbiliti]	n.	能力，容积
segregation	[ˌsegriˈgeiʃən]	n.	种族隔离，隔离
collateralize	[kəˈlætərəlaiz]	v.	以……作抵押，质押
jurisdiction	[ˌdʒuərisˈdikʃən]	n.	权限，司法权，司法管辖
governing	[ˈgʌvəniŋ]	n.	控制，操纵，管辖，约束
adherence	[ədˈhiərəns]	n.	粘着，忠诚，遵守，坚持
incorporation	[inˌkɔːpəˈreiʃən]	n.	结合，合并，形成法人组织，组成公司（或社团）
multiple	[ˈmʌltipl]	a.	多样的，多重的，复合的
		v.	成倍增加
facilitate	[fəˈsiliteit]	v.	（不以人作主语）使容易，使便利，推动，促进，便利
amendment	[əˈmendmənt]	n.	改善，改正，修改
modification	[ˌmɔdifiˈkeiʃən]	n.	更改，修改，修正
utilization	[ˌjuːtilaiˈzeiʃən]	n.	利用，使用
courier	[ˈkuriə]	n.	送快信的人，送递快件的信差
shipment	[ˈʃipmənt]	n.	装船，出货，一批货物发运
integrity	[inˈtegriti]	n.	正直，诚实
commonsense	[ˌkɔmənˈsens]	a.	具有常识的，共识的，常识的
elapse	[iˈlæps]	v.	（时间）过去，消逝，流逝，消失
validity	[vəˈliditi]	n.	有效性，合法性，正确性，有效期
irregularity	[iˌregjuˈlæriti]	n.	不规则，无规律，不规则
commitment	[kəˈmitmənt]	n.	委托事项，许诺，承担义务，承诺
cancellation	[kænsəˈleiʃən]	n.	取消，撤销
subsidiary	[səbˈsidjəri]	a.	辅助的，补充的

Chapter 6 Letter of Credit

		n.	附属公司
substitute	['sʌbstitjuːt]	n.	代用品, 代替者, 替代品
		v.	代替, 替换, 替代
incur	[in'kəː]	v.	招致, 发生, 引起
fractionable	['frækʃənəbl]	a.	可分割的
assignable	[ə'sainəbl]	a.	可转让的
transmissible	[trænz'misəbl]	a.	可转让的, 可传送的
render	['rendə]	v.	致使
disregard	[ˌdisri'gɑːd]	v.	不理, 漠视
		n.	漠视, 忽视, 不予考虑
outlay	['autlei]	n.	费用, 开销, 开支, 花费
designate	['dezigneit]	v.	指明, 指出, 任命, 指派, 指定, 规定
assignment	[ə'sainmənt]	n.	分配, 委派, 任务, 转让
waiver	['weivə]	n.	[律] 自动放弃, 放弃, 弃权, 弃权证书
intermediary	[ˌintə'miːdiəri]	a.	中间的, 媒介的
		n.	中间人, 中介方
retainment	[ri'teinmənt]	n.	保留, 保持
stipulate	['stipjuleit]	v.	规定, 保证规定
signify	['signifai]	v.	颇为重要, 表示, 表明
renew	[ri'njuː]	v.	使更新, 使恢复, 更新, 重新开始, 续期
reinstate	['riːin'steit]	v.	恢复, 重新使用
procurement	[prə'kjuəmənt]	n.	获得, 取得

definite undertaking   确定的承诺, 明确的承诺
effect payment   执行付款
have no regard for   不考虑
be in a position to   能做……, 处于……状态
security agreement   保障协议
credit backing   信用支持
credit standing   信用状况
legislative law   立法
codified law   成文法
decision law   裁决法
contractual law   合同法
customary law   习惯法
case law   判例法
bank association   银行协会
banking personnel   银行职员
trade facilitation   贸易便利, 促进贸易

duly honored   及时支付
expiry date   有效期
guarantee payment   保证付款
silent confirmation   未授权保兑
relevant document   有关单据
usance credit   远期信用证
deferred payment   延期付款
freely negotiable   自由议付
applicable law   有关法律
deferred payment credit   延期付款信用证
automatic revolving credit   自动循环信用证
notice revolving credit   通知循环信用证
periodic revolving credit   定期循环信用证
cumulative revolving   累计循环
non-cumulative revolving   非累计循环
commencing with   从……开始

issuing bank 开证行	successive month 下一个月
advising bank 通知行	back-to-back credit 背对背信用证
confirming bank 保兑行	reciprocal credit 对开信用证
nominated bank 指定的银行	commercial credit 商业信用证
transferring bank 转让行	red clause documentary credit 红条款信用证
negotiating bank 议付行	aggregate amount 总金额
proceed with 继续	at the ruling rate of exchange 按当前汇率
face-to-face negotiation 面对面商谈	foreign exchange hedging 外汇套期保值
document package 全体单据,所有单据	irrevocable straight documentary credit 不可撤销的直接信用证
reimbursement agreement 偿付协议	
precision instrument 精密仪器	irrevocable negotiation documentary credit 不可撤销的议付信用证
excessive detail 过多的细节	
"police" the commercial transaction "监督"该笔交易	honor draft 兑付汇票,支付汇票
inconsistent with one another 互相不一致	stamp duty 印花税
affiliated part 联营机构	incur a liability 承担责任
payment order 支付命令	courier service 快邮

Notes

1. The former has security to get paid provided he presents impeccable documents while the latter has the security to get the goods required through the documents he stipulated in the credit. 前者只要提供了符合条件的单据就可以取得付款,而后者通过其信用证里所规定的单据也可以保证得到自己所要求的货物。
此处的"impeccable"意为"faultless",即"无瑕疵的",在该句中表示"与信用证相符的"。

2. The documentary credit or letter of credit is an undertaking issued by a bank for the account of the buyer (the applicant) or for its own account, to pay the beneficiary the value of the draft and/or documents provided that the terms and conditions of the documentary credit are complied with. 跟单信用证或简称为信用证,是由银行为买方(申请人)或以其自己的名义出立的一种保证,保证在符合信用证的一切条件下,将汇票或单据的金额支付给受益人。

3. The documentary credit achieves a commercially acceptable compromise between the conflicting interests of buyer and seller by matching time of payment for the goods with the time of their delivery. 跟单信用证通过将付款和交货的时间结合起来,取得了一种解决买卖双方之间利益矛盾的商业上的折中方式。

Chapter 6　Letter of Credit　143

4. May not require actual segregation of cash, since the buyer is not always required to collateralize his documentary credit obligation to the issuing bank.　可能不需实际动用现金，因为（开立信用证时）银行并不一定要求买方向开证行对他在跟单信用证项下所承担的义务提供抵押品。
   "collateralize"在这里表示"为……提供担保/抵押"；"segregation"的本意为"隔离，分离"，这里的"segregation of cash"则指"动用现金"。

5. ICC Uniform Customs and Practices for Documentary Credits　《跟单信用证统一惯例》
   它是由国际商会所制定的约束信用证业务的一套规则，尽管不是强制各国遵守，但大多数国家的银行和贸易公司都普遍接受它作为约束信用证业务的规则。

6. The buyer is confident that payment will only be made to the seller after the terms and conditions of the documentary credit and the UCP rules are complied with.　买方可以确信，只有在符合信用证条件和《跟单信用证统一惯例》规则的情形下才会对卖方付款。
   该句中的"confident"和"assured"意思相同。

7. It is, nevertheless, a precision instrument, and must be properly handled by all concerned.
   然而，信用证是一种必须认真处理的业务，各有关当事人都必须妥善处理它。
   该句的"precision instrument"本义为"精密仪器"，这里是指"需要认真处理的业务"。

8. His instructions to the issuing bank must be clear, correct and precise, and free from excessive details.　他对开证行的指示必须清楚、准确无误，并且不要包含过多的细节。
   这里的"free from"表示"不受……影响的"、"无……的"，例如"free from debt"（免除债务）。

9. If the advising bank confirms the credit, it must pay without recourse to the seller when the documents are presented, provided they are in order and the credit requirements are met.　如果通知行对信用证进行了保兑，对于卖方所提供的单据，只要它们是正确的并且符合信用证的要求，通知行就必须无追索权地进行付款。

10. Under this credit, the beneficiary will receive payment at sight and the discount charges and acceptance commission are for the account of the applicant.　对于假远期信用证，受益人可以取得即期付款，而贴现的费用和承兑手续费是由申请人支付。
    "for the account of"表示"由……支付"。

11. It is a credit under which the beneficiary (the first beneficiary) may request the bank authorized to pay, incur a deferred payment undertaking, accept or negotiate (the transferring bank), or in the event of a freely negotiable credit, the bank specially authorized in the credit as the transferring bank to make the documentary credit available in whole or in part to one or more other beneficiary(ies) (second beneficiary).　它（可转让信用证）是指受益人可以要求受委托付款、承担延期付款责任、承兑或者议付的银行，或在自由议付信用证的情况下，银行经特别授权作为转让行，将该信用证的全部或部分转让给一个或多个受益人。

12. Whenever payment is made, it becomes a final payment without any right of recourse. The paying bank is authorized to debit the issuing bank's account if an account is opened with the bank, or the advising bank may claim reimbursement from the issuing bank by cable. 无论什么时候进行付款，都将视为最终付款，且无追索权。如果开证行在付款行开有账户，付款行被授权借记开证行的账户，或者通知行可通过电报向开证行索偿。

13. "Should the negotiating bank not be advised of stopping renewal within … days after each negotiation, this credit shall be renewed to the original amount the next month until the total payment reaches _____ USD." "每次议付后……天之内，议付行未接到停止循环的通知时，本信用证将自动恢复到原来的金额，直至其总金额达到……美元"。

14. The exporter, namely, the beneficiary of the first credit, offers it as a security to the advising bank or his banker for the issuance of a second credit. In other words, the two credits are put "back to back", the one being issued on the security of the other. 出口商，即第一信用证的受益人，将其作为开立第二信用证时向通知行或其银行提供的保障。换句话说，两个信用证"背对背"开出，一个信用证以另一信用证为担保开出。

15. It is a credit with a special clause added thereto that authorizes the advising bank or any other nominated banks to make advances to the beneficiary before his submission of documents. 它是一种包含有特殊条款的信用证，该条款授权通知行或其他指定的银行在受益人交单之前对其预先垫款。

16. "The negotiating bank is hereby authorized to make advance to the beneficiary up to an aggregate amount of USD200,000 (20% of the amount of L/C). The advances, with the interest at the ruling rate of exchange at the time of payment of such advance, are to be deducted from the proceeds of the drafts drawn under this credit." "兹授权通知行给受益人预支信用证项下的款项，其金额不超过 200 000 美元（为本信用证金额的 20%）。本信用证项下的预支款按付款当天公布的汇率折算并加付利息，并应从本信用证项下的汇票金额中扣除。"

17. The standby credit is a documentary credit or similar arrangement, however named or described, which represents an obligation to the beneficiary on the part of the issuing bank to: ① repay money borrowed by the applicant, or advanced to or for the account of the applicant, ② make payment on account of any indebtedness undertaken by the applicant, or ③ make payment on account of any default by the applicant in the performance of an obligation. 无论如何命名或描述，备用信用证是一种跟单信用证或类似的安排。它代表开证行对受益人所承担的以下一项义务：① 偿还申请人的借款或偿还对申请人给予的垫款，② 代申请人支付其所承担的任何债务，或③ 对申请人在履行义务时的毁约承担付款之责。

18. It is of advantage to the seller in that he does not have to wait until the issuing bank reviews the documents to get paid the proceeds under the credit. 它对卖方有利，这是因为他无须等到开证行审查单据以后才可取得付款。

即：由于这类信用证的开证行授权其他的银行进行议付，那么，被授权议付的银行在审查单据无误以后便可对受益人付款，受益人便可以提早收到款项。

1. **Define the following terms.**

   (1) letter of credit
   (2) confirmed letter of credit
   (3) revolving credit
   (4) confirming bank
   (5) applicant of the credit

2. **Translate the following terms or sentences into English.**

   (1) 未授权保兑
   (2) 有效地点为开证行所在地的柜台
   (3) 凭代表物权的单据付款
   (4) 信用证以银行信用代替了商业信用。
   (5) 信用证独立于它所代表的商业合同。

3. **Decide whether the following statements are true or false.**

   (1) Under documentary credit, the negotiating bank has no obligation to examine documents. (   )
   (2) Usually the advising bank is the bank resides in the same city as the buyer. (   )
   (3) Credit, by its nature, is a separate transaction from the sales contract or other contracts on which it was based, and banks are in no way concerned with or bound by such contracts. (   )
   (4) A revocable credit cannot be amended. (   )
   (5) Unless otherwise stipulated in the credit, a transferable credit can be transferred only once. (   )
   (6) A transferable credit can be transferred only to one party. (   )
   (7) Under assignment, the beneficiary assigns his right to perform under the credit to a third party. (   )
   (8) An irrevocable confirmed credit gives the beneficiary a double assurance of payment. (   )
   (9) Reciprocal credits will be effective only when each of the two parties receives a credit from the opposite side. (   )

(10) In a red clause credit, the advising bank itself gives a packing loan to the beneficiary. (   )

(11) Under a red clause credit, the onus of repayment of the advance lies with the applicant. (   )

(12) Banks run greater risks when they open a revolving credit, therefore they usually specify a total amount available in this type of credit. (   )

(13) A transferable credit is one that authorizes the beneficiary to transfer part of the right under the credit to third party or parties. (   )

(14) An irrevocable credit cannot be amended, revoked or cancelled. (   )

(15) Under a straight credit, the issuing bank is under no obligation to the advising bank. (   )

4. Choose the best answer to each of the following statements or questions.

(1) A letter of credit is ____.
   A. a formal guarantee of payment
   B. a conditional undertaking to make payment
   C. an unconditional undertaking to make payment
   D. a two bank guarantee of payment

(2) With an unconfirmed irrevocable letter of credit, ____.
   A. the terms and conditions can be amended or cancelled unilaterally by any party
   B. only the exporter can amend the credit
   C. the advising bank transmits details without commitment to the beneficiary
   D. the issuing bank has the ability to cancel the credit at any time

(3) A confirmed irrevocable letter of credit ____.
   A. carries the confirmation of the issuing bank
   B. always involves at least two banks
   C. is issued by the advising bank
   D. creates the highest level of security against sovereign risk

(4) Confirmation of a credit may be given by ____.
   A. the beneficiary at the request of the importer
   B. the advising bank at the request of the issuing bank
   C. the advising bank after the receipt of correct documentation
   D. the issuing bank after the receipt of correct documentation

(5) In any dispute over the terms and conditions of a credit, which interpretation will prevail?
   A. Uniform Customs and Practice.   B. Incoterms.
   C. Statute law.   D. International law.

(6) A stand-by letter of credit ____.
   A. is never revoked

B. is not a letter of credit

C. is invoked in the event of non-compliance by buyer or seller with the terms of an original credit

D. is invoked in the event of non-compliance by the buyer or seller with the terms of the sales contract

(7) The beneficiary of a transferred credit is ____.

A. the paying/accepting/negotiating bank B. the shipper

C. the middleman D. the actual supplier

(8) The sum of the transferred credit will not be ____.

A. the same as in the credit before transfer

B. less than in the credit before transfer

C. more than in the credit before transfer

D. equal to the original credit

(9) Which of the following details on the transferred credit may not be different to that of the credit before transfer?

A. The shipping date. B. The expiry date of the credit.

C. The description of the goods. D. The name of the applicant.

(10) A back-to-back credit exposes the bank issuing the second credit to risk because ____.

A. the beneficiary under the second credit may not ship goods

B. the documents presented under the second credit may not exactly conform to the terms of the first credit

C. the bank has already paid the beneficiary under the second credit before it receives documentation from the beneficiary under the first credit

D. the bank has already paid the beneficiary of the first credit before it receives documentation from the beneficiary under the first credit

(11) Under the red clause credit, on which party does the final responsibility lie for reimbursement if the terms and conditions are not fulfilled by the beneficiary?

A. The issuing bank. B. The advising bank.

C. The beneficiary. D. The applicant.

(12) An applicant must reimburse an issuing bank unless he finds that ____.

A. goods are defective

B. goods are not as ordered in the sales contract

C. documents received do not allow him to clear the goods through customs

D. documents do not conform on the face to the terms and conditions of the credit

(13) A revocable credit cannot be amended or cancelled only after ____.

A. the documents under it have been honored

B. it has been amended once

C. the advising bank has notified the beneficiary of its opening

D. it has been confirmed by a correspondent bank

(14) According to the beneficiary's instructions, a transferable credit may be made available to ____.
    A. one party   B. two parties   C. more parties   D. any of the above
(15) A bank is obligated to transfer the credit only after ____.
    A. being instructed
    B. being instructed as well as paid
    C. receiving the credit
    D. the credit is confirmed
(16) Under ____, the obligation of the issuing bank is extended only to the beneficiary in honoring draft(s)/document(s) and usually expires at the counters of the issuing bank.
    A. the irrevocable credit
    B. the revocable credit
    C. the confirmed credit
    D. irrevocable straight credit
(17) ____ gives the beneficiary double assurance of payment.
    A. The irrevocable credit
    B. The revocable credit
    C. The confirmed credit
    D. The irrevocable confirmed credit
(18) The revolving credit can be revolved in relation to ____.
    A. time   B. value   C. time and value   D. time or value
(19) The credit may only be confirmed if it is so authorized or requested by ____.
    A. the issuing bank
    B. the supplier
    C. the advising bank
    D. the beneficiary
(20) The red clause credit is often used as a method of ____.
    A. providing the buyer with funds prior to shipment
    B. providing the seller with funds prior to shipment
    C. providing the buyer with funds after shipment
    D. providing the seller with funds after shipment

L/C Practice

信用证实务

> 📢 **In this chapter, you will learn:**
> ☑ Import credit operation
> ☑ Export credit operation
> ☑ Credit financing

7.1 The Operation of Import Credit 进口信用证实务

7.1.1 Application of Documentary Credit 跟单信用证的申请

When the importer applies for the issue of a documentary credit, he is requesting his bank to make a promise of payment to the supplier. Obviously, the bank will generally only agree to this request if it can rely on the reimbursement by the applicant. The applicant must therefore either have adequate funds in his account with the issuing bank or have been granted a credit line sufficient to cover the amount.

It is in the importer's interest to formulate the terms and conditions of the credit with care. He is well advised to seek advice from the bank's specialist. It is not just a question of ensuring that the credit complies with the terms of payment stipulated by the supplier; It is equally important that the buyer's own requirements be taken into account. Complete and precise terms and conditions in the credit offer the best assurance that the ordered goods will be dispatched promptly, in good condition and at the agreed price, or, in the case of service transaction, that the service will be rendered as agreed.[1]

A further reason for care in drawing up the credit terms is that the credit is legally quite independent of the underlying transaction. Banks deal in documents and not goods.[2] Once the bank has issued the credit, its obligation to pay is conditional solely on the presentation of the stipulated documents within the prescribed time limit. The applicant cannot prevent a bank from honoring the documents on grounds that the delivery of the goods or other obligations of the beneficiary have not been performed in accordance with the terms of the contract.

Rules to follow:

(1) Refer to documents only. The buyer's instructions to the issuing bank should be given in clear, professional wording, and should pertain only to documentation, not to the goods themselves.

(2) Be clear and concise. The wording in a documentary credit should be simple but specific. The more detailed the documentary credit is, the more likely the seller will reject it as too difficult to fulfill, the more likely that banks will find a discrepancy in the details, thus voiding the credit.

(3) Do not specify impossible documentation. The documentary credit should not require documents that the seller cannot obtain; nor should it call for details in a document that are beyond the knowledge of the issuer of the document.

The application should include, amongst other details, the following elements.

① The full (and correct) name and address of the applicant.

② The Issuing bank. The name of the issuing bank may be expected to be pre-printed on the standard application form when it is provided by the issuing bank for the convenience of the applicant. The beneficiary's bank does not have to be specified. It is better for the issuing bank to send the credit to a bank of its own choice in the beneficiary's country.

③ Date of application for the credit.

④ The expiry date and place for presentation of documents. Every credit, whether revocable or irrevocable, must bear an expiry date, which is the latest date for the presentation of documents.

⑤ Beneficiary. The name and address of the beneficiary must be stated precisely.

⑥ - ⑧ The mode of transmitting the credit. Depending on the degree of urgency and cost, the issuing bank transmits the credit by airmail, brief advice by tele-transmission or by tele-transmission.

⑨ Whether it is transferable. To be transferable, a credit must expressly have been designated as "transferable" by the applicant.

⑩ Confirmation.

- It has to be agreed between the applicant and the beneficiary whether the credit is to be a "confirmed" as well as an "irrevocable" one.
- If the applicant marks the "requested" box, he indicates that he wants the issuing bank to authorize or request a nominated bank to confirm the credit to the beneficiary and thereby enter into an undertaking as referred to in UCP 600 Article 8.
- If the applicant marks the "authorized if requested by the beneficiary" box, he indicates that he wants the issuing bank to instruct the nominated bank to advise the credit to the

beneficiary without their confirmation but, if the beneficiary subsequently requests that the credit be confirmed, then the nominated bank is authorized to add their confirmation and enter into an undertaking as referred to in UCP 600 Article 8.

⑪ Amount.
- The amount of the credit should be expressed both in words and figures.
- The currency in which the credit is to be issued should be indicated as shown in the ISO currency code.
- The applicant may specify an exact total number, a maximum amount or an approximate amount that permits variation by a given percentage in either direction. Under UCP 600, Article 30, when words such as "about", "circa", "approximately", or similar expressions are used precedent of the drawing amount, it means that the applicant wants to allow the 10% more or 10% less tolerance of the amount of drawing.

⑫ Availability.
- Unless the credit stipulates that it is available only with the issuing bank, all credits must nominate the bank which is authorized to pay, to incur a deferred payment undertaking, to accept draft(s) or to negotiate (unless the credit is "freely negotiable").
- Credit available: by payment at sight;
    by deferred payment at XX days;
    by acceptance;
    by negotiation.

These settlement terms should also have been agreed between the applicant and the beneficiary at the time of entering into the sales contract for which the credit is intended to be the payment mechanism.³

⑬ Whether partial shipment is allowed. It is recommended that the applicant be specific.

⑭ Transshipment. Before deciding whether to allow or prohibit transshipment, the applicant must determine the method of shipment or transport that will be utilized to deliver the goods to the consignee. If it is not allowed, the applicant should stipulate this clearly in its application.

⑮ Insurance. If there is no indication in the credit of the insurance coverage required, the amount of insurance coverage must be at least 110% of the CIF or CIP value of the goods.

⑯ Transport details. It refers to the place where the goods are to be dispatched, taken in charge, or loaded on board, as the case may be, and the place of final destination, or the port of discharge.

⑰ A brief description of the goods, including details of quantity and unit price, if any. Banks should discourage applicants from including an excessively detailed description of the goods, since this could lead to confusion and misunderstanding. The process of the credit should not be delayed by unnecessarily extensive checks and controls. However, a brief description of the goods is essential; as a rule, the quantity and price are also stated.

⑱ Trade terms. This space is to be used to indicate the relevant trade terms. It is recommended that the applicant consult Incoterms 2000 (ICC publication No. 560.)

⑲ – ㉓ Details of the documents required. The applicant should require the exporter to produce only such documents as the latter can procure without difficulty. He can safeguard himself to a large extent against the delivery of inferior goods by stipulating, for example, a certificate of analysis or quality.

㉔ Latest shipping date. It refers to the period of time after the date of shipment within which the documents must be presented for payment, acceptance, or negotiation. If a latest shipping date is stated, it should allow sufficient time for the documents to be presented before the expiry date of the credit. Account must be taken of postal delivery times between the place of dispatch, the address of the seller and address of the correspondent bank, and also of possible losses of the time through formalities.[4]

㉕ Additional instructions. If there is any additional instruction, indicate in this box.

㉖ Settlement. This will normally be to the debit of the applicant's account as authorized in the printed text of the standard documentary credit application.

㉗ Signature. The application form is to be duly signed and dated as indicated in the form.

Some of the above are not applicable when the documentary credit is to cover payment of services.

SAMPLE 7-1

Irrevocable Documentary Credit Application

Applicant: ①	Issuing Bank ②
Date of Application: ③ ⑥ ☐ Issue by (air) mail ☐ With brief advice by teletransmission (see UCP 600 Aricle 11) ⑦ ⑧ ☐ Issue by teletransmission (see UCP 600 Article 11) ⑨ ☐ Transferable Credit — as per UCP 600 Article 38	**Expiry Date and Place for Presentation of Documents** Expiry Date: ④ Place for Presentation: **Beneficiary:** ⑤
Confirmation of the Credit: ☐ not requested ☐ requested ☐ authorised if requested by Beneficiary ⑩	**Amount in figures and words:** (Please use ISO Currency Codes) ⑪
Partial Shipments ☐ allowed ☐ not allowed ⑬ Transhipments ☐ allowed ☐ not allowed ⑭ Please refer to UCP 600 transport Articles for exceptions to this condition ☐ Insurance will be covered by us ⑮ **Shipment** From: For transportation to: ⑯ Not later than:	**Credit available with Nominated Bank:** ☐ by payment at sight: ☐ by deferred payment at: ☐ by acceptance of drafts at: ⑫ ☐ by negotiation: **Against the documents detailed herein:** ☐ and Beneficiay's draft(s) drawn on:
Goods (Brief description without excessive details) ⑰	**Terms:** ☐ FAS ☐ CIF ⑱ ☐ FOB ☐ Other terms: ☐ CFR as per INCOTERMS

Commercial invoice ☐ signed original and ☐ copies
Transport Document:
☐ Multimodal Transport Document covering at least two different modes of transport
☐ Marine/Ocean Bill of Lading covering a port-to-port shipment
☐ Non-Negotiable Sea Waybill covering a port-to-port shipment
☐ Air Waybill, original for the consignor
☐ Other transport document:
☐ to the order of
☐ endorsed in blank
☐ marked freight   ☐ prepaid   ☐ payeble at destination
☐ notify

Insurance Document:
☐ Policy ☐ Certificate   ☐ Declaration under an open cover. Covering the following risks:
Certificates:
☐ Origin
☐ Analysis
☐ Health   ⑲-㉓
☐ Other
Other Documents:
☐ Packing List
☐ Weight List

Documents to be presented within ☐ days after the date of shipment but within the validity of the Credit ㉔
Additional instructions: ㉕	We request you to issue on our behalf and for our account your Irrevocable Credit in accordance with the above instructions (marked(x)where appropriate). ㉖ This Credit will be subject to the Uniform Customs and practice for Documentary Credits(2007 Revision. Publication No.600 of the International Chamber of Commerce, Paris, France),insofar as they are applicable Name and signature of the Applicant ㉗

7.1.2 Security Arrangement 保障协议

Before issuing a credit, the issuing bank must know quite well the financial standing and integrity of the applicant as well as his past record of doing similar transactions. It may happen that the applicant does not have sufficient funds to reimburse the credit after the issuing bank has honored its undertaking against correct documents. As a precautionary measure, security for opening a credit is usually required from the applicant by the issuing bank. The security arrangement may take the following forms.

(1) Margins. It may take the form of cash or advance deposit placed at the issuing bank. The amount of margins may be a percentage of the credit amount or the total value of it depending on the applicant's credit standing. The cash or partial cover is placed on a special account in the issuing bank as security.

(2) Line of credit. The issuing bank may extend a line of credit to the applicant in the same way as an overdraft or a loan facility to be used for effecting payment on requirements if the credit standing of the applicant is satisfactory.

(3) Third party guarantee. The applicant may obtain guarantee from his parent company or business associates if the latter's credit-worthiness is sound.

7.1.3 Issuance of the Credit 信用证的开立

1. Reviewing the Documentary Credit Application

When the issuing bank is satisfied that he can open the credit for the beneficiary and the security agreement has been made, he can issue the documentary credit according to the clauses in the application made by the applicant and advise the credit through another bank. He should carefully check the application for the following points.

(1) Review the terms and conditions of the proposed documentary credit to ensure that they are in compliance with the policies of the bank and in accordance with the legal requirements or regulations of the issuing bank.

(2) Review the application to see if every detail is correctly completed.

(3) Review the applicant's instructions to see whether they are acceptable or whether the bank is authorized to choose its own correspondent for advising the credit.

(4) Review the application to see whether it requires to submit any documents, the performance or production of which is totally dependent on the performance by a third party not controlled by the beneficiary, or whether there are any "non-documentary conditions" stated in the application.[5] The issuing bank should also discourage the applicant from including too much detail in the credit.

2. Completion of the Standard Documentary Issuance Form

SAMPLE 7-2

Noted Irrevocable Documentary Credit Form (Advice for the Beneficiary)

Name of Issuing Bank:	Irrevocable Documentary Credit ①	Number ②
Place and Date of Issue: ③ **Applicant:** ⑤	**Expiry Date and Place for Presentation of Documents** Expiry Date: ④ Place for Presentation:	
Advising Bank: Reference No. ⑦	**Beneficiary:** ⑥ **Amount:** ⑧	
Partial shipments ☐ allowed ☐ not allowed ⑩ Transhipment ☐ allowed ☐ not allowed ⑪ ☐ Insurance covered by buyers ⑫ **Shipment** From: For transportation to: ⑬ Not later than:	**Credit available with nominated Bank:** ☐ by payment at sight ☐ by deferred payment at ☐ by acceptance of drafts at ⑨ ☐ by negotiation **Against the documents detailed herein:** ☐ and Beneficiary's draft(s) drawn on:	
14-20		
Documents to be presented within ☐ days after the date of shipment but within the validity of the Credit ㉑		
We hereby issue the Irrevocable Documentay Credit in your favour. It is subject to the Uniform Customs and Practice for Documentary Credits (2007 Revision International Chamber of Commerce, Paris, France, Publication No.600) and engages us in accordance with the terms thereof. The number and the date of the Credit and the name of our bank must be quoted on all drafts required if the Credit is available by negotiation, each presentation must be noted on the reverse side of this advice by the bank where the Credit is available. ㉓		
㉔ This document consists of ☐ signed page(s)	㉕ Name and signature of the Issuing Bank	

① Type of the credit.

② Credit number.

③ Place and date of issue.

④ Date and place of expiry: the latest date for presentation of the documents.

⑤ Applicant. The applicant is the customer at whose request and on whose instructions a bank is to issue a documentary credit.

⑥ Beneficiary. It refers to the party in whose favor the credit is to be issued and the party that must comply with the terms and conditions of the credit.

⑦ Advising bank. When the applicant fails to state beneficiary's bank, the issuing bank will choose its own correspondent bank in beneficiary's country.

⑧ Amount of the credit. The amount should be expressed both in words and figures. The currency should be indicated in the ISO currency code, e. g. USD, GBP, DEM and CNY, etc.

⑨ Nominated bank and credit availability. This is the area where the credit will indicate the nominated bank and the details of its availability.

⑩ Partial shipment. Please refer to UCP 600 Article 31, if the credit does not stipulate otherwise, either the "allowed" or the "not allowed" box should be X-marked.

⑪ Transshipment. The "allowed" or "not allowed" box should be X-marked.

⑫ Insurance clause. This area should state the percentage of insurance and the party that effects the insurance.

⑬ Shipment. This section should indicate where the goods must be shipped, loaded on board/dispatched/taken in charge and to which destination they must be transported. This section should also indicate the latest date for shipment, loading on board/dispatched/taken in charge.

Points to remember:
- Avoid abbreviations;
- Avoid vagueness;
- State the country rather than a specific points or port.

⑭ – ⑳ Blank center space. This area is for the variable details of the credit, instructions about the documents to be presented. State precisely:
- What documents?
- How many of each?
- Originals or copies?
- Sequence of documents should be: commercial invoice;
  transport document;
  insurance document;
  other documents.

㉑ The latest date for presentation of the documents.

㉒ Advising instruction (on advise bank only). An X-mark is to be placed in one of the three boxes to indicate whether the advising bank is requested to advise the credit:
- Without adding its confirmation;
- Adding its confirmation;
- Authorized to add its confirmation, if requested by the beneficiary.

Attention should be given to the possibility that a bank may not be prepared to add its confirmation; in such a situation, the advising bank is not to advise the credit without adding its confirmation.

㉓ Bank-to-bank instructions (on advise bank only). The issuing bank should use this space to indicate where, how and when reimbursement is to be obtained by the bank which, under UCP 600 Article 13, has been nominated in the credit as the paying, accepting or negotiating bank, e.g.:
- Debit our account with you.
- We shall credit your account with us.
- Claim reimbursement from ... (the issuing bank's agent, the reimbursing bank).

㉔ Number of pages. The issuing bank should always indicate in how many pages the credit is issued.

㉕ Signature. The issuing bank's signature is to be placed both on the advice for the advising bank and the beneficiary.

Note: Some of the above details are not applicable when the documentary credit is to cover payment of services.

3. Transmitting the Documentary Credit

As soon as the issuing bank opens the credit, he must forward it to his branch or his correspondent in the place of the beneficiary. If a letter of credit is issued by airmail, it ought to be authenticated by authorized signatures, and by test key or SWIFT authentic key when issued by cable/telex/SWIFT.

(1) Issue by mail. Usually cost and time factors will decide whether the credit is to be issued by mail, possibly preceded by a brief advice by teletransmission.

(2) Brief advice by teletransmission. The function of a brief advice by teletransmission is to insure that the beneficiary is informed of the issuance and the main details of the credit. The operative credit will be the mail advice subsequently sent.

(3) Issue by teletransmission. It includes transmission by cable, telex, telegram, telefax, and transmission by data communication network. Unless otherwise indicated within the message, the teletransmission is the full operative credit (see UCP 600 Article 11).

7.1.4 Amendment of the Credit 信用证的修改

When the beneficiary receives the documentary credit, he must examine it closely to see if the terms and conditions reflect the agreement of the buyer and the seller and can be met within the time limit stipulated. If there is anything he disagrees with, he must contact the applicant and the issuing bank for amendment. Sometimes the buyer or his bank may also want to amend some of the terms and conditions of the credit.

1. Problems the Beneficiary May Often Find

(1) The seller might disagree with some terms and conditions.

(2) The seller might find himself unable to meet specific requirements of the credit.

2. Procedure for Amendment of the Credit

(1) The seller requests that the buyer make an amendment to the credit. This can be made by a telephone call, a fax, or by face-to-face negotiation.

(2) If the buyer agrees, he orders the issuing bank to issue the amendment.

(3) The issuing bank amends the credit and notifies the advising bank of the amendment.

(4) The advising bank notifies the seller of the amendment.

3. The Standard Amendment Form

① Number. It refers to number of the credit which is being amended.

② Date of amendment. This is usually the issuance date of amendment. When used as the operative amendment to a previously teletransmitted message, the date should be as stated in the teletransmission. If no date has been stated in the teletransmission, the date should be that of the teletransmission.

③ Place and date of issue. It is the same as the credit being amended.

④ Applicant. It is the same as the credit being amended.

⑤ Beneficiary. It is the same as the credit being amended.

⑥ Advising bank. UCP 600 states that a bank using the services of another bank or banks (advising bank) to have the credit advised must use the services of the same bank(s) for advising any amendments.

⑦ Central blank space. It is the area to contain the details of the amendment(s).

⑧ Signature. The issuing bank's authorized signature is to be placed both on the advice for the advising bank and advice for the beneficiary.

⑨ Advising bank's notification. It is for the use of the advising bank intending to advise the credit amendment without its own covering letter or advice.

SAMPLE 7-3

Noted Irrevocable Documentary Credit Amendment Form

Name of Issuing Bank:	Amendment to Documentary Credit	Number ①
Date of amendment ②	Place and date of issue ③	
Applicant: ④	Beneficiary: ⑤	
Advising Bank: Reference No. ⑥	This amendment is to be considered as part of the above-mentioned Credit and must be attached thereto.	
The above-mentioned Credit is amended as follows: ⑦ All other terms and conditions remain unchanged. The above-mentioned Documentary Credit is subject to the Uniform Customs and Practice for Documentary Credits(2007 Revision International Chamber of Commerce, Paris, France, Publication No.600)		
Please advise the Beneficiary ⑧ Name and signature of the Issuing Bank	Advising Bank's notification ⑨ Place, date, name and signature of the Advising Bank	

7.1.5 Examination of Documents and Dishonor 审单和拒付

1. General Principle

The principles for examining documents are based upon the UCP 600 rules, by the International Chamber of Commerce and the International Banking Committee throughout the world, that is, the documents must comply with the terms and conditions of the letter of credit on the one hand and they must be consistent with each other on the other hand.

The bank examiner should first read the letter of credit so as to have the knowledge of what documents it requires and then see whether he has received all of them. Then he should go over the letter of credit point by point, making sure that each requirement has been complied with by the documents. Moreover, he has to check whether the documents are consistent with each other.

The Rule to follow: Whatever the letter of credit stipulated must be carried out.

There are some important principles to keep in mind.

(1) Banks deal exclusively with documents. They are not in a position to verify whether the goods supplied are actually identical with those specified in the credit. They are only concerned with whether the documents presented are in conformity with the terms and conditions of the credit or not.[6]

(2) Banks observe the rule of "strict compliance". It is imperative for the banks to make certain that the documents presented are exactly in compliance with those specified in the credit so that their interests will be protected.

(3) Banks assume no responsibility for authenticity, form or validity of the documents.

(4) Banks assume no responsibility for the act of the third parties taking part in the credit operations.

2. General Checklist

The following are points of consistency that all the parties should be aware of when preparing or examining documents of a documentary transaction.

Does information on all documents agree as to ... ?

(1) Name and address of the seller/shipper/beneficiary.

(2) Name and address of the buyer/consignee/importer.

(3) Issuing bank's name and address.

(4) Quantity and description of the goods.

(5) Country of origin of the goods.

(6) Country of destination of the goods.

(7) Invoice numbers, documentary numbers.

(8) Certifications.

(9) Legalizations.

(10) Shipping marks and numbers.
(11) Net weight, gross weight, volume.
(12) Number of packages or containers.
(13) Documents that are required are legally certified or legalized.
(14) All documents are in complete sets and of the number specified in the credit.

7.1.6 Accepting/Paying/Reimbursing 承兑/付款/偿付

Upon receipt of the documentation sent by the bank abroad, the issuing bank should check them carefully. If the documents meet the credit requirements, the issuing bank has to either effect payment, or make reimbursement, as stipulated, to the confirming bank or any other bank that has paid, accepted or negotiated under the credit. If the issuing bank considers that these documents appear on their face not to be in compliance with the terms and conditions of the credit, it must inform the bank sending the documents of the refusal of payment.

1. Review the Documents

When the issuing bank examines the documents, he must pay attention to the following points.

(1) Banks must examine all documents stipulated in the credit with reasonable care, to ascertain whether or not they appear, on the face, to be in compliance with the terms and conditions of the credit. Compliance of the stipulated documents on the face with the terms and conditions of the credit shall be determined by international standard banking practice and UCP rules. Documents, which appear on the face to be inconsistent with one another, will be considered as not appearing on the face to be in compliance with the terms and conditions of the credit.

(2) Documents not stipulated in the credit will not be examined by banks. If they receive such documents, they shall return them to the presenter or pass them on without responsibility.

(3) The issuing bank, the confirming bank, if any, or nominated bank acting on their behalf, shall each have a reasonable time, not to exceed five banking days following the date of receipt of the documents, to examine the documents and determine whether to take up or refuse the documents and to inform the party from which it received the documents accordingly.

(4) If the issuing bank decides to refuse the documents, it must give to that effect by telecommunication, or, if that is not possible, by other expeditious means, without delay but not later than the close of the fifth banking day following the date of receipt of the documents.

(5) Such notice must state all discrepancies in respect of which the bank refuses the documents and must also state whether it is holding the documents at disposal of, or is returning them to, the presenter.

2. Discrepant Documents and Procedures to Be Taken by the Issuing Bank

The issuing bank has up to five banking days following the receipt of the documents presented by another bank to examine and notify the result. If it finds discrepancies in the documents, it can choose from several options.

(1) Refuse to accept the documents and return them to the advising or the confirming bank so that the beneficiary can correct them and represent them during the period of validity under the documentary credit.

(2) If it feels the discrepancy is not material to the transaction, it can ask the buyer/applicant for a waiver for specific discrepancy, but must do so within seven banking days.

(3) The seller may request the opening bank to present the documents to the buyer on a collection basis.

(4) To pay, negotiate or accept with reserve or against indemnity. That is to say, if the applicant refuses to pay the discrepant document, the bank has recourse to the beneficiary.

3. Reimbursement Under a Letter of Credit

Payment and reimbursement under the letter of credit are very important procedures in the letter of credit transaction. When the correspondent bank forwards the documents to the issuing bank and requests reimbursement, either immediately or at a later date (depending on the terms of the credit), the issuing bank must check the documents and reimburse it according to their arrangement. If the transaction is conducted on the local currency of the correspondent bank, this bank can debit the amount to the issuing bank's account. If the amount of the credit is expressed in the currency of the issuing bank's country, the issuing bank will credit the amount of the correspondent bank. In the case of a documentary credit issued in a third currency, settlement is not quite simple. The issuing bank has to authorize a bank in the respective currency area to credit or transfer the owed amount on demand to the correspondent bank.

If it is a sight credit, the reimbursement methods are as follows:

1) T/T reimbursement

(1) Claim on the issuing bank. If the credit indicates the reimbursement by the issuing bank, the clauses are as follows:

"We shall credit your ... account with ... on receipt of your authenticated wire confirming that all the terms and conditions of the credit have been complied with."

"We shall remit the proceeds according to your instructions on receipt of your cable confirming documents fully complying with the credit."

(2) Claim on the reimbursing bank. If a reimbursing bank is nominated in the reimbursement method, claims should be made on the reimbursing bank. The common reimbursement clause is as follows:

"Please claim reimbursement from ... (reimbursing bank) by cable."

"The negotiating bank is authorized to claim their reimbursement by cable on ... (reimbursing bank)."

"Kindly reimburse yourselves for payment under this credit on ... (reimbursing bank) by

cable."

2) Reimbursement by airmail

If the credit stipulates reimbursement is to be made by airmail, the negotiating bank should claim on the issuing bank, the drawee bank or the reimbursing bank by airmail. The reimbursement clause may be as such:

"The negotiating bank is authorized to reimburse on the drawee bank by sending beneficiary's drafts to them together with the negotiating bank's certificate stating that all terms and condition of the credit have been complied with."

"You are authorized to reimburse yourselves to the amount of your negotiations by airmail on ... (reimbursing bank) under advice to us."

3) Reimbursement by debiting the issuing bank's account with the negotiating bank or the paying bank

The reimbursement clause in the credit is:

"We authorize you to debit our account with you under advice to us."

"You are authorized to debit our account with you."

4) Reimbursement by electronic transfer system

Nowadays, electronic transfer systems are used by the world financial centers for transmitting payments among members. Member banks send and receive on-line payment messages to one another through a main computer system installed in and operated by clearing houses such as CHIPS, CHAPS, SWIFT, and CHATS, etc. The instructions are similar to the above ones.

If it is a usance credit, the reimbursement clauses are as follows:

"Draft drawn on us at ... days after sight, payment will be made at ... days after acceptance of draft for the draft amount."

"Draft at ... days sight drawn on ... (paying bank). In reimbursement, drawee bank will at maturity pay the credit amount in the currency of the credit in accordance with the negotiating banks instructions."

"This credit is payable at ... days from date of B/L for 100% of invoice value. Please reimburse yourselves by drawing on a sight basis on our account with ... (reimbursing bank) ... at maturity."

"... available by acceptance of your draft at ... days sight drawn on us. Payment under this credit will be on a sight basis. Discount charges being for the opener account."

When the issuing bank determines that the documents they have received are in compliance, or if the applicant agrees to accept the discrepant documents, the issuing bank must reimburse the bank from which he has received the documents without delay according to the above arrangement they made in the letter of credit. Then the documents are released to the buyer against payment of the amount due, either immediately or at a later date depending on the terms of the credit. On the strength of the documents, the buyer can now take possession of the goods and proceed with the import formalities. [7]

7.2 The Operation of Export Credit 出口信用证实务

7.2.1 Review of the Credit 审证

Upon receiving the letter of credit opened by the overseas correspondent bank, the advising bank should check the signature or the test code of the credit to determine the apparent authenticity of the credit and then advise the credit to the beneficiary. Although, the UCP articles stipulate that the advising bank has no liability to check it further, such banks usually review the clauses of the credit for the purpose of good banking service. [8] The beneficiary must also carefully review the credit. It is usually for the beneficiary to check with his bank together.

Points to be checked:

(1) The documentary credit appears to be a valid documentary credit;

(2) The type of the credit and its terms and conditions are in accordance with the sales contract;

(3) The documents required by the credit are obtainable and presentable under the documentary credit;

(4) The credit does not contain any conditions, which are unacceptable or impossible to comply with;

(5) The goods description or unit prices, if any, are as stated in the sales contract;

(6) There are no conditions indicated in the credit requiring payment of interest, charges, or expenses not contracted for in the sales contract;

(7) The shipping and expiry dates indicated in the credit and the period for presentation of the documents are sufficient to enable the beneficiary to comply with them in order to obtain payment;

(8) The port of loading, taking in charge, or place of dispatch and the port of discharge or delivery correspond to the sales contract;

(9) The insurance requirement (whether is to be covered by the beneficiary or the buyer) is declared in the documentary credit.

7.2.2 Advising/Confirming 通知/保兑

1. Advising/Confirming

After the seller's bank has checked the credit and found it is in order, he must advise the beneficiary without delay.

If the correspondent bank is instructed merely to advise the credit, it forwards the prescribed text to the beneficiary without engagement on its own part. [9]

The correspondent bank may, on the instructions of the issuing bank, add its own confirmation to an irrevocable credit, thereby committing itself to make payment to the beneficiary if the terms of the credit are met. Obviously, it will give such an undertaking if it has full confidence in the issuing bank.

SAMPLE 7-4 is the standard form for the Notification of Irrevocable Unconfirmed Letter of Credit.

SAMPLE 7-5 is the standard form for the Notification of Irrevocable Confirmed Letter of Credit.

2. Utilization by the Beneficiary

Utilization is the process of the seller shipping the goods, presenting the documentation and getting paid.

The beneficiary does not have to accept the documentary credit expressly. He is deemed to have accepted it if he presents the required documents to the correspondent bank or issuing bank on time. Upon receipt of the credit, he prepares the goods and dispatches them on time. Before the beneficiary presents the documents to his bank he must ensure that they meet all the requirements laid down in the credit. The following "3C principle" applies to the exporter's documentation.

(1) Completeness. All the documents called for must be presented.

(2) Correctness. The documents must not contravene any stipulation of the credit.

(3) Consistency. They must not be at variance with each other.

When checking the documents prior to presentation, the beneficiary must first make sure that:

(1) The name of the presenter corresponds with that of the beneficiary named in the credit;

(2) The credit is still valid and the latest date for shipment (if stipulated) has not exceeded;

(3) All the stipulated documents are presented in the required numbers;

(4) The shipping marks, the number of packages and the indications of weight are identical in all documents.

👉 SAMPLE 7-4

Irrevocable Unconfirmed Documentary Credit Advice

Name of Advising Bank: The American Advising Bank 456 Commerce Avenue Tampa, Florida **Reference Number of Advising Bank:** 2417 **Place and Date of Notification:** January 14, 2019, Tampa	Notification of Irrevocable Documentary Credit
Issuing Bank: The French Issuing Bank 38 rue Francois ler Paris, France	**Beneficiary:** The American Exporter Co., Inc. 17 Main Street Tampa, Florida
Reference Number of the Issuing Bank: 12345	**Amount:** USD100,000 — One hundred thousand US Dollars

We have been informed by the above-mentioned Issuing Bank that the above-mentioned Documentary Credit has been issued in your favour. Please find enclosed the advice intended for you.

Check the Credit terms and conditions carefully. In the event you do not agree with the terms and conditions, or if you feel unable to comply with any of those conditions, kindly arrange an amendment of the Credit through your contracting party (the Applicant).

Other information:

☒ This notification and the enclosed advice are sent to you without any engagement on our part.

☐ As requested by the Issuing Bank, we hereby add our confirmation to this Credit in accordance with the stipulations under UCP 600 Aritcle 8.

The American Advising Bank

SAMPLE 7-5

Irrevocable Confirmed Documentary Credit Advice

Name of Advising Bank: The American Advising Bank 456 Commerce Avenue Tampa, Florida **Reference Number of Advising Bank:** 2417 **Place and Date of Notification:** January 14, 2019, Tampa	Notification of Irrevocable Documentary Credit
Issuing Bank: The French Issuing Bank 38 rue Francois ler Paris, France	**Beneficiary:** The American Exporter Co., Inc. 17 Main Strret Tampa, Florida
Reference Number of the Issuing Bank: 12345	**Amount:** USD100,000 — One hundred thousand US Dollars

We have been informed by the above-mentioned Issuing Bank that the above-mentioned Documentary Credit has been issued in your favour. Please find enclosed the advice intended for you.

Check the Credit terms and conditions carefully. In the event you do not agree with the terms and conditions, or if you feel unable to comply with any of those conditions, kindly arrange an amendment of the Credit through your contracting party (the Applicant).

Other information:

☐ This notification and the enclosed advice are sent to you without any engagement on our part.

☒ As requested by the Issuing Bank, we hereby add our confirmation to this Credit in accordance with the stipulations under UCP 600 Aritcle 8.

The American Advising Bank

7.2.3 Examination of Documents 审单

The seller prepares and presents all the documents as required by the credit to the nominated bank. The advising/confirming bank reviews the document package making certain the documents are in conformity with the terms and conditions of the credit and pays the seller/accepts his draft/negotiates his documents according to the terms of the credit. Then the advising/confirming/negotiating/accepting bank sends the documents to the issuing bank by mail or by courier or other telegraphic means. For the general principles and general checks, please refer to 7.1.5 in this chapter.

1. Examining a Draft

When examining a draft, the following points should always be noted.

(1) Is the L/C number required on the draft absent or incorrect?
(2) Is presentation of the draft after the expiry date?
(3) Does the amount of the draft agree with the credit amount and invoice?
(4) Is the tenor the same as shown in the credit?
(5) Is the draft drawn by the beneficiary?
(6) Is the drawer's signature presented on the draft?
(7) Is the draft drawn on the nominated party in the credit?
(8) Is the draft endorsed by the payee or endorsed correctly?
(9) Are the amount in words and amount in figures identical?
(10) Is there any interest clause?
(11) Does the draft contain any or all notations as stipulated in the credit?

2. Examining the Commercial Invoice

The following points should always be noted.

(1) Is it issued by the beneficiary named in the credit?
(2) Is it issued to the correct name and address as named in the credit?
(3) Does the description of the goods in the invoice correspond exactly to what is described in the credit?
(4) Does the quantity of the goods in the invoice correspond exactly to what is described in the credit?
(5) Does the value/unit price/total price of the goods correspond exactly to what is specified in the credit?
(6) Does the invoice amount exceed the amount of the credit?
(7) Does the currency used in pricing the invoice match that of the credit?
(8) Does the invoice state the delivery terms, and does it correspond to what is described in the credit?
(9) Is the invoice signed?
(10) If required by the credit, does it bear proper certifications, authorizations, or legalizations?
(11) If required by the credit, does the invoice contain any special marks, numbers, or other notations?

3. Examining the Transport Documents

The following points should always be noted when examining the transport documents.

(1) Does it contain a "clean, shipped on board" notation?
(2) Does it contain the correct name and address of the consignee in the credit?
(3) Does the transport document contain the correct transport details stated in the credit (the vessel, the port of loading, port of destination, buyer's premises)?

(4) If required by the credit, is the "notify party" listed?

(5) Was the transport document issued within the period specified in the credit?

(6) Is the full set of originals being presented?

(7) Is the transport document not a charter party document, unless otherwise authorized by the credit?

(8) Is the quantity and description of the goods consistent with those on other documents of this transaction?

(9) Are the shipping marks and numbers consistent with those on other documents?

(10) Is the freight terms consistent with those stipulated in the documentary credit?

(11) Does the transport document meet the stipulations of the credit with regard to transshipment?

(12) If the transport document states "on deck" stowage, is it allowed by the credit?

4. Examining the Insurance Document

The following points should always be noted when examining the insurance document.

(1) Is the insurance document issued and signed by an insurance company, underwriter, or their agent?

(2) Is it the correct type of the insurance document as stated in the credit?

(3) Has the document covered all the risks stipulated in the credit?

(4) Does the document cover the full period of transit?

(5) Is the information in the insurance document concerning mode of transport and transport route consistent with the documentary credit?

(6) Is the currency of the insurance document the same as that shown in the credit?

(7) Is the percentage of the insurance the same as specified in the credit?

(8) Is the merchandise description consistent with that shown in the credit?

(9) Are the transport details the same as stated in the credit (the vessel, the port of loading, port of destination, buyer's premises)?

(10) If endorsement is required, is the document properly endorsed?

(11) Is the full set of insurance documents presented?

5. Most Common Discrepancies in Examination of Documents

Perhaps the greatest problem associated with documentary credits is discrepancies with documents as they are prepared, presented and examined by sellers, buyers, and the banks. All parties have the obligation to check the documents to make certain they are in order and all parties are at risk for failing to do so properly. The most common discrepancies occurring in a credit transaction are as follows:

(1) Bill qualified (unclean bill of lading);

(2) No evidence of goods actually "shipped on board";

(3) Shipment made between ports other than those stated in the credit;

(4) Goods shipped on deck;

(5) Presentation of an insurance document of a type other than that required in the credit;

(6) Insurance risks covered not as specified in the credit;

(7) Under-insured;

(8) Insurance not effective from the date shown on the shipping document;

(9) Documents inconsistent with each other;

(10) Description of goods on the invoice different from that shown in the credit;

(11) Weight different between documents;

(12) Amount shown on the invoice not identical with that indicated on the bill of exchange;

(13) Marks and numbers inconsistent between documents;

(14) Credit amount exceeded/under drawn;

(15) Credit expired;

(16) Late presentation;

(17) Late shipment;

(18) Short shipment;

(19) Absence of some documents called for in the credit;

(20) Bill of exchange drawn on a wrong party;

(21) Bill of exchange payable on an indeterminable date;

(22) Absence of signatures required on documents;

(23) Drafts/Bills of lading/Insurance documents not endorsed or not endorsed correctly;

(24) Insufficient number of copies presented.

7.2.4 Discrepancies in the Documents 单据的不符点

Irregular documents must be returned by the bank to the beneficiary within a reasonable time (usually within five working days). It must sometimes be possible for the beneficiary to amend the documents or get them corrected and to resubmit them before the credit expires. The credit does not automatically become void when the documents are rejected by the bank. The advising bank/confirming bank has several options in dealing with discrepant documents.

(1) The advising or confirming bank can refuse to accept the documents and return them to the beneficiary so that they can be corrected or replaced.[10]

(2) The correspondent bank notifies the issuing bank of the discrepancies by telex and requests authorization to effect payment despite them.

(3) The correspondent bank suggests to the beneficiary that he send the documents to the issuing bank for approval. In this way, the buyer will gain possession of the documents only against payment of the value of the goods.

(4) The correspondent bank may — though it is under no obligation to do so — honor the documents "under reserve". If the buyer or issuing bank then refuses to make payment against the documents because of the discrepancies, the beneficiary must refund the amount, plus commissions, expenses and interest, to the bank.[11]

7.2.5 Accepting/Paying/Negotiating 承兑/付款/议付

Once the correspondent bank has examined the documents and found them to be in order, it will not hesitate to honor any credit to which it has added its confirmation. If the credit is unconfirmed, the correspondent bank that advised the credit is not bound to honor the documents, but in the interest of his customer, it will usually do so. Depending on the agreed method of settlement, the correspondent bank either pays out the credit amount, accepts the bill of exchange or — in the event of a deferred payment credit — issues an undertaking to make payment at a later date. In the first case, the beneficiary obtains liquid funds immediately. If the credit is available by acceptance, he can either wait for the accepted bill to maturity or convert it into cash by discounting it at his bank.

(1) Negotiation. It means the giving of value for the draft(s) and/or document(s) by the bank authorized to negotiate. Mere examination of the documents without giving value does not constitute a negotiation. The draft drawn under a negotiation credit can be a sight draft/usance draft drawn on the issuing bank or nominated bank, but it can't be drawn on the applicant.

In a negotiation credit, the issuing bank may authorize the advising bank or another bank to negotiate the documents under the credit; it may be authorized to be freely negotiable by any bank. When banks negotiate the credit, they deduct the interest from the negotiation date to the agreed payment date and give the net amount to the beneficiary, then remit the documents to the issuing bank or nominated reimbursing bank for reimbursement.[12]

(2) Payment. If the sight credit stipulates "the credit is payable at the counters of the advising bank", the advising bank then becomes the nominated paying bank. As soon as the beneficiary submits the complying documents, the advising bank can effect payment to the beneficiary and then send the documents to the issuing bank or nominated reimbursing bank for reimbursement.

If the credit is a deferred payment credit, there is no need to draw a draft. The deferred payment is made by the issuing bank, confirming bank or nominated paying bank. It is better for the beneficiary to require that the credit be confirmed. The export bank will ask for reimbursement from the issuing bank after his deferred payment to the beneficiary.

(3) Acceptance. If the acceptance credit stipulates the advising bank or another bank as the drawee of the draft under the credit, the advising bank can accept the draft and make payment at the maturity when he is sure that the credit terms are complied with. The acceptance bank will ask for reimbursement after he has paid the draft.

7.2.6 Claim 索偿

1. Claim for Reimbursement

The correspondent bank forwards the documents to the issuing bank and requests reimbursement, either immediately or at a later date depending on the terms of reimbursement.

If the transaction is conducted in the local currency of the correspondent bank, this bank can debit the amount to the issuing bank's account (vostro account). If the credit amount is expressed in the currency of the issuing bank's country, the issuing bank will credit the account of the correspondent bank (nostro account from the correspondent bank's point of view). Examples of this type of reimbursement instructions are:

"You are requested at sight/at maturity to credit the above total sum to us/our H. O. account with you under telex/airmail advice to us."

"We have today debited the above total sum to your account with us/our H. O. Beijing."

"Please authorize us/our H. O. Beijing by cable/airmail to debit your account with the above total sum."

In the case of a documentary credit issued in a third currency, settlement is not quite so simple. The issuing bank has to authorize a bank in the respective currency area to credit or transfer the owed amount to the correspondent bank. Examples of this type of reimbursement instructions are:

"Please pay/remit the proceeds by T/T or airmail to XX bank for the credit of us/our H. O. account with them under their telex/airmail advice to us."

"We have requested XXX bank by telex/airmail to debit your account and credit us/our H. O. account with the above proceeds."

"We have claimed reimbursement as per our telex of today requesting you (or reimbursing bank) to credit the above sum under your (their) telex/airmail advice to us."

2. Payment Refused by the Issuing Bank

If the documents presented by the correspondent meet the credit requirements, the issuing bank then has to effect payment or make reimbursement, as stipulated, to the confirming bank or any other bank that has paid, accepted or negotiated under the credit. If the issuing bank considers that these documents appear on their face not to be in compliance with the terms and conditions of the credit, it must inform the bank sending the documents of the refusal of payment.

If the irregularities in the documents put forward by the issuing bank are not reasonable, the paying bank, accepting bank or negotiating bank shall mail/cable the issuing bank immediately, following the banks' regular practice or the UCP rules to urge the latter to effect payment promptly, together with the interest caused by the delay payment, if any.

It occasionally happens that an issuing bank without a reputable credit standing may collude with the applicant to refuse payment. In that case, the beneficiary and negotiating bank must be cautious and take certain measures to press the issuing bank for making payment.

If actual discrepancies do exist, the beneficiary must present again the correct documents immediately or contact the opener directly, asking him to accept the documents and effect payment.

Whenever the issuing bank refuses payment or places a reservation for an alleged discrepancy, the paying, accepting or negotiating bank must cooperate of one mind with the beneficiary to make every effort to receive payment as soon as possible.

3. Settlement with the Applicant

The issuing bank checks the documents to ensure that they meet the requirements of the credit. If they are in order, the documents are released to the buyer against payment of the amount due, either immediately or at a later date depending on the terms of the security agreement. On the strength of the documents, the buyer can now take possession of the goods and proceed with the import formalities.

7.3 Credit as a Means of Finance 信用证融资

7.3.1 Finance to the Exporter 对出口商的融资

The situation often arises that an exporter/supplier is able to or has concluded a contract to deliver goods to an importer/buyer, but is unable to finance the purchase or production of the goods that are to be delivered out of its own liquidity.

It is in such cases, where the customer will or has received a letter of credit, that banks are requested to pre-export financing so that the exporter may fulfill his contractual obligations and profit from the transaction.

There are a number of methods that may be applied to meet the exporter's needs, such financing arrangements include: red clause letter of credit and transferable credit that have been covered in Chapter 6. Other arrangements include:

(1) Packing loan;
(2) Negotiation and outward bill purchased.

1. Packing Loan

It is a finance extended to the exporter by the exporter's bank against the original credit received from overseas banker together with the sales contract. In other words, the original credit and the sales contract are used as securities for the exporter to obtain the said loan. It is so called because the loan is extended at the stage of production and packing and it enables the exporter to obtain payment before shipment is made.

Having received the letter of credit from the importer's bank, the exporter will approach his bank seeking finance on the strength of the letter of credit in his favor. If agreeable, the bank will then advance normally an amount of 80% of the credit amount with the time limit within 3 months or no longer than 21 days after the expiry date of the credit. After shipping the goods to the importer, the exporter will submit documents under the credit to the bank. The bank will in turn obtain payment under the letter of credit (assuming the credit terms are complied with) and apply the funds against the cash advance with the balance being paid out to the exporter.

2. Negotiation and Outward Bill Purchased

Negotiation means the bank authorized or choosing to negotiate gives value to the draft(s) drawn on the issuing bank at the time when the exporter presents the documents to him. Similar to negotiation under collection, the negotiation bank will become the holder in due course who has the right of recourse against the exporter when the draft is dishonored by the drawee. However, under the credit, the drawee is a bank rather than a trader (the importer). Therefore, the negotiating bank is more secured to get compensation in the sense that he has a payment undertaking from the issuing bank rather than from a trader (the importer) under collection.

3. Bank's Considerations When Granting Finance

(1) Creditworthiness of borrower:
- balance sheets;
- reputation;
- financial standing;
- nature of business;
- track record;
- future outlook.

(2) Security of letter of credit:
- standing/reputation of the issuing bank;
- country risk;
- authenticity;
- terms of credit;
- confirmed/unconfirmed.

(3) Foreign exchange risks:
- hedging.

(4) Supplier:
- standing & ability;
- reputation;
- track record;
- nature of business/goods.

4. How to Minimize Risks

(1) Always try to obtain the original letter of credit.

(2) Ensure that the letter of credit is genuine (signature, test key), if in doubt contact the issuing bank for their confirmation.

(3) If the letter of credit was advised through another bank, inform the advising bank that your customer has authorized you to "handle" this transaction.

(4) Consider the status of the issuing bank.

(5) Examine terms of the credit, can the bank lend against the credit?

(6) Always obtain a copy of the exporter's proforma invoice that has been sent to the ultimate seller. If in doubt, contact the seller to "confirm" the transaction.

(7) If deemed necessary, try and obtain copies of the related contracts between all parties.

(8) Try and ensure that payment to the seller is made directly to the seller's bank.

(9) If possible, don't advance the whole purchase price but rather 80% thereof.

(10) Upon receipt of the documents, ensure that they conform to the credit terms.

7.3.2 Finance to the Importer 对进口商的融资

1. Deposit Margin for Issuing a Credit

It is a kind of finance extended by the issuing bank to the importer. At the time of applying for the issuance of a credit, the deposit margin required to place with the issuing bank is just a certain percentage of the credit amount, and normally it is from 10% to 80%. This means that the importer can utilize the full credit amount against a partial margin. The importer is financed in the sense that the occupancy of his flow of funds is greatly reduced. And in some cases, the importer may enjoy greater benefits when no margin is required on the part of the importer when the credit is issued at his request.

2. Advance against Inward Documentary Bills

This is a kind of finance extended to the importer by the issuing bank at the time when the issuing bank receives complying documents sent from the exporter or his banker. The importer is financed because the payment is made by the issuing bank on his behalf, the importer should then reimburse the issuing bank against the complying documents.

3. Advance against Trust Receipt

This kind of finance is extended to the importer by the issuing bank at the time when the importer is supposed to make payment to the complying documents but faces some financial difficulties, or when under a usance credit where the physical goods are at the port of destination long before the maturity of the documents.

Under this arrangement, the bank will release the documents to the importer against Trust Receipt under which he will clear the goods as a "trustee" of his bank. Thus, payment is deferred and the importer will obtain goods at once.

7.4 Risk Protection of L/C 信用证的风险防范

As we have seen, letters of credit enjoy a peculiar status in the payment cycle. Because they guarantee the underlying commercial transaction, they have to be a legally independent vehicle from that transaction. This means that if the supporting documents give every appearance of being genuine, banks are obliged by international law to pay against them.

Effectively this changes the status of the back-up documentation for an L/C. It means that a bill of lading is a negotiable document, and a counterfeit copy could well be worth millions of dollars. It is strange, that traders do not realize this. There is often an implicit trust in international trade, but the key message to all our clients, when entering into a new relationship, should be caveat emptor.

Documents supporting L/Cs that are susceptible to forgery are: bills of lading, commercial invoices, insurance certificates and certificates of quality.[13]

The potential fraudster has a series of options open. He could ship, for instance, substandard goods or even rubbish inside the correct packing cases and then, using the genuine bill of lading, obtain payment through the L/C.

Alternatively, and frequently much cheaper, if he can obtain an entire set of forged backing documents, including the bill of lading, he may present them to the bank negotiating the L/C and obtain payment.

The crime would, in both instances, not normally be detected until after the ship had reached its destination, weeks, sometimes months after the payment had been made. Therefore, whenever being approached by an unusual transaction with unknown parties, importers and banks should exercise extreme caution to avoid becoming involved in fraudulent transactions. The best way to avoid fraud is to have a detailed investigation about the creditworthiness of the prospective trader.[14]

New Words and Expressions

formulate	[ˈfɔːmjuleit]	v.	设计，规划
pertain	[pə(ː)ˈtein]	v.	关于，属于
reimbursement	[ˌriːimˈbəːsmənt]	n.	付还，退还，偿付
discrepancy	[disˈkrepənsi]	n.	差异，矛盾，不符合
variation	[ˌvɛəriˈeiʃən]	n.	变更，变化，变异
tolerance	[ˈtɔlərəns]	n.	公差，增减幅度
certification	[ˌsəːtifiˈkeiʃən]	n.	证明，证书
legalization	[ˌliːgəlaiˈzeiʃən]	n.	合法化，得到法律认可，立法，法规
safeguard	[ˈseifˌgɑːd]	v.	维护，保护
		n.	安全措施，防范
integrity	[inˈtegriti]	n.	正直，诚实，完整
margin	[ˈmɑːdʒin]	n.	利润，差数，保证金
imperative	[imˈperətiv]	a.	命令的，强制的，急需的，必要的
completeness	[kəmˈpliːtnis]	n.	完全，完整
correctness	[kəˈrektnis]	n.	正确
consistency	[kənˈsistənsi]	n.	一致性，连贯性
stowage	[ˈstəuidʒ]	n.	装载，装载费
proceeds	[ˈprəusiːdz]	n.	收益，货款
contravene	[ˌkɔntrəˈviːn]	v.	违反，违背（法规，习俗等），反驳
fraudster	[ˈfrɔːdstə]	n.	骗子

grant a credit line　给予信贷额度　　　　bank examiner　银行审单人员
be well advised to　最好……　　　　　　international standard banking practice　标准国际银行惯例
within the prescribed time limit　在规定的时间限度内　　expeditious means　快捷的方法

in professional wording 用专业语言	without delay 毫不延误
ISO currency code 国际标准化组织的货币符号	claim on the issuing bank 向开证行索偿
notional profit 名义利润	electronic transfer system 电子支付系统
precedent of 在……之前	clearing house 清算所，清算行
port of discharge 卸货港	reimbursing bank 偿付行
on-line payment 网上支付	apparent authenticity of the credit 信用证表面的真实性
document package 所有的单据	dispatch the goods 发运货物
balance sheet 资产负债表	strict compliance 严格相符
enjoy a peculiar status 有奇怪的特征	interest clause 利息条款
inferior goods 劣质商品	delivery terms 交货条件
certificate of analysis 质量分析证书	clean, on board bill of lading 清洁的已装船提单
postal delivery 邮寄	notify party 被通知方
latest shipping date 最迟装运日期	transport route 运输路线
precautionary measure 预防措施	qualified/unclean bill of lading 不洁提单
security arrangement 保障安排	under reserve 有保留（这里指保留追索权）
overdraft/loan facility 透支/贷款便利	collude with 与……共谋
parent company 母公司	alleged discrepancy 无证据，给不出证据的不符点
business associate 贸易伙伴	be at variance with each other 互相矛盾，互不一致
claim reimbursement 索偿	caveat emptor 买主须自行当心（货物售出概不退换）
make reimbursement 偿付	counterfeit copy 伪造品（这里指伪造的单据）
operative credit 有效的信用证	susceptible to forgery 容易伪造
mail advice 邮寄通知	sub-standard goods 不符合标准的货物
data communication network 信息交换系统	short shipment 短装（指数量少于规定的数量）

Notes

1. Complete and precise terms and conditions in the credit offer the best assurance that the ordered goods will be dispatched promptly, in good condition and at the agreed price, or, in the case of service transaction, that the service will be rendered as agreed. 在信用证里面完整准确地规定各种条件和条款可以最大限度地保障所订购的货物能及时、完好并按约定的价格提供；如果是劳务交易，则可以最大限度地保障能按照约定的条件提供劳务。

2. A further reason for care in drawing up the credit terms is that the credit is legally quite independent of the underlying transaction. Banks deal in documents and not goods. 在制定信用证条款时要谨慎的另一个原因是：在法律上，信用证完全独立于它所基于的交易。银行处理的是单据而不是货物。

3. These settlement terms should also have been agreed between the applicant and the beneficiary at the time of entering into the sales contract for which the credit is intended to be the payment mechanism. 这些结算条款也应由申请人和受益人在签订销售合同并规定用信用证作为支付方式时约定好。

   该句中的"for which the credit is intended to be the payment mechanism"作为定语修饰"the sales contract"。

4. Account must be taken of postal delivery times between the place of dispatch, the address of the seller and address of the correspondent bank, and also of possible losses of the time through formalities. 应考虑单据从发运地、卖方所在地到往来行所在地所花的邮寄时间，同时还应考虑这些手续可能耽误的时间。

5. Review the application to see whether it requires to submit any documents, the performance or production of which is totally dependent on the performance by a third party not controlled by the beneficiary, or whether there are any "non-documentary conditions" stated in the application. 审查开证申请书以确定它是否要求提供某些单据，这些单据的提供或制作完全取决于受益人无法控制的第三方，或者是否存在任何非单据化（不能以单据体现）的条款。

6. They are not in a position to verify whether the goods supplied are actually identical with those specified in the credit. They are only concerned with whether the documents presented are in conformity with the terms and conditions of the credit or not. 它们不会验证所提供的货物是否实际与信用证里规定的相符。它们只关心所提交的单据是否与信用证的条件和条款相符。

   "in a position to ..."意为"be able to ...", 表示"能够……"。

7. On the strength of the documents, the buyer can now take possession of the goods and proceed with the import formalities. 凭单据，买方现在可以获得对货物的所有权，从而办理货物的进口手续。

   "on the strength of"表示"凭借……，依靠……"之意，例如：

   I bought it on the strength of his advise. 我因他的建议买了它。
   I did it on the strength of your promise. 我凭着你的诺言而做此事。

8. Although, the UCP articles stipulate that the advising bank has no liability to check it further, such banks usually review the clauses of the credit for the purpose of good banking service. 尽管《跟单信用证统一惯例》的条款规定，银行没有义务进一步对单据进行审查。但是，从提供优质服务的角度考虑，这些银行还是会审查信用证的条款。

9. If the correspondent bank is instructed merely to advise the credit, it forwards the prescribed text to the beneficiary without engagement on its own part. 如果往来行只被指示通知信用证，它只需将规定的内容（此处指信用证）通知受益人，自身无须承担任何责任。

10. The advising or confirming bank can refuse to accept the documents and return them to the beneficiary so that they can be corrected or replaced. 通知行或保兑行可以拒绝接受单据

并将这些单据退还受益人，以便修改或替换新的单据。

11. The correspondent bank may — though it is under no obligation to do so — honor the documents "under reserve". If the buyer or issuing bank then refuses to make payment against the documents because of the discrepancies, the beneficiary must refund the amount, plus commissions, expenses and interest, to the bank. 往来行可以（尽管没有义务这样做）有保留地对单据进行付款。如果买方或开证行因单据存在不符点而拒绝付款，受益人必须将本金、利息、佣金及其他费用一起归还银行。
此处的"有保留地"是指"保留对受益人的追索权"。

12. When banks negotiate the credit, they deduct the interest from the negotiation date to the agreed payment date and give the net amount to the beneficiary, then remit the documents to the issuing bank or nominated reimbursing bank for reimbursement. 当银行议付信用证时，它们扣除议付日至约定的付款日之间的利息，并将余款付给受益人，然后将单据寄往开证行或指定的偿付行要求偿付。

13. Documents supporting L/Cs that are susceptible to forgery are: bills of lading, commercial invoices, insurance certificates and certificates of quality. 信用证有关单据中容易出现伪造的有：提单、商业发票、保险单和质量检验证书。

14. Therefore, whenever being approached by an unusual transaction with unknown parties, importers and banks should exercise extreme caution to avoid becoming involved in fraudulent transactions. The best way to avoid fraud is to have a detailed investigation about the creditworthiness of the prospective trader. 因此，无论什么时候遇上某个不熟悉的客户，觉得该笔交易不正常，进口商和银行都应该特别小心，尽量避免做这笔带有欺诈性的交易。防止被欺骗的办法就是详细调查未来的贸易商的信誉。

Exercises

1. Fill in the blanks to complete each sentence.

（1）When the beneficiary presents the documents to his bank, he must follow the "3C principle" in his documentation, the "3C" represents _____, _____, _____.

（2）The credit is legally quite independent of the _____.

（3）If a letter of credit is issued by airmail, it ought to be authenticated by _____ and when issued by cable/telex it is authenticated by _____.

（4）The documents of the credit must _____ the terms and conditions of the letter of credit on the one hand and they must _____ with each other on the other hand.

(5) The currency in which the credit is to be issued should be indicated as shown in the _____.

2. **Translate the following terms or sentences into English.**

(1) 信用证表面的真实性
(2) 标准国际银行惯例
(3) 信息交换系统
(4) 有足够的资金来支付信用证
(5) 买方考虑自己的要求也同样的重要。

3. **Decide whether the following statements are true or false.**

(1) If a credit is issued by airmail, it ought to be authenticated by test key. (   )

(2) The issuing bank's signature is only to be placed on the advice for the beneficiary. (   )

(3) Utilization of the credit is the process of the seller shipping the goods, presenting the documents and getting informed. (   )

(4) If the credit is advised by a certain bank, the amendment must also be advised by the same bank. (   )

(5) In examination of the documents, banks should follow the rule of "strict compliance". (   )

(6) The credit is legally quite independent of the underlying transaction. (   )

(7) An issuing bank must always reimburse the advising bank if the latter pays the credit. (   )

(8) If the tele-transmission states "full details to follow", then it will not be deemed to be the operative credit instrument. (   )

(9) Banks will not accept a document bearing a date of issuance prior to that of the credit. (   )

(10) If the credit is a deferred payment credit, there is no need to draw a draft. (   )

4. **Choose the best answer to each of the following statements.**

(1) In addition to stipulating an expiry date for presentation of documents, every credit should also stipulate a specified period of time after the date of shipment during which presentation must be made. If no such period of time is stipulated, banks will not accept documents presented to them ____.

　　A. later than 15 days after the date of shipment
　　B. later than 12 days after the date of shipment
　　C. later than 21 days after the date of shipment
　　D. later than 7 days after the date of shipment

(2) If the credit stipulates shipment on or about Jan. 10, 2020, then the date of on board

bill of lading may be ____.
A. Jan. 13, 2020 B. Jan. 6, 2020
C. Jan. 10, 2020 D. B or C

(3) If a credit stipulating total amount available is about USD100,000.00, then bank will refuse the invoice that bears the amount of ____.
A. USD100,000.00 B. USD100,500.00
C. USD120,000.00 D. USD99,900.00

(4) The ____ informs the beneficiary another bank has issued a credit in his favor without adding its own engagement.
A. confirming bank B. advising bank
C. issuing bank D. presenting bank

(5) The beneficiary must do two things to be paid. He must present documents which conform to the credit, ____.
A. and must present them on the expiry date
B. and must present them before the expiry date
C. and must present them on or before the expiry date
D. and must present them around the expiry date

(6) The expiry date is Feb. 25. The beneficiary presents his documents on Feb. 25. The bank examines the documents and finds the insurance certificate was made out for too little. ____.
A. The bank will not pay the beneficiary
B. The bank will not pay the beneficiary for documents presented expired
C. The bank will not pay the beneficiary for documents presented not in order
D. Both B and C

(7) ____ is obligated to reimburse the paying bank under a confirmed irrevocable credit.
A. The issuing bank B. The negotiating bank
C. The reimbursing bank D. The advising bank

(8) Amendments to a letter of credit must be applied by ____.
A. the account party B. the beneficiary
C. the confirming bank D. the issuing bank

(9) ____ must approve any amendments to a confirmed irrevocable letter of credit.
A. The beneficiary B. The confirming bank
C. The issuing bank D. A and B and C

(10) In L/C transactions, the account party is the ____.
A. issuing bank B. seller C. importer D. both A and C

(11) In a letter of credit, the bank pays the seller for ____.
A. documents which agree with the credit
B. merchandise which the buyer ordered
C. merchandise which agrees with the contract

D. documents which agree with the contract

(12) J. A. Smith applies to his bank for a letter of credit. The bank issues the credit and mails it to C. Thomas. Mr. Smith is the ____.

A. issuer　　　　B. seller　　　　C. beneficiary　　　　D. applicant

(13) The security arrangement of a credit may take the following forms except ____.

A. margins　　　　　　　　　　B. line of credit

C. thirty party guarantee　　　　D. protest

(14) If a credit is issued with brief advise by tele-transmission, the operative credit will be the ____.

A. mail advise subsequently sent　　B. the brief advise

C. the application form　　　　　　D. the SWIFT message

(15) Under a letter of credit, the account party is obligated to repay ____ provided that the terms and conditions of the credit are complied with.

A. the negotiating bank　　　　B. the issuing bank

C. the advising bank　　　　　D. the seller

Chapter 8

Documents under the Credit

信用证项下的单据

> 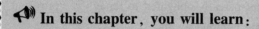 In this chapter, you will learn:
> ☑ The importance of documents in international settlements
> ☑ Some major documents used in documentary credits
> ☑ Sample documents

8.1 Introduction to Documents 单据概述

8.1.1 Importance of Documents in International Settlements
单据在国际结算中的重要性

In the process of international trade settlements, the relevant parties are dealing with documents, not goods. Banks will generally pay against documents; exporters will only receive payment by handling over the required documents; importers will only rely on documents. Documents are at the heart of all forms of international payment. It is, therefore, essential to have a good knowledge of the function of the different kinds of documents, their limitations as well as the specific problems that may possibly arise when handling them.

The documents called for by a payment method will differ somewhat according to the nature of the transaction, the goods and the countries of exporters and importers. Some documents, however, such as bill of lading and commercial invoice, are required in all transactions.

8.1.2 Some Issues Relating to Documents under the Credit
信用证项下有关单据的一些问题

1. Ambiguity as to Issuers of Documents

According to the UCP rules, if terms such as "first class", "well-known", "qualified", "independent", "official", "competent", or "local" are used in a documentary credit to refer to the issuer of a required document, banks are authorized to accept whatever documents that are presented, provided that they appear on the face to be in compliance with the credit and were not issued by the seller (beneficiary).[1]

2. Originals

The originals of specified documents should be provided unless copies are called for or allowed. If more than one originals are required, the buyer should specify in the credit how many are necessary.

Unless otherwise noted in the credit, banks are authorized to accept documents as originals, even if they were produced or appear to have been produced on a copy machine, by a computer system, or are carbon copies, provided they have the notation "original" and are, when necessary, signed.[2]

3. Authentication

Banks are not responsible for the verification of the certification or authorized signature. Certificates must usually bear the signature of the issuer. Unless otherwise stipulated in the credit, banks are authorized to accept documents that appear to satisfy the requirement.

4. Signature

Banks are authorized to accept documents that have been signed by facsimile, perforated signature, stamp, symbol, or any other mechanical or electronic method.

5. Unspecified Issuers or Contents of Documents

If the credit does not name a specific content of a document (other than transport documents, insurance documents, and commercial invoice), banks are authorized to accept documents as presented so long as the data contained in the documents are consistent with the credit and other stipulated documents.

6. Issuance Date

Unless otherwise noted in the documentary credit, banks are authorized to accept documents dated prior to the issuance date of the credit, so long as all other terms of the credit are complied with.

8.2 Types of Documents 单据的种类

8.2.1 Financial Documents 资金单据

(1) Draft.
(2) Promissory note.
(3) Check.

8.2.2 Commercial Documents 商业单据

(1) Commercial invoice.
(2) Proforma invoice.
(3) Receipt invoice.
(4) Sample invoice.
(5) Consular invoice.

(6) Customs invoice.
(7) Legalized or visaed invoice.

8.2.3　Shipping Documents　运输单据

(1) Marine/Ocean bill of lading.
(2) Non-negotiable ocean waybill.
(3) Rail-way bill.
(4) Road waybill.
(5) Air waybill.
(6) Post parcel receipt.
(7) Combined/multi-modal transport document.

8.2.4　Insurance Documents　保险单据

(1) Insurance policy.
(2) Insurance certificate.
(3) Cover note.
(4) Combined certificate.

8.2.5　Miscellaneous Documents　其他单据

(1) Certificate of origin.
(2) Health certificate.
(3) Certificate of inspection.
(4) Export/import license.
(5) Packing list.
(6) Weight list.

8.3　Invoice　发票

8.3.1　Definition of Commercial Invoice　商业发票的定义

The commercial invoice is the key accounting document describing the commercial transaction between the buyer and the seller. It is a document giving details of goods, service, price, quantity, settlement terms and shipment.[3] It includes the following elements.

(1) Name and address of seller.
(2) Name and address of buyer.
(3) Date of issuance.
(4) Invoice number.
(5) Order or contract number.
(6) Quantity and description of the goods.
(7) Unit price, total price, other agreed upon charges, and total invoice amount stated in the currency of the documentary credit.

(8) Shipping details: including weight of the goods, number of packages, and shipping marks and numbers.

(9) Terms of delivery and payment.

(10) Any other information as required in the documentary credit (e.g. country of origin). Stipulations about a commercial invoice in UCP 600 are as follows:

(1) A commercial invoice:

- must appear to have been issued by the beneficiary (except as provided in article 38);
- must be made out in the name of the applicant (except as provided in sub-article 38 (g));
- must be made out in the same currency as the credit;
- need not be signed.

(2) A nominated bank acting on its nomination, a confirming bank, if any, or the issuing bank may accept a commercial invoice issued for an amount in excess of the amount permitted by the credit, and its decision will be binding upon all parties, provided the bank in question has not honoured or negotiated for an amount in excess of that permitted by the credit.

(3) The description of the goods, services or performance in a commercial invoice must correspond with that appearing in the credit.

SAMPLE 8-1

Stanley International Trading Co., Ltd
Commercial Building Manila, the Philipines
Tel: (65) 2210001   Tele-fax: (65) 2210425

Commercial Invoice

Date: 10th August, 2019
Invoice No.: 01-12345
Consignee (name/address): Messrs Powell International Trading Co., Ltd., Malaysia
Shipped by: Stanley International Trading Co., Ltd
Shipment per: Medaley Container Co.   Payment terms: FOB Malaysia
Port of shipment: Manila, the Philippines
Destination: Malaysia
Order/Contract No.: 01-45678
L/C No.: MS01-1821

Marks & Numbers	Description of Merchandise	Quantity	Unit Price	Value
▼ MP 1821 Malaysia 1/30	1. Spare Parts HTE - TYPE I 2. Spare Parts HTP - TYPE II 3. Spare Parts HTP - TYPE III	10 SETS 10 SETS 10 SETS	F.O.B. Malaysia USD 2,000 USD 3,000 USD 5,000	20,000 30,000 50,000
			Total:	USD100,000

Say: One Hundred Thousand US Dollars Only
Drawn Under: L/C NO.: MS01-1821 Issued by Commercial Bank Malaysia Dated 10th May, 2019
Insurance: Insurance to be effected by the Buyer

Stanley International Trading Co., Ltd
Manila, the Philippines
Signature

8.3.2 Customs Invoice 海关发票

A customs invoice is a special invoice required by the importing customs for the purpose of determining the value and origin of the imported goods. It is prepared by the exporter. It is also called certified invoice, combined certificate of value and origin, etc.

The customs invoice of each country will have its own form and content. Certain elements are likely to be included in all customs invoices.

(1) Name and address of the seller.

(2), (4), (8), (10) can be left blank.

(3) Date of issuance and invoice number.

(5) Consignee.

(6) Buyer, if other than consignee.

(7) Country of origin of the goods.

(9) Terms of sale, payment, commission and discount.

(11) Currency used. It should be in the same currency as stated in the invoice.

(12) Exchange rate.

(13) Date on which the order is accepted.

(14) Shipping marks.

(15) Number of packages.

(16) Full description of goods.

(17) Quantity.

(18) Domestic market price.

(19) Invoice price.

(20) Invoice total.

(21) Production detail.

(22) Packing cost.

(23) Ocean or international freight.

(24) Domestic freight charges.

(25) Insurance cost.

(26) Other costs.

(27) Declaration of the seller/shipper. A, B are declarations; C is the signature of the seller.

☞ **SAMPLE 8-2**

CUSTOMS INVOICE

1. SELLER	2. DOCUMENT NO.		3. INVOICE NO. AND DATE	
5. CONSIGNEE	4. REFERENCES			
8. NOTIFY PARTY	6. BUYER			
10. ADDITIONAL TRANSPORTATION INFORMATION	7. ORIGIN OF GOODS			
	9. TERMS OF SALE, PAYMENT AND DISCOUNT			
	11. CURRENCY USED	12. EXCH, RATE	13. DATE ORDER ACCEPTED	
14. MARKS	15. NUDMBER OF PACKAGES	16. FULL DESCRIPTION OF GOODS	17. QUANTITY	UNIT PRICE		20. INVOICE TOTALS
				18. HOME MARKET	19. INVOICE	
21. If the production of these goods involved furnishing goods or services to the seller(e.g. assists such as dies, molds, tools.) and the value is not included in the invoice price, check box (21) and explain below.			22. PACKING COSTS	
			23. OCEAN OR INTERNATIONAL FREIGHT	
27. DECLARATION OF SELLER/SHIPPER(OR AGENT)			24. DOMESTIC FREIGHT CHARGES	
I declare: (A) ☐ If there any are rebates, drawbacks or bounties allowed upon the exportation of goods, I have checked box (A) and itemized separately below.	(B) ☐ If the goods were not sold or agreed to be sold, I have checked box (B) and have indicated in column 19 the price I would be willing to receive.		25. INSURANCE COSTS	
			26. OTHER COSTS (Specified below)	
I further declare that there is no other invoice differing from this one (unless otherwise described below)and that all statements contained in this invoice and declaration are true and correct.	(C) SIGNATURE OF SELLER / SHIPPER (OR AGENT):			

8.3.3 Manufacturer's Invoice 厂方发票

It is an invoice issued in domestic currency by the manufacturer to the exporter. The description of goods must be the same as those in the commercial invoice except that the price should be lower. It is used to understand the domestic market condition in the exporting country. If the exporter himself is the manufacturer, he may indicate in the commercial invoice "we, ourselves, are the manufacturer."

SAMPLE 8-3

Manufacture's Affidavit

IRS#: _____

Entry Number: _____

Dated: _____

Dear Sir,

We (name of person making the declaration) do hereby declare that we are the manufacturers of the articles covered by the above captioned entry and that these articles were manufactured by us in the United Stated of America.

(DESCRIPTION AND VALUE OF THE ARTICLES)

We hereby declare that no drawback has been found thereon, nor on any part thereof, that no drawback will be claimed, nor any certificate of delivery has been made or will be issued.

(NAME OF COMPANY)
(SIGNATURE OF AN OFFICER OF THE COMPANY)
(TITLE)

8.3.4 Consular Invoice 领事发票

A consular invoice is an invoice covering a shipment of goods certified (usually in triplicate) in the country of export by a local consul of the country for which the merchandise is destined.

The consular invoice of each country will have its own form and content. Certain elements are likely to be included in all consular invoices.

(1) Name and address of seller.
(2) Name and address of buyer.
(3) Date of issuance.
(4) Country of origin of the goods shipped.
(5) Country of final destination of the goods.
(6) Quantity and description of the goods.
(7) Shipping details including: weight of the goods, number of packages, and shipping marks and numbers.

SAMPLE 8-4

Consular Invoice

Shipper(name / address / phone): _____   Date: _____
                                                Invoice No.: _____
Consignee(name / address): _____   Order / Contract No.: _____
Shipment per: _____   Payment terms: _____
Port of shipment: _____
Destination: _____
Partial shipment: __(yes or no)__   License No.: _____

Marks & Numbers	Description of Merchandise	Quantity	Unit Price	Value
				Total:

Merchandise Origin _____
Manufactured by _____
Tran-shipped/Re-exported at _____

The Undersigned swear that the contents and value of this Invoice are true and correcet in every respect.

Authorized Signature of the shipper
_____

For Consul General

Signature
_____

_____
Place

8.3.5 Legalized Invoice 签证发票

A legalized invoice plays the same role as the consular invoice. It is required by some countries, particularly by those in the Middle East. Here the commercial invoice must be stamped and signed by the importing country's embassy or consulate in the exporting country, so as to become a legalized invoice, for which a fee is to be charged by the embassy or consulate. In China, the competent institution for legalizing the commercial invoice is China Council for Promotion of International Trade.

📌 SAMPLE 8-5

Stanley International Trading Co., Ltd
Commercial Building Manila, the Philipines
Tel: (65)2210001　　　Tele-fax: (65)2210425

Legalized Invoice

Date: 10th August, 2019
Invoice No.:   01-12345
Consignee (name/address):   Messrs Powell International Trading Co., Ltd., Malaysia
Shipped by: Stanley International Trading Co., Ltd
Shipment per: Medaley Container Co.   Payment terms: FOB Malaysia
Port of shipment: Manila, the Philippines
Destination: Malaysia
Order / Contract No.:   01-45678
L/C No.:   MS01-1821

Marks & Numbers	Description of Merchandise	Quantity	Unit Price	Value
▼ MP 1821 Malaysia 1/30	4. Spatre Parts HTE - TYPE I 5. Spare Parts HTP - TYPE II 6. Spare Parts HTP - TYPE III	10 SETS 10 SETS 10 SETS	F.O.B. Malaysia USD 2,000 USD 3,000 USD 5,000	20,000 30,000 50,000
				Total: USD100,000

Say: One Hundred Thousand US Dollars Only
Drawn Under: L/C NO.: MS01-1821 Issued by Commercial Bank Malaysia Dated 10th May, 2019
Insurance: Insurance to be effected by the Buyer

Stanley International Trading Co., Ltd.
Manila, the Philippines
Signature
_____

The Undersigned certified that the contents and value of this Invoice are true and correct in every respect.

For Consul General of the Philippines
Seal/Signature

8.4 Transport Documents 运输单据

Many of the problems arising in payment transactions have to do with transport documents. Often, the buyer stipulates a type of transport document that is not appropriate to the mode(s) of carriage.

8.4.1 Bill of Lading 提单

A bill of lading is a document issued by a carrier to a shipper, signed by the captain, agent, or owner of a vessel, providing written evidence regarding receipt of the goods (cargo), the conditions on which transportation is made (contract of carriage), and the engagement to deliver goods at the prescribed port of destination to the lawful holder of the bill of lading. [4]

A bill of lading is both a receipt for merchandise and a contract to deliver the goods.

1. Basic Functions of a Bill of Lading

(1) As a receipt of the goods from the shipping company to the exporter.

(2) As evidence of the contract for carriage between the exporter and the carrier.

(3) As a quasi negotiable document.

(4) As document of title.

2. Specimen Bill of Lading

A bill of lading usually embodies the following details.

(1) The name of the carrier.

(2) The name of the shipper, usually the exporter or his agent.

(3) The name of the consignee.

(4) The address of the notify party, the person whom the shipping company will notify on arrival of the goods.

(5) The name of the carrying vessel.

(6) Transport details, including the port of loading, the port of discharge, and the place where the goods is taking in charge, etc.

(7) The shipping marks. The marks and numbers will appear on the cases in which the goods are contained, so that it is quite clear which cases are covered by this bill of lading.

(8) A brief description of the goods.

(9) The details of the freight.

(10) The number of original bills of lading.

(11) This bill of lading is an original, because it is signed on behalf of the shipping company.

(12) The date on which the goods are received for shipment and/or loaded on board the vessel.

(13) This shows the bill of lading is a clean one. When there is no indication of damage to the goods, a bill of lading is said to be clean.

SAMPLE 8-6

Bill of Lading
Multimodal Transport or Port to Port Shipment

PAGE 2   **Hapag-Lloyd**

Carrier: ① Hapag-Lloyd Contarner Linie Gmbh, Hamburg	Hapag-Lloyd Reference: 14813696	B/L-No: HLCUOAK980300049
Shipper: ② WATSON / SHAKLEY RICE INTERNATIONAL 8176 WILLOW STREET WINDOSR, CALLIFORNIA CA 95492-9305	Export References: SHPR REF: JFC(UK) LTD FWOR REF: SF01078226 C. H. B. NO: 5118	
Consignee or Order: ③ TO THE ORDER BANK OF LLOYDS LONDON L/C# 3892XVGR012965	Forwarding Agent: F. M. C. NO: 0087 NALDUZAK ASSOCIATES, INC. 5088A DIAMOND HEIGHTS BLVD, SAN FRANCISCO, CA 94131-1605	
	Consignee's Reference:	
Notify Address CONNOLLY (UK) LIMITED #1 1000 NORTH CIRCLE ROAD EAST ④ STAPLES CORNER LONDON NW2 7JP ENGLAND	Place of Receipt:	

Pre-Carriage by:	Place of Receipt by Pre-Carrier	Place of Delivery:
Ocean Vessel: ⑤ 50E04 HFTNFI RFRG EXPRES	Port of Loading: OAKLAND, CA	
Port of Discharge TAMESPORT ⑥	Place of Delivery by On-Carrier	

Container, Seal Nos. Marks and Nos. ⑦ HLCU 2254295 SEAL: 136427	Number and kind of Packages: ⑧ Description of Goods 1 FCL / FCL 20' CONTAINER STC; 1420 PACKAGES MILLED RICE COMMODITY: 1006000000	Gross Weight(kg) 43020# 19513K	Measurement (cbm)

SHIPPED ON BARRD DATE: MAR/05/2019
PORT OF LOADING: OAKLAND, CA
VESSEL NAME: KOELN EXPRESS
⑫
SHIPMENT PURSUANT TO SC NO, 98-302
SHIPPER'S LORD: STOWAGE AND COUNT
FREIGHT PREPAID — ORIGIN TERMINAL CHARGE PREPAID
NO S.E.O. REQUIRED, SECTION 30.39 FTSR, C.A.S. - JL.
THESE COMMODITIES, TECHNOLOGY OR SOFTWARE WERE EXPORTED FROM
THE UNITED STATES IN ACCORDANCE WITH THE EXPORT ADMINISTRATION
REGULATIONS, DIVERSION CONTRARY TO U.S. LAW PROHIBITED, NLP

Above Particulars as declared by Shipper. Without responsibility or warranty as to correctness by carrier(see clause11(1) and 11(2))   **ORIGINAL**

Total No. of Containers / Packages received by the Carrier: 1	Shipper's declared value (see clause 7(1) and 7(2) hereof):	Received by the Carrier from the Shipper in apparent good order and condition (unless otherwise noted herein) the total number or quantity of Containers or other packages or units indicated in the box opposite entitled "Total No. of Containers hereof (Including the Terms and Conditions on the Reverse hereof and the Terms and Conditions of the Carrier's Applicable Tariff)" from the Place of Receipt or the Port of Loading, whichever is applicable, to the Port of Discharge or the Place of Delivery, whichever is applicable. One original Bill of Lading, duly endorsed, must be surrendered by the Merchant to the Carrier in exchange for the Goods or a delivery order. In accepting this Bill of Lading the Merchant expressly accepts and agrees to all its terms and conditions whether printed stamped or written, or otherwise incorporated, not withstanding the non-signing of this Bill of Lading by the Merchant. ⑬ In Witness whereof the number of original Bills of Lading stated below all of this tenor and date has been signed, one of which being accomplished the others to stand void.
Movement FCL / FCL	Currency USD	

Charge	Rate	Basis	WT/MEA/VAL	Payment Amount
THO	420.00	CTR	1	P	420.00
SEA	1530.00	CTR	1	P	1530.00
BAF	40.00	CTR	1	P	40.00
CAF	6.00	CTR	1530	P	91.00
THD	185.00	CTR	1	P	185.00

⑨

		Place and Date of Issue: CORTE MADERA, CA MAR/05/2019
Total Freight Prepaid 2081.80	Total Freight Collect 185.00	Total Freight 2266.80	Freight Payable at: CORTE MADERA, CA	Number of original Bs/L: 3/3 ⑩ For above named carrier ⑪ Hapag-Lloyd(America)Inc. (as agent)

3. Different Types of Bill of Lading

(1) Multi-modal/Combined transport bill of lading. It is a bill of lading covering two or more modes of transport, such as shipping by rail and by sea. It evidences that the goods have been collected from a named inland place and have been dispatched to a port or inland container

depot in the country of import.

(2) Transshipment bill of lading. These are used when the goods have to be transferred from one ship to another at a named transshipment port. The carrier has full responsibility for the full journey, and these are documents of title if the appropriate negotiable wording appears on the bill.

(3) Container bill of lading. When goods are packed in containers, the shipping company will issue bill of lading that acts as a receipt for containers. This kind of bill of lading can be issued to cover goods being transported on a traditional port-to-port basis, or they can cover transport from an inland container depot in the exporter's country to an inland container depot in the importer's country.

(4) Straight bill of lading. This kind of document indicates that the shipper will deliver the goods to the consignee. The document itself does not give title to the goods (non-negotiable). The consignee need only identify himself to claim the goods.

(5) Shipper's order bill of lading. It is a kind of title document to the goods, issued "to the order of" a party, usually the shipper, whose endorsement is required to effect its negotiation. Because it is negotiable, a shipper's order bill of lading can be bought, sold, or traded while the goods are in transit. This is favored for documentary credit transactions.

(6) Marine bill of lading/Conventional ocean bill of lading. This bill of lading is issued when the goods are being transported from one port to another by ship.

(7) Short form bill of lading. This type of bill of lading does not contain the full details of the contract of the carriage on the back. However, they fulfill all the other functions of bills of lading, and in particular they are considered to be documents of title. The opposite is long form B/L.

(8) Charter party bill of lading. A charter party bill of lading is issued by the hirer of a ship to the exporter. The terms of this kind of bill of lading are subject to the contract of hire between the ship's owner and hirer. Such a bill is usually marked subject to charter party, therefore it is not usually considered to be document of title.[5]

(9) Liner bill of lading: This kind of document fulfils all the normal functions of a bill of lading, including that of document of title. The liner bill of lading indicates that goods are being transported on a ship that travels on a scheduled route and has a reserved berth at destination; thus the exporter can reasonably assume that his goods will reach the buyer's country by a fixed date.

8.4.2 Marine/Ocean/Port to Port Bill of Lading
海洋运输提单/港到港运输提单

A marine bill of lading is a transport document covering port-to-port shipments of goods (for carriage of goods solely by sea).

The marine bill of lading contains the following key elements.

(1) Name of carrier with a signature identified as that of carrier, or ship's master, or agent for or on behalf of either the carrier or ship's master.

(2) An indication or notation that the goods have been loaded "on board" or shipped on a named vessel. Also, the date of issuance or date of loading.

(3) An indication of the port of loading and the port of discharge as specified in the original documentary credit.

(4) A sole original, or if issued in multiple originals, the full set of originals.

(5) The terms and conditions of carriage or a reference to the terms and conditions of carriage in another source or document.

(6) No indication that the document is subject to a charter party and/or an indication that the named vessel is propelled by said only.

(7) Meets any other stipulations of the documentary credit.

☞ **SAMPLE 8-7**

Specimen of a Marine/Ocean/Port-to-port Bill of Lading

NOL Bill of Lading	NEPTUNE ORIENT LINES LIMITED HEAD OFFICE 456 Alexandra Road #06-00 NOL Building Singapore 0511	
SHIPPER / EXPORTER (COMPLETE NAME AND ADDRESS)	BOOKING NO.	BILL OF LADING NO.
	EXPORT REFERENCES	
CONSIGNEE(COMPLETE NAME AND ADDRESS)	FORWARDING AGENT, F.M.C. NO.	
	POINT AND COUNTRY OF ORIGIN OF GOODS	
NOTIFY PARTY (COMPLETE NAME AND ADDRESS)	ALSO NOTIFY — ROUTING & INSTRUCTIONS	
LOCAL VESSEL (WHEN TRANSHIPMENT IS INVOLVED)	PLACE OF RECEIPT BY PRE-CARRIER	
OCEAN VESSEL VESSEL VOY FLAG	PORT OF LOADING	LOADING PIER / TERMINAL
PORT OF DISCHARGE	PLACE OF DELIVERY BY ON CARRIER	FINAL DESTINATION (FOR MERCHANTS REFERENCE ONLY)

PARTICULARS FURNISHED BY SHIPPER				
MARKS & NOS / CONTAINER NOS.	NO. OF PKGS	DESCRIPTION OF PACKAGES AND GOODS	GROSS WEIGHT LBS / KGS	MEASUREMENT M³
		"SAMPLE"		

CHECKS IN PAYMENT OF FREIGHT AND OTHER CHARGES FOR THIS B/L COLLECTABLE IN THE U.S.A AND CANADA MUST BE PAID TO THE ORDER OF NEPTUNE ORIENT LINES LTD.

SHIPPERS DECLARED VALUE $ SUBJECT TO EXTRA FREIGHT AS PER TARIFF AND CARRIER'S LIABILITY LIMITS.			APPLICABLE ONLY WHEN USED AS THROUGH BILL OF LADING	
FREIGHT & CHARGES	BASIS	RATE	PREPAID	COLLECT
Received by the Carrier from the Shipper in apparent good order and condition (unless otherwise noted herein)the total number of Containers or other packages or units enumerated above and said by the Shipper to contain the Goods specified above (weight,quantity, contents, condition, quality and value unknown) for Carriage, subject to all the terms hereof (INCLUDING THE TERMS ON THE REVERSE HEREOF AND THE TERMS OF THE CARRIER'S APPLICABLE TARIFF) from the Place of Receipt or the Port of Loading, whichever is applicable, to the Place of Delivery or Port of Discharge, whichever is applicable.The Merchant in accepting this Bill of Lading or in presenting it to the Carrier expressly accepts and agrees to all its terms,conditions and exceptions, whether printed, stamped, or written or otherwise incorporated, notwithstanding the non-signing of this Bill of Lading by the Merchant.			TOTAL	TOTAL
			IN WITNESS WHEREOF the Master or Agent of said vessel hath affirmed to _____ Bills of Lading, all of this tenor and date, one of which being accomplished,the other(s) to stand void. DATED AT_____ ON_____ BY_____ As Agent	
FOR OTHER TERMS AND CONDITIONS SEE REVERSE SIDE			FOR NEPTUNE ORIENT LINES LIMITED, As Carrier	

Please note that this type of document must by issued, signed or authenticated as required in **UCP 600, article 20**.

8.4.3 Non-negotiable Sea Waybill/Ships Waybill 不可转让的海运单

A transport document issued by the shipping company covering port-to-port shipment.

The functions of a waybill are similar to those of a bill of lading, except that a waybill is not negotiable and it is not a title document. On arrival at the destination, the goods will be released by the shipping company to the named consignee against identification. The consignee can then collect the goods without the need to produce the waybill.[6]

SAMPLE 8-8

Non-Negotiable Waybill for Combined Transport Shipment or Port-to-port Shipment	
Shipper	Waybill No.
	Booking Ref.:
	Shipper's Ref.:
Consignee	**P&O Containers** (Incorporating the business of ASSOCIATED CONTAINER TRANSPORTATION(Australia) LTD, and THE SHIPPING CORPORATION OF NEW ZEALAND LTD
Notify Party / Address	Place of Receipt
Vessel and Voy. No.	Place of Delivery
Port of Loading	
Port of Discharge	

Marks and Nos; Container Nos	Number and kind of Packages; description of Goods	Gross Weight (kg)	Measurement (cbm)

Above particulars as declared by Shipper, but not acknowledged by the Carrier

Total No. of Containers / Packages received by the Carrier

Movement

Freight and Charges (indicate whether prepaid or collect):
Origin Inland Haulage Charge ....
Origin Terminal Handling / LCL
Service Charge ....
Ocean Freight ....
Destination Terminal Handling / LCL
Service Charge ....
Destination Inland Haulage Charge ....

Place and Date of Issue

IN WITNESS whereof this Waybill is signed

This Waybill is issued subject to the CMI Uniform Rules for Sea Waybills.
SHIPPED ON BOARD PER
OCEAN VESSEL ....
AT.............ON...............
FOR P & O CONTAINERS LTD.
p & o CONTAINERS LTD, Beagle House, Breabam Street, London E18EP
046011 ....

ANZ WB2 11/92

8.4.4　Air Waybill　空运单

The air carrier bill of lading is known as an air waybill or a consignment note, which is a document evidencing shipment or dispatch or receipt of goods.

The air waybill contains the following elements.

(1) Name of carrier with a signature identified as that of carrier or named agent for or on behalf of the carrier.

(2) An indication or notation that the goods have been accepted for carriage. Also, the date of issuance or date of loading.

(3) An indication of the actual date of dispatch if required by the documentary credit. If the actual date of dispatch is not required by the credit, the issuance date of the document is deemed to be the date of shipment.

(4) An indication of the airport of departure and airport of destination.

(5) Appears on its face to be the original for consignor/shipper regardless of wording in the documentary credit stipulating a full set of originals.

(6) The terms and conditions of carriage or a reference to the terms and conditions of carriage in another source or document.

(7) Meets any other stipulations of the documentary credit.

SAMPLE 8-9

[Air Waybill sample document from Swissair — Shipper: SWISS EXPROT LTD, AIRFREIGHT DIVISION, ZUERICH; Consignee: IMPORT KONTOR VIENNA; Issuing Carrier's Agent: FORWARDING LTD BASLE; Airport of Departure: BSL-VIE; Flight: SR436/8.7; 8 pieces, Gross Weight 200.6 kg, Commodity Item No. 6750, Chargeable Weight 201, Rate 1.90, Total 381.90; CHEMICALS NOT RESTRICTED, CONTRACT No 100-15-2; Total Prepaid 15.00, Total Collect 381.90; executed 07.07. at BASLE; No.3—ORIGINAL For SHIPPER; 085-7260 2751]

8.4.5 Charter Party Bill of Lading 租船合约提单

A charter party bill of lading is a transport document covering port-to-port shipments of goods issued by a party chartering a vessel (as opposed to a named carrier or shipping line).

The charter party bill of lading contains the following elements.

(1) An indication that the bill of lading is subject to a charter party.

(2) A signature or authentication by the ship's master or owner, or agent for or on behalf of

either the ship's master or owner.

(3) Unless otherwise stated in the documentary credit, does not name the carrier.

(4) An indication or notation that the goods have been loaded "on board" or shipped on a named vessel. Also, the date of issuance or date of loading.

(5) An indication of the port of loading and the port of discharge as specified in the original documentary credit.

(6) A sole original, or if issued in multiple originals, the full set of originals.

(7) No indication that the named vessel is propelled by sail only.

(8) Meets any other stipulations of the documentary credit.

SAMPLE 8-10

Charter Party Bill of Lading

CODE NAME: "CUMENTVIYBILL" Shipper	BILL OF LADING	B/L No. Page 2
	Reference No.	
Consignee		
Notify address		
Vessel	Port of loading	
Port of discharge		
Shipper's description of cargo		Gross weight

Issued pursuant to CHARTER-PARTY dated...... Freight payable in accordance therewith FREIGHT ADVANCE. Received on account of freight	SHIPPED at the Port of Loading in apparent good order and condition on board the Vessel for carriage to the Port of Discharge of so near thereto as she may safely get the goods specified above. Weight, measure, quality, quantity, condition, contents and value unknown. IN WITNESS whereof the Master or Agent of the said Vessel has signed the number of Bills of Lading indicated below all of this tenor and date, any of which being accomplished the others shall be void. FOR CONDITIONS OF CARRIAGE SEE	
Printed and sold by Fr.G.Knudtzons Bogtrykkeri A/S, 55 Toldbodgade, DK-1253 Copenhagen K, by authority of The Baltic and International Maritime Council(BIMCO). Copenhagen, Copyright	Freight payable at	Place and date of Issue
	Number of original Bs/L	Signature
	Please note that this type of document must be issued, signed or authenticated as required in **UCP 600, article 22.**	

8.4.6 Road or Inland Waterway Transport Documents 公路、内河航运单据

UCP 600, Article 24 discusses in detail the requirements of a road, rail or inland waterway transport document for presentation under a documentary credit. Please refer to it for details.

(1) For transport by road, the applicant should stipulate a truck bill of lading or waybill.

(2) For transport by inland waterway, the applicant should stipulate an inland waterway bill of lading, waybill, or consignment note.

8.4.7 Cargo Receipt/Railway Bill 货运收据/铁路运输单

When the goods are dispatched by railway, a cargo receipt or a railway bill may be issued. A cargo receipt is not a document of title, just an acknowledgement of receipt of goods for dispatch, so it is non-negotiable.

A cargo receipt contains the following elements.

(1) Date of issue.

(2) Name and address of sender and consignee.

(3) Name of the originating railway station/place designated for delivery.

(4) Ordinary description of goods and method of packing and, in the case of dangerous goods, its generally recognized description.

(5) Gross weight of goods or its quantity.

(6) Carriage charges.

(7) Requisite instructions for customs and other formalities.

8.4.8 Courier Receipt 快邮收据

A courier receipt is a document issued by a courier or expedited delivery service evidencing receipt of goods for delivery to a named consignee.

In documentary credit transactions courier receipts should include the following elements.

(1) Appears on its face to name the issuer.

(2) Appears on its face to be stamped, signed, or authenticated by the service.

(3) Name and address of the shipper (seller).

(4) Name and address of the consignee (buyer).

(5) The date of pick-up or receipt of the goods by the service.

(6) Meets any other stipulations of the documentary credit.

SAMPLE 8-11

[Courier Waybill form - OCS]

8.4.9 Post Receipt 邮包收据

A post receipt is a document issued by the postal service of a country evidencing receipt of goods for delivery to a named consignee.

Please refer to UCP 600, Article 25 for details about courier receipt, post receipt or certificate of posting.

🖘 **SAMPLE 8-12**

Post Receipt

CHINA POST No. of Parcel: Category of parcel ☐ Air ☐ Surface ☐ SAL		The parcel may be opened officially.		
	☐ Commercial sample ☐ Document ☐ Gift			
	Insured Value	RMB	DTS Others	
	Total gross weight	Charges	Person take in charge	
Name and address of sender		Name and address of addressee		
Telephone number		Telephone number		
Itemized list of contents (including number of items)	Country of origin of goods	Net weight (kg)	Value (Customs)	Stamp (Customs)

Sender's instructions in case of non-delivery
☐ Return immediately to sender
☐ Return to sender after ___ days
☐ Treat as abandoned
☐ Redirect to address Below
☐ Return/redirect   ☐ By surface/S.A.L.
                              ☐ By air
    Address: _____
				Office of origin and date of posting
				
				I certify that the particulars given in the customs declaration are correct and that this item does not contain any dangerous articles prohibited by postal regulations as well as those forbidden for exportation by the Customs of P.R.C. I also agree to pay the costs related to adjacent instruction in case of non-delivery.
				
				Date and sender's signature

8.4.10 Combined Transport Documents（CTD） 混合运输单据

A combined (multimode) transport document is a bill of lading covering two or more modes of transport, such as shipping by rail and by sea.

SAMPLE 8-13

Bill of Lading Multimodal Transport Document

PAGE2 **Hapag-Lloyd**

Shipper:	Hapag-Lloyd Reference:	B/L-No.:
	Export Reference:	
Consignee or Order:	Forwarding Agent:	
	Consignee's Reference:	
Notify Address (Carrier not responsible for failure to notify: see clause 20 [1] hereof):	Place of Receipt: (Applicable only when document used for Multimodal transport)	

Pre-Carriage by:	Place of Receipt by Pre-Carrier	Place of Delivery: (Applicable only when document used for Multimodal transport)
Ocean Vessel:	Port of Loading	
Pre of Discharge:	Place of Delivery by On-Carrier:	

Container, Seal Nos: Marks and Nos.	Number and kind of Packages Description of Goods	Gross Weight (kg)	Measurement (cbm)

COPY

Above Particulars as declared by Shipper.

Total No. of Containers / Packages received by the Carrier:	Shipper's declared value (see clause 7(3) hereof) :	Received by the Carrier from the Shipper in apparent good order and condition (unless otherwise noted herein) the total number or quantity of Containers or other packages or units indicated in the box opposite entitled "Total No. of Conditions hereof (Including the Terms and Conditions on the Reverse hereof and the Terms and Conditions of the Carrier's Applicable Tariff" from the Place of Receipt or the Port of Loading, whichever is applicable, to the Port of Discharge or the Place of Delivery, whichever is applicable. One original Bill of Lading, duly endorsed, must be surrendered by the Merchant to the Carrier in exchange for the Goods or a delivery order. In accepting this Bill of Lading the Merchant expressly accepts and agrees to all its terms and conditions whether printed stamped or written, or other wise incorporated, not withstanding the non-signing of this Bill of Lading by the Merchant.
Movement	Currency	
Charge	Rate	Basis	WT / MEA / VAL	Payment Amount	

In Witness whereof the number of original Bills of Lading stated below all of this tenor and date has been signed, one of which being accomplished the others to stand void.

			No. Original	Place and Date of Issue:
Total Freight Prepaid	Total Freight Collect	Total Freight	Freight Payable at:	For the Carrier
			Loading Pier / Terminal	

8.5 Insurance Documents or Certificates
保险单据或保险证明

8.5.1 Introduction to Insurance Documents 保险单据介绍

An insurance document is a contract whereby the insurer (insurance company) undertakes to indemnify the insured in a manner and to the extent thereby agreed, against certain losses, that is to say, the losses incidental to carriage "adventure".[7] It is a document indicating the type and amount of insurance coverage in force on a particular shipment. Used to assure the consignee that insurance is provided to cover loss of or damage to cargo while in transmit.

UCP 600, Article 28 is about stipulations of insurance document and coverage.

(1) An insurance document, such as an insurance policy, an insurance certificate or a declaration under an open cover, must appear to be issued and signed by an insurance company, an underwriter or their agents or their proxies. Any signature by an agent or proxy must indicate whether the agent or proxy has signed for or on behalf of the insurance company or underwriter.

(2) When the insurance document indicates that it has been issued in more than one original, all originals must be presented.

(3) Cover notes will not be accepted.

(4) An insurance policy is acceptable in lieu of an insurance certificate or a declaration under an open cover.

(5) The date of the insurance document must be no later than the date of shipment, unless it appears from the insurance document that the cover is effective from a date not later than the date of shipment.

(6) ① The insurance document must indicate the amount of insurance coverage and be in the same currency as the credit.

② A requirement in the credit for insurance coverage to be for a percentage of the value of the goods, of the invoice value or similar is deemed to be the minimum amount of coverage required.

If there is no indication in the credit of the insurance coverage required, the amount of insurance coverage must be at least 110% of the CIF or CIP value of the goods.

When the CIF or CIP value cannot be determined from the documents, the amount of insurance coverage must be calculated on the basis of the amount for which honour or negotiation is requested or the gross value of the goods as shown on the invoice, whichever is greater.

③ The insurance document must indicate that risks are covered at least between the place of taking in charge or shipment and the place of discharge or final destination as stated in the credit.

(7) A credit should state the type of insurance required and, if any, the additional risks to be covered. An insurance document will be accepted without regard to any risks that are not covered if the credit uses imprecise terms such as "usual risks" or "customary risks".

(8) When a credit requires insurance against "all risks" and an insurance document is presented containing any "all risks" notation or clause, whether or not bearing the heading "all

risks", the insurance document will be accepted without regard to any risks stated to be excluded.

(9) An insurance document may contain reference to any exclusion clause.

(10) An insurance document may indicate that the cover is subject to a franchise or excess (deductible).

SAMPLE 8-14

Insurance Policy

INVOICE NO. _____
POLICY NO. _____
DATE OF ISSUANCE _____

This Policy of Insurance witnesses that _____ Company of _____ (hereinafter called The Insurer), at the request of _____ (hereinafter called The Insured) and in consideration of the agreed premium paid to the company by the Insured, underakes to insure the under-mentioned goods in transportation subject to the conditions of this policy as per the clauses printed and other special clauses attached hereon.

Marks & Nos.	Quantity Package	Description of Goods	Amount Insured

Total Amount Insured _____
Premium: _____ Rate: _____
As arranged _____ Per conveyance s.s. _____
Sailing on _____ From _____ To _____
Conditions/Special Coverage: _____

 Claims, if any, are payable to the holder on surrender of this Policy together with other relevant documents.

 In the event of an accident where-by loss or damage may result in a claim under this Policy immediate notice applying for survey must be given to the Insurer's agent as mentioned hereunder.

 Claim payable at _____

_____ Insurance Co.
Signature

8.5.2 Contents of Insurance Policy 保单的内容

(1) The name of the insurer.
(2) The name of the insured or some person who effects the insurance on his behalf.
(3) Subject matter.
(4) Risk insured against.
(5) The voyage or period of time or both, as the case may be, covered by the insurance.

(6) The sum insured.

(7) Premium.

(8) Surveyor.

(9) The date and place of issuing the insurance policy.

(10) The signature of the insurer.

8.5.3　Classification of Insurance Documents　保单的分类

1. Insurance Policy

An insurance policy is a document issued by an insurance company, covering the goods being shipped against specified risks (e.g. fire, water, damage, etc.) during the whole or part of the journey between the seller and the buyer.

2. Insurance Certificate

An insurance certificate is a document issued to the insured certifying that insurance has been effected. It contains the same details as an insurance policy except that the version of the provisions of the policy is abbreviated. In some countries, an insured person must have a policy before he can take legal action against an insurer. A certificate alone is insufficient evidence on which to base a legal action.

3. Floating Policy

This policy is issued for fixed conditions of insurance, where each cargo is not insured individually. Each shipment can be declared by the insured for goods shipped on a named vessel. As each shipment is made the value of the sum insured is reduced accordingly until it is exhausted.

4. Open Cover

This refers to an agreement between the insurer and the insured where the coverage, liabilities and premium are set out without a lump sum stipulated as the case of floating policy, whereas the maximum sum for each shipment is limited. An insurance certificate is issued after the declaration by the insured of each shipment.

5. Cover Note

It is a document normally issued to give notice that insurance has been placed pending the production of a policy or a certificate. Such document does not contain full details of the insurance to be effected. In most cases, this applies to transactions insured by the importer under FOB or CFR terms.

8.6　Miscellaneous Documents　其他单据

8.6.1　Certificate of Origin　原产地证书

A document issued by an authority, as stated in the documentary credit, stating the country of origin of goods. Certificate of origin Form A, specifically, is a document required by the customs authorities of many developed nations to prove eligibility of imported merchandise under duty-free import programs such as the Generalized System of Preferences (GSP).

A GSP (Generalized System of Preference) certificate of origin is a certificate used to obtain the treatment of preference customs duty imposed by the developed country on the developing countries. China began to use it since 1978, the main documents under GSP used in China are:

(1) Generalized System of Preference Certificate of Origin Form A;

(2) Certificate of Origin — Textile Products;

(3) Certificate in regard to textile handicrafts and traditional textile products of the cottage industry (to be issued by China Inspection Bureau);

(4) Export License — Textile Products.

In documentary credit transactions a certificate of origin should include the following elements.

(1) Key details (typically consignor, consignee, and description of goods) regarding the shipment. Also, such details to be in conformity with other documents (e.g. documentary credit, commercial invoice).

(2) A statement of origin of the goods.

(3) The name, signature and/or stamp or seal of the certifying authority.

8.6.2 Certificate of Inspection 检验证书

A document issued by an authority, as stated in the documentary credit, indicating that goods have been inspected (typically according to a set of industry, customer, government, or carrier specifications) prior to shipment and the results of the inspection.

Inspection certificates are generally obtained from neutral testing organizations (e.g. a government entity or independent service company).

In documentary credit transactions an inspection certificate should include the following elements.

(1) Key details (typically consignor, consignee, and description of goods) regarding the shipment. Also, such details to be in conformity with other documents (e.g. documentary credit, commercial invoice).

(2) Date of inspection.

(3) Statement of sampling methodology.

(4) Statement of the results of the inspection.

(5) The name, signature and/or stamp or seal of the inspection entity.

SAMPLE 8-15

```
              DEPARTMENT OF THE TREASURY              Approved through 12/31/96
              UNITED STATES CUSTOMS SERVICE                  OMB No. 1515-0240
           NORTH AMERICAN FREE TRADE AGREEMENT        See back of form for Paper-
                    CERTIFICATE OF ORIGIN             work Reduction Act Notice.

   Please Print or type                    19 CFR 181.11, 181.22
   1. EXPORTER NAME AND ADDRESS            2. BLANKET PER100 (DD/MM/YY)
                                           FROM
                                           TO
   3. PRODUCER NAME AND ADDRESS            4. IMPORTER NAME AND ADDRESS

   TAX IDENTIFICATION NUMBER               TAX IDENTIFICATION NUMBER:
```

5. DESCRIPTION OF GOOD(S)	6. HS TARIFF CLASSIFICATION NUMBER	7. PREFERENCE CRITERION	8. PRODUCER	9. NET COST	10. COUNTRY OF ORIGIN

I CERTIFY THAT:
* THE INFORMATION ON THIS DOCUMENT IS TRUE AND ACCURATE AND I ASSUME THE RESPONSIBILITY FOR PROVING SUCH REPRESENTATIONS, I UNDERSTAND THAT I AM LIABLE FOR ANY FALSE STATEMENTS OR MATERIAL OMISSIONS MADE ON OR IN CONNECTION WITH THIS DOCUMENT;

* I AGREE TO MAINTAIN. ADN PRESENT UPON REQUEST, DOCUMENTATION NECESSARY TO SUPPORT THIS CER-TIFICATE. AND TO INFORM, IN WRITING, ALL PERSONS TO WHOM THE CERTIFICATE WAS GIVEN OF ANY GHANGES THAT COULD AFFECT THE ACCURACY OR VALIDITY OF THIS CERTIFICATE.

*THE GOODS ORIGINATED IN THE TERRITORY OF ONE OR MORE OF THE PARTIES, AND COMPLY WITH THE ORIGIN REQUIREMENTS SPECIFIED FOR THOSE GOODS IN THE NORTH AMERICAN FREE TRADE AGEREEMENT.AND UNLESS SPECIFICALLY EXEMPTED IN ARTICLE 411 OR ANNEX 401, THERE HAS BEEN NO FURTHER RRO-DUCTION OR ANY OTHER OPERATION OUTSIDE THE TERRITOR IES OF THE PARTIES; AND

* THIS CERTIFICATE CONSISTS OF (   ) PAGES, INCLUDING ALL ATTACHMENTS.

	11a. AUTHORIZED SIGNATURE	11b. COMPANY	
11.	11c. NAME (Print or Type)	11d. TITLE	
	11e. DATE (DD/MM/YY)	11f. TELEPHONE NUMBER	(Voice)	(Facsimile)

Customs Form 434 (121793)

When examining the Inspection Certificate, the bank concerned must pay attention to the following aspects.

(1) The description and mark of the goods must be the same as those mentioned in the commercial invoice and other documents to ascertain that the goods inspected are exactly those exported.

(2) The wording on the inspection certificate must be exactly the same as those mentioned in the invoice and must be in compliance with the terms and conditions of the credit.

(3) The inspection date must be earlier than B/L's date or conform to that stipulated in the letter of credit. If the credit stipulates inspection to be made upon shipment, the inspecting date must be the same as the bill of lading date or prior to it.

SAMPLE 8-16

Certificate of Inspection

```
          IMPORT & EXPORT COMMODITY INSPECTION BUREAU
COUNTRY & PLACE
_____
TELEX _____
TEL _____     Certificate of Inspection
DATE _____       CERTIFICATE NO. _____
1. APPLICANT _____
   ADDRESS _____ TELEX _____ TEL _____
2. COMMODITY DESCRIPTION _____
3. SPECIFICATION _____
4. QUANTITY _____
5. AVERAGE NET WEIGHT / NO. OF PIECES PER PACKAGE _____
_____
6. TOTAL NET WEIGHT _____
7. MANUFACTURER _____
8. EXPORTER _____
9. TRANSPORT DETAIL _____
10. INSPECTION LABEL NO. _____
11. DATE OF INSPECTION _____
12. INSPECTION RESULTS _____
_____
_____
13. REMARKS _____
14. IT IS HEREBY CERTIFIED THAT THE COMMODITY LISTED ABOVE HAS BEEN
    INSPECTED AND PASSED. THIS CERTIFICATE IS VALID ONLY WHEN THE
    COMMODITY IS EXPORTED BEFORE_____.

IMPORT & EXPORT                SIGNATURE OF AUTHORIZED OFFICER
COMMODITY INSPECTION
BUREAU                         _____

CHOP
```

8.6.3 Packing List/Weight List 装箱单/重量单

A packing list is a document prepared by the shipper listing the kinds and quantities of merchandise in a particular shipment.

The packing list should include the following elements.

(1) Name and address of seller.

(2) Name and address of buyer.

(3) Date of issuance.

(4) Invoice number.

(5) Order or contract number.

(6) Quantity and description of the goods.

(7) Shipping details, including weight of the goods, number of packages, and shipping

Chapter 8   Documents under the Credit   209

marks and numbers.

(8) Quantity and description of contents of each package, carton, crate or container.

(9) Any other information as required in the documentary credit (e. g. country of origin).

SAMPLE 8-17

Certificate of Measuring and/or Weight

| REPORT NO. _____ |
| APPLICANT _____ |
| CONTRACT NO._____ INVOICE NO. _____ |
| NAME OF CARRY VESSEL_____ DATE OF SAILING _____ |
| PORT OF LOADING _____ PORT OF DISCHARGING _____ |
| COMPLETION DATE OF MEASURED AND/OR WEIGHT_____ |
| LOCATION AT _____ |
| GOODS DESCRIPTION _____ |
| STYLE NO. _____ |
| WE HEREBY CERTIFY THAT THE GOODS WERE MEASURED AND / OR WEIGHED BY OUR MEASURERS AS FOLLOWS: |

CARTON NO.	QTY PER CTN	DESIGNS COLORS	SIZE ASSORTMENT FOR CTN	PCS/SETS PER CTN	TOTAL PCS/SETS	GR.WT PER CTN (KGS)	NET WT PER CTN (KGS)	MEASURE-MENT PER CTN (KGS)	M

TOTAL QUANTITY _____ PCS/SETS   PACKED IN _____ CARTONS ONLY
GROSS WEIGHT _____ KGS   NET WEIGHT ____ KGS

INTERNATIONAL INSPECTION AND
TESTING CENTRE
SIGNATURE
_____

8.6.4 Export License   出口许可证

An export license is a document prepared by a government authority of a nation granting the right to export a specific quantity of a commodity to a specified country. This document is often required for the exportation of certain natural resources, national treasures, drugs, strategic commodities, and arms and armaments.

Certain elements are likely to be included in all export licenses.

(1) Name and address of seller.

(2) Name and address of buyer.

(3) Date of issuance.

(4) Validity date.
(5) Description of goods covered by license.
(6) Name of country of origin.
(7) Name of country of ultimate destination.

8.6.5 Beneficiary's Statement 受益人证明

It is a statement issued and signed by the beneficiary, certifying that he has done some work according to the stipulations in the credit, such as airmailing the copy of shipping documents, cabling the issuing bank that shipments have been effected, etc.

8.6.6 Cable Copy 电报副本

If a letter of credit stipulates that the exporter should cable the details of the shipment immediately after the goods are shipped, the exporter must do so accordingly. In that case, the cable copy must be presented to the negotiating bank along with the shipping documents if documentary credit so stipulates.

New Words and Expressions

ambiguity	[ˌæmbiˈgjuːiti]	n.	含糊，不明确，含义模糊
original	[əˈridʒənəl]	a.	最初的，原始的
		n.	原物，原作，正本
notation	[nəuˈteiʃn]	n.	符号，批注
verification	[ˌverifiˈkeiʃn]	n.	确认，查证，作证，证实
facsimile	[fækˈsimili]	n.	摹写，传真，摹本
customs	[ˈkɑːstəmz]	n.	海关
embassy	[ˈembəsi]	n.	大使馆，大使
consulate	[ˈkɔnsjulət]	n.	领事馆
shipper	[ˈʃipə]	n.	托运人，发货人
embody	[imˈbɔdi]	v.	具体表达，包括
freight	[freit]	n.	货物，船货，运费，货运
consignor	[kənˈsainə]	n.	委托者，发货人
consignee	[kɔnsaiˈniː]	n.	受托者，收件人，收货人
vessel	[ˈvesl]	n.	船，容器，船只
indication	[ˌindiˈkeiʃn]	n.	指示，迹象，注明
waybill	[ˈweibil]	n.	运货单，提货单
propel	[prəˈpel]	v.	推进，驱使
underwriter	[ˈʌndəraitə]	n.	保险业者，保险商，承保人
indemnify	[inˈdemnifai]	v.	赔偿，补偿
eligibility	[ˌelidʒəˈbiliti]	n.	合格，合格性
ascertain	[ˌæsəˈtein]	v.	确定，探知，验证

Chapter 8 Documents under the Credit

handicraft	[ˈhændikrɑːft]	n.	手工艺,手工艺品,手艺
armament	[ˈɑːməmənt]	n.	军备,武器
authentication	[ɔːθentiˈkeiʃən]	n.	证明真实性

pay against documents 凭单据付款
carbon copy 复写本,副本
perforated signature 穿孔签字,透字签名
financial documents 金融单据,资金单据
commercial documents 商业单据
commercial invoice 商业发票
proforma invoice 形式发票
receipt invoice 收讫发票
sample invoice 样品发票
consular invoice 领事发票
customs invoice 海关发票
legalized/visaed invoice 签证发票
shipping documents 运输单据
marine/ocean bill of lading 海运提单
non-negotiable ocean waybill 不可转让的海运单
rail waybill 铁路运输单
road waybill 公路运输单
air waybill 空运单
post parcel receipt 邮包收据
combined/multi-modal transport document 联合运输单
cover note 暂保单
combined certificate 联合凭证
insurance policy 保险单,大保单
domestic currency 本币
description of goods 货物描述
scheduled route 固定的航线
prescribed port of destination 规定的目的地
lawful holder 合法持有人
shipping line 轮船公司,运输公司
quasi-negotiable document 准流通单据
transport detail 运输细节
port of discharge 卸货港
take in charge 负责
shipping mark 唛头
original bill of lading 正本提单
received for shipment 收受待运
multi-modal transport bill of lading 多式联运提单
transshipment bill of lading 转运提单
container bill of lading 集装箱提单
straight bill of lading 直达提单
short form bill of lading 简式提单
long form bill of lading 全式提单
charter party bill of lading 租船合约提单
document of title 物权单据
reserved berth 预订的泊位
liner bill of lading 班轮提单
ship's master 船长
sole original 单张正本
multiple originals 多张正本
airport of departure 起运机场
waterway transport 水运
cargo receipt 货物收据
railway bill 铁路运输单
carrier receipt 承运人收据
expedited delivery service 特快专递
post receipt 邮包收据
insurance carrier 保险商
General System of Preference 普惠制
cottage industry 家庭工业
China Inspection Bureau 中国商检局
export license 出口许可证
certificate of origin 原产地证书
government entity 政府机构
sampling methodology 抽样方式
strategic commodity 战略产品
China Council for Promotion of International Trade 中国国际贸易促进委员会
inspection certificate of quality 质量检验证书
inspection certificate of health 健康检验证书

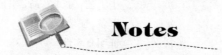

Notes

1. According to the UCP rules, if terms such as "first class", "well-known", "qualified", "independent", "official", "competent", or "local" are used in a documentary credit to refer to the issuer of a required document, banks are authorized to accept whatever documents are presented, provided that they appear on the face to be in compliance with the credit and were not issued by the seller (beneficiary). 根据《跟单信用证统一惯例》的条款，如果使用诸如"第一流的"、"著名的"、"合格的"、"独立的"、"正式的"、"有资格的"、"当地的"及类似的词语来描述信用证项下的出单人，只要这些单据的表面与信用证相符并且不是由卖方（受益人）出具的，银行将照予接受。

2. Unless otherwise noted in the credit, banks are authorized to accept documents as originals, even if they were produced or appear to have been produced on a copy machine, by a computer system, or are carbon copies, provided they have the notation "original" and are, when necessary, signed. 除非信用证另有规定，银行将有权接受下述方法或从表面上看是用下述方法制作的单据作为正本单据：影印、计算机系统处理或复写等方法，但条件是上述方法制作的单据须加注"正本"的字样，并且如有必要，须在表面签名。

3. The commercial invoice is the key accounting document describing the commercial transaction between the buyer and the seller. It is a document giving details of goods, service, price, quantity, settlement terms and shipment. 商业发票是描述买卖双方某笔交易的一种主要的计账单据。它列出了商品、劳务、价格、数量、付款条件和装运的有关细节。

4. A bill of lading is a document issued by a carrier to a shipper, signed by the captain, agent, or owner of a vessel, providing written evidence regarding receipt of the goods (cargo), the conditions on which transportation is made (contract of carriage), and the engagement to deliver goods at the prescribed port of destination to the lawful holder of the bill of lading. 提单是由承运人开给发货人，并由船长、运输代理或船主签字，作为收到货物进行运输的证明，以及承诺将货物运往指定的目的地并交给提单的合法持有人的书面凭证。

5. A charter party bill of lading is issued by the hirer of a ship to the exporter. The terms of this kind of bill of lading are subject to the contract of hire between the ship's owner and hirer. Such a bill is usually marked subject to charter party, therefore it is not usually considered to be document of title. 租船合约提单是由船只的承租人开给出口商的提单。此类型提单的运输条款受制于船主与承租人之间的租船合同。这种提单上通常注明受制于租船合同，因此它通常不被视为物权单据。

6. The functions of a waybill are similar to those of a bill of lading, except that a waybill is not

negotiable and it is not a title document. On arrival at the destination, the goods will be released by the shipping company to the named consignee against identification. The consignee can then collect the goods without the need to produce the waybill. 海运单的功能类似于正规提单，只是它不可转让，因此不是物权单据。货物到达目的地以后，只需验证收货人的身份便可以交货。因此，收货人无须出示提单便可以提货。

7. An insurance document is a contract whereby the insurer (insurance company) undertakes to indemnify the insured in a manner and to the extent thereby agreed, against certain losses, that is to say, the losses incidental to carriage "adventure". 保险单是保险商和投保人之间的保险合同，由保险商向投保人承诺如发生某些风险（也就是在运输过程中发生的某些损失），由保险商按约定方式赔偿投保人。

1. Define the following terms.

(1) commercial invoice
(2) export license
(3) bill of lading
(4) inspection certificate
(5) consular invoice

2. Translate the following terms into English.

(1) 战略产品
(2) 普惠制
(3) 有预订的泊位
(4) 多式联运提单
(5) 抽样方式

3. Decide whether the following statements are true or false.

(1) A commercial invoice is a kind of title documents. （　）
(2) A cover note can be transferred so it is a negotiable instrument. （　）
(3) A short form bill of lading is document of title. （　）
(4) An unclean bill of lading is one which bears any clause or notation. （　）
(5) Cover notes issued by brokers will not be accepted, even specifically authorized in the credit. （　）
(6) Banks will not accept a document bearing a date of issuance prior to that of the credit. （　）
(7) If a credit calls for an insurance certificate, banks will not accept an insurance policy.

(8) Unless otherwise stipulated in the credit, the insurance document must be expressed in the same currency as the credit. (　)

(9) Commercial invoice need not be signed. (　)

(10) A clean bill of lading is one that is not stained. (　)

4. Choose the best answer to each of the following statements or questions.

(1) Which of the following transport documents is negotiable?
   A. Marine bill of lading.
   B. Air waybill.
   C. Rail waybill.
   D. FIATA Forwarder Certificate of Receipt.

(2) A bill of lading is a receipt for goods. When is a bill of lading issued?
   A. When the shipper makes up the order.
   B. When the carrier receives the goods.
   C. When the producer manufactures the goods.
   D. When the carrier delivers the goods to the consignee.

(3) The shipper wants assurance that the goods will reach their destination. The bill of lading gives him this assurance. It thus serves as a ____.
   A. title document   B. negotiable instrument
   C. receipt for goods   D. contract for delivery

(4) The bill of lading is evidence of ownership. It thus functions as a ____.
   A. title document   B. non-negotiable instrument
   C. receipt for goods   D. contract for delivery

(5) A commercial invoice is ____.
   A. a contract for delivery of the merchandise
   B. demand for payment
   C. a statement describing the merchandise, its cost, and shipping charges
   D. a promise of payment

(6) A bill of lading that states "consigned to J. Smith" is a ____.
   A. short form bill of lading   B. negotiable bill of lading
   C. straight bill of lading   D. long form bill of lading

(7) Under FOB terms, the bill of lading would state ____.
   A. goods loaded on board, freight paid
   B. goods received for shipment, freight payable at destination
   C. goods loaded on board, freight payable at destination
   D. goods received for shipment, freight paid

(8) Marine insurance policies do not always cover ____.
   A. all deliberate losses

B. all accidental total losses

C. all partial losses

D. voluntary losses to save ship from danger

(9) If a bill of lading is dated March 5, 2020, the insurance should be covered ____.

A. on March 5, 2020
B. before March 5, 2020
C. after March 5, 2020
D. on or before March 5, 2020

(10) Commercial invoice must be made out in the name of ____.

A. the applicant
B. the beneficiary
C. the issuing bank
D. the advising bank

(11) A bill of lading that bears a wording "bale broken" is ____.

A. a short form bill of lading
B. a clean bill of lading
C. a stale bill of lading
D. an unclean bill of lading

(12) A bank will not accept ____.

A. an insurance policy
B. an insurance certificate
C. an open cover
D. a cover note

(13) If a credit calls for an insurance policy, banks will accept ____.

A. an insurance policy
B. an insurance certificate
C. both A and B
D. open policy

(14) The minimum amount of the insurance cover under the letter of credit must be ____.

A. 110% of CIF value
B. 100% of CIP value
C. 110% of invoice value
D. 110% of FOB value

(15) ____ a railway receipt ____ an air consignment note is a document of title to goods in the same way that a bill of lading is.

A. Neither … nor
B. Either … or
C. Not only … but also
D. Both … and

(16) A consular invoice is an invoice signed by ____.

A. a consul of the importing country in the country from which the goods are consigned
B. a consul of the exporting country in the country from which the goods are consigned
C. the chamber of commerce of the exporting country
D. the chamber of commerce of the importing country

(17) ____ is the person or company that holds himself or itself liable to compensate the assured in the event of a loss to the insured property proximately caused by a peril insured against.

A. The broker
B. The insurer
C. The carrier
D. The claimant

(18) The bill of lading is evidence of the contract of carriage ____.

A. between the shipper and the carrier
B. between the issuing bank and the carrier
C. between the applicant and the carrier

D. between the exporter and the importer

(19) Which one of the following documents is not a quasi-negotiable instrument?
   A. A draft.
   B. An invoice.
   C. A bill of lading.
   D. A bill of exchange.

(20) When the exporter agrees to sell on open account terms, he should ask the shipping company to issue ____.
   A. combined transport documents
   B. bills of lading
   C. air waybill
   D. ships waybill

International Factoring and Forfeiting
国际保理与福费廷

> **In this chapter, you will learn:**
> - ☑ Definition, procedures of factoring
> - ☑ Advantages and disadvantages of factoring
> - ☑ Definition, characteristics, procedures of forfeiting
> - ☑ Advantages and disadvantages of forfeiting

Selling your export accounts receivable can enhance your global competitiveness and can help you better manage your cash flow. The practice of receivables financing is fundamental to the operation of the capitalist system. In the most developed countries the bulk of corporate wealth is locked up in receivables. Receivables financing allows funds to be released without the need to wait for the debts to mature. This can be accomplished through the use of forfeiting houses and factoring houses. Whether you use a forfeiting house (forfeiter) or a factoring house (factor), you will end up with a stronger balance sheet as outstanding receivables are reduced and cash is accelerated.[1] Forfeiters and factors also remove some or all of the risk associated with collection. At the same time, each enables you to offer your foreign customer terms that are longer in duration than those you could normally afford to offer.

9.1 Factoring 账款保理

9.1.1 Definition of Factoring 保理的定义

Since the 1960s factoring has been more widely used in international trade. Factoring is a form of trade financing that allows sellers to sell their products to overseas buyers essentially on an open account basis.

In simple terms, factoring is the purchase of claims, arising from sales of goods, by a specialized company known as factoring company or factor. It is in fact a three-party transaction between a financial institution (the factor) and a business entity (the client, i.e. the exporter) selling goods or providing services to foreign debtors (the client's customer, i. e. the importer).[2] The factor purchases his client's (the exporter's) account receivables, normally without recourse, controls the credit extended to the importer and administers his client's bookkeeping and collections. The factor will provide a package of financial services including export trade finance, maintenance of exporter's sales ledger, collection of receivables and evaluation of the importer's credit standing.[3]

1. The Essence of Factoring

The essence of factoring is the discounting of acceptable accounts receivable on a recourse or non-recourse and notification basis. Accounts receivable are sold outright to the factor, who assumes the responsibility for collection as well as the risk of credit losses. In a way, a factoring transaction represents a division of labour between the exporter and the financial house, whereby the former concentrates in his core business, which is trade, and the latter assumes the burden of streamlining the flow of funds between the trading parties. Especially in the context of international trade it is often useful to interpose between the exporter and the importer someone who has experience in commercial transactions in the home jurisdictions of the parties and who is better equipped to assess credit risks and collect funds. The factor may not restrict itself to a price collection service on behalf of the exporter, but may also provide credit management services. According to the provisions in the factoring agreement the factor may handle the internal credit control and sales accounting of the exporter. These facilities, where agreed, will be included in the factor's charges.

2. The Services Provided by the Factor

The factor acts as a manager of exporter's sales and provides his client with finance based on the level of sales and on the other hand evaluates the importer's creditworthiness either by himself or with the aid of his correspondent or agent, so as to ensure the final payment.[4] The services in the service package offered by the factors are closely related to one another. They are to minimize the risks on the part of the factors in the process.

1) Evaluation of the importer's credit standing

The factor should evaluate the importer's credit standing and conclude a preliminary credit assessment. Based on it, the factors can set a credit approval for a certain period of time for each order prior to its shipment. Credit approval means the amount for each transaction should be kept within the approved credit line and any such approved amount will be called approved account receivables by which the factor will assume the responsibility of payment. Any transaction beyond the credit approval will become unapproved receivables and the risk of bad debts will be borne by the exporter himself. This method can protect the factors from the risk of the importer's non-payment.

2) Export trade finance

It is up to the exporter whether or not to apply for trade finance from the export factor. If the exporter chooses to do so and if a transaction is within the credit approval, the export factor may

Chapter 9　International Factoring and Forfeiting

grant finance to the exporter prior to the maturity of the invoice by negotiating without recourse the latter's account receivables. The payment is advanced and the exporter's turnover is speed up. When the account receivables are assigned to the factor, the ownership to the goods will also be transferred to him.

3) Maintenance of sales ledger

Once the invoice is sent to a factor, he will set up corresponding sales ledger in his computer record system if the exporter is a new customer, or he will update the sales ledger for his old clients. Professional services such as book keeping, calculation and making statements will be carried out by the factor.

4) Collection of receivables

At maturity of the invoice, the importer factor will collect payment from the importer. The proceeds will be credited to the exporter if they have not been advanced to the exporter. In the event that the importer fails to make payment on due date and if the payment is not advanced, the import factor will make payments to the exporter, plus doubled interest calculated from the due date to the date of actual payment.

9.1.2　Functions of Factoring　保理的功能

1. Credit Approval

The factor acts as the client's credit department to evaluate the importer's credit standing to determine a credit line for his client's customer so that he can exercise the function of pre-approving orders prior to shipment. If the importer appears not to be a reliable one as a result of this evaluation, the factor will not approve this transaction.

2. Credit Protection

By purchasing the client's accounts receivables without recourse, factoring can protect the clients from risk of loss so long as merchandise quality, quantity and terms meet the requirements of sales contract between the client and his customer. However, the client takes full responsibility if the goods are claimed to be defective or any disputes occur concerning the shipment.

3. Management of Accounts Receivable

Upon shipment, the client invoices his customer and sends a copy to the factor. The invoice indicates that it is payable to the factor. At maturity of the invoice, the factor will collect payment from the client's customer.

4. Financing

The factor may grant financing to the client prior to the maturity of the invoice by purchasing the latter's accounts receivables.

9.1.3　Costs of Factoring　保理的成本

The cost of factoring consists of commission and interest.

(1) Commission. The factor charges the client a fee for his services based on four basic elements: annual sales volume, average invoice size, quality of client's customer list and length of trade terms. Normal range is from 0.75% to 1.75%.

(2) Interest. Interest is charged solely on a money-in-use basis.

9.1.4 Procedures of Factoring 保理的流程

A factoring agreement will be signed after an assessment of the exporter has been made by the factor, based on the written information including the business conditions, the balance sheet and other required information presented by the exporter and the investigation made by the factor.

A factoring consists of the following procedures.

1. Application for Credit Approval

(1) The sales contract is concluded between the buyer and the seller on open account terms.
(2) The seller applies to a financial institution (usually a bank) for credit approval.
(3) The bank acting as a factor makes a credit assessment of the customer/buyer.
(4) The factor agrees to the credit limit/cover.

Figure 9-1 illustrates the procedure of application for credit approval.

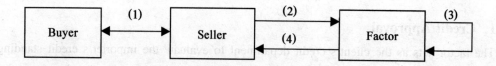

Figure 9-1 The procedure of application for credit approval

2. Delivery of Goods and Making out Invoice

(1) The seller delivers the goods and makes out the invoice to the buyer.
(2) The seller forwards a copy of invoice to the factor.
(3) The factor updates the sales ledger.
(4) The factor generally makes 80% of invoice value available to the seller.
(5) The factor notifies the buyer of the status of the creditor.

Figure 9-2 illustrates the procedure of delivery of goods and making out invoice.

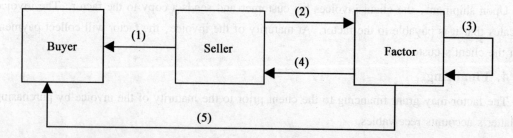

Figure 9-2 The procedure of delivery of goods and making out invoice

3. Payment Collection

(1) The factor performs the collection activity when the invoices fall due.
(2) The buyer effects payment to the factor.
(3) The factor updates the sales ledger.
(4) The factor pays the balance to the seller.

Figure 9-3 illustrates the procedure of payment collection.

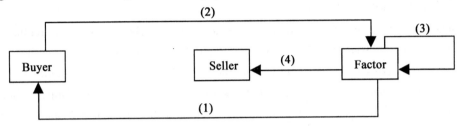

Figure 9-3   The procedure of payment collection

4. Conclusion

In a factoring business the factor assumes financial and administrative responsibility for the invoice including credit cover against customer's insolvency. Generally 80% of the invoice value is immediately available to the seller. The balance is payable within a fixed number of days after the invoice date or when the customer makes his payment.

9.1.5   Types of Factoring   保理的分类

There are various methods under which international factoring can be organized. The different types of factoring affect the organization of the deal and the legal consequences but they all share the same function described above. The choice of type is usually a matter of convenience. The important element is the intention of the parties who can structure the arrangement in such a way that it best reflects their individual circumstances. To begin with, factoring can be disclosed or undisclosed. Further, factoring can be on a recourse or non recourse basis according to the individual contracts. Generally, there are three main methods of factoring international debts, the two factor system, direct import and export factoring and back to back factoring.

1. Disclosed and Undisclosed Factoring

Disclosed factoring is the arrangement under which the exporter enters into a factoring agreement with the financial house and assigns the benefit of the debts created by the sales transaction to them. The importer is then notified and effects payment to the factor. The arrangement is usually on a non-recourse basis. This means that the factor cannot claim the assigned funds from the exporter if the importer fails to pay, in other words, he assumes the credit risk in the transaction. Those debts that are not approved by the factor are assigned on a recourse basis, so he can claim against the exporter in case of any default of the importer.

Recourse factoring is more accurately described as invoice discounting. Factoring arrangements are usually made on a whole turnover basis. This arrangement connotes an obligation of the exporter to offer all his receivables to the factor who receives a commission. Undisclosed factoring, which is usually undertaken on a recourse basis, does not involve the importer. The agreement is made between the factor and the exporter and the importer remains bound to pay as agreed under the sales contract. In receipt of payment, the exporter holds the funds in a separate bank account as trustee for the factor.

2. The Two Factor System

An international factoring transaction involves a number of elements that differentiate it from a domestic factoring transaction. The most important differentiations are the possibly different languages of the parties to the sales contract and the difficulty in assessing the credit standing of a foreign party. In answer to these considerations the two factor system was developed. This entails the use of two factors, one in each country, dealing with the exporter and the importer respectively. The export factor on obtaining the information from the exporter on the type of his business and the proposed transaction will contact the import factor designated by the importer and agree the terms of the deal. The importer advances funds to the import factor who then transmits them to the export factor, minus his charges. In the two factor system the import factor and the importer do not come into direct contact. The system involves three agreements, one between the exporter and the importer, one between the export factor and the exporter and one between the factors themselves. It is important to bear in mind that the import factor's obligations are to the export factor alone and they include determining the importer's credit rating and the actual collection of the debts. The import factor assumes the credit risk in relation to approved debts and is responsible for the transfer of funds to the export factor. On the other hand, the export factor is responsible to the import factor for the acceptance of any recourse.

The two factor system is supported by the existence of chains of correspondent factors. These where established for the purpose of facilitating the cooperation between import and export factors by the development of common rules and accounting procedures. There are members of factoring chains in most major trading nations. Some of them restrict their membership to one factor per country (closed chains), while others are open to the participation of multiple factors in the same country (Factors Chain International).

The two factor system has various advantages. The main ones concentrate around efficiency and speed. The import factor is in a better situation to assess the credit capabilities of the importer and communicate effectively with him. He knows the legal and business environment in the country and is in a position to take swift action in the case of any default. This may help to avoid misunderstandings and preempt disputes. The use of the import factor alleviates the pressure on the export factor and streamlines the procedure. The same elements make the system preferable to the exporter who is spared the inconvenience of dealing with a foreign factor. Further, there is the possibility of the client receiving lower discount charges if the import factor makes payments at the rate of discount charge in his country (if these are lower than the ones in the exporter's home jurisdiction). Finally, use of this system can help in reducing the exchange risk involved in international trade by speeding up the circulation of funds. The speedier the flow of funds from the buyer to the seller, the smaller the risk of exchange rate fluctuations between the date of shipment and the date of payment.

The main disadvantage of the system is the expense involved. The increased cost of employing two factors makes the arrangement unsuitable for transactions of low value. Also there is the possibility of delays in the transmission of funds and the duplication of some records is unavoidable. However, the use of chains of factors makes the transactions speedier through the use of a clearing system. Further, electronic forms of record transmission can help in alleviating the need for double record keeping.

3. Direct Import and Export Factoring

Direct import factoring connotes the situation where the exporter assigns debts to a factor in the country of the debtor. This is usually the case where there is a substantial volume of exports to a specific country. This solution is a cheap and time efficient method of debt collection but it does not serve the aim of providing finance to the exporter. The factor provides a debt collection service and does not enquire into the creditworthiness of the importer. Prepayments are not possible because that would expose the factor to high risks.

Direct export factoring on the other hand, does operate as an alternative to the two factor system. In this situation, the factor is appointed in the exporter's own country and deals with all the aspects of the factoring arrangement including the provision of financing and the assessment of the financial position of the importer. This system is inexpensive and facilitates the communication between the exporter and the factor. However, all the advantages of the two factor system relating to the import factor's proximity to the importer and his jurisdiction can be listed here as disadvantages. Communication problems with the debtor, credit risks and the occurrence of disputes are the most important problems.

4. Back to Back Factoring

Back to back factoring is an arrangement most suitable for debts owed by the exclusive distributors of products to their suppliers. The structure of the agreements is similar to the ones already considered with one material difference. The exporter enters into a factoring agreement with the export factor who contracts with the import factor in the usual way. The difference lies in the existence of a separate factoring agreement between the import factor and the distributor.

Included in that arrangement is a right to set off credits arising from the domestic sales of the distributor with his debts to the supplier. This is to guard against default by the distributor due to the fact that the goods have already been sold to third parties and thus the supplier cannot take a security interest over them to guarantee repayment of the debts.

9.1.6 Advantages to Exporters of Factoring 保理对出口商的有利方面

(1) The seller gets access to finance linked to his current levels of business. By contrast, the amount available under a traditional overdraft arrangement is based on the historic balance sheet

ratios. When a company is up against its overdraft limit and yet confident of its sales prospects, the factoring can finance a higher level of sales.

(2) The seller is in a position to improve the relationship with his suppliers through prompt payment and to extract the optimum terms when making his purchases, for example, through bulk purchase discounts or simply for cash payment.

(3) Factoring furnishes finance for growth to the seller, without requiring an injection of new equity from external sources or any additional guarantees from the management.

(4) The seller saves the cost of maintaining his own administrative department.

(5) The seller can get assistance from the factor by latter's providing an assessment of the creditworthiness of the overseas buyers as well as by latter's offering credit protection and collection service. Thus, the exporter is free to concentrate on international sales and development of new markets because the factor has assumed responsibility for sales accounting and collection of funds.

(6) The seller will increase sales through factors' knowledge of the market and ability to offer credit lines.

(7) Open account agreements with the buyer, guaranteed by the factor, are made possible. That is, the factor guarantees the credit risk of the foreign buyer. In this way, the seller will be able to offer competitive open account selling terms in the highly competitive market.

(8) Seller's bad debts will be eliminated. That is to say, all delinquent account receivable risks are eliminated for the exporter and assumed by the factor.

9.2　Forfeiting　福费廷

9.2.1　Definition of Forfeiting　福费廷的定义

The word "forfeiting" comes from the French "à forfait" and conveys the idea of surrendering rights, which is of fundamental importance in forfeiting. This expression is rendered by "Forfaitierung" in German, "le forfaitage" in French, "la forfetizzazione" in Italian and "la forfetizacion" in Spanish.

Simply speaking, forfeiting is the term generally used to denote the purchase of obligations falling due at some future date, arising from deliveries of goods and services — mostly export transactions — without recourse to any previous holder of the obligation.[5] It is the purchase of a series of credit instruments such as drafts drawn under time letters of credit, bills of exchange, promissory notes, or other freely negotiable instruments on a "non-recourse" basis (non-recourse means that there is no comeback on the exporter if the importer does not pay). The Forfeiter deducts interest (in the form of a discount), at an agreed rate for the full credit period covered by the notes. The debt instruments are drawn by the exporter (seller), accepted by the importer (buyer), and will bear an aval, or unconditional guarantee. The guarantee will normally be issued by the importer's bank, but some strong corporates can be accepted without a bank guarantee.

In exchange for the payment, the Forfeiter then takes over responsibility for claiming the debt from the importer. The Forfeiter either holds the notes until full maturity (as an investment), or sells them to another investor on a non-recourse basis. The holder of the notes then presents each receivable to the bank at which they are payable, as they fall due.

9.2.2　Origins of the Forfeiting Market　福费廷市场的起源

The origins of the forfeiting market lay in changes in the world economic structure that took place during the late fifties and early sixties of the 20th century, when the seller's market for capital goods gradually changed into a buyer's market.

A considerable expansion in international trade took place, accompanied by an increasing tendency for importers to demand periods of credit extending beyond the traditional 90 or 180 days.

In addition, these times saw the lowering of trade barriers created in the prewar years of depression and the cold-war era. The resurgence of trade between the West and Eastern Europe coupled with the growing importance of the developing countries of Africa, Asia and Latin America created many financial problems for the West European exporters.

Furthermore, the arrival of these markets came at a time when the heavy investment commitments of exporting firms prevented them from financing such medium-term supplier credits out of their funds, and the existing banks were unable to offer the services the exporters desired. Forfeit finance was thus created to satisfy growing demands in international finance.

9.2.3　Characteristics of Forfeiting　福费廷的特征

(1) The goods involved in forfeiting are usually capital goods.

(2) Forfeiting is a medium-term business in the sense that only those maturities from six months to five or six years are to be considered. However, every forfeiter will impose his own limits, to be determined largely by market conditions and his assessment of the risks involved in a particular transaction.

(3) The purchase of bills of exchange or promissory notes falling due on some future date by a forfeiter is without recourse to any previous holder if the drawee of the draft/maker of the promissory note (importer) fails to pay it at maturity.

(4) Forfeiting is a relatively inexpensive and attractive alternative to other forms of export financing for the exporter. By forfeiting the exporter wishes to pass all risks and responsibilities for collection to the forfeiter in exchange for immediate cash payment. The exporter virtually converts his credit-based sale into a cash transaction.

(5) Unless the credit standing of the importer (drawee) is first class, any forfeited bill must carry a collateral security in the form of an "aval" or an unconditional and irrevocable bank guarantee acceptable to the forfeiter ensuring the holder thereof that the importer will pay it at maturity. The fulfillment of this condition is of the utmost importance in view of the non-recourse aspect of the business, for the forfeiter can only rely on this form of bank guarantee as his sole security in the event of non-payment of the obligor.

(6) The purchase of bills in forfeiting is carried out by discounting, namely by deduction of the interest (discount) in advance for the unmatured draft. Discounting takes place the moment the forfeiter has received the draft, i.e. the agreed discounting interest for the corresponding maturities

is deducted from the nominal amount and the net amount is paid by the forfeiter. Discounting rate in forfeiting is higher because the forfeiting bank bears more risks than the discount bank.

9.2.4 Procedures of Forfeiting 福费廷的流程

(1) The exporter, after obtaining a commitment from the forfeiter to finance the transaction at a fixed interest rate, will then proceed to validate the commercial contract.

(2) The importer, after receiving the shipping documents, signs a series of promissory notes with maturities fixed according to the repayment terms, usually at six-month intervals to reflect the installment, then gets the notes endorsed or guaranteed by a bank which is acceptable to the forfeiter. The endorser-bank or the guarantor bank becomes the primary obligor of these notes, just as in the case of banker's acceptance.

(3) The forfeiter purchases the series of notes from the exporter without recourse on discounting basis.

(4) At the maturity of each note, the importer pays the amount due. If the importer fails to pay, the endorser-bank or the guarantor bank will be responsible for the due payment of the amount of the note together with the interest and losses incurred.

Figure 9-4 shows an example of forfeiting transaction.

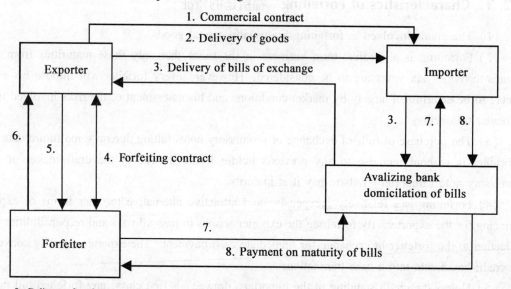

5. Delivery of exchange
6. Cash payment of face value less discount charges
7. Presentation of bills of exchange for payment on maturity

Figure 9-4 An example of forfeiting transaction

9.2.5 Advantages and Disadvantages of Forfeiting 福费廷的利与弊

1. Advantages of Forfeiting to the Exporter

Forfeiting offers the following advantages to the exporter.

(1) Forfeiting relieves the balance sheet of contingent liabilities. The finance is without recourse, so there is no need for any contingent liability on the exporter's balance sheet. Forfeiting does not affect any other facilities, e. g. overdraft.

(2) The exporter receives cash in full at the outset. Forfeiting improves liquidity and the exporter has an increased borrowing capacity. The financing costs can be passed on to the buyer if the exporter is in a strong bargaining position.

(3) Forfeiting avoids possible losses through only partial state or private insurance cover and the negation of possible liquidity problems unavoidable under the claim period with insurance cover.

(4) Forfeiting involves no interest rate risk for the exporter. The rate of discount applied by the forfeiter is fixed, and subsequent changes in the general level of interest rates do not affect the discount.

(5) Under forfeiting there is no risk of fluctuations in the exchange rate and no changes in the status of the debtor. All exchange risks, buyer risks, and country risks are removed.

(6) Under forfeiting there are no credit administration and collection problems and related risks and costs.

(7) The facility is flexible. The documentation can be set up in a matter of hours, whereas Export Credit Guarantee Department (ECGD) buyer credit guarantees can take up to three months to arrange. In suitable cases, the forfeit facility can cover the full amount of the contract price.

2. Disadvantages of Forfeiting

(1) Costs can be high, and there is no interest rate subsidy such as the consensus rates.

(2) It may be difficult to find an institution that will be willing to be prepared to guarantee the importer's liabilities. Sometimes the guarantor institution may charge a high commitment fee if the buyer is not considered undoubted.

9.3 Differences between Factoring and Forfeiting
保理与福费廷的不同之处

(1) Factors usually want access to a large percentage of an exporter's business, while most forfeiters will work on a one-shot basis.

(2) Forfeiters generally work with medium and long-term receivables (180 days to 10 years), while factors work with short-term receivables (up to 180 days). Payment terms usually reflect the type of product involved: forfeiters usually work with capital goods, commodities, and large projects; factors work mostly with consumer goods.

(3) Most factors do not have strong capabilities in developing regions of the world where legal and financial frameworks are inadequate and credit information is not readily available through affiliate factors. However, since forfeiters usually require a bank guarantee, most factoring houses are willing to work with receivables from these higher risks, emerging markets.

New Words and Expressions

factoring	[ˈfæktəriŋ]	n.	（账款）保理
forfeiting	[fəˈfetiŋ]	n.	福费廷
factor	[ˈfæktə]	n.	保理行
insolvency	[inˈsɔlvənsi]	n.	无力偿还，破产
streamline	[ˈstriːmlain]	a.	流线型的
interpose	[ˌinəˈpəuz]	v.	提出
preliminary	[priˈliminəri]	a.	预备的，初步的
connote	[kəˈnəut]	v.	含言外之意，意味着
duplication	[ˌdjupləˈkeiʃən]	n.	副本，复制
alleviate	[əˈliːvieit]	v.	使（痛苦等）易于忍受，减轻
resurgence	[riˈsəːdʒəns]	n.	苏醒，复兴
collateral	[kəˈlætərəl]	a.	间接的，附属的
		n.	担保品，抵押品
validate	[ˈvæləˌdeit]	v.	[律] 使有效，使生效，确认，证实，验证

trade financing 贸易融资
accounts receivable 应收账
credit approval 信用审查
credit investigation 信用调查
sales ledger 销售分类账
credit assessment 信用评估
credit limit 信用额度
credit cover 信用准备金
capital goods 资本货物，生产资料
supplier credit 卖方信贷
without recourse 无追索权的
credit standing 信用状况

contingent liability 或有负债
balance sheet 资产负债表
buyer's market 买方市场
face value 面值
division of labour 劳动分工
disclosed factoring 公开保理，明保理
undisclosed factoring 暗保理
two factor system 双保理商模式
direct import factor system 直接进口保理商形式
indirect export factor system 间接出口保理商形式
optimum terms 最适宜的条件，最优惠的条件

Notes

1. Whether you use a forfeiting house (forfeiter) or a factoring house (factor), you will end up with a stronger balance sheet as outstanding receivables are reduced and cash is accelerated.
无论你利用保理商还是福费廷公司的服务，你的资产负债表的状况都会得到改善，因为应收账款余额减少了而现金快速增加了。

Chapter 9 International Factoring and Forfeiting

2. In simple terms, factoring is the purchase of claims, arising from sales of goods, by a specialized company known as factoring company or factor. It is in fact a three-party transaction between a financial institution (the factor) and a business entity (the client, i.e. the exporter) selling goods or providing services to foreign debtors (the client's customer, i.e. the importer). 简单地说，账款保理是由被称之为保理公司或保理行的专业公司购买由于货物销售而产生的债权。实际上，保理是金融机构（保理行）与销售货物或提供服务给国外债务人（客户的客户，即进口商）的企业实体（客户，即出口商）之间的三方交易。

3. The factor will provide a package of financial services including export trade finance, maintenance of exporter's sales ledger, collection of receivables and evaluation of the importer's credit standing. 保理商将会提供一揽子的金融服务，其中包括出口贸易融资、出口商销售账户的管理、应收账款的收取和出口商信用的评估等。

4. The factor acts as a manager of exporter's sales and provides his client with finance based on the level of sales and on the other hand evaluates the importer's creditworthiness either by himself or with the aid of his correspondent or agent, so as to ensure the final payment. 保理行充当出口商销售的管理者，并根据销售额水平向其客户提供融资，另一方面，由其自己或借助其代理行或代理人对进口商的资信状况进行评估，以确保最后的货款交付。

5. Simply speaking, forfeiting is the term generally used to denote the purchase of obligations falling due at some future date, arising from deliveries of goods and services — mostly export transactions — without recourse to any previous holder of the obligation. 简而言之，福费廷通常是指买进因商品和劳务的转让（主要是出口交易）而产生的在将来某一个日子到期的债务，这种购买对原先的票据持有人无追索权。

Exercises

1. **Fill in the blanks to complete each sentence.**

   (1) The essence of factoring is the discounting of _____ on a _____ basis.
   (2) Factor assumes the responsibility for _____ without recourse to the client.
   (3) The factor acts as a manager of exporter's sales and provides his client with finance based on _____ as well as an evaluator of the importer's creditworthiness.
   (4) The origins of the forfeiting market lay in _____ that took place during the late fifties and early sixties of the 20th century, when the seller's market for capital goods gradually changed into a buyer's market.
   (5) Forfeit finance was thus created to satisfy _____ in international finance.

(6) By _____ without recourse, factoring can protect the clients from risk of loss so long as merchandise quality, quantity and terms meet the requirements of sales contract between the client and his customer.

(7) In a factoring business the factor assumes _____ responsibility for the invoice including credit cover against customer's insolvency.

(8) Generally 80% of the invoice face value is immediately available to the seller. The balance is payable within a fixed number of days after _____ or when _____.

(9) Forfeiting is a medium-term business in the sense that only those maturities from six months to five or six years are to be considered. However, every forfeiter will impose his own limits, to be determined largely by _____ and _____.

(10) Under forfeiting there is no risk of _____ and no changes _____. All exchange risks, buyer risks, and country risks are removed.

2. **Define the following terms.**

   (1) factoring
   (2) forfeiting

3. **Translate the following terms into English.**

   (1) 或有负债   (2) 信用额度
   (3) 卖方信贷   (4) 无追索权的
   (5) 信用审定   (6) 资本货物
   (7) 买方信贷担保   (8) 福费廷融资便利
   (9) 贸易壁垒   (10) 大宗采购折扣

4. **Choose the best answer to each of the following statements.**

   (1) Clients of a factoring are thus able to eliminate or reduce the need for credit, ____ and other related administrative activities.
      A. knowledge of the market   B. bookkeeping
      C. competitive open account selling terms   D. bad debts

   (2) The factor may grant financing to the client prior to the maturity of the invoice by ____.
      A. purchasing the latter's accounts receivables
      B. sending a copy of invoice to the factor
      C. indicating that the invoice is payable to the factor
      D. collecting payment from the client's customer

   (3) The factor charges the client a fee for his services based on elements such as annual sales volume, ____, quality of client's customer list and length of trade terms.
      A. creditworthiness   B. credit standing
      C. interest   D. average invoice size

   (4) In a factoring, the seller gets access to finance linked to his ____.

A. overdraft limit   B. historic balance sheet ratios
C. current levels of business   D. sales prospects

(5) The seller can get assistance from the factor by latter's providing an assessment of the creditworthiness of the overseas buyers as well as by latter's offering credit protection and ____.

A. sales accounting   B. development of new markets
C. international sales   D. collection service

Letter of Guarantee
银行保函

> 📢 **In this chapter, you will learn:**
> ☑ Definition, parties and types of guarantee
> ☑ Contents and procedure of guarantee
> ☑ Main types of guarantees

10.1 Introduction to Letter of Guarantee 保函概述

10.1.1 An Overview of Letter of Guarantee 保函概览

1. The Necessity of Guarantee in International Trade

In international trade, on the one hand, the buyer wants to be certain that the seller is in a position to honor his commitment as offered or contracted. The former therefore makes it a condition that appropriate security be provided. On the other hand, the seller must find a way to be assured of receiving payment if no special security is provided for the payment such as in open account business and documentary collections. Such security may be obtained through banks in the form of guarantee.

2. Definition

A bank guarantee is used as an instrument for securing performance or payment especially in international business. A bank guarantee is a written promise issued by a bank at the request of its customer, undertaking to make payment to the beneficiary within the limits of a stated sum of money in the event of default by the principal.[1]

A bank guarantee may also be defined as an independent obligation where the guarantor (a bank/financial institution/surety) has to make a special agreement with its customer, ensuring that it will be refunded by him for any payment to be effected under the contract of guarantee.

3. Main Point of Guarantee

The main point of guarantee does not consist in assuming the debtor's liability (by the guarantor) in the latter's interest, but in recouping the beneficiary for any damage caused by faulty performance.

4. Basic Functions of Guarantees

The two basic functions of guarantees are as follows:

(1) Guarantees are used as secure mechanism for payment of the contract amount;

(2) A contractor uses a guarantee as default instrument that covers the risk of non-performance or defective performance by the contractor.

5. Counter Guarantee

A counter guarantee refers to any guarantee or other payment undertaking of the instructing party given in writing for the payment of money to the guarantor on presentation in conformity with the terms of the undertaking of a written demand for payment and other documents specified in the counter guarantee.[2]

Counter guarantees are by their nature separate transactions from the guarantees to which they relate and from any underlying contract or tender conditions, and instructing partners are in no way concerned with or bound by the related guarantees.

10.1.2 Parties and Obligation of Letter of Guarantee 保函的主要当事人及义务

Usually, there are three parties involved in a guarantee practice.

1. Beneficiary

Beneficiary is the party in whose favor the guarantee is issued. He is secured against the risk of the principal's not fulfilling his obligations towards the beneficiary in respect of the underlying transaction for which the demand guarantee is given. He will not obtain a sum of money if the obligations are not fulfilled.

2. Principal

The principal is the person at whose request the guarantee is issued, e.g. in tender guarantee/bond the principal is the party tendering or the party to whom the contract has been awarded. The principal will be claimed if he is in breach of his obligations.

3. Guarantor

The guarantor is a surety, a bank or financial institution that issues a letter of guarantee undertaking to make payment to the beneficiary in the event of default of the principal against the presentation of a written demand and other specified documents. He is not required to decide whether the beneficiary and principal have or have not fulfilled their obligations under the underlying transaction with which the guarantor is not concerned. That is to say, the guarantor is willing to meet its commitment in terms of the guarantee, without becoming involved in possible disputes between beneficiary and principal regarding correct performance by the principal of his obligations.

4. Instructing Party

Sometimes, a bank or a financial institution or any other body acting as an instructing party issues a counter guarantee acting on the instruction of a principal in favor of a bank or a financial institution located in the beneficiary's country. The instructing party instructs the bank or a financial institution located in the beneficiary's country to issue a letter of guarantee on behalf of the principal in favor of a specified party named therein.

10.1.3 Types of Bank Guarantee 银行保函的种类

There are a number of different types of guarantees or bonds from different points of view and according to different requirements.[3]

1. In Terms of the Relationship with the Underlying Transaction

In terms of the relationship with the underlying transaction, guarantees can be classified into accessory guarantee and independent guarantee.

Accessory guarantee is an accessory contract by which the guarantor undertakes to answer for the debt, default or miscarriage of another person known as the principal debtor. An accessory guarantee necessarily involves some other person being primarily liable. A person may be a guarantor either by undertaking liability for the principal debtor's debt or giving security on behalf of the principal debtor. The accessory guarantee is a traditional guarantee which is a secondary undertaking, and a promise to carry out someone else's obligation if the party primarily responsible fails to do so. Such obligations are accessory to and dependent on the contract in respect of which they are given.

Independent guarantee is a principal obligation; it is a promise to pay a sum of money against presentation of the beneficiary's demand and stipulated documentation, if any. They are independent of the underlying contract. The guarantor is not concerned to determine whether or not default has occurred on the commercial deal. Their payment is triggered by presentation of a claim complying with the formal requirements of the instrument itself.

2. In Terms of Methods of Issuing the Guarantee

In terms of the methods of issuing the guarantee, a guarantee may be divided into direct guarantee and indirect guarantee.

A direct guarantee occurs when the client authorizes the bank to issue a guarantee directly to the beneficiary, as Figure 10-1 shows.

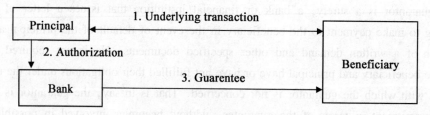

Figure 10-1 Direct guarantee

An indirect guarantee is a guarantee where a second bank is involved. This bank (usually a foreign bank located in the beneficiary's country of domicile) will be requested by the initiating bank to issue a guarantee in return for the latter's counter-guarantee. Thus the initiating bank protects the foreign bank from the risk of a loss which could result from the beneficiary submitting a claim under the foreign bank's guarantee. The initiating bank must formally pledge to pay the amount claimed by the beneficiary under the guarantee upon demand by the guaranteeing bank.

Indirect guarantees (as Figure 10-2 shows) are mainly used in connection with international business.

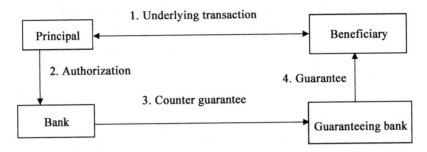

Figure 10-2 Indirect guarantee

3. In Terms of the Conditions for a Claim

In terms of the conditions for a claim, a guarantee or bond may be classified into unconditional bond and conditional.

Unconditional bonds can be called at the sole discretion of the buyer. The bank must pay if called upon to do so, even in circumstances where it may be clear to the exporter that the claim is wholly unjustified. If the bank has to pay under the bond, it will debit the customer's account under the authority of the counter indemnity. The exporter will then be left with the unenviable task of claiming reimbursement in the courts of the buyer's country. It must be stressed that banks never become involved in contractual disputes. If payment is called for, which conforms to the terms of the bond, the bank must pay.

Conditional bonds can be divided into two types: ① conditional bonds requiring documentary evidence and ② conditional bonds that do not require documentary evidence. Conditional bonds requiring documentary evidence give maximum protection to the exporter. Payment can only be called for by the buyer against production of a specified document, such as a certificate of award by an independent arbitrator. Unfortunately, this type of conditional bond is often unacceptable, particularly in the case of Middle East buyers.

Conditional bonds that do not require documentary evidence are less better than unconditional bonds from the exporter's point of view. Such bonds often specify that payment must be made in the event of default or failure on the part of the contractor to perform his obligations under the above-mentioned contract.

4. In Terms of the Payment Prerequisite under Guarantee

In terms of the payment prerequisite under guarantee, a guarantee is subdivided into payment guarantee and credit guarantee.

Payment guarantee is a security mechanism for payment of the contract amount. Under a payment guarantee, it is stipulated that the bank undertakes to pay, provided the documents presented are in strict compliance with the terms and conditions of the guarantee. In this case, the issuing bank is primarily liable to the beneficiary. Included in this category are payment bond, deferred payment bond, guarantee for compensation trade, loan guarantee, overdraft guarantee, leasing guarantee, and payment guarantee for commission or any other charges.

Credit guarantee is a default instrument that covers the risk of non-performance or defective performance by the contractor. Credit guarantees often include a bid bond, performance bond, advance payment guarantee, quality guarantee, maintenance guarantee, etc.

5. In Terms of the Purposes of Guarantees

There are different types of guarantees issued by banks to serve different purposes. Some of them guarantee the performance of a contract; others guarantee the payment of importing goods under open account terms or under documents against acceptance collection; still others guarantee the payment due under a lease, or the repayment of money borrowed by the account party. The following is a list of the different types of guarantees under different categories.

(1) Guarantees under international trade: tender guarantee, performance guarantee, advance/down payment guarantee, quality or maintenance guarantee, payment guarantee, deferred payment guarantee, guarantee for compensation trade, guarantee for processing, leasing guarantee.

(2) Guarantees under international construction/engineering contracting: bid (tender) bond or guarantee, performance guarantee, maintenance guarantee, customs guarantee (duty free guarantee), retention money guarantee, and overdraft guarantee.

(3) Stand-by letter of credit.

(4) Other guarantees.

10.1.4 Contents of Bank Guarantee 银行保函的内容

The contents of a guarantee are the most important part of the guarantee. All instructions for the issuance of guarantees and amendments thereto and guarantees and amendments themselves should be clear and precise and should avoid excessive detail. The contents of a guarantee generally contain the following elements.

(1) Guarantee purpose.

(2) Parties involved: the principal, the beneficiary and guarantor.

(3) The underlying transaction requiring the issue of guarantee. Since the bank guarantee is independent of the underlying transaction, a precise definition of how the principal defaulted on the contract in question is not necessary, and the beneficiary's claim is all that is needed to elicit payment.

(4) Amount of the guarantee (the maximum amount and its currency). The amount payable under a guarantee shall be reduced by the amount of any payment made by the guarantor in satisfaction of a demand in respect thereof.

(5) The expiry date or expiry event of the guarantee. The guarantee should be worded to expire on a definite date for the guarantor's benefit. The guarantee should also state that claims

must be received not later than a certain date, and indicate where they must be presented. According to ICC No. 458, expiry date shall be on a specified calendar date or on presentation to the guarantor of the documents specified for the purpose of expiry. If both an expiry date and an expiry event are specified in a guarantee, the guarantee shall be expired on whichever of the expiry date or expiry event occurs first.

(6) Payment mechanism or terms for demanding payment. The guarantee may insert the required conditions to trigger payment. According to ICC No. 458 any demand for payment under the guarantee shall be in written and shall be supported by a written statement stating that the principal is in breach and other documents as specified in the guarantee.

(7) Assignment. Depending on the applicable law the benefit of a guarantee may be assignable by the beneficiary. The guarantors generally do not like such assignments, preferring to restrict their guarantee undertaking to beneficiaries who are known at the time of issue.

(8) Other provisions: reduction of the amount, the governing law and jurisdiction.

10.1.5 Procedures of Bank Guarantee 银行保函的业务流程

(1) The underlying contract is entered into by and between the principal and the beneficiary.

(2) The principal applies to a bank and requests the issuance of the guarantee.

(3) If the guarantor (usually a bank) is satisfied that joining in a guarantee is justified, it then issues a letter of guarantee undertaking to make payment to the beneficiary in compensation in the event of default of the principal against the presentation of a written demand and other specified documents.

(4) At the same time, the principal will be asked to sign a counter indemnity to authorize the guarantor to debit the account with the cost of any payments under the guarantee.

(5) In case the principal does not fulfil his obligations towards the beneficiary in respect of the underlying transaction for which the guarantee is given, the principal is claimed and so the guarantor answers for the debt, default of the principal (in case of accessory guarantee). The payment is triggered by presentation of a claim complying with the formal requirements of the instrument itself (in case of independent guarantee).

(6) The guarantor debits the principal's account as previously authorized in the counter indemnity signed by the principal with any money paid out under the guarantee.

10.2 Bid Bond 投标保函

10.2.1 Definition 定义

Bid bond is an undertaking given by a bank at the request of a tenderer in favor of a party inviting tenders abroad, whereby the guarantor undertakes to make payment to the beneficiary within the limit of a stated sum of money in the event of default by the principal in the obligations resulting from the submission of tender.

10.2.2 Functional Terms and Conditions 功能条款

The guarantor will pay the total amount stated in the guarantee on first demand, if the beneficiary of the guarantee informs him that the offer is withdrawn before its expiry date or the tenderer has failed to accept the contract awarded or the bid bond is not replaced by a performance bond after the contract has been awarded.

Tender bond is designed to ensure that the tenderer does not withdraw its bid before adjudication, and does not fail or refuse to accept the award of contract in its favor. A tender bond is usually for between 2% and 5% of the contract value. Failure to take up the contract results in a penalty for the amount of the bond. Tender bonds serve to prevent the submission of frivolous tenders.

10.2.3 Form 通用格式

The following is a sample of bid bond.

SAMPLE 10-1

UBS

Bid bond

Example AG
Mr John Example
P.O. Box
CH-8000 Zurich

UBS AG
Trade Finance
Guarantees
P.O. Box
CH-8098 Zurich
Tel. +41-1-234 11 11

Bid bond no. _____

26 May 2019

SPECIMEN

Amount _____
(in words _____)

We have been informed that _____ submitted on _____
their offer no. _____ for _____ under your bid invitation no. _____ dated _____ according to the tender conditions a bid bond has to be supplied.

This being stated, we, UBS AG, _____, irrespective of the validity and the legal effects of the above mentioned bid and waiving all rights of objection and defense arising therefrom, hereby irrevocably undertake to pay to you, on your first demand, any amount up to the above mentioned maximum amount, upon receipt of your duly signed request for payment stating that _____

- have withdrawn their offer before its expiry date without your consent, or
- have failed to sign the contract awarded to them in the terms of their offer, or
- have failed to provide the performance bond foreseen in the tender upon signing the contract.

For the purpose of identification your request for payment must bear or be accompanied by a signed confirmation of one of our correspondent banks stating that the latter has verified your signature(s) appearing on the said request for payment.

Your claim is also acceptable if transmitted to us in full by duly encoded telex/swift through one of our correspondent banks confirming that your original claim has been forwarded to us by registered mail or courier service and that the said bank has verified your signature(s) appearing thereon.

Our guarantee is valid until _____

and expires in full and automatically, should your written request for payment or telex/SWIFT not be in our possession at our above address on or before that date, regardless of such date being a banking day or not.

Our guarantee will be reduced by each payment made by us as a result of a claim.

This guarantee is governed by Swiss law, place of jurisdiction and performance is _____

UBS AG

10.3 Performance Bond 履约保函

10.3.1 Definition 定义

A performance guarantee (bond) is an undertaking given by a bank (the guarantor) at the request of a supplier of goods or services or a contractor (the principal) to a buyer or an employer (the beneficiary), whereby the guarantor undertakes to make payment to the beneficiary within the limit of a stated sum of money in the event of default by the supplier or the contractor in due performance of the terms of a contract between the principal and the beneficiary.

10.3.2 Functional Terms and Conditions 功能条款

A performance bond is issued when the contract has been awarded. It gives the employer an indication of the contractor's creditworthiness and affords a remedy in case of default. A performance bond payable on demand is issued for a specified sum, usually between 5% and 10% of the project value.

10.3.3 Form 通用格式

☞ SAMPLE 10-2

※ UBS

Performance bond

Performance bond no. ▇▇▇▇▇

UBS AG
Trade Finance
Guarantees
P.O. Box
CH-8098 Zurich
Tel. +41-1-234 11 11

Example AG
Mr John Example
P.O. Box
CH-8000 Zurich

SPECIMEN

26 May 2019

Amount ▇▇▇▇▇▇▇▇▇▇▇▇▇▇▇▇▇▇
(in words ▇▇▇▇▇▇▇▇▇▇▇▇▇▇▇▇▇▇▇▇▇▇▇▇▇▇▇▇▇▇▇▇▇▇▇▇▇)

We have been informed that you concluded on ▇▇▇▇ a contract ▇▇▇▇ with ▇▇▇▇ for ▇▇▇▇ at a total price of ▇▇▇▇. According to this contract, ▇▇▇▇ are required to provide you with a performance bond.

This being stated, we, UBS AG, ▇▇▇▇▇▇, irrespective of the validity and the legal effects of the above mentioned contract and waiving all rights of objection and defense arising therefrom, hereby irrevocably undertake to pay to you, upon your first demand, any amount up to the above mentioned maximum amount, upon receipt of

your duly signed request for payment stating that ▇▇▇▇▇▇ have failed to fulfil their contractual obligations.

For the purpose of identification your request for payment must bear or be accompanied by a signed confirmation of one of our correspondent banks stating that the latter has verified your signature(s) appearing on the said request for payment.

Your claim is also acceptable if transmitted to us in full by duly encoded telex/swift through one of our correspondent banks confirming that your original claim has been forwarded to us by registered mail or courier service and that the said bank has verified your signature(s) appearing thereon.

Our guarantee is valid until ▇▇▇▇▇▇▇▇

and expires in full and automatically, should your written request for payment or telex/SWIFT not be in our possession at our above address on or before that date, regardless of such date being a banking day or not.

Our guarantee will be reduced by each payment made by us as a result of a claim.

This guarantee is governed by Swiss law, place of jurisdiction and performance is ▇▇▇▇▇▇▇.

UBS AG

10.4 Advance Payment Bond 预付款保函

10.4.1 Definition 定义

An advance payment bond is issued at the request of the exporter to the importer (the beneficiary) when the advance payment is required by the latter. The guarantee ensures the repayment of the advance by the exporter in the event of the non-performance of his contractual obligations.

10.4.2 Functional Terms and Conditions 功能条款

In most large projects the contractor requires an advance payment on the contract price to finance operations. Typically such payments range from 5 to 20 per cent of the total price. It is somewhat like the repayment guarantee under the contract guarantees. The guaranteed amount is the amount of the advance payment, which is, as a rule, automatically and proportionally reduced following each shipment. In some instances the amount of the bond may be reduced as work proceeds.

10.4.3 Form 通用格式

☞ **SAMPLE 10-3**

❋ **UBS**

Advance payment guarantee

Example AG
Mr. John Example
P.O. Box
CH-8000 Zurich

Advance payment guarantee no.

UBS AG
Trade Finance
Guarantees
P.O. Box
CH-8098 Zurich
Tel. +41-1-234 11 11

26 May 2019

SPECIMEN

Amount
(in words)

We have been informed that ▮▮▮▮▮▮▮▮ (hereinafter called "the Principal"), has entered into contract no. ▮▮▮▮▮▮▮▮ dated ▮▮▮▮▮▮▮▮ with you, for the supply of

Furthermore, we understand that, according to the conditions of the contract, an advance payment is to be made against an advance payment guarantee.

This being stated, we, UBS AG, ▮▮▮▮▮▮▮▮, irrespective of the validity and the legal effects of the above mentioned contract and waiving all rights of objection and defense arising therefrom, hereby irrevocably undertake to pay to you, upon your first demand, any sum or sums not exceeding in total the above mentioned maximum amount, upon receipt by us of

your duly signed demand for payment in writing stating that the Principal is in breach of his obligation(s) under the underlying contract and the respect in which the Principal is in breach.

It is a condition for any claim and payment to be made under this guarantee that the advance payment referred to above must have been received by the Principal into his account held with us.

For the purpose of identification your request for payment must bear or be accompanied by a signed confirmation of one of our correspondent banks stating that the latter has verified your signature(s) appearing on the said request for payment.

The amount of this guarantee will automatically be reduced in proportion to the value of each shipment upon presentation by the Principal to us of copies of the commercial invoice and the corresponding shipping document.

This guarantee shall expire once it has been reduced to nil or on ▮▮▮▮▮▮▮▮ at the latest.

This guarantee will be reduced by each payment made by us as a result of a claim.

This guarantee is subject to the Uniform Rules for Demand Guarantees, ICC Publication No. 458.

UBS AG

10.5 Standby Letter of Credit 备用信用证

10.5.1 Definition 定义

A standby letter of credit is a clean letter of credit that generally guarantees the payment to be made for an unfulfilled obligation on the part of the applicant. It is payable on presentation of a draft together with a signed statement or certificate by the beneficiary that the applicant has failed to fulfil his obligation.

10.5.2 Functional Terms and Conditions 功能条款

Therefore, the standby letter of credit is actually an alternative issued by the bank in favor of the importer, promising to pay a given amount against specified documents, usually a formal default claim. From a bank's viewpoint, a standby letter of credit is better than a guarantee because it is subject to UCP for documentary credits rather than Uniform Rules for Demand Guarantee.

10.6 Repayment Guarantee 还款保函

10.6.1 Definition 定义

A repayment guarantee is an undertaking given by a bank (the guarantor) at the request of a supplier of goods or services or other contractor (the principal) to a buyer or an employer (the beneficiary) whereby the bank undertakes to make payment to the beneficiary within the limits of a stated sum of money in the event of default by the principal to repay, in accordance with the terms and conditions of a contract between the principal and the beneficiary, any sum or sums advanced or paid by the beneficiary to the principal.[4]

10.6.2　Form　通用格式

☞ **SAMPLE 10-4**

Repayment Guarantee

To：

Advised through：

Dear Sirs，

Our Irrevocable Letter of Guarantee No. _____

With reference to Contract No. _____ (hereinafter called the Contract) signed on _____ between your goodselves and _____ (hereinafter called the Seller) covering the sale to you of _____ and at request of the Seller, we hereby establish in your favor an irrevocable Letter of Guarantee No. _____ for an amount not exceeding _____ equivalent to _____ % of the price of the contract.

In the event that the seller fails to deliver the equipment under the contract, we shall, within _____ days after receipt of your written notice, immediately refund to you the advance payment previously made by you, plus interest at the rate of _____ % per annum calculated from the date of your advance payment up to the date of our repayment.

This Letter of Guarantee shall come into force as from the date when the Sellers receives the advance payment and shall remain valid until the Sellers have delivered completely the equipment under the contract. The validity of this Letter of Guarantee, however, expires on _____ at the latest, by which date any claim must have reached us. You are kindly requested to return to us this Letter of Guarantee upon its expiry date.

This guarantee is personal to yourselves and is not transferable or assignable.

This guarantee shall be governed by and construed in accordance with the law of England.

　　　　　　　　　　　　　　　　　　　　　　　　For　　　　　　　BANK

10.7　Overdraft Guarantee　透支保函

10.7.1　Functional Terms and Conditions　功能条款

　　If a bank provides the overdraft facility for its overseas customer, sometimes a letter of guarantee issued by an overseas bank on behalf of this customer is needed. Under the guarantee the overseas bank undertakes to refund the bank providing the overdraft facility, should the customer fail to repay in due time the amount overdrawn in the account.

10.7.2 Form 通用格式

SAMPLE 10-5

Overdraft Guarantee

To:

Re: Our Irrevocable Letter of Guarantee No. ...

At the request of _____, we hereby issue this Letter of Guarantee in your favor to the extent of _____ _____ (say _____ only) for the purpose of your providing the overdraft facility to the account held by _____ with your bank.

We hereby undertake to refund you, should _____ fail to repay you in due time the due amount which they have overdrawn in the A/M account, the amount not exceeding the above-mentioned sum upon our receipt of your written claim dispatched within the validity of this L/G.

This guarantee remains valid until _____

Upon its expiration please confirm us by your tested telex for our cancellation.

This guarantee is personal to yourselves and is not transferable or assignable.

This guarantee shall be governed by and construed in accordance with the law of England.

                                                                For   BANK

10.8 Others 其他保函

Besides, there are also some other types of bank guarantees, such as guarantees in connection with credit cards, guarantees in connection with legal proceedings, guarantees in favor of tax authorities, etc., which are not going to be discussed here in detail. Several common types will be introduced briefly here.

10.8.1 Import Guarantee 进口保函

It is issued at the request of the importer to guarantee his effecting payment in accordance with the terms and conditions of the relative contract. It is mainly employed to secure the payment on an open account basis. Should the importer fail to make payment wholly or partially within the time limit as stipulated in the contract, the guarantor bank undertakes to effect payment for the unpaid value of goods delivered by the exporter plus interest, if any.

10.8.2　Loan Guarantee　贷款保函

The guarantee is issued at the request of the borrower (the principal) in favor of the lender (the beneficiary). The bank guarantees that, after the lender has extended a loan to the borrower as stipulated in the contract, the latter will repay the former the loan plus interest at ...% per annum within the time limit in accordance with the terms and conditions of the contract if the principal fails to repay the loan.

10.8.3　Leasing Guarantee　租赁保函

The guarantor bank guarantees to the beneficiary that the lessee will pay the rent in accordance with the terms and conditions of the lease agreement. Should the lessee fail to pay the rent within the time limit as stipulated in the lease agreement, the bank undertakes to effect payment for the unpaid rent plus defaulted interest, if any.

10.8.4　Retention Bonds　保留款保函

Retention bonds enable retention moneys, which would otherwise be held by the buyer beyond the completion of the contract, to be released early. These bonds guarantee the return of these retention moneys to the buyer in the event of non-performance of post completion obligations by the exporter.[5]

New Words and Expressions

principal	[ˈprinsəp(ə)l]	n.	负责人，本金，委托人
guarantor	[ˌgærənˈtɔː]	n.	[律] 保证人，担保人
beneficiary	[beniˈfiʃəri]	n.	受惠者，受益人
surety	[ˈʃuəriti]	n.	保证人，担保人
security	[siˈkjuəriti]	n.	担保（品），抵押
recoup	[riˈkuːp]	v.	赔偿，补偿，扣除，补偿损失
elicit	[iˈlisit]	v.	得出，引出，抽出，引起
trigger	[ˈtrigə]	v.	引发，引起，触发
		n.	扳机
construe	[kənˈstruː]	v.	解释，分析，直译

letter of guarantee　担保书，保函	quality guarantee　质量保函
counter indemnity　反担保	maintenance guarantee　维修保函
underlying transaction　基础交易	payment bond　付款保函

Chapter 10 Letter of Guarantee

demand guarantee 见索即付保函	deferred payment bond 延期付款保函
counter guarantee 反担保	loan guarantee 贷款保函
accessory guarantee 附属保函	guarantee for compensation trade 补偿贸易保函
independent guarantee 独立担保	overdraft guarantee 透支保函
bid bond 投标保函	leasing guarantee 租赁保函
performance bond 履约保函	standby letter of credit 备用信用证
advance payment guarantee 预付款保函	

Notes

1. A bank guarantee is a written promise issued by a bank at the request of its customer, undertaking to make payment to the beneficiary within the limits of a stated sum of money in the event of default by the principal. 银行担保书是银行应其客户的要求而开立的书面承诺,保证在委托人违约时向受益人支付规定的货币金额。

2. A counter guarantee refers to any guarantee or other payment undertaking of the instructing party given in writing for the payment of money to the guarantor on presentation in conformity with the terms of the undertaking of a written demand for payment and other documents specified in the counter guarantee. 反担保是指示人出具的任何书面保证或其他付款承诺,凭提交与承诺条款相符的书面付款要求及反担保内容规定的其他文件,支付款项给担保人。

3. 依据不同的标准,可以对担保进行不同的分类。
   (1) 就与基础交易的关系(Relationship with the Underlying Transaction)而言,可分为附属担保(Accessory Guarantee)和独立担保(Independent Guarantee)。
   (2) 就开立担保的方法(Methods of Issuing the Guarantee)而言,可分为直接担保(Direct Guarantee)和间接担保(Indirect Guarantee)。
   (3) 就索偿的条件(Conditions for a Claim)而言,可分为无条件的担保(Unconditional Bond)和有条件的担保(Conditional Bond)。
   (4) 就担保项下支付的先决条件(Payment Prerequisite under Guarantee)而言,可分为支付担保(Payment Guarantee)和信用担保(Credit Guarantee)。
   (5) 就担保的目的(Purposes of Guarantees)而言,担保可分为:
     ① 国际贸易项下的担保(Guarantees under International Trade);
     ② 国际工程承包项下的担保(Guarantees under International Engineering Contracting);
     ③ 备用信用证(Stand-by Letter of Credit);
     ④ 其他担保(Other Guarantees)。

4. A repayment guarantee is an undertaking given by a bank (the guarantor) at the request of a

supplier of goods or services or other contractor (the principal) to a buyer or an employer (the beneficiary) whereby the bank undertakes to make payment to the beneficiary within the limits of a stated sum of money in the event of default by the principal to repay, in accordance with the terms and conditions of a contract between the principal and the beneficiary, any sum or sums advanced or paid by the beneficiary to the principal. 还款担保书是指银行（担保人）应货物或服务的供应商或其他承包商（委托人）的要求，向买方或雇主（受益人）提供的一种担保，在担保书中银行承诺在委托人不能按委托人和受益人之间的合约条款退还受益人预付或支付给委托人的任何金额时，由银行向受益人支付或退还在规定的货币金额限额内的款项。

5. Retention bonds enable retention moneys, which would otherwise be held by the buyer beyond the completion of the contract, to be released early. These bonds guarantee the return of these retention moneys to the buyer in the event of non-performance of post completion obligations by the exporter. 留置金保函使本应该在合同完成以后由买方扣留的留置金提前给予卖方。担保人向买方保证如果卖方没有履行其售后服务的职责，由担保人退还其留置金。

Exercises

1. Fill in the blanks to complete each sentence.

(1) The two basic functions of guarantees are that guarantees are used as _____ of the contract amount and _____ that covers the risk of non-performance or defective performance by the contractor.

(2) The principal is the person at whose request the guarantee is issued, e.g. in tender guarantee the principal is the _____ or the party to whom _____. The principal will be claimed if he is in breach of his obligations.

(3) Independent guarantee is a principal obligation and is independent of the underlying contract. It is a promise to pay a sum of money against _____.

(4) A direct guarantee occurs when the client authorized the bank to _____.

(5) _____ can be called at the sole discretion of the buyer. The bank must pay if called upon to do so, even in circumstances where it may be clear to the exporter that the claim is wholly unjustified.

(6) Tender bond is designed to ensure that the tenderer does not _____ before adjudication, and does not fail or refuse to _____. A tender bond is usually for _____ of the contract value.

(7) From a bank's viewpoint, a standby letter of credit is better than a guarantee because it is subject to _____ rather than _____.

(8) _____ bond ensures the repayment of the advance by the exporter in the event of the non-performance of his contractual obligations.

(9) The loan guarantee is issued at the request of the _____ in favor of _____.

(10) While the bank is issuing a guarantee, the principal will be asked to sign a _____ to authorize the guarantor to debit the account with the cost of any payments under the guarantee.

2. Define the following terms.

(1) bank guarantee
(2) beneficiary
(3) indirect guarantee
(4) performance bond
(5) standby letter of credit

3. Translate the following terms into English.

(1) 履约保函   (2) 担保书
(3) 反赔偿   (4) 附属保函
(5) 备用信用证   (6) 工程承包
(7) 基础交易   (8) 见索即付保函
(9) 延期付款保函   (10) 反担保

4. Choose the best answer to each of the following statements.

(1) A ____ refers to any guarantee, bond or other payment undertaking of the instructing party given in writing for the payment of money to the guarantor on presentation in conformity with the terms of the undertaking of a written demand for payment and other documents specified.
   A. demand guarantee   B. counter guarantee
   C. conditional guarantee   D. dependent guarantee

(2) Under indirect guarantees, the ____ must formally pledge to pay the amount claimed by the beneficiary under the guarantee upon demand by the guaranteeing bank.
   A. initiating bank   B. beneficiary
   C. guaranteeing bank   D. principal

(3) Conditional bonds requiring documentary evidence give maximum protection to the ____. Payment can only be called for by the ____ against production of a specified document, such as a certificate of award by an independent arbitrator.
   A. exporter...importer   B. importer...importer
   C. importer...exporter   D. exporter...exporter

(4) ____ is not included in the category of payment guarantee.
   A. Deferred payment bond   B. Guarantee for compensation trade
   C. Loan guarantee   D. Bid bond

(5) Payment guarantee is a security mechanism for payment of the contract amount. In this case, the ____ is primarily liable to the beneficiary.
   A. contractor   B. exporter
   C. issuing bank   D. instructing party

(6) A bond is a guarantee to ____ that ____ will fulfil his contractual obligations.
   A. the exporter ... the buyer   B. the beneficiary ... the principal
   C. the guarantor ... the buyer   D. the exporter ... the guarantor

(7) A tender or bid bond is usually for ____ of the contract value.
   A. 2%   B. 5%
   C. between 2% to 5%   D. 10%

(8) Advance payment bonds undertake to ____ .
   A. make payments
   B. make payments if the goods
   C. refund any advance payments
   D. refund any advance payments if the goods or services are unsatisfactory

(9) "On Demand" bonds can be called ____ .
   A. at the sole discretion of the seller   B. at the sole discretion of the buyer
   C. at the sole discretion of the bank   D. at the discretion of both the buyer and the seller

(10) ____ guarantee the return to the buyer of these retention moneys in the event of non-performance of post-completion obligations by the exporter.
   A. Retention Bonds   B. Recourse Bonds
   C. Refund Bonds   D. Stand-by credits

Chapter 11

Rules of International Payments and Settlements
国际支付与结算的规则

> 📢 **In this chapter, you will learn:**
> ☑ Application, major content and improvement of URC
> ☑ Application, major content and improvement of UCP
> ☑ Application, major content and improvement of ICC 525
> ☑ Application, major content and improvement of URDG
> ☑ Basic features of rules for international settlements

11.1 URC 《托收统一规则》

11.1.1 General Introduction 概述

Although documentary collections, in one form or another, have been in use for a long time, questions arose about how to effect transactions in a practical, fair, and uniform manner.

The Uniform Rules for Collection (URC) are the internationally recognized codification of rules that unify banking practice regarding collection operations for drafts and for documentary collections.[1] URC are not incorporated in national or international law, but become binding on all parties because all bank authorities (especially the collection order) will state that the collection is subject to URC. URC will apply unless the collection order states otherwise or the laws in one of the countries concerned specially contradict them.

The Uniform Rules for Collections were developed by the International Chamber of Commerce in Paris. It is revised and updated from time-to-time; the current valid version is ICC publication No. 522.

11.1.2 Application 适用范围

The Uniform Rules for Collections, 1995 Revision, ICC Publication No. 522, shall apply to all collections where such rules are incorporated into the text of the "collection instruction" and are binding on all parties thereto unless otherwise expressly agreed or contrary to the provisions of a national, state or local law and/or regulation which can not be departed from.[2]

Banks shall have no obligation to handle either a collection or any collection instruction or subsequent related instructions.

If a bank elects, for any reason, not to handle a collection or any related instructions received by it, it must advise the party from whom it received the collection or instructions by telecommunication, or if that is not possible, by other expeditious means, without delay.

11.1.3 Major Contents 主要内容

Uniform Rules for Collection (ICC Publication No. 522) consists of seven parts with 26 articles altogether.[3]

1. Part A: General Provisions and Definitions

This part consists of Articles 1–3, including the application of URC 522, definitions of collections and documents, and parties to a collection.

2. Part B: Form and Structure of Collections

It has been made clear in the URC that ICC Publication No. 522 is binding on all parties concerned only if it is stated in the collection instructions that the collection is subject to URC 522. The form and information items of collection are stipulated in detail. The liability and responsibility of the instructing party and the instructed party are also made clear.

3. Part C: Form of Presentation

This part is made up of Articles 5–8, specifying the procedure, methods and precautions of presentation, stipulating the time limit for the presenting bank to handle sight/tenor collection presentation, etc.

4. Part D: Liabilities and Responsibilities

This part is composed of Articles 9–15, including the liability and responsibility banks shall assume for the goods, services or performances related to documents. This part also stipulates disclaimer for acts of an instructed party, disclaimer on documents received, disclaimer on effectiveness of documents, disclaimer on delays, loss in transit and translation, and force majeure.

5. Part E: Payment

Articles 16 to 19 constitute Part E, requiring that amounts collected should be made available without delay to the party from whom the collection instruction was received. This part is also about different operations under "payment in local currency", "payment in foreign currency" and "partial payment".

6. Part F: Interest, Charges and Expenses

This part made up of Articles 20-21 is about the collection of interest, charges and expenses and the corresponding provisions in collection instruction.

7. Part G: Other Provisions

Articles 22-26 make up Part G, involving acceptance, protest, case-of-need and advice — form and method of advice, and advice of payment, acceptance, non-payment and non-acceptance.

11.1.4 Improvement 改进

1. Necessity of Drawing up URC

With the development of international economy and trade early in the 20th century, collection received increasing importance and gradually became a settlement method. Many disputes and conflicts arose from the different understanding of the obligations and rights of respective parties and from different operations in handling the collections.

2. 1956 Version of URC (ICC Publication No. 192)

The International Chamber of Commerce (ICC) deemed it necessary to draw up the "Uniform Rules for Collection of Commercial Paper". This was implemented in 1956, and the Uniform Rules came into force in 1958 (ICC Publication No. 192), and these rules were adopted by a great number of banks throughout the world, though not so universally as in the case of the Uniform Customs.

3. 1968 Version of URC (ICC Publication No. 254)

In 1967, the ICC submitted a revised text of the Uniform Rules for adoption by the banks in the various countries, and it was put into force on January 1, 1968. These revised Uniform Rules for the Collection of Commercial Paper (ICC Publication No. 254) differed from the previous regulations mainly in their construction and terminology. These new Uniform Rules comprised, in a uniform "code", all provisions relating to the collection of commercial paper, in contrast with the previous regulation of 1956, which contained rules on commercial paper in general and the special (additional) rules to be applied to documentary remittances.

4. 1979 Version of URC (ICC Publication No. 322)

After almost ten years of practical application, and with the development of international trade and improvement of international collection, these Rules were further developed, mainly by changes in the titles and the wording of the text and by inclusion of some provisions deemed to be necessary. This is the Uniform Rules for Collection (ICC Publication No. 322) that came into effect on January 1, 1979. Uniform Rules for Collection No. 322 were adopted by banks in many countries and played a positive role in facilitating the international trade.

5. 1995 Version of URC (ICC Publication No. 522)

However, the limitations and inadaptability of the rules became increasingly obvious. It was essential that the previous regulation should be revised and complemented in order to keep up with new developments in international finance, trade, transportation and computer technology. The revised regulations were published in July 1995 and came into force on January 1, 1996 (ICC Publication No. 522) and these are the current Uniform Rules for Collection. This development has interested bankers throughout the world since the new Rules replaced the previous ones. In making revision, the ICC's Banking Commission took into account both the evolutions in practice since 1979 and specific problems that have arisen and could not be solved by the existing rules. This revision reflected the policy of the ICC to keep abreast of changes in international commerce.

6. Table of Improvement of URC

Table 11-1 is a summary of the improvements of URC and may be of some help.

Table 11-1 A summary of the improvements of URC

Time of Adoption/Operation	Full Name	Short Name	Features
1956/1958	Uniform Rules for Collection of Commercial Paper	ICC Publication No. 192	Containing rules on commercial paper in general and the special (additional) rules to be applied to documentary remittances, these rules were adopted by a great number of banks throughout the world.
1967/January 1968	Uniform Rules for Collection of Commercial Paper	ICC Publication No. 254	Different from ICC No. 192 mainly in their construction and terminology, ICC No. 254 comprise in a uniform "code" all provisions relating to the collection of commercial paper.
1978/January 1979	Uniform Rules for Collection	ICC Publication No. 322	With the development of international trade and improvement of international collection, these Rules were further developed, mainly by changes in the titles and the wording of the text and by inclusion. Adopted by banks in many countries, these rules played a positive role in facilitating the international trade.
July 1995/January 1996	Uniform Rules for Collection.	ICC Publication No. 522	Taking into account both the evolutions in practice since 1979 and specific problems, ICC No. 522 has interested the bankers throughout the world.

11.2 UCP 《跟单信用证统一惯例》

11.2.1 General Introduction 概述

Although documentary credits, in one form or another, have been in use for a long time, questions arose about how to effect transactions in a practical, fair, and uniform manner.

The Uniform Customs and Practice for Documentary Credits (UCP) is the internationally recognized codification of rules unifying banking practice regarding documentary credits. The UCP was developed by a working committee attached to the International Chamber of Commerce in Paris. It is revised and updated from time-to-time.

UCP rules affect all parties involved in transactions covered by documentary credits including:

(1) banks and other institutions that issue, confirm or otherwise process them;

(2) buyers (applicants) who cause them to be issued;

(3) sellers (beneficiaries) who look to them for payment;

(4) service providers such as forwarders, carriers, customs brokers who provide or use the documents that the credits stipulate.

11.2.2　Application　适用范围

The Uniform Customs and Practice for Documentary Credits, 1993 Revision, shall apply to all Documentary Credits (including to the extent to which they may be applicable, Standby Letter(s) of Credit) where they are incorporated into the text of the Credit. They are binding on all parties thereto, unless otherwise expressly stipulated in the credit.[4]

11.2.3　Major Contents　主要内容

Concerning the structure and articulation of the regulation, the UCP 600 commences with "General Provisions and Definitions", which refers in the first place to the permissive (non-mandatory, "dispositive") character of the customs and practices; then it gives the definition of documentary credit and further stresses some basic principles.

The second part deals with the "Form and Notification of Credits", explaining the different forms of documentary credits, i.e. revocable, irrevocable and confirmed and the distinguishing features of each.

Among the provisions contained in the following articles under the title "Liabilities and Responsibilities" another basic principle is emphasized, i.e. in documentary credit operations all parties concerned deal in documents and not in goods. It is the bank's duty to comply strictly with the terms and conditions determined in the text of the credit when taking up documents, and to reject and withhold payment for the ones which are not in accordance with such terms and conditions.

The following part "Documents" stresses that it is for the applicant to specify what he wants in the way of documents, and not for the bank to guess. It goes on to define the conditions, which in the absence of any specific requirements laid down by the applicant, the documents prescribed must fulfill.

"Miscellaneous Provisions" is about the definitions and interpretations of terms, which, lacking such definitions and uniformity of interpretation, have in the past hampered the smooth working and successful operation of documentary credits.

Finally, it deals comprehensively with the "Transfer of credits", and "Assignment of proceeds", a special form of passing all or part of the benefit or proceeds of a credit to a third party.

11.2.4 Improvement 改进

1. 1929 UCP Version(ICC No.74)

At the Amsterdam Congress of the ICC in 1929, Uniform Rules for Commercial Documentary Credits were approved and published in 1930 as ICC Publication No. 74. Though the standard was imperfect and was put into practice by banks only in Paris and Belgium, the Uniform Rules were still of great importance for they gave a uniform definition of documentary credit, and explained some terms and the rights and obligations of parties concerned.

2. 1933 UCP Version(ICC No.82)

After complete revision, the Uniform Customs and Practice for Commercial Documentary Credits (ICC publication No. 82) adopted at the Vienna Congress of the ICC in 1933 was accepted by banks throughout Continental Europe.

3. 1951 Version of UCP (ICC No.151)

After World War Two, the need to take note of American practice and the necessity of altering certain matters of detail in the light of experience led to further revision, adopted at the 1951 Lisbon Congress. This version secured the collective adherence of the banks in some thirty countries. This was ICC Publication No. 151 and was put into practice on January 1, 1952.

4. 1962 Version of UCP (ICC No.222)

In 1962, the Uniform Rules of 1951 were revised at Mexican City Congress, and Uniform Customs and Practice for Documentary Credits (UCP) were adopted by banks from more than 100 countries. This was ICC Publication No. 222, which came into force on July 1, 1963. UCP 222 was published in English rather than in French, which further established UCP as a worldwide practice.

5. 1974 Version of UCP (ICC No.290)

Due to the rapid development of international cargo transportation, containerized traffic came into wide use and great changes took place in international waybill practices. This led to further revision adopted at the 1974 Madrid Congress. This was ICC Publication No. 290, which was put into practice on October 1, 1975 with 47 articles. It was adopted by banks from more than 160 countries.

6. 1983 Version of UCP (ICC No.400)

After the publication of UCP 290, the rapid development of multi-transportation and containerized traffic, the increasingly frequent use of non-negotiable waybills/transport documents, the electronic inter-bank communication and the rapid development of stand-by letters of credit led to another revision of the UCP in 1983. This was ICC Publication No. 400 with 55 articles that came into force on October 1, 1984.

7. 1993 Version of UCP (ICC No. 500)

The UCP 1993 Revision, ICC Publication No. 500[5] with 49 articles came into force on January 1, 1994. In other words, each L/C opened is automatically subject to UCP 500. Compared with the previous standards, UCP 500 was only intended to:

(1) simplify the rules;

(2) make them coincide with banking practices;

(3) emphasize the bank's responsibility;

(4) decide what to do with non-documentary conditions;

(5) clarify the documents for each kind of transport.

8. 2007 Version of UCP (ICC No. 600)

UCP 600 will replace the current UCP 500 as from July 1, 2007. UCP 600 incorporates a number of major changes from UCP 500 which you as a banker, importer, exporter, service provider and business professionals (such as lawyers and consultants) need to know. Amongst key new or changes in UCP 600 rules, which you should know are:

(1) a reduction in the number of articles from 49 to 39;

(2) new articles on "Definitions" and "Interpretations" to provide more clarity and precision in the rules;

(3) the replacement of the phrase "reasonable time" for acceptance or refusal of documents by a firm period of five banking days;

(4) new provisions which allow for the discounting of deferred payment credits;

(5) a definitive description of negotiation as "purchase" of drafts of documents;

(6) re-drafted transport articles aimed at resolving confusion over the identification of carriers and agents.

The Modifications and Changes in General:

(1) Given 14 definitions at first and 12 interpretations to clarify the meaning of ambiguous terms, refer to Article 2 & 3. And we need pay attention to the change about "negotiation".

(2) Agreed that the issuing bank must reimburse the nominated bank even though the documents are lost in the transmitting however, the presentation must be complying.

(3) Denied the practice that banks stipulate the clause about which the amendment should be accepted by beneficiary who did not send any rejected advice in certain time, refer to sub-article 10(f).

(4) Five banking days replaced reasonable time and seven banking days, refer to sub-article 14(b).

(5) Two kinds of form about refusing have been added in UCP600, refer to sub-article 16(c)(iii).

(6) Banks can now accept an insurance document that contains reference to any exclusion

clause, refer to sub-article 28(i).

(7) The insurance document could be issued by proxies, refer sub-article 28(a).

(8) The clause for transport documents issued by Freight Forwarders has been deleted.

(9) The clause about carrying vessel propelled by sail only has been deleted since that kind of sailboat has dropped out of ocean transport.

(10) The expression is straightaway, precise and compact, for example, the wording for "unless the credit expressly stipulates..." is not used in UCP 600.

(11) The clause about shipment date has changed, refer to sub-article 19(a)(ii), 20(a)(ii), 21(a)(ii) and 22(a)(ii), especially to note the effect to received bill of lading.

(12) Canceled the blocking frame about the form of clauses.

(13) The number of the clauses has decreased to 39 from original 49.

(14) The deferred payment credit could be discounted or purchased.

(15) Added the acts of terrorism as a kind of Force Majeure, refer to Article 36.

(16) Confirmed that the issuing bank may be a transferring bank, refer to sub-article 38(b).

9. ISBP 681

ISBP stands for International Standard Banking Practice for the Examination of Documents under Documentary Credits. Since the approval of International Standard Banking Practice (ISBP) by the ICC Banking commission in 2002, ICC Publication 645 has become an invaluable aid to banks, corporates, logistics specialists and insurance companies alike, on a global basis. Participants in ICC seminars and workshops have indicated that rejection rates have dropped due to the application of the 200 practices that are detailed in ISBP.

However, there have also been comments that although the ISBP Publication 645 was approved by the Banking Commission its application had no relationship with UCP 500. With the approval of UCP 600 in October 2006, it has become necessary to provide an updated version of the ISBP. It is emphasized that this is an updated version as opposed to a revision of ICC Publication 645. Where it was felt appropriate, paragraphs that appeared in Publication 645 and that have now been covered in effectively the same text in UCP 600 have been removed from this updated version of ISBP(681).

As a means of creating a relationship between the UCP and ISBP, the introduction to UCP 600, states: "During the revision process, notice was taken of the considerable work that had been completed in creating the International Standard Banking Practice for the Examination of Documents under Documentary Credits (ISBP), ICC Publication 645. This publication has evolved into a necessary companion to the UCP for determining compliance of documents with the terms of letters of credit. It is the expectation of the Drafting Group and the Banking Commission that the application of the principles contained in the ISBP, including subsequent revisions thereof, will continue during the time UCP 600 is in force. At the time UCP 600 is implemented, there will be an updated version of the ISBP to bring its contents in line with the substance and style of the new rules."

The international standard banking practices documented in this publication are consistent with

UCP 600 and the Opinions and Decisions of the ICC Banking Commission. This document does not amend UCP 600. It explains how the practices articulated in UCP 600 are applied by documentary practitioners. This publication and the UCP should be read in their entirety and not in isolation.

11.3　ICC 525　《跟单信用证项下银行偿付统一规则》

11.3.1　General Introduction　概述

ICC 525 means the Uniform Rules for Bank-to-Bank Reimbursements under Documentary Credits (ICC Publication No. 525). The 1974 revision of the UCP, updating the 1962 version, reflected the increasing importance of currency markets in international trade and first made specific reference to the involvement of a "third bank" in processing the claims for reimbursement of payments made under documentary credits.

The definition of the functions of the reimbursing bank was further developed in the 1983 UCP revision and updated in the current UCP 500. To meet the need for international standards and to assist trade facilitation, the ICC Banking Commission in 1993 established a Working Party to draft a suitable framework for a new set of rules. The publication of ICC 525 is the result of its efforts.

11.3.2　Application　适用范围

The Uniform Rules for Bank-to-Bank Reimbursements under Documentary Credits, ICC Publication No. 525, shall apply to all Bank-to-Bank Reimbursements where they are incorporated into the text of the Reimbursement Authorization. They are binding on all parties thereto, unless otherwise expressly stipulated in the Reimbursement Authorization. The Issuing Bank is responsible for indicating in the Documentary Credit that Reimbursement Claims are subject to these Rules.

In a Bank-to-Bank Reimbursement subject to these Rules, the Reimbursing Bank acts on the instructions and/or under the authority of the Issuing Bank. These Rules are not intended to override or change the provisions of the ICC Uniform Customs and Practice for Documentary Credits.

11.3.3　Major Contents　主要内容

The Uniform Rules for Bank-to-Bank Reimbursements under Documentary Credits, ICC Publication No. 525 (URR 525), define explicitly and explain in detail for the first time reimbursement authorization, reimbursement undertakings, expiry of a reimbursement authorization, and authenticity of reimbursement claims, etc.

URR 525 also offers a basis to solve the problems and disputes that have long existed regarding the respective rights, obligations and responsibilities involved in bank-to-bank reimbursements. ICC Publication No. 525 consists of four parts with 17 articles.

1. Part A: General Provisions and Definitions

This part stipulates the application of URR 525 and gives standard definitions to parties concerned, documents and practices. This part also makes clear the relationship between bank-to-bank reimbursement authorizations under documentary credits and the documentary credits themselves.

2. Part B: Liabilities and Responsibilities

This part lays emphasis upon the liabilities and responsibilities of both the issuing bank and the reimbursing bank.

3. Part C: Form and Notification of Authorizations, Amendments and Claims

This part includes the details about the issuance and receipt of reimbursement authorizations and reimbursement amendment, and amendment or cancellation of reimbursement authorizations. In addition, there are also concrete provisions as regards reimbursement undertakings and standards for and processing of reimbursement claims. Finally the duplication of reimbursement authorizations is clearly explained.

4. Part D: Miscellaneous Provisions

This part includes foreign laws and usages, disclaimer on the transmission of message, force majeure, charges and interest claim/loss of value.

11.3.4 Improvement 改进

(1) Provisions regarding bank-to-bank reimbursements under documentary credits appeared as early as in Article 13 of ICC Publication No. 290, which was adopted in 1974 and put into practice on October 1, 1975.

(2) Rules and procedures of bank-to-bank reimbursements under documentary credits were laid down in the United States in 1981.

(3) Based on Article 13 of the ICC 290, bank-to-bank reimbursements under documentary credits were complemented in Article 21 of ICC 400.

(4) New developments of business led to further revision by the US in 1989 of the rules and procedures of bank-to-bank reimbursements drawn up in 1981.

(5) The 19th Article in ICC 500 made further elaboration and exposition on bank-to-bank reimbursements.

However, the clauses tended to be too simple, the content was applicable only to certain districts and the structure was loose. All these drawbacks in the rules were not completely eliminated. With the development of international trade and banking, it was urgent that a set of complete, systematic and uniform rules for international bank-to-bank reimbursements under documentary credits should be laid down.

(6) After years of arduous work, Uniform Rules for Bank-to-bank Reimbursements under Documentary Credits, ICC Publication No. 525, as complement and perfection to Article 19 of UCP 500 came into force on July 1, 1996.

Chapter 11 Rules of International Payments and Settlements

11.4 URDG 《见索即付担保统一规则》

11.4.1 Application 适用范围

Uniform Rules for Demand Guarantees, ICC Publication No. 458 apply to any demand guarantee and amendment thereto which a guarantor has been instructed to issue and which states that it is subject to ICC Publication No. 458 and binding on all parties thereto except as otherwise expressly stated in the Guarantee or any amendment thereto.

11.4.2 Major Contents 主要内容

In Uniform Rules for Contract Guarantee (ICC Publication No. 325), it is stipulated that if a guarantee does not specify the documentation to be produced in support of a claim or merely specifies only a statement of claim by the beneficiary, the beneficiary must submit either a court decision or an arbitral award justifying the claim or the approval of the principal in writing to the claim. Such stipulations are unfavorable to the creditor and are time consuming to get a judgment from judicial or arbitral tribunal whenever there is a dispute in the transaction.

Many Articles in ICC Publication No. 458 are somewhat similar to those mentioned in UCP Publication No. 500, such as Articles 9, 10, 11, 12 and 14. Like a letter of credit the Rules are binding on all parties thereto if the guarantee indicates that it is issued subject to the Uniform Rules for Demand Guarantee.

Uniform Rules for Demand Guarantee, ICC Publication No. 458 reflect more closely international practice in the use of demand guarantees and at the same time preserve the goal of the original rules to balance the interests of the different parties and to curb abuses in the calling of guarantees. The duty of making payment by the guarantor or issuer under Publication No. 458 lies in the presentation of a written demand and any other documents specified in the guarantee, not conditional on proof of default by the principal in the underlying transaction such as a judgment or arbitral award as a condition of the beneficiary's right to payment as mentioned in Publication No. 325. Publication No. 458 is intended to apply worldwide to the use of demand guarantee.

11.4.3 Improvement 改进

1. Necessity of Coordinating Guarantees

With the increasingly wide use of bank guarantees in international finance, trade, services exports, engineering contracting and other economic activities, and due to the fact that partners with different legal and cultural backgrounds are called on to do business together, more and more disputes under guarantees occurred. The understanding and concept of the nature and characteristics of guarantee, payment obligation, and rules for guarantee vary from country to country in their respective domestic laws. International guarantee will inevitably involve the interests of two or more parties from different countries or regions. In view of this, some international organizations such as the International Chamber of Commerce gradually realized the necessity of coordinating guarantees.

2. Improvement

(1) Uniform Rules for Contract Guarantee (ICC Publication No. 325) were the first international uniform rules issued by ICC in 1978. ICC Publication No. 325 aimed at producing a fair balance between the legitimate interest of the different parties concerned — beneficiary, principal and guarantor — to define the rights and obligations of the three parties with sufficient precision to avoid disputes.

(2) At the same time, ICC also issued "Model Forms for Contract Guarantee No. 406". According to ICC Publication No. 325, a claim shall only be made and honored if the beneficiary has a legal right to make the claim based on a failure of the principal to perform or correctly perform the underlying contract. Because the principle and provisions of ICC Publication No. 325 were quite different from the practice of guarantee, ICC Publication No. 325, though published for many years, did not gain general acceptance and recognition from the prevailing banking and commercial practice or from world financial and trade circles.

(3) For this reason, ICC drafted Uniform Rules for Guarantee in 1988 in which the overemphasis of the balanced rights and interests between the beneficiary and the principal was abandoned and more common practices and actual needs were taken into account. However, Uniform Rules for Guarantee were not officially issued due to various reasons.

(4) In order to avoid being involved in the trade disputes, the guarantor usually stipulates that the payment under guarantee should be based on the presentation of the document(s) required in guarantee rather than the fact of default.

(5) In 1992, ICC issued Uniform Rules for Demand Guarantee, ICC Publication No. 458 to take the place of ICC Publication No. 325. Accessory guarantee whose uniform rules are difficult to be agreed upon and under which the payment is based on the actual performance of the underlying transaction was completely abandoned. ICC Publication No. 458 does not apply to those guarantees according to which the guarantors make payment only when there is any default on the part of the principal. However, for the time being the old one — ICC Publication No. 325 — will continue to be used to some extent, so as to be available for those who may wish to use it in preference to the new rules.

11.5 Basic Features of International Settlement Rules
国际结算规则的基本特征

(1) All settlement rules, whether UCP, URC, URDG or ICC 525, have specific application, the rules are binding on all parties thereto unless otherwise expressly stipulated in

Chapter 11 Rules of International Payments and Settlements

the rules.

(2) All settlement rules have in general gained general acceptance and recognition from the prevailing banking and commercial practice and from world financial and trade circles, for these settlement rules reflect closely the international financial and trade practice.

(3) All settlement rules contribute to effect transactions in a practical, fair, and uniform manner. With the increasing development of international finance, trade, services exports, engineering contracting and other economic activities, and due to the fact that partners with different legal and cultural backgrounds are called on to do business together, disputes naturally occur. The understanding and interpretation of the nature, characteristics and operations of a certain business activity vary from country to country in their respective domestic laws. International business will inevitably involve the interests of two or more parties from different countries or regions. In view of this, some international organizations such as the International Chamber of Commerce realized the necessity of coordinating the international business by drafting and issuing some uniform rules.

(4) All settlement rules were revised and updated from time-to-time to keep abreast of changes in international commerce.

After years of practical application, and with the development of international finance and trade, the limitations and inadaptability became increasingly obvious. It was essential that the previous rules should be revised and complemented in order to keep up with new developments in international finance, trade, transportation and computer technology.

In making revision, the ICC's Banking Commission took into account both the evolutions in practice and specific problems that had arisen and could not be solved by the existing rules. The revision reflected the policy of the ICC to keep abreast of changes in international commerce.

New Words and Expressions

disclaimer	[dis'kleimə]	n.	放弃，拒绝，放弃者，不承诺
implement	['implimənt]	v.	贯彻，实现，执行
submit	[səb'mit]	v.	(使)服从，(使)顺从，提交，递交
construction	[kən'strʌkʃən]	n.	解释，意义，结构
terminology	[ˌtəːmi'nɔlədʒi]	n.	术语
positive	['pɔzətiv]	a.	肯定的，积极的，绝对的，确实的
inadaptability	['inəˌdæptə'biləti]	n.	无适应性，非适合性
abreast	[ə'brest]	ad.	并肩地，并排地
articulation	[ɑːˌtikju'leiʃən]	n.	清晰度
hamper	['hæmpə]	v.	妨碍，牵制

comprehensive	[ˌkɔmpriˈhensiv]	a.	全面的，广泛的，能充分理解的
override	[ˌəuvəˈraid]	v.	不顾，不考虑（某人的意见、决定、愿望等）
duplication	[ˌdjuːpliˈkeiʃən]	n.	副本，复制
arduous	[ˈaːdjuəs]	a.	费劲的，辛勤的，险峻的
codification	[ˌkɔdifiˈkeiʃən]	n.	法典编纂，法律成文
contradict	[ˌkɔntrəˈdikt]	v.	同……矛盾，同……抵触
incorporate	[inˈkɔːpəreit]	a.	合并的，一体化的
		v.	合并，使组成公司
expeditious	[ˌekspiˈdiʃəs]	a.	迅速的，敏捷的
proxy	[ˈprɔksi]	n.	代理人
propel	[prəˈpel]	v.	推进，驱使
facilitation	[fəˌsiliˈteiʃən]	n.	简易化，助长
elaborate	[iˈlæbərit]	a.	精心制作的，详细阐述的
		v.	精心制作，详细阐述
exposition	[ˌekspəuˈziʃən]	n.	博览会，展览会，说明

URC 《托收统一规则》
arbitral award 仲裁书，仲裁判决书
arbitral tribunal 仲裁庭
codification of rules 规则汇编
collection order 托收委托书
collection instruction 托收指示
sight collection presentation 即期托收提示
general provisions 总则
tenor collection presentation 远期托收提示
UCP 《跟单信用证统一惯例》

reimbursement authorization 偿付授权
reimbursement claim 索偿
International Chamber of Commerce (ICC) 国际商会
Uniform Rules for Demand Guarantee
《见索即付担保统一规则》
Uniform Rules for Contract Guarantee
《合约担保统一规则》
Uniform Rules for Bank-to-bank Reimbursements under Documentary Credits
《跟单信用证项下银行偿付统一规则》

Notes

1. The Uniform Rules for Collections (URC) are the internationally recognized codification of rules that unify banking practice regarding collection operations for drafts and for documentary collections. 《托收统一规则》(URC)是国际上规范银行汇票托收和跟单托收业务的公认的规则。

2. The Uniform Rules for Collections, 1995 Revision, ICC Publication No. 522, shall apply to all collections where such rules are incorporated into the text of the "collection instruction" and are binding on all parties thereto unless otherwise expressly agreed or contrary to the provisions

Chapter 11 Rules of International Payments and Settlements

of a national, state or local law and/or regulation which can not be departed from. 《国际商会第 522 号出版物》，即《托收统一规则》（1995 年修订本），将适用于"托收指示"中所包含的规则中的所有托收项目。除非另有明确的约定，或与某一国家、某一政府，或与当地法律和尚在生效的条例有所抵触，本规则对所有的关系人均具有约束力。

3. Uniform Rules for Collection (ICC Publication No. 522) consists of seven parts with 26 articles altogether. 《托收统一规则》（国际商会第 522 号出版物）包括 7 个部分，共 26 项条款。7 个部分具体是如下。

    A 部分：总则与定义（General Provisions and Definitions），第 1～3 条。
    B 部分：托收的形式与结构（Form and Structure of Collection），第 4 条。
    C 部分：提示的构成（Form of Presentation），第 5～8 条。
    D 部分：责任和任务（Liabilities and Responsibilities），第 9～15 条。
    E 部分：付款（Payment），第 16～19 条。
    F 部分：利息、手续费和费用（Interest, Charges and Expenses），第 20～21 条。
    G 部分：其他条款（Other Provisions），第 22～26 条。

4. The Uniform Customs and Practice for Documentary Credits, 1993 Revision, ICC Publication No. 500, shall apply to all Documentary Credits (including to the extent to which they may be applicable, Standby Letter(s) of Credit) where they are incorporated into the text of the Credit. They are binding on all parties thereto, unless otherwise expressly stipulated in the credit. 《跟单信用证统一惯例》（1993 年修订本），即国际商会第 500 号出版物，适用于所有在信用证文本中标明按本惯例办理的跟单信用证（包括本惯例适用范围内的备用信用证），除非信用证中另有明确规定，本惯例对一切有关当事人均具有约束力。

5. 《跟单信用证统一惯例》（1993 年修订本）（即 UCP 500）的主要结构如下。
    A. 总则与定义（General Provisions and Definitions）第 1～5 条。
    B. 信用证的形式与通知（Form and Notification of Credits），第 6～12 条。
    C. 责任义务（Liabilities and Responsibilities），第 13～19 条。
    D. 单据（Documents），第 20～38 条。
    E. 杂项规定（Miscellaneous Provisions），第 39～47 条。
    F. 可转让信用证（Transfer of credits），第 48 条。
    G. 款项让渡（Assignment of proceeds），第 49 条。

Exercises

1. **Fill in the blanks to complete each sentence.**

    (1) The Uniform Rules for Collections are the internationally recognized codification of rules

unifying banking practice regarding _____.

(2) ICC No. 522, shall apply to _____ where such rules are incorporated into the text of the "_____" and are binding on all parties thereto unless otherwise expressly agreed or contrary to the provisions of a national, state or local law and/or regulation which can not be departed from.

(3) ICC Publication No. 500 shall apply to _____ (including to the extent to which they may be applicable, Standby Letter (s) of credit) where they are incorporated into the text of the _____. They are binding on all parties thereto, unless otherwise expressly stipulated in the credit.

(4) The Uniform Rules for Bank-to-Bank Reimbursements under Documentary Credits, ICC Publication No. 525, shall apply to _____ where they are incorporated into the text of the _____. They are binding on all parties thereto, unless otherwise expressly stipulates in the Reimbursement Authorization.

(5) ICC Publication No. 458 apply to _____ which a guarantor has been instructed to issue and which states that it is subject to ICC Publication No. 458 and are binding on all parties thereto except as otherwise expressly stated in the _____.

(6) In documentary credit operations all parties concerned deal in _____ and not in _____. It is the bank's duty to comply strictly with the _____ determined in the text of the credit when taking up documents.

(7) The Uniform Customs and Practice for Documentary (UCP) is the internationally recognized _____ developed by a working committee attached to ICC unifying _____.

(8) After years of practical application, and with the development of international finance and trade, it was essential that the previous rules should be revised and complemented in order to keep up with new development in _____.

(9) Because the principle and provisions of ICC Publication No. 325 were _____, ICC Publication No. 325 has not yet gained general acceptance and recognition from the prevailing _____ practice or from world financial and trade circles.

(10) ICC Publication No. 525 also offers basis to solve the problems and disputes that have long existed regarding the respective rights, obligations and responsibilities involved in _____.

2. Translate the following terms into English.

(1) 索偿
(2) 仲裁书
(3) 银行委员会
(4) 多式联运
(5) 偿付保证
(6) 银行惯例
(7) 集装箱运输
(8) 非转让运输单据
(9) 远期托收提示
(10) 国际商会

Chapter 11 Rules of International Payments and Settlements   265

3. Fill in the following table of the improvement of UCP.

Time of Adoption/Operation	Full Name	Short Name	Features
1929 ICC Amsterdam Congress/1930			
1933 ICC Vienna Congress			
1951 ICC Lisbon Congress/1952			
1962 ICC Mexican City Congress/July 1963			
1974 ICC Madrid Congress/October 1975			
In 1983/October 1984			
In 1993/January 1994			
July 2007			

4. Choose the best answer to each of the following statements or questions.

(1) The Uniform Rules for Collections were developed by the International Chamber of Commerce in Paris. It is revised and updated from time-to-time; the current valid version is ____.
  A. ICC No. 322   B. ICC No. 522
  C. ICC No. 400   D. ICC No. 525

(2) Compared with the previous, UCP 500 was only concerned to simplify the rules, ____, decide what to do with non-documentary conditions, and clarify the documents for each kind of transport.
  A. reject and withhold payment
  B. emphasize mostly on bank's responsibility
  C. make them coincide with banking practices
  D. both B and C

(3) As far as rules for international settlements are concerned, there are some basic features. Which of the following is not a basic feature?

   A. All settlement rules have specific application.
   B. The rules are binding on all parties thereto unless otherwise expressly stipulates in the rules.
   C. All settlement rules generally still have not gained general acceptance and recognition.
   D. All settlement rules were revised and updated from time-to-time to keep abreast of changes in international commerce.

(4) Provisions regarding bank-to-bank reimbursements under documentary credits appeared as early as in ____ of ICC Publication No. 290 that was adopted in 1974 and put into practice on October 1, 1975.

   A. Article 13   B. Article 19
   C. Article 21   D. Article 18

(5) Rules and procedures of bank-to-bank reimbursements under documentary credit ____.

   A. tended to be too simple
   B. were loose
   C. were applicable only to certain districts
   D. were complete, systematic and uniform

International Payment Systems
国际支付体系

> 📢 **In this chapter, you will learn:**
> ☑ An overview of payment systems
> ☑ Concept, benefits, operation of SWIFT
> ☑ CHIPS
> ☑ CHAPS
> ☑ Fed Wire

12.1 Introduction to International Payment Systems 国际支付体系概述

12.1.1 Definition of Payment Systerm 支付体系的定义

A payment system is the means whereby cash value is transferred between a payer's bank account and a payee's bank account. It includes:

(1) policies and procedures, including rules for crediting and debiting balances;

(2) a medium for storing and transmitting payment information;

(3) financial intermediaries for organizing information flow, carrying out value transfer instructions, and generally administering payment activities.

12.1.2 Facilities of Payment Systerm 支付体系的便利

There are four types of value transfer (coin and currency, check, wire, and automated clearing house). These are designated as primary payment systems because each one alone is sufficient to transfer value from one party to another. There are also different types of secondary payment systems that convey payment information but ultimately require one of the primary payment systems to transfer value.

12.2 Some Major Payment Systems 几种主要的支付体系

12.2.1 SWIFT 环球银行同业电子电讯系统

1. The SWIFT Concept

1) Establishment

SWIFT (Society for Worldwide Inter-bank Financial Telecommunication) is a computerized international telecommunications system that, through standardized formatted messages, rapidly processes and transmits financial transactions and information among its members around the world.[1]

The need for this type of system was first recognized in the late 1960s. A study of international inter-bank transactions was conducted by a group of European and North American banks. As a result, in 1973, 239 of the largest European and North American banks from 15 countries joined together to establish SWIFT, a Belgian bank-owned nonprofit cooperative society. The Bank of New York was the first American bank to connect to SWIFT.

2) Development

The SWIFT network has grown considerably since 1973. SWIFT has been in continuous operations since May 9, 1977, four years after the foundation of the company in May 1973.

This system by 1983 connected over a thousand banks in various countries and carried an average of 400,000 messages per day.

Its membership now consists of nearly 8,100 international financial institutions (including branches) in over 207 countries. SWIFT members include banks, broker-dealers and investment managers. The broader SWIFT community also encompasses corporates as well as market infrastructures in payments, securities, treasury and trade. Over the past ten years, SWIFT message prices have been reduced over 80%, and system availability approaches 5×9 reliability — 99.999% of uptime. It currently carries an average of 12.49 million messages per day and on 1 March, 2007, messages carried is 14,729,184.

SWIFT is a step forward to improve the cooperation among international correspondent banks. The lengthy pipelines and slow response time of paper and mail-based systems are no longer considered adequate. Much of the paper produced by the banks is already computer generated, and on receipt at the destination bank the same information has to be transferred from the paper to the bank's computer system.

The network covers most of Western Europe, North America, parts of South America and the Far East. It is a four-center financial transaction control system, with banks connecting their terminals to programmable concentrators in each country.

2. The SWIFT Benefits

SWIFT benefits[2] are many and apply not only to SWIFT members but also to their correspondent banks and customers. The system enables member banks to transmit between themselves international payments, statements and other transactions associated with international banking. The use of the network is more convenient and reliable than past methods of communication (mail, telex and cable), and enables the banks to offer a better service to their customers.

SWIFT is an international communications network connecting the world major banks, enabling its members from different countries to get in touch with each other. The banks use computer systems to speed up the transfer of international payments and other business. Financial messages will be passed on, stored, with test keys added automatically. When the test keys have been verified, messages will be categorized and handled automatically, too. This switching system operates 24 hours, seven days a week and can achieve same-day transfer. It has demonstrated to the world its high speed and accuracy. The principal function of SWIFT is to provide its member banks with access to the system for the settlement of international money transfers.

However, SWIFT itself is not a system allowing member banks to settle payments among them; settlements among banks still require an international clearing house such as CHIPS.

Some of the beneficial features of SWIFT are given as follows:

(1) Faster, more reliable communication. SWIFT messages can be transmitted worldwide within seconds. SWIFT service is available to its members 24 hours a day.

(2) Reduced transaction errors. Standardized formats decrease the potential for misinterpreted information.

(3) Lower transmission costs. The cost of a SWIFT transaction is much less than the cost of other methods of electronic communication.

(4) Greater efficiency. SWIFT's standardized formats permit automated handling of transactions, eliminating the need for operator intervention.

(5) Better statistics. Detailed transaction statements provide auditable records of incoming and outgoing transactions.

(6) Increased security. All SWIFT transmissions are encrypted to insure their integrity. In addition, funds transfer-type messages are verified through a SWIFT "Authenticator", thus providing further protection from fraud.

3. The SWIFT Messages

SWIFT is a fully integrated computer transmission system where messages can be transmitted in a standard format. The SWIFT system imposes certain standards for procedures and message formats. This, coupled with the ability to transmit and receive messages in computer-readable form, facilitates the automation of the banks' international payment business. The problem of account reconciliation is also eased as the system can be used for the frequent transmission of statements.

Message Test Standards have been designed and users are able to transmit all types of customer and bank transfers as confirmation of foreign exchange deals, statements, collection and documentary credit messages.

All SWIFT messages are formalized, containing routine and systematic information, as well as text. For each message type, a format is defined by specifying a number of fields, the presence of which may be mandatory or optional. Field contents are governed by the rules laid down in the Message Text Standards.

Although each operating center features fully duplicated computer configurations, a four-center design is used for increased security, should one center become unavailable through natural catastrophe, industrial action or sabotage. Each configuration has enough capacity to handle the entire traffic load.

4. The SWIFT Operation

SWIFT messages are transmitted from country to country via central, interconnected to operating centers located in Brussels, Amsterdam, and Culpeper of Virginia.[3] These operating centers are in turn connected by international data-transmission lines to regional processors in most member countries.

Banks in an individual country use the available national communication facilities to send messages to the regional processor. Technically, a member bank in SWIFT has computer "hook-ups" in the systems that permit banks to relay funds to one another simultaneously.

Message flow is like this, as Figure 12-1 shows.

(1) The appropriate SWIFT message type is selected, prepared, addressed and released by the sender to the SWIFT network via the bank's SWIFT interface.

(2) The message is then sent to the sender's local SWIFT Regional Processor.

(3) The input Regional Processor forwards the SWIFT message to a Slice Processor.

(4) If the message is properly formatted, it is sent to the Receiver's local SWIFT Regional Processor. (Messages that are improperly formatted are returned to the sender along with an explanation of the error.)

(5) The output Regional Processor then sends the message to the Receiver. Usually the message is received a few seconds after it has been transmitted by the Sender. If the Receiver is unable to accept the message, it is periodically retransmitted.

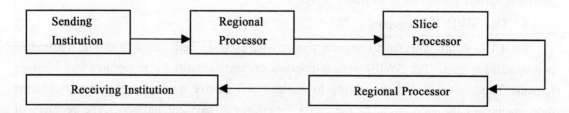

Figure 12-1　The message flow of SWIFT

5. Types of Transfers

SWIFT message types are identified by a three-digit number. The first digit identifies the category and the second and third digits identify the message's type. This three-digit number allows the receiver to direct the message to an appropriate area within its organization.[4] The common SWIFT messages are divided into ten types.

(1) Customer transfer.

(2) Financial institution transfers.

(3) Collection cash letters.

(4) Foreign exchange deal and loan.

(5) Securities.

(6) Precious metals and syndication.

(7) Traveler's checks.

(8) Documentary credit and guarantees.

(9) Statement.

(10) SWIFT cables.

Table 12 – 1 shows an example of funds transfer type messages.

Table 12 – 1 An example of funds transfer type messages

Category	Three Digit Number	Message Type
(1) Customer Transfer	100	Customer Transfer
(2) Financial Institute Transfer	200 201 202 203	Financial Institution Transfer for Its Own Account Multiple Financial Institution Transfer for Its Own Account General Financial Institution Transfer Multiple General Financial Institution Transfer

12.2.2 CHIPS 票据交换所银行同业清算系统

1. CHIPS: a Settlement System

In New York City, a pseudo-wire system handles an enormous volume of cash flow between local financial institutions. CHIPS stands for Clearing House Inter-bank Payment System. It is a settlement system involving primarily about 135 New York City financial institutions and is operated by the New York Clearing House Association. Many other institutions have access to CHIPS through offices or correspondents in New York City.

2. CHIPS: a Netting System

CHIPS works as a netting system (see Figure 12-2). This means that only information, and not value, is transferred during a specified time period. At the end of the time period (for CHIPS the period is one business day) only the net amount is actually transferred from one party to the other.[5] If bank A sends $10,000,000 in transfers to bank B and bank B sends $8,000,000 in transfers to bank A, only the net amount of $2,000,000 is transferred at the end of the day.

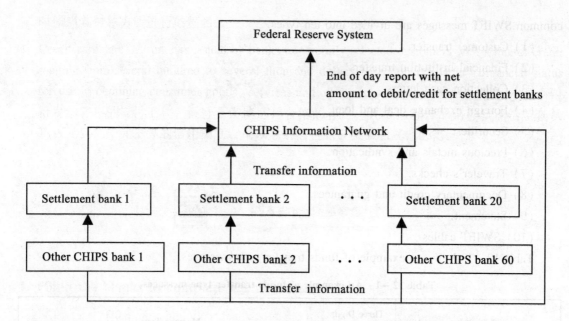

Figure 12-2 CHIPS netting system

3. Operation of CHIPS

During the day, member banks send instructions to CHIPS regarding transfers that they wish to make to other banks in New York City. Only information flows during the day. In the evening, value transfer occurs. There are two classes of banks in CHIPS. Settlement banks are the largest New York City banks. At the end of the day CHIPS reports to the Federal Reserve Bank of New York the net amounts to debit and credit at each of the settlement banks. Non-settlement banks use the larger settlement banks as correspondents to settle their accounts with CHIPS.

4. Daily Volume of CHIPS

CHIPS processes over 320,000 payments a day with a gross value of \$1.6 trillion. It is a premier payments platform serving the largest banks from around the world, representing 19 countries world wide. Over its 37 year history, CHIPS has developed and maintained a reputation of reliability, efficiency and innovation in the marketplace by processing over 95% of the USD cross-border payments. Most international dollar-based transactions flow through New York correspondent banks that clear transactions through CHIPS. And now, with new value-added features CHIPS is the leading system for all large value payment needs—both international and domestic.

12.2.3 CHAPS 票据交换所自动支付系统

1. What Is CHAPS?

1) Definition of CHAPS

CHAPS (Clearing House Automated Payment System) is an electronic transfer system for sending same-day value payments from bank to bank. It operates in partnership with the Bank of

England in providing the payment and settlement service. CHAPS was developed in 1984, and is one of the largest real-time gross settlement systems in the world, second only to Fed Wire in the US.

2) Services offered by CHAPS

CHAPS offers its members and their participants an efficient, risk-free, reliable same-day payment mechanism. Every CHAPS payment is unconditional, irrevocable and guaranteed. CHAPS is available nationwide in Britain and is operated by a number of settlement banks who communicate directly through computers. Payments sent through the system are guaranteed and unconditional, and cleared on a same-day basis. Inter-bank settlement is effected electronically at the end of each day through the settlement banks' accounts held at the Bank of England.

3) New development of CHAPS

Since 4 January 1999, the CHAPS Clearing Company has operated two separate clearings, CHAPS Sterling and CHAPS Euro. The CHAPS Company is managed by a board of directors drawn from its member banks, led by a Company Chairman and the CHAPS Company Manager.

4) Operation of CHAPS

The system operates as follows (see Figure 12-3): Each bank sends instructions of the payments to be made to the other banks through a so-called "gateway". This uses common software and there is no central executive on computer. Once the messages have been accepted in the system as being authentic they cannot be revoked. This allows same day transfer throughout the clearing system. Larger companies may be able to link their own technology into the system and operate payments and receipts electronically. Small companies can instruct their banks to make these payments in the usual way—by telephone call. CHAPS also means that the expensive telegraphic transfer need no longer be used. At the same time, treasurers of companies are able to monitor their cash positions more easily.

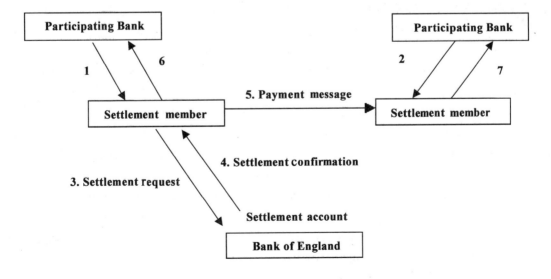

Figure 12-3 Operation of CHAPS

2. CHAPS Members

The following 20 member banks currently participate in the euro and/or sterling clearings.

Abbey National	Den Norske Bank
ABN AMRO Bank	Deutsche Bank
Bank of America	Dresdner Bank
Bank of England	First Union National Bank
Bank of Scotland	HSBC Bank
Bank of Tokyo — Mitsubishi	Lloyds TSB Group
Barclays Bank	National Westminster Bank
Chase Manhattan	National Australia Bank
Citibank	Royal Bank of Scotland
Co-operative Bank	Standard Chartered Bank

12.2.4 Fed Wire/Fedwire 联储银行支付系统

1. Brief Introduction

This is a fund transfer system operated nationwide in the USA by the Federal Reserve System (the Fed, Central Bank of the USA). This fund-transfer network handles transfers from one financial institution to another with an account balance held with the Fed. The transfer of reserve account balances is used for the buying and selling of Fed funds, and credit transfers on behalf of bank customers. An institution that maintains an account at a Reserve Bank generally is allowed to be a Fedwire participant. These institutions include Federal Reserve member banks, nonmember depository institutions, and certain other institutions, such as US branches and agencies of foreign banks.

Participants use Fedwire to instruct a Reserve Bank to debit funds from the participant's own Reserve Bank account and credit the Reserve Bank account of another participant. Fedwire processes and settles payment orders individually throughout the operating day. Payment to the receiving participant over Fedwire is final and irrevocable when the amount of the payment order is credited to the receiving participant's account or when the payment order is sent to the receiving participant, whichever is earlier. Fedwire participants send payment orders to a Reserve Bank on line, by initiating an electronic message, or off line, via telephone. Payment orders must be in the proper syntax and meet the relevant security controls. An institution sending payment orders to a Reserve Bank is required to have sufficient funds, either in the form of account balances or overdraft capacity, or a payment order may be rejected.

In 2005, Fedwire processed an average daily volume of approximately 528,000 payments, with an average daily value of approximately \$2.1 trillion. The distribution of these payments is highly skewed, with a median value of approximately \$32,000 and an average value of approximately \$3.9 million. Roughly 10 percent of Fedwire payments are for more than \$1 million. Approximately 7,500 depository institutions are eligible to initiate or receive funds transfers over Fedwire. Use of Fedwire, however, is also highly skewed. Ninety-four participants

Chapter 12 International Payment Systems

account for 80 percent of the volume of payments, and twenty-four participants account for 80 percent of the value of payments.

2. Fund Transfer Operations under Fed Wire

(1) In making a Fedwire transfer, a payer gives instructions to a bank in which the payer has an available balance.

(2) The paying bank passes instructions on to the Fed to move value from the bank's reserve balance account to the reserve balance account of another bank in which the payee has an account.

(3) Though initially generated by voice, paper instructions, or electronic means, the actual transfer of value is merely a bookkeeping entry at the Fed. The Fed credits the reserve account of the payee's bank and debits the reserve account of the payer's bank.

(4) Wires also provide a confirmation number to the payer so that the transaction can be traced.

(5) When a bank receives an incoming wire, the receiving firm is given notification that value has been received. This is also an important feature for many types of transactions. No other mechanism provides confirmation help and notification to the parties in a payment transaction.

3. Drawback

Unfortunately, wires do not permit much additional information to be carried along with the wire information. It is not uncommon for a firm to receive a wire payment and to be in the dark concerning the purpose of the payment.

New Words and Expressions

configuration	[kənˌfigjuˈreiʃən]	n.	构造，结构，配置，外形
hook-up	[ˈhukˌʌp]	n.	连接（电脑）
administer	[ədˈministə]	v.	管理，给予，执行
format	[ˈfɔːmæt]	n.	版式，格式
netting	[ˈnetiŋ]	n.	净额结算
pipeline	[ˈpaipˌlain]	n.	管道，传递途径
terminal	[ˈtəːminl]	n.	终点站，终端，接线端
encrypt	[inˈkript]	v.	加密，将……译成密码
integrity	[inˈtegriti]	n.	完整，完全，完整性
gateway	[ˈgeitwei]	n.	门，通路，网关
encompass	[inˈkʌmpəs]	v.	包围，环绕，包含或包括某事物
uptime	[ˈʌptaim]	n.	（计算机等的）正常运行时间
relay	[ˌriːˈlei]	v.	（消息、货物等）分程传递，使接替，转播，得到接替
interface	[ˈintəfeis]	n.	[地质] 分界面，接触面，[物、化] 界面
skew	[skjuː]	a.	歪斜的
median	[ˈmiːdiən]	a.	中央的
		n.	中部，当中，[数学] 中线，中值

account reconciliation 账户调节，账目核对	Abbey National 伦敦阿比国民银行
payment system 支付体系	Den Norske Bank 挪威银行
cash value 现金价值	ABN AMRO Bank 荷兰银行
bank account 银行账户	Deutsche Bank 德意志银行
payment information 支付信息	Bank of America 美洲银行
test key 密码，密押	Dresdner Bank 德国德累斯顿银行
automated clearing house 自动票据交换所	Bank of England 英格兰银行
cash position 现金头寸	First Union National Bank 第一联合国民银行
secondary payment system 次支付体系	Bank of Scotland 苏格兰银行
settlement bank 结算银行	HSBC Bank 汇丰银行
bookkeeping entry 簿记入账	Lloyds TSB Group 劳合TSB银行
customer transfer 客户汇款	Barclays Bank 巴克莱国际银行
Fed Wire/Fedwire 联储银行支付系统	Chase Manhattan 大通曼哈顿银行
financial intermediary 金融中介	National Australia Bank 澳大利亚国民银行
CHAPS 票据交换所自动支付系统	Citibank 花旗银行
non-settlement bank 非结算银行	Royal Bank of Scotland 苏格兰皇家银行
primary payment system 主支付体系	Co-operative Bank 台湾合作银行
fund transfer system 资金调拨系统	Bank of Tokyo-Mitsubishi 东京－三菱银行
reserve balance account 储备余额账户	Standard Chartered Bank 标准渣打银行（麦加利银行）
CHIPS 票据交换所银行同业清算系统	precious metals and syndication 贵金属和辛迪加
Federal Reserve System 联邦储备系统	foreign exchange deal and loan 外汇买卖和放款
financial institution transfers 银行头寸调拨	non-profit cooperative society 非盈利性合作协会
National Westminster Bank 国民西敏斯特银行	

Notes

1. SWIFT (Society for Worldwide Inter-bank Financial Telecommunication) is a computerized international telecommunications system that, through standardized formatted messages, rapidly processes and transmits financial transactions and information among its members around the world. 环球银行金融电讯协会（SWIFT）是一个计算机化的国际电信系统，通过标准化的、格式化的信息，该系统能迅速处理并在全球会员银行间传递金融业务与信息。

2. SWIFT 具有许多优点。
   （1）Faster, more reliable communication. 沟通更快、更可靠。
   （2）Reduced transaction errors. 交易错误锐减。
   （3）Lower transmission costs. 传递成本更低廉。

Chapter 12 International Payment Systems

(4) Greater efficiency.　效率更高。

(5) Better statistics.　统计更精确。

(6) Increased security.　安全系数更高。

3. SWIFT messages are transmitted from country to country via central, interconnected to operating centers located in Brussels, Amsterdam, and Culpeper of Virginia.　环球银行金融电讯协会与三个分别位于布鲁塞尔、阿姆斯特丹、弗吉尼亚州库尔佩珀市的操作中心互相连接,通过中枢系统将电文从一国传送到另一国。

4. SWIFT message types are identified by a three-digit number. The first digit identifies the category and the second and third digits identify the message's type. This three-digit number allows the receiver to direct the message to an appropriate area within its organization.
SWIFT的信息由三位数来识别,第一位数识别范畴,第二和第三位数识别信息类型。这个三位数使信息接收者能将信息发至组织内部适当的部门。

5. CHIPS works as a netting system. This means that only information, and not value, is transferred during a specified time period. At the end of the time period (for CHIPS the period is one business day) only the net amount is actually transferred from one party to the other.
票据交换所银行间支付系统(CHIPS)是一个净额交易系统,即在一个规定的时间内传递的只是信息而非价值,在该期限末(对CHIPS而言,该期限为一个营业日),仅有净额才发生由一方至另一方的实际转移。

1. Fill in the blanks to complete each sentence.

(1) There are different types of secondary payment systems that convey _____ but ultimately require one of the primary payment systems to _____.

(2) Fedwire provides a _____ to the payer so that the transaction can be traced. When a bank receives an incoming wire, the receiving firm is given notification that value has been received. No other mechanism provides _____ to the parties in a payment transaction.

(3) The fact that the SWIFT system imposes certain standards _____ and the ability to transmit and receive messages in _____ form facilitates the automation of the banks' international payment business.

(4) CHIPS works as a netting system, which means that only _____, not _____, is transferred during a specified time period. At the end of one business day only the

_____ is actually transferred from one party to the other.

(5) SWIFT network system operates 24 hours for seven days a week on end and can achieve same-day transfer, and has been displaying to the world its _____.

(6) The principal function of SWIFT is to provide its member banks with _____.

(7) Some of the beneficial features of SWIFT are as follows: _____, reduced transaction errors, _____, greater efficiency and better statistics, and increased security.

(8) SWIFT itself is not a system allowing member banks to settle payments among them; settlements among banks would still require _____ such as CHIPS.

(9) SWIFT's _____ decrease the potential for misinterpreted information and permit automated handling of transactions, eliminating the need for operator intervention.

(10) CHAPS stands for _____, it is an electronic transfer system for sending same-day value payments from bank to bank. It operates in partnership with _____ in providing the payment and settlement service.

2. **Define the following terms.**

   (1) payment system
   (2) SWIFT
   (3) CHIPS
   (4) CHAPS
   (5) Fed Wire

3. **Translate the following terms into English.**

   (1) 现金头寸　　　　　　　　　　(2) 入账
   (3) 金融中介　　　　　　　　　　(4) 客户汇款
   (5) 账目核对　　　　　　　　　　(6) 联储银行支付系统
   (7) 非结算银行　　　　　　　　　(8) 资金调拨系统
   (9) 次支付体系　　　　　　　　　(10) 储备余额账户
   (11) 自动票据交换所　　　　　　　(12) 银行头寸调拨
   (13) 非盈利性合作协会　　　　　　(14) 外汇买卖和存放款
   (15) 票据交换所银行同业清算系统

4. **Decide whether the following statements are true or false.**

   (1) Non-settlement banks use the larger settlement banks as correspondents to settle their accounts with CHIPS. (　)

   (2) Under CHIPS, each bank sends instructions of the payments to be made to the other banks. Once the messages have been accepted in the system as being authentic they cannot be revoked. (　)

   (3) Three-digit number identifies SWIFT message types. The first digit identifies the type and the second and third digits identify the message's category. This three-digit number allows the receiver to direct the message to an appropriate area within its organization.

( )

(4) If the message sent to the Receiver's local SWIFT Regional Processor is improperly formatted, it will be returned to the sender along with an explanation of the error. ( )

(5) Since each operating center of SWIFT features fully duplicated computer configurations, should one center become unavailable through natural catastrophe, industrial action or sabotage, each configuration has too limited capacity to handle the entire traffic load. ( )

5. Choose the best answer to each of the following statements or questions.

(1) A payment system includes policies and procedures, a medium for storing and transmitting payment information and ___.
   A. rules for crediting and debiting balances
   B. financial intermediaries
   C. financial transactions and information
   D. financial institution transfers

(2) The purpose of financial intermediaries is to organize information flow, ___, and generally administer payment activities.
   A. carry out value transfer instructions
   B. process financial transactions
   C. authenticate the system
   D. settle payments

(3) Each primary payment system alone is sufficient to transfer value from one party to another. Which of the following is not a primary payment system?
   A. Coin and currency.   B. Check.
   C. Wire and automated clearing house.   D. Charge card.

(4) The SWIFT network by now carries an average of ___ messages per day.
   A. 400,000   B. 12.49 million
   C. 3,000   D. 200,000

(5) Unfortunately, wires do not permit much additional information to be carried along with the ___. It is not uncommon for a firm to receive a wire payment and to be in the dark concerning the purpose of the payment.
   A. confirmation number   B. notification
   C. wire information   D. bookkeeping entry

Chapter 13

International Non-trade Payments and Settlements
国际非贸易支付与结算

> **In this chapter, you will learn:**
> ☑ Definition and parties of traveler's check
> ☑ Procedure and advantage of traveler's check
> ☑ Definition and parties of credit card
> ☑ Procedure and function of credit card

International payment and settlement include trade settlement, the settlement of visible trade (exports and imports of goods and commodities) and non-trade settlement, the settlement of invisible trade. Invisible trade is the part of international trade that does not involve the transfer of goods or tangible objects. It is mostly generated by the overseas activities of tertiary industries. Invisible trade is comprised of invisible imports and invisible exports. International non-trade settlement includes the following items.

(1) Credit cards (entrusted cashing and issuance).
(2) Remittance.
(3) Traveler's checks in FX.
(4) Traveler's letter of credit.
(5) Exchange bills, etc.

13.1 Traveler's Check 旅行支票

13.1.1 Definition 定义

A traveler's check is a specially printed form of check issued by a financial institution, leading hotels, and other agencies in preprinted denominations for a fixed amount to a customer for use when he is going to travel abroad.[1] The issuer commits himself to pay the stated sum to any payee and undertakes to repay the purchaser if the check is lost or stolen before it is cashed. A traveler's check is actually a draft on a bank or other agency, which is self-identifying and may be cashed at banks, hotels, etc., either throughout the world or in particular areas only.

13.1.2 Parties 当事人

There are five parties to a traveler's check, namely, the issuer, the selling agent or office, the purchaser or the holder, the paying agent or the person who encashes the traveler's check and the transferee.[2]

1. Issuer

The issuer is the financial institution, leading hotels or other agencies issuing the traveler's check. If the issuer is a bank, it is called the issuing bank or the drawee bank, for the check is drawn on the issuer. The name and address of the issuer usually appear on the upper part of the check. A valid traveler's check should bear the printed facsimile of the issuer's authorized signature.

2. Selling Agent or Office

The selling agent or office is one that sells the traveler's check. If the issuer sells the check by itself, then it is acting as the selling agent or office. If the issuer dispatches its traveler's checks to its branches or correspondents in other countries for sale, the latter is acting as its selling agents. All dispatches of the traveler's checks are to be advised to their selling agents by the issuer. Receipt is to be acknowledged by the selling agent, usually on a form attached to the advice of dispatch. If the traveler's checks do not reach the selling agent in due time, he must inform the issuer by cable. The selling agents shall keep separate accounts to record the total amount of checks that they have received and sold. The sales proceeds must be remitted to the issuer at once.

3. Purchaser or Holder

The purchaser is a person who buys a traveler's check from the issuer or his selling agent. When purchasing the check, he must sign his name thereon at the counter of the issuer or his selling agent, thereby making himself a holder of the instrument. Any unused checks may be returned to the issuing bank or the selling agent for refund.

4. Paying Agent

The paying agent is one that undertakes by arrangement with the issuer to pay the latter's traveler's checks when presented by the holder. The paying agent, on honoring a check, pays the holder in local currency at the current rate of exchange, then sends the check forward for collection and instructs the issuing bank to pay the proceeds either to its account or to some other bank for credit to its account.

5. Transferee

The transferee is one to whom the traveler's check is transferred. If the purchaser or the holder makes use of the traveler's check to pay a bill of any hotel or restaurant or an invoice of any shop, the hotel, restaurant, or shop becomes the transferee.

13.1.3 Procedures 结算的流程

1. Purchase

(1) The traveler first fills in an application form in which the total amount and denominations needed are indicated, requesting the issuer or his selling agent to sell him the traveler's checks.

(2) The clerk or the bank teller then takes out the checks from the inventory and records the number (each traveler's check is numbered) of the check to be sold on the purchaser's purchase receipt along with the purchaser's name and address.

(3) The purchaser signs his name on the face of each check in a designated place in the presence of the clerk or the teller and pays the amount equivalent to the total value of the checks plus a small commission, usually one percent or less.

(4) The purchaser receives the checks, together with a list of the checks' serial numbers of which it is advisable to be carried separately from the checks.

2. Encashment

(1) Whenever the traveler desires to cash one or more of the traveler's checks during a trip, he or she countersigns on each check in a designated place in the presence of the cashier of a store, a hotel or a bank.[3]

(2) The cashier then compares this signature with that already signed thereon. If the two signatures are identical with each other, the cashier encashes the traveler's check. If the countersignature differs slightly from the initial signature, the holder may be requested to endorse his name on the back of the check in the presence of the cashier. The encashment by the paying agent is subject to the endorsement, which should be identical with the initial signature. Sometimes the submission of the presenter's passport or some other official identity with his photograph affixed may be required.

3. Claims

One of the most important features of the traveler's check favorable to the purchaser or the holder is that in case the checks are lost or stolen, they will be replaced. Once the checks are lost the loser should notify the issuer either directly or more often through one of its local selling agent. The issuer will replace the lost checks as quickly as possible, frequently within hours. If the losers fail to keep a separate listing of their check numbers, they may encounter a delay in time in obtaining the replaced checks, for the issuer will seek to identify the missing check numbers from computer records.

13.1.4 Advantages 优点

(1) Traveler's checks are safer than foreign bank notes and coins. The issuer will soon replace the lost or stolen checks which have not been encashed.

(2) Traveler's checks are readily encashable at banks, hotels, railway stations, airports and many commercial firms abroad because of their wide acceptability.

(3) Different denominations of traveler's checks facilitate their use by the traveler to meet his needs during a trip.

(4) Traveler's checks are not as bulky as an ordinary wallet full of bank notes for the same total amount.

(5) No time limit is set to the circulation of the traveler's checks, for in general, no expiry date is specified in the check.

13.2　Credit Card　信用卡

13.2.1　Definition　定义

Credit cards are instruments issued by banks to carefully selected customers with a line of credit ranging from several hundred to several thousand dollars based on the latter's financial status for use in obtaining consumer goods, services and other necessities on credit.[4] They may be used, in effect, as a substitute for money. By using these cards commodities can be bought, hotel bills paid, and airfares met without paying any cash in many regions of the world.

In other words, credit cards are a short-term small amount consumer's credit extended by a bank. Credit cards are often used by those who have a current account with the card-issuing bank and whose credit is good. A credit card is a small plastic with the name of the bank printed on it, a specimen of the user's signature, the number of the card and the expiry date, embossed with the cardholder's name, his signature, account number and an expiry date for card.

The best known cards in the world are American Express Card, Diners Club Card, Visa Card, Master Card, Federal Card, etc.

13.2.2　Parties　当事人

1. Issuing Bank

The bank issues the card that extends a small amount of short-term credit to its customers, first by careful selection and evaluation of the customers and then issuance of a line of credit.

2. Cardholder

It refers to the customer who has a current account with the card-issuing bank and whose credit is good, and who based on his financial status can obtain, on credit, consumer goods, services and other things when necessary.

3. Merchant

It refers to store, hotel or restaurant that is bound to have a pre-arrangement with the card-issuing bank and is willing to accept the credit card for payment of commodities sold or services rendered.

13.2.3　Procedures　结算的流程

Credit cards provide control and also smooth the relationship between the issuing bank, cardholder and the merchant in terms of payment. The issuing bank plays a dominant role in the process of issuance, application and clearing of cards while keeping in close contact with the individual users and merchants. The procedure goes as follows:

1. The Issuance of Cards

a. The client fills in an application form according to the requirements and regulations set forth by the bank.

b. The bank investigates and examines the annual income and the credit standing of the client before approving the issuance of cards. An entrance fee and/or annual membership dues may be charged to the cardholder. Some credit cards are given to the holders free of charge.

2. Setting up Relations with Merchants and Authorization

Credit cards have to be widely accepted by what is called the merchant or assigned merchant, i.e. shops, hotels, restaurants, airports, that agree to accept credit cards prior to an agency agreement signed between the bank and the merchant. This agreement is a promise made by the merchant. Accordingly, the bank becomes the merchant bank and the merchant becomes assigned merchant. Rights, duties and obligations shall be expressly stipulated in the agreement. Staff members of the merchant are to be trained by the bank and the merchant as to the essential steps of handling credit cards.

Authorization is an important step by which the bank controls the credit of the cardholder in the process of its circulation and a means by which the bank bridges the relations between the individual and the merchant through the consumption of goods or services by the cardholder. In the agreement between the merchant and the bank, a credit limit is usually set out for the customer. Much larger limits can be granted to selected customers. The cardholder is expected not to exceed the ceiling limit in using the card; otherwise the merchant has to contact the acquirer and obtain permission to accept the largest amount.

3. Clearing and Settlement

The bank is the center dealing with the clearing and settlement between the cardholder, merchant and the bank. Steps necessary in the actual use of the card are as follows:

a. When the cardholder purchases goods or services from the merchant, he should sign a sales slip and hand it together with his card to the merchant.

Sales slips are provided to record all the details of each transaction. A part of the required information is hand-written on the sales slip and the remaining obtained by processing the credit card and sales slip through an imprinter provided by the card-issuing bank. While processing, the imprinter will record on the sales slip the cardholder's name and account number, card expiration date, merchant's name and account number. Other information such as date, description of merchandise purchased or services rendered, total amount, etc., is filled in by the clerk.

b. The merchant examines the card carefully to determine whether the card is a valid or a forged one, and whether it is expired or not. If the card is valid, the merchant then delivers the goods to the cardholder.

c. The merchant presents to the bank the sales slip bearing the signature of the cardholder.

d. The bank effects payment of the amount on the slip, less a discount ranging from one to

Chapter 13 International Non-trade Payments and Settlements

several percent allowed to the bank. The discount depends on the volume of the credit card sales generated by the merchant, the types of goods sold or services rendered and the competitiveness among banks in the area.

e. The bank issues monthly bills to the cardholder for his purchases.

f. The cardholder repays the amount to the bank. He has the option of paying the bill in full within a grace period (usually 25 days) without interest or drawing revolving credit with an interest usually higher than a 90-day commercial paper discount rate.

Figure 13-1 illustrates the procedure of credit card.

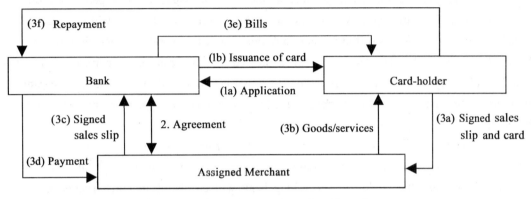

Figure 13-1 The procedure of credit card

13.2.4 Functions 功能

Credit cards have been in fashion for decades and are currently issued in various countries that are active in tourism. They contribute to the development of new contrivances for the benefit of consumers, tourism and business travels and for the generation of foreign exchange. As is well known to all, a credit card is one of the most popular banking instruments in the conduct of retailing banking business nowadays. Specifically, a credit card avoids the need of carrying too much cash or bulky traveler's checks, allows cash to be drawn at banks as and when required without planning it beforehand, and serves as a useful "back-up" if traveler's checks or bank notes are lost or stolen.

In general, as an important financial tool credit card offers the following benefits.

(1) They can be safer and more convenient to use and carry than cash.

(2) Credit cards offer the ability to buy goods and services now and pay for them later.

(3) They have valuable consumer protections under the law.

(4) Major credit cards are accepted by merchants around the world.

(5) They may provide a source of cash or payment in an emergency.

(6) Credit cards can guarantee hotel or travel reservations.

(7) If you are not happy with a purchase you made using a credit card, you may have the right to withhold payment until the problem is resolved.

13.3 Traveler's Letter of Credit 旅行信用证

Traveler's letter of credit is another form of the credit instrument to be used to avoid both the trouble and the risk of carrying a large sum in cash when a tourist travels abroad. But nowadays most tourists use traveler's checks and credit cards. So we only discuss this instrument briefly.

A tourist, when applying for a traveler's letter of credit, will be called upon to inform the issuing bank of the particular places he wishes to visit. The Issuing bank then advises its branches or correspondents located there of the letter of credit issued and sends each of them a specimen of the beneficiary's signature. In some cases, a document known as a "letter of indication" containing a specimen of the beneficiary's signature may be issued. The issuing bank may require the applicant to pay the full credit amount at the time of issue, or may permit a "drafts as presented" basis for settlement. As soon as the credit is issued, the traveler will be given a list of branches and correspondents of the issuing bank throughout the world from which drawings under this credit can be made. The letter of credit addressed to "the branches or correspondents of the bank", will imply an authority to encash drafts drawn hereunder, designate the drawee bank, fix the total amount available and its currency, set the expiry date, and bear the number and date of the credit.

The reimbursement method of the traveler's letter of credit is the same as other commercial letters of credit, such as claim on the issuing bank, claim on the reimbursing bank, etc.

When encashing the credit, the encashing bank will check the authorized signatures of the issuing bank on the credit to ensure the authenticity of the document. Each drawing is recorded on the back of the credit together with the encashing bank's stamp and date, so as to make certain that the credit limit will not be exceeded. A draft drawn on the issuing bank and signed by the beneficiary is to be paid by the encashing bank after verifying the beneficiary's signature to be identical with that shown in the letter of indication. The draft is then sent by the encashing bank to the issuing bank for reimbursement.

New Words and Expressions

emboss	[imˈbɔs]	v.	饰以浮饰，使浮雕出来
inventory	[ˈinvəntri]	n.	详细目录，存货，财产清册，总量
commit	[kəˈmit]	v.	约定，承诺，提交
facsimile	[fækˈsimili]	n.	摹写，传真
dispatch	[disˈpætʃ]	v.	分派，派遣
		n.	派遣
refund	[riˈfʌnd]	v./n.	归还，退还（资金）
denomination	[diˌnɔmiˈneiʃən]	n.	命名，（长度、大小、币值的）单位
countersignature	[ˌkauntəˈsignətʃə(r)]	n.	复签，连署
imprinter	[imˈprintə]	n.	盖印，印刻
option	[ˈɔpʃən]	n.	选项，选择权，[经] 期权
contrivance	[kənˈtraivəns]	n.	发明，发明才能，想出的办法，发明物

Chapter 13 International Non-trade Payments and Settlements

tertiary industry 第三产业，服务业	consumer's credit 消费者信贷
traveler's check 旅行支票	current account 往来账户
grace period 宽限期	American Express Card 美国运通卡
authorized signature 签字印鉴	Diners Club Card 大莱卡
selling agent 售票代理，售票行	Visa Card 签证卡，维萨卡
paying agent 兑付代理人	Federal Card 发达卡，联邦卡
purchase receipt 购货收据	credit standing 信用状况，资信情况
check's serial number 支票顺序号码	Master Card 万事达卡
initial signature 初签	membership dues 会员费
foreign bank note 外钞	assigned merchant 商户
commercial firm 商店，商行	merchant bank 商人银行
credit card 信用卡	entrance fee 入会费
line of credit 信用额度	sales slip 签购单，购物单
financial status 财务状况	description of merchandise 品名
on credit 以赊账或挂账的方式	retailing banking business 零售银行业务
consumer goods 消费品	

1. A traveler's check is a specially printed form of check issued by a financial institution, leading hotels, and other agencies in preprinted denominations for a fixed amount to a customer for use when he is going to travel abroad.   旅行支票是由金融机构、大型饭店及其他机构向顾客发行的一种某一固定面额的预先特别印制的支票，以供其在国外旅行过程中使用。

2. 旅行支票(Traveler's Check)有5个关系人：
   (1) 发行人(Issuer)；
   (2) 售票代理人或售票行(Selling Agent or Office)；
   (3) 购票人或持票人(Purchaser or Holder)；
   (4) 兑付代理人(Paying Agent)；
   (5) 受让人(Transferee)。

3. Whenever the traveler desires to cash one or more of the traveler's checks during a trip, he or she countersigns on each check in a designated place in the presence of the cashier of a store, a hotel or a bank.   旅游者在旅行过程中希望兑现一张或更多的旅行支票时，他（她）需要当着商店、饭店或银行出纳的面在每张支票的指定位置上复签。
   旅行支票的签名不同于其他票据，它有两次签名：初签（Initial signature）和复签（Counter Signature）。初签是在购买支票的时候由客户在支票正面签名，复签是在客户兑现支票的时候当着付款方所进行的签名。

4. Credit cards are instruments issued by banks to carefully selected customers with a line of credit ranging from several hundred to several thousand dollars based on the latter's financial status for use in obtaining consumer goods, services and other necessities on credit. 信用卡是由银行发给客户的支付工具，银行要谨慎选择合格的客户，并根据客户的财务状况给予其从几百元到几千元不等的信用额度，用以赊购消费品、服务和其他必需品。

Exercises

1. Fill in the blanks to complete each sentence.

(1) One of the most important features of the traveler's check favorable to the _____ is that in case the checks are lost or stolen, they will be _____.

(2) The purchaser of a traveler's check signs his name on the face of each check in a designated place in the presence of the _____ and pays the amount equivalent to the total values of the checks plus _____, usually one percent or less.

(3) The cashier compares _____ with _____. If the two signatures are identical with each other, the cashier encashes the traveler's check.

(4) As it is well known to all, a credit card is one of the most popular _____ in the conduct of _____ banking business nowadays.

(5) Credit cards have to be widely accepted by what is called _____, i.e. shops, hotels, restaurants, airports, that agree to accept credit cards.

(6) The bank investigates and examines the _____ of the client before approving the issuance of cards.

(7) The issuing bank plays a dominant role in the process of _____ of cards while keeping in close contact with the individual users and merchants.

(8) Credit cards are a short-term small amount _____ extended by a bank and are often used by those who have a _____ with the card-issuing bank and whose credit is good.

(9) If the card losers fail to keep a _____, they may encounter a delay in time in obtaining the replaced checks for the issuer will seek to identify the missing check numbers from the computer records.

(10) As far as the repayment of the amount to the bank is concerned, the credit card holder has the option of _____ within a grace period without interest or _____ with an interest usually higher than a 90 days commercial paper discount rate.

Chapter 13　International Non-trade Payments and Settlements

2. **Define the following terms.**

    (1) traveler's check
    (2) paying agent
    (3) credit cards
    (4) cardholder
    (5) merchant

3. **Translate the following terms into English.**

    (1) 初签
    (2) 入会费
    (3) 售票代理
    (4) 商户
    (5) 旅行支票
    (6) 购货收据
    (7) 往来账户
    (8) 签购单，购物单
    (9) 兑付代理人
    (10) 会员费
    (11) 消费者信贷
    (12) 签字印鉴
    (13) 美国运通卡
    (14) 非贸易结算
    (15) 零售银行业务

4. **Decide whether the following statements are true or false.**

    (1) The transferee is one to whom the traveler's check is transferred. If the purchaser or the holder makes use of the traveler's check to pay a bill of any hotel or restaurant or an invoice of any shop, the hotel, restaurant, or shop becomes the transferee. ( )

    (2) Any unused checks may not be returned to the issuing bank or the selling agent for refund. ( )

    (3) It is advisable for the purchaser to carry the list of check's serial numbers separately from the checks. ( )

    (4) In the agreement between the merchant and the bank, a credit limit is usually set out for the customer. The cardholder is expected not to exceed the ceiling limit in using the card. ( )

    (5) An entrance fee and/or annual membership dues are to be charged to the cardholder, so no credit cards are given to the holders free of charge. ( )

5. **Choose the best answer to each of the following statements or questions.**

    (1) There are five parties to a traveler's check, namely, the issuer, the selling agent or office, the purchaser or the holder, the ＿＿ or the person who encashes the traveler's check and the transferee.

    　　A. cardholder　　　　　　　　B. paying agent
    　　C. merchant　　　　　　　　　D. issuer

    (2) Traveler's checks have some advantages. Which of the following is not an advantage?

    　　A. Great safety and convenience.　　B. Wide acceptability.
    　　C. Different denominations.　　　　D. Short time limit.

(3) The ____ is the center dealing with the clearing and settlement of credit card.
   A. bank   B. cardholder
   C. merchant   D. transferee

(4) ____ is an important step by which the bank controls the credit of the cardholder in the process of its circulation and a means by which the bank bridges the relations between the individual and the merchant through the consumption of goods or services by the cardholder.
   A. Application   B. Verification
   C. Authorization   D. Test key

(5) Credit cards, currently issued in various countries that are most active in tourism, contribute to the development of new contrivances for the benefit of consumers, ____ and business travels and the generation of foreign exchange.
   A. financial industrial   B. tourism
   C. non-trade settlement   D. investment

Cyber-payments
电子支付

> 📢 **In this chapter, you will learn:**
> ☑ Introduction to cyber-payments
> ☑ Transfer of money in Internet
> ☑ Control of the electronic money
> ☑ Prospect of cyber-payment

14.1 Introduction to Cyber-payments 电子支付概述

14.1.1 Phenomenal Growth of E-commerce 电子商务的迅猛发展

International trade has undergone explosive growth in the past decade, and it is now possible to purchase goods and services from many more places and in more ways than ever before. Electronic commerce — the ability to purchase goods and services electronically, over the Internet, from around the world at any time of day or night — is currently experiencing phenomenal growth.[1] The World Wide Web (the Web) is quickly developing into a medium of high-speed digital transactions. A growing number of companies are taking advantage of the Web by selling products and services of all sorts, both to consumers and to other businesses. Although electronic commerce is now merely a fraction of total international trade, all indications are that there has been a virtual deluge of companies jumping into the arena.[2]

14.1.2 Internet: Parent of Cyber-payments 互联网：电子支付之母

The Internet is the parent of cyber-payments, and cyber-payments are the tactical method of buying goods and services over the Internet. Today, the Internet is reshaping the way business transactions are conducted. It is empowering both consumers and businesses by providing expanding markets and choices to not only national, but also international communities. It enriches competition in products and prices, and it drives change and improvement, given its ability to provide information and comparative choices.[3]

The Internet is a vast new frontier of consumer-to-business and business-to-business commerce. For consumers, Internet-based shopping holds an attraction because of its breadth of coverage and ease of use. For corporations, Internet-based commerce represents an as-yet largely untapped medium for expanding and growing of their business.

14.1.3　The Internet Demand Side　电子商务的需求

E-commerce activity over the Internet is currently at a relatively small fraction of what it will become. It is expected to grow almost 15 times from USD105 billion in 1999 to USD1.4 trillion by 2003, according to Jupiter Research. This is the Internet demand side of the equation of exchange. Buyers looking for the best deals may purchase goods from Singapore, Argentina or South Africa. With the Internet, the globalization of commerce has arrived, and both consumers and corporations have more choice to address their personal and corporate purchasing requirements. It raises global trade and global economic growth.

14.1.4　The Internet Supply Side　电子商务的供给

For the supply side, economies of scale take on a whole new meaning. Sellers of goods and services can expect not only local opportunities, but also national and global reach. The Internet expands opportunities to small producers with worthy products, and thrusts them into competition with their multinational big brothers.

14.1.5　Necessity of Developing Cyber-payments　发展电子支付的必要性

Putting up a Web site to promote and display products, and then luring online shoppers in to look around at the offerings, however, is only one dimension of conducting business via the Internet. To realize the true potential of electronic commerce, an effective method of receiving payment for products sold or delivered through the Internet is a necessity. Developing and implementing effective and simple "cyber-payment" methods is a major focus of current Internet-related research.

Terms like "electronic commerce", "e-cash", "cyber-money" and similar general and proprietary terms are tossed about casually in the press and in daily conversation, with little attention to just what these terms mean. Since there is as yet no standard terminology for the new forms of electronic-based payments, and the practitioners and specialists in various financial sectors apply their own special (and often different) technical definitions to common terms, there is great confusion.

14.1.6　Types of Electronic Cash Technologies　电子货币技术的种类

There are basically two types of electronic cash technologies: stored-value products (such as a JR Orange Card or an NTT telephone card) and access products (that process a transaction online, such as a bank ATM card). The concept of cyber-payments encompasses means of payment that use either (or a combination of both) of these technologies to effect fund transactions.

Primitive forms of electronic-based transaction systems have been around since last century (consider wiring "money" via telegraph).

A more recent form of electronic transactions that we are all familiar with is credit cards and ATM cards, which contain an encoded magnetic stripe that enables access to a line of credit or bank account, commonly by transmitting the encoded information over a phone line or network for approval.

Another common form is a magnetic stripe card that can store value (such as telephone cards). And being developed today are microchip-embedded "smart cards" that offer increased storage capacity, security, and applicability.

14.1.7　Role of Cyber-payments in E-commerce　电子支付在电子商务中的作用

Internet-based payment systems take the concept of electric commerce further, though, by facilitating financial transactions with other users. Since the personal computer that serves as the user's interface for Internet transactions can also store value, like the smart card it can act as both an access device and a stored-value device.

14.2　Cyber-payments Today　电子支付的现状

14.2.1　Definition of Cyber-payment　电子支付的定义

The term "cyber-payment" is just one of many used to describe systems that facilitate the transfer of financial value (i.e. digital currency, e-money). In fact, these developments may alter the means by which all types of financial transactions are conducted and financial payments systems are operated. This new technology will change many of the fundamental principles associated with a "cash" oriented society. Such transactions may occur via the Internet or through the use of "smart cards" which unlike debit or credit cards actually contain a microchip, which stores value on the card. Some cyber-payments systems use both. So the term "cyber-payment" can be used to define methods that have been implemented to transfer money. Cyber-payments refer to evolving new methods of financial transactions as today banks already can transfer money with computers. Cyber-payment is going to change the way people make payments. These payments could happen in Internet or in stores with "smart cards" that contain microchip, where the value of the card is stored.[4]

14.2.2　Advantages of Cyber-payments　电子支付的优点

The common element is that these systems are designed to provide the transacting parties with immediate, convenient, secure and potentially anonymous means by which to transfer financial value. When fully implemented, this technology will impact users worldwide and provide readily apparent benefits to legitimate commerce. These systems have been designed to give both to consumer and vendor a fast, easy to use, secure and possibly anonymous way to transfer money. After this system has been implemented completely, it'll affect users globally and enables normal commerce to profit from it.[5]

While it is currently possible to make purchases over the Internet, this form of commerce has not yet gained sufficient popularity to deem it a significant factor in foreign trade. Still, it does have potential.

The ability to order and pay for products over the Internet can revolutionize international trade. It can provide purchasers in one country with access to goods and services from another of which they might otherwise not even be aware.

Since many governments restrict imports of certain products and regulate advertising and other marketing tools within their national borders, purchasers are often forced to choose from a limited — or even monopolistic — supply of a desired product. With Internet access, purchasers can scour the world in minutes to find the right product at the best price.[6]

14.2.3 Disadvantages of Cyber-payments 电子支付的缺点

However, when fully implemented, this technology may also have the potential to facilitate the international movement of illicit funds. Unfortunately, after completely implemented, this system also has undesired side effects, as international transfer of illicit money becomes easier to do.

As home banking and Internet payment systems are more commonly used there are fewer and fewer face-to-face transactions. This makes it hard for the financial institutions to really know their customers. These faceless transactions make it harder to control and analyze movements of money, as transfers could be anonymous and paperless.[7]

Until recently, however, suppliers used the Internet primarily for advertising purposes. All orders were taken either over the telephone or by mail. While this certainly opened the door and paved the way for Internet commerce, it still required that business be conducted through traditional methods.

14.3 Transfer of Money on Internet 网上支付

Shopping at these days is easy and convenient with home shopping networks and mail order catalogs. What has been added is Internet shopping. As you surf in the Internet and come across to some vendor's home page you'll be able to purchase commodities.

14.3.1 Methods of Payment 支付的方法

In the Internet there are two common ways to make payments: phone orders and credit card orders.

In the case of phone orders, vendors use Web only for advertising and endorsing products. To order customers have to phone in their orders. The vendor takes order in as the contact had been made in TV, in newspaper or somewhere else.

Credit card orders means by using some secure methods of transferring credit card information to vendor. For some customers the idea of sending credit card information over Internet is not appealing.

14.3.2　Categories of Purchases　采购的分类

1. Small Purchases

Pay-per-view articles and information could be considered to be small purchases. The value of the transaction is often so small that they don't warrant the use of credit cards. Several solutions exist for micro-payments.

2. Medium and Large Purchases

These kinds of payments are the normal usage for credit cards. Sums usually range from tens to thousands. For these kinds of payments credit cards are probably the most often used method. Sums are high enough that it is warranted to use credit cards for payment. Credit card companies have tried for security reasons to come up with a scheme that could answer to this issue.

3. Private Purchases

People everywhere are concerned about what kind of trace is left from their purchases to the "Big Brother". Among these purchases might be special gifts that customer doesn't want his/her spouse to see or people just don't want authorities to mingle their life. In these cases electronic cash is a convenient way to provide anonymity.

14.3.3　Risks in Internet Paying　互联网支付的风险

Will customers and vendors risk investments into a service that is just coming onto the markets? If customers don't use system, vendors don't provide products and if vendors don't provide products, customers don't use services. This seems to be a newer ending circle.

Customers that are willing to make purchases are worried about the security in the Internet. They don't want to give their credit card information to someone without knowing who can use that information. It is interesting that people easily give credit card information over telephone conversation when buying items but don't like to do it from their computer.

Some of the systems have a very strict policy on privacy as power users of the Internet feel that privacy is the most important thing in the Internet. The rest of the users on the contrary have become very open to buy with credit cards.

14.3.4　Electronic Cash in the Internet　互联网上的电子现金

1. What Is Gained with This Scheme?

Most on-line transactions systems involve the debit of a customer's credit or debit card account. This type of system works well, but giving away a credit card or bank account number can expose purchasers to unnecessary risk of theft when used in an unsecured medium like the Internet. Several companies have developed systems to allow transactions to be conducted entirely over the Internet. In order to be effective, these systems must be able to validate the transaction, provide for non-repudiation by either party, and ensure at least some level of privacy for the parties to the transaction.

Electronic cash systems use digital signatures, which can be quickly verified with the entity that issued them to validate that the electronic currency represents actual value. A digital signature is a way to encrypt a message so that the recipient can decode it and be certain of the authenticity of the transaction. A measure of privacy can be added to the signature technology by utilizing a blind signature — digital signature with an additional number built-in and known only by the party owning it.

One of the biggest advantages of e-cash also draws much criticism. It offers the user complete anonymity, so the seller never knows who the buyer is — only that the buyer's e-cash is valid. On the other hand, since it is a cash-based system, buyers in countries that restrict capital outflow can more freely purchase goods and services from other countries without detection by the authorities.

Since this system is one of the most technologically simple, and coupled with the complete anonymity it offers, it is well placed to take advantage of the great increases anticipated in electronic commerce over the next few years. A number of companies have developed systems to facilitate electronic commerce; each system offers some advantages and some disadvantages.

Digital money makes it possible for customer to transfer money to their account to be used for making purchases over the Internet. Some systems make it possible to convert money to electronic cash, which is then stored to users' hard drive. This electronic cash is used when a customer makes purchase over the Internet, provided that seller is willing to accept that kind of payment. Seller then converts the electronic cash to money by sending needed information to system provider.

What is gained with this scheme?

(1) Privacy. By using electronic cash customer doesn't leave trace of himself/herself. System cannot link used electronic cash to customers. It is impossible to identify customers of the system. System provides total anonymity of the customer and so himself/herself doesn't have to worry about getting added to unwanted mailing lists. Of course if customer has purchased something that has to be delivered there is going to be trace left from the transaction. But when the merchandise is information that is sent over Internet there is no trace left after the purchase.

(2) Limited liability. If, for some reason, something goes wrong user only looses that amount of money that was stored into the hard drive. And in some cases even in this case lost money can be saved. People will more easily use system, if the only risk is loosing money in the electronic wallet compared to sending credit card information, that has 10,000 limit on it, over Internet.

2. Types of Electronic Cash

There are two different kinds of electronic cash: identified and anonymous.

Identified electronic cash contains information of its user. With identified electronic cash, both offline or online, the bank can always reconstruct the path the electronic cash went through the economy. The bank will know what everyone bought, where he or she bought it, when he or she bought it, and how much he or she paid for it. And what the bank knows, the IRS (taxation authority) knows.

Anonymous electronic cash is like notes. After it has been withdrawn from bank you can use it without trace.

The big difference between offline anonymous electronic cash and offline identified electronic cash is that the information accumulated with anonymous electronic cash will only reveal the transaction trails if the electronic cash is double spent. If the anonymous electronic cash is not double spent, the bank cannot determine the identity of the original spender nor can it reconstruct the path the electronic money went through the economy.

If everyone would use identified money there was no need to file tax returns, as government already would know every transaction you have done or have taken a part. Wouldn't that be nice?

14.3.5 Credit Cards in the Internet 互联网上的信用卡

Customers will be using credit cards as they have done it so far and companies will continue to offer this service to them. With credit cards customers can make purchases directly from vendors. What has changed is that major credit card companies have introduced a new way of securing transactions. In this system customer doesn't send credit card information to vendor. Instead what is sent is a token that vendor can deliver to credit card company. The credit card company then uses this token to get the credit card information and validates the usage of the card. Vendor can be sure that card is good and deliver the wanted merchandise to customer. Also customer gets a digital receipt from the transaction. This system is essentially more secure than traditional one.

1. Advantages

Customer's money is at the bank. If the card is lost account still have link to customer unlike in electronic cash systems where if customer looses his/her electronic cash it is gone. In this scheme customer doesn't have to open a new account at the bank. They can use credit card they have already had, unlike in electronic cash systems where customer have to open a new account.

2. Disadvantages

Lack of privacy: unlike in electronic cash systems where transactions hide the identity of the customer, in this scheme transaction always links customer's name to purchase. System so cannot maintain anonymity of the customer. There also could be a risk that customer's name is added to unwanted mailing lists.

14.3.6 Checks and the Internet 支票与互联网

There have been attempts to transfer electronic checks over Internet, but these systems have not been developed as far as other forms of money transfer. In a simplest scheme electronic version of the check could be an email that authorizes vendor to draw funds from customer's bank account. Identification of the customer is done by digital signature and attached certificates. This system looks like a compromise between credit card and electronic cash payments.

1. Advantages

(1) Processing. Electronic checks can be processed by the normal methods. The appearance of the check is different but it will still be a check.

(2) Making change. Electronic checks can be made out to exact amount of money needed.

(3) Money is in the bank. Customers don't have to worry about their money, as it is stored safely at the bank.

2. Disadvantages

Privacy: electronic check reveals the real user of the money.

14.3.7 Smart Cards and the Internet 灵通卡与互联网

1. What Are Stored Value Cards (Smart Cards)?

The evolution of cyber-payments systems has not been a straight-line progression from one financial transaction system to another. It has been the multi-lateral development of hybrid systems. Essentially, the first electronic based transaction systems were credit cards and Automatic Teller Machine (ATM) cards containing a magnetic stripe that allowed the user to gain access to a line of credit or bank account. At the same time, there was development of magnetic stripe cards that could store value. The addition of microchip technology to cards increased the storage, security and applicability of the cards. The stored value card (smart card) is both an access device and a self-contained store of value. Internet-based payment systems use the Internet's telecommunications capability to facilitate financial transactions with other users. However, the personal computer that serves as the user's interface with the Internet payment system can also store value and is therefore, both an access device and self-contained store of value.

Banks in Australia, Europe, and Japan are already issuing "smart cards", which combine credit, debit, and stored value on a single card. Smart cards are micro-processor-equipped cards that work with card readers installed in the computers of consumers. The buyer slips his card in the reader and the transaction is secure and guaranteed, making Internet purchasing tremendously alluring to both businesses and consumers. A single smart card can carry many applications — it can function as a credit, debit, and/or ATM card, while at the same time store a cardholder's medical insurance information, frequent flyer mileage information, and other financial data. The cardholder's information is accessed by a card acceptance device only if that terminal is programmed to read the card or if the cardholder has authorized access via use of a Personal Identification Number (PIN) or virtual "fingerprint". The security of a chip card is far greater than that of the currently popular magnetic strip cards because use of the chip allows encryption of the vital information.

2. How Are Smart Cards Used?

Smart cards are used to store critical medical records and treatment histories; smart phone cards store account and PIN numbers so that the same cellular phone can be used by different people who simply insert or swipe through their smart card to activate the phone; and airline and hotel chains use smart cards to store passenger frequent flyer and frequent guest credits.

Most importantly, smart cards are already being used in international commerce to keep track of transportation records such as bills of lading. It is anticipated that soon they will be able to store all the payment information relating to an international trade transaction, thus enabling traders to quickly and effectively undertake secure payment arrangements.

14.4 Control of the Electronic Money 电子货币的管理

Introduction of Internet has fuelled the change from physical method of paying to electronic version. It can be seen that electronic cash is going to evolve into a commonly acceptable method, but there are still open issues that have to be solved.

14.4.1 Secured Electronic Transactions Standards 电子交易安全标准

1. Necessity of SET

Two major issues kept international businesses from flocking en masse to the Internet: trust and security. Both buyers and sellers must have confidence in the infrastructure of the Internet for it to support electronic commerce. Today's Internet infrastructure is both insecure and untrusted. Until recently, adequate technology simply did not exist to remedy these problems. There simply wasn't a readily available method of preventing fraud or theft when using a credit card to purchase goods over the Internet. But, with the release in mid-1997 of the Secured Electronic Transactions (SET) Standards the whole world should benefit from a tremendous increase in electronic commerce.

2. What Is SET?

SET is a single technical standard for safeguarding credit (and in the near future debit) card purchases made over the open networks of the Internet. It is an international protocol that details how credit card (and debit card) transactions on the Internet will be secured using encryption technology and digital certification. Developed by a consortium including IBM, VISA, Master Card, Microsoft, Netscape Communications, VeriSign and VeriFone, and GTE, among others, SET provides internationally approved and available cryptography that complies with minimum requirements to ensure the effectiveness of a global authentication service. The SET specifications include business requirements, technical specifications, and a programmer's guide.

3. Significance of SET

The publication of the SET standard opens the electronic marketplace to participating banks, and to buyers and sellers around the world. SET is a huge step forward in securing credit and debit card transactions over the Internet, and it should certainly pave the way for establishing the necessary trust of buyers and sellers conducting electronic commerce.

14.4.2　Law Enforcement and Cyber-payments　执法与电子支付

The overall efficiency and security of the system influence customers' opinions in favor of the system. These features make it also very vulnerable against those who are willing to exploit it for illicit purposes. It also makes it difficult for the law enforcement agencies to get enough information of its users.

Why are cyber-payments a law enforcement concern? The speed which makes the systems efficient and the anonymity that makes them secure are positive characteristics from the public's perspective as well as law enforcement in protecting the systems from being compromised. However, these same characteristics make these systems equally attractive to those who seek to use it for illicit purposes and increased anonymity while providing security, may actually impede law enforcement from obtaining necessary information to detect illegal activity.

14.5　Cyber-payments in the Future　电子支付的未来

14.5.1　Cyber-payments: Future Method for All Payments
电子支付：未来的支付方法

While nobody is certain what the future will bring, we do know that the Internet recognizes no national borders. Electronic commerce is global in nature, so the Internet cannot help but to dramatically increase international trade. As trust and security issues are resolved — as they continue to be each day — companies around the world will add the software and hardware tools required to conduct their business on-line.

The future of online payments is certain. One thing is clear: new payment mechanisms for both consumers and corporations will drive the development of new cyber-cash management techniques. With technology advancing ever more quickly, and old methods of business being replaced by newer, faster, digital models, current cash management payment and collection methods that are now called "alternative" will soon be the norm. Cyber-payments will be the method for all payments among the new technologies emerging in the coming few years. Electronic commerce as a term means trade that is made in electronic way. Electronic commerce makes it possible to sell commodities in a cheap, efficient, easy and global way.

14.5.2　Secure Payment Methods: Crucial to E-commerce
安全的支付方法：电子商务的关键

Electronic commerce can only be done if the payment methods are secure and usable. Also possible juridical issues have to be solved before commerce can be done on a global scale.

As we can see, the number of people using Internet is increasing by 100% each year. Very soon just plain surfing isn't going to be enough for them. Internet access providers, service providers, vendors and companies involved in Internet development have to come up with fast, secure, anonymous and easy to use solution to be used by customer, in order to make payments, who want to fully exploit Internet.[8] The first company that hits global market with application that is accepted by everyone (customers, vendors, official agencies, etc.) is going to be a major player.[9]

Electronic systems like the Internet that facilitates the transfer of financial value promise to alter the means by which we conduct transactions. A common element of cyber-payment systems is that they are designed to provide transacting parties with immediate, convenient, and secure (even potentially anonymous) means of transferring financial value. When fully implemented, the new technologies will provide users worldwide with numerous benefits for legitimate commerce. Unfortunately, these technologies carry with them many of the theft/tampering, fraud, and privacy abuse dangers of traditional cash-based commerce, while creating new potentials for abuse as well. How, and to what extent, governments should and must become involved in regulating electronic commerce is an issue that is only now starting to surface.

14.5.3 Further Work for Full Operation of E-payments System
电子支付系统业务的全面开展

The ever-changing technology in electronic commerce and the introduction of new hardware, software, and service technology forces market participants to quickly and readily adjust their basic business strategies. Companies who want to participate in the worldwide electronic commerce revolution must adapt their electronic commerce service capabilities and product offerings to the requirements of the electronic commerce marketplace[10], or rely on revenues from more traditional business services, hoping these continue to be profitable.

There is an active movement under way to enable trusted intermediaries — such as banks and other financial institutions — to underwrite transactions by offering guarantees and recourse, much as they do with today's documentary letters of credit. At present, the bill of lading, which is almost universally used in international sales transactions, operates as the document of title, and this requires an original document to operate effectively. There is thus no electronic mechanism available today to eliminate the possibility of fraudulently selling goods to which title has already passed. Further work is necessary in the field of documentary (or rather, documentless) credits before an electronic payments system is fully operational. However, research is at hand to allow documentary credit rules and procedures to be applied by a bank electronically to international transactions.

New Words and Expressions

Internet	[ˈintənet]	n.	因特网，国际互联网络
phenomenal	[fiˈnɔminəl]	a.	显著的，现象的，惊人的
deluge	[ˈdeljuːdʒ]	v.	大量涌至
multinational	[mʌltiˈnæʃənəl]	a.	跨国的
untapped	[ʌnˈtæpt]	a.	未开发的，未利用的
lure	[ljuə(ː)]	v.	引诱，吸引

offering	[ˈɔfəriŋ]	n.	提供，出售物
interface	[ˈintə(ː)feis]	n.	界面
illicit	[iˈlisit]	a.	违法的，不正当的
vendor	[ˈvendɔː]	n.	卖主，卖方
monopolistic	[mənɔpəˈlistik]	a.	独占的，垄断的
scour	[ˈskauə]	v.	搜索
mingle	[ˈmiŋgl]	v.	使混合
anonymity	[ˌænəˈnimiti]	n.	匿名，作者不明（或不详）
encrypt	[inˈkript]	v.	加密，将……译成密码
hybrid	[ˈhaibrid]	a.	混合的，杂种的
alluring	[əˈljuəriŋ]	a.	迷人的，吸引人的，诱惑的
fuel	[fjuəl]	n.	燃料
		v.	激起，刺激
flock	[flɔk]	v.	聚集，成群地去（或来）
en masse	[aŋˈmæs]	ad.	全体地，一同地
protocol	[ˈprəutəkɔl]	n.	草案，议定书，协议
consortium	[kənˈsɔːtjəm]	n.	企业集团
cryptography	[kripˈtɔgrəfi]	n.	密码系统，密码术
compromise	[ˈkɔmprəmaiz]	n./v.	妥协，折中；泄漏（秘密）
juridical	[dʒuəˈridikəl]	a.	裁判的，司法的
surfing	[ˈsəːfiŋ]	n.	冲浪游戏，网络冲浪
tampering	[ˈtæmpəriŋ]	n.	窜改，损坏

e-cash 电子现金
cyber-money 电子货币
cyber-payment 电子支付
electronic wallet 电子钱包
World Wide Web 万维网
electronic commerce 电子商务
stored-value product 储值产品
encoded magnetic stripe 加密的磁卡
access device 存取设备
digital currency 数字化货币
e-money 电子货币
debit card 借记卡
side effect 副作用
virtual fingerprint 虚拟指纹
cellular phone 移动电话
IBM 国际商用机器公司
Netscape Communications 网景通信
online payment 在线支付
economies of scale 规模经济
ATM (Automated Teller Machine) 自动出纳机，自动柜员机
microchip-embedded smart card 微芯片埋置式灵通卡
IRS (Internal Revenue Service) （美国）国内税务局
personal identification number (PIN) 个人身份识别号
Secured Electronic Transactions Standards (SETS) 电子交易安全标准
GTE (General Telephone and Electronics Corp.) 通用电话和电子设备公司

Chapter 14 Cyber-payments

Notes

1. Electronic commerce — the ability to purchase goods and services electronically, over the Internet, from around the world at any time of day or night — is currently experiencing phenomenal growth.　电子商务，即以电子方式通过互联网在任何时候从全球各地购买货物或获得服务的能力，现在正在经历着惊人的增长。

2. Although electronic commerce is now merely a fraction of total international trade, all indications are that there has been a virtual deluge of companies jumping into the arena.
尽管电子商务现在仅占国际贸易总量的一小部分，但是所有迹象表明，到 20 世纪末，公司已如潮涌般地涉足这一领域。

3. It enriches competition in products and prices, and it drives change and improvement, given its ability to provide information and comparative choices.　因互联网能够提供相关信息和对比选择机会，从而强化了产品和价格的竞争，促进着变革与提高。

4. So the term "cyber-payments" can be used to define methods that have been implemented to transfer money. Cyber-payments refer to evolving new methods of financial transactions as today banks already can transfer money with computers. Cyber-payment is going to change the way people make payments. These payments could happen in Internet or in stores with "smart cards" that contain microchip, where the value of the card is stored.　因此，电子支付这个术语可用来定义资金转移的方法。电子支付指发展金融交易的新方法，正如当今银行用计算机调拨资金一样。电子支付将改变人们支付的方法，这些支付可在互联网上或商场进行，在商场中可用内存有微型芯片的"灵通卡"。

5. These systems have being designed to give both to consumer and vendor a fast, easy to use, secure and possibly anonymous way to transfer money. After this system has been implemented completely, it'll affect users globally and enables normal commerce to profit from it.　这些系统的设计旨在使消费者和商家获得一种快捷、简便、安全及匿名的付款方式。这种系统完全实施后，会对全球的用户产生影响，而且能使正常的商业活动从中受益。

6. Since many governments restrict imports of certain products and regulate advertising and other marketing tools within their national borders, purchasers are often forced to choose from a limited — or even monopolistic — supply of a desired product. With Internet access, purchasers can scour the world in minutes to find the right product at the best price.　由于许多政府对某些产品的进口及其国内广告和其他营销手段实施了某些限制，消费者被迫从非常有限甚或垄断性的产品供应中进行选择。但是，由于可以在互联网上进行访问，消费者就可以在数分钟内搜遍全球，以最优的价格找到合适的产品。

7. As home banking and Internet payment systems are more commonly used there are fewer and

fewer face-to-face transactions. This makes it hard for the financial institutions to really know their customers. These faceless transactions make it harder to control and analyze movements of money, as transfers could be anonymous and paperless. 随着内部银行业务和互联网系统支付越来越普遍地运用，面对面的业务日益减少。这使得金融机构真正了解客户越来越困难。这些不见面的业务使控制并分析资金动向更加困难，因为资金转移是匿名的、无纸化的。

8. Very soon just plain surfing isn't going to be enough for them. Internet access providers, service providers, vendors and companies involved in Internet development have to come up with fast, secure, anonymous and easy to use solution to be used by customer, in order to make payments, who want to fully exploit Internet. 用不了多久，仅在网上冲浪对他们而言是不够的。互联网网络供应商、服务提供商、供货商及与互联网开发有关的公司必须设计出快捷、安全、匿名且易于操作的方法来进行支付，以满足那些希望充分利用互联网的顾客的需要。

9. The first company that hits global market big time, with application that is accepted by everyone (customers, vendors, official agencies, etc.), is going to be a major player. 凡能迎合有利可图的全球市场的第一家公司（其应用程序被顾客、供货商及官方机构等接受），将成为行业主导者。

10. Companies who want to participate in the worldwide electronic commerce revolution must adapt their electronic commerce service capabilities and product offerings to the requirements of the electronic commerce marketplace… 希望参与全球电子商务大变革的公司必须能使其电子商务服务能力和产品适应电子商务市场的要求……

Exercises

1. **Fill in the blanks to complete each sentence.**

   (1) A growing number of companies are taking advantage of the Web quickly developing into a _____ by selling products and services of all sorts, both to consumers and to other businesses.

   (2) The Internet is a vast new frontier of consumer-to-business and _____ commerce. For consumers, Internet-based shopping holds an attraction because of _____.

   (3) _____ to promote and display products, and then _____ to look around at the offerings, however, is only one dimension of conducting business via the Internet.

   (4) Terms like "electronic commerce", _____, _____ and similar general terms are tossed about casually in the press and in daily conversation, with little attention to just what these terms mean.

Chapter 14　Cyber-payments

(5) There are basically two types of electronic cash technologies: _____ and _____.

(6) The term "cyber-payment" is just one of many used to describe systems that facilitate the _____ (i.e. digital currency, e-money).

(7) Until recently, however, suppliers used the Internet primarily for _____ purposes.

(8) In the Internet there are two common ways to make payments: _____ and _____.

(9) Electronic cash systems use _____, which can be quickly verified with the entity that issued them to validate that the electronic currency represents actual value.

(10) Most on-line transactions systems involve the debit of a customer's credit or _____.

2. **Define the following terms.**

(1) electronic commerce

(2) cyber-payment

(3) SET

(4) digital signature

(5) smart cards

3. **Translate the following terms into English.**

(1) 电子支付　　　　　　　　(2) 电子现金
(3) 信用额度　　　　　　　　(4) 数字化货币
(5) 电子钱包　　　　　　　　(6) 自动出纳机
(7) 商务的全球化　　　　　　(8) 个人身份识别号
(9) 微芯片埋置式灵通卡　　　(10) 电子交易安全标准
(11) 电子商务　　　　　　　 (12) 加密的磁条
(13) 存取设备　　　　　　　 (14) 借记卡
(15) 虚拟指纹

4. **Decide whether the following statements are true or false.**

(1) The evolution of cyber-payments systems has been a straight-line progression from one financial transaction system to another. (　)

(2) The first electronic based transaction systems were credit cards and ATM cards containing a magnetic stripe that allowed the user to gain access to a line of credit or bank account. (　)

(3) The common element is that the cyber-payment systems are designed to provide the transacting parties with immediate, convenient, secure and potentially anonymous means by which to transfer financial value. (　)

(4) When fully implemented, the new cyber-payment technologies will not carry with them many of the theft/tampering, fraud, and privacy abuse dangers of traditional cash-based commerce. (　)

(5) A single smart card can carry many applications — it can function as a credit, debit, and/or ATM card, while at the same time store a cardholder's medical insurance

information, frequent flyer mileage information, and other financial data. (　)

(6) The stored value card (smart card) is both an access device and a self-contained store of value. Internet-based payment systems use the Internet's telecommunications capability to facilitate financial transactions with other users. (　)

(7) Smart cards are already being used in international commerce to keep track of transportation records such as bills of lading. (　)

(8) The speed which makes the systems efficient and the anonymity that makes them secure are negative characteristics from the public's perspective as well as law enforcement in protecting the systems from being compromised. (　)

(9) Whether new payment mechanisms for both consumers and corporations will drive the development of new cyber-cash management techniques is still not clear. (　)

(10) E-commerce can be done even if the payment methods are not secure and usable as long as the Internet that facilitates the transfer of financial value promises to alter the means by which we conduct transactions. (　)

5. Choose the best answer to each of the following statements.

(1) What is gained with e-cash in the Internet is ____.
　　A. privacy and limited liability　　　　B. convenience
　　C. speed　　　　　　　　　　　　　　D. ease of use

(2) There are two different kinds of electronic cash: ____.
　　A. stored-value products and access products
　　B. identified and anonymous
　　C. NTT telephone cards and ATM cards
　　D. JR Orange Cards and ATM cards

(3) With ____ electronic cash, both offline or online, the bank can always reconstruct the path the electronic cash went through the economy.
　　A. illicit　　　　　　　　　　　　　　B. secure
　　C. identified　　　　　　　　　　　　D. anonymous

(4) Credit card orders means by using some secure methods of transferring credit card information to ____. For some customers the idea of sending credit card information over Internet is not appealing.
　　A. Internet access providers　　　　　B. service providers
　　C. customers　　　　　　　　　　　　D. vendors and companies

(5) The big difference between offline anonymous electronic cash and offline identified electronic cash is that the information accumulated with anonymous electronic cash will only reveal the ____ if the electronic cash is double spent.
　　A. transaction system　　　　　　　　B. transaction online
　　C. transaction standard　　　　　　　D. transaction trail

(6) Being developed today are/is ____ that offer increased storage capacity, security, and

applicability.

A. wiring "money" via telegraph
B. credit cards and ATM cards
C. microchip-embedded "smart cards"
D. magnetic stripe cards

(7) Internet-based payment systems take the concept of electric commerce further ____.

A. providing expanding markets and choices to national and international communities or by selling products and services of all sorts
B. by facilitating financial transactions with other users
C. utilizing a blind signature or using some secure methods of transferring credit card information to vendor
D. by transmitting the encoded information over a phone line or network for approval

(8) Two major issues kept international businesses from flocking en masse to the Internet are trust and ____.

A. security
B. speed
C. privacy
D. honor

(9) Companies who want to participate in the worldwide e-commerce revolution must adapt ____ to the requirements of the e-commerce marketplace, or rely on revenues from more traditional business services, hoping these continue to be profitable.

A. their e-commerce service capabilities
B. their product offerings
C. cyber-cash management techniques
D. both A and B

(10) At present, there is no electronic mechanism available to eliminate the possibility of fraudulently selling goods to which ____ has already passed.

A. documentary letters of credit
B. title
C. a documentless credit
D. a bill of exchange

References
参考文献

[1] HINKELMAN E G. International settlements[M]. Novato, CA: The Syndicate of World Trade Press, 2000.

[2] 叶玉军,王甘霖. 国际贸易结算实务操作与技巧[M]. 北京:中国金融出版社,1994.

[3] 许罗丹,陈平. 国际结算[M]. 广州:中山大学出版社,2000.

[4] 徐秀琼,沈锦昶,李宝华,等. 国际支付与结算[M]. 上海:上海外语教育出版社,1994.

[5] 颜世廉,邵新莉,丁华南,等. 国际结算[M]. 长沙:中南工业大学出版社,1998.

[6] 汤红庆. 国际结算原理研究[M]. 广州:暨南大学出版社,2001.

[7] 汤劲松,吴啸风. 国际结算[M]. 北京:中国商业出版社,1997.

[8] 苏宗祥,张林森. 国际结算[M]. 北京:中国金融出版社,2001.

[9] 宋毅英. 国际贸易支付方式:信用证[M]. 香港:超文植字公司,1993.

[10] 赵薇. 国际贸易融资支付办法[M]. 南京:东南大学出版社,2003.